The Hidden Tree
by
Valton Brown

ISBN: 978-1-914933-84-4

Copyright 2023

All rights reserved. No part of this publication may be reproduced, stored in a retrieval system, or transmitted in any form or by any means, electronic, mechanical, photocopy, recording or otherwise, without prior written consent of the copyright owner. Nor can it be circulated in any form of binding or cover other than that in which it is published and without similar condition including this condition being imposed on a subsequent purchaser. The right of Valton Brown to be identified as the author of this work has been asserted in accordance with the Copyright Designs and Patents Act 1988. A copy of this book is deposited with the British Library.

Published By: -

i2i
PUBLISHING
i2i Publishing. Manchester.
www.i2ipublishing.co.uk

Contents

Introduction _____ ix

Trading in The Souls of Men _____ 1

The Soil – The Blood of Abel _____ 15

The Nutrients or Toxins? _____ 18

The Root System _____ 29

   Man vs Machine – Transition from the 18th to 19th Century (First and Second Industrial Revolution) _____ 29

The Evangelists _____ 47

   Francis Galton _____ 50

      The Galton Institute and its Eugenics Past _____ 55

      Phrases and words coined by Francis Galton _____ 56

   Julian Sorell Huxley _____ 58

      Phrases and words coined by Julian S Huxley _____ 64

   Charles Davenport _____ 65

   Clarence Gamble _____ 71

      Pathfinder Distance Themselves from Clarence Gamble 75

   Margaret Higgins Sanger _____ 76

      Planned Parenthood Remove Margaret Sanger's Name _ 82

      Phrases and words coined by Margaret Sanger _____ 83

The Hidden Tree _____ 85

   The Materials _____ 91

      Racial Laws | Racial Politics _____ 91

- Psychology | Psychiatry ... 91
  - Mental Testing | Racial Testing ... 102
  - Psychometric Testing and Sociology ... 104
  - Education ... 110
  - Economics ... 116
  - Genetics ... 120
- Apostles of Apostasy ... 125
  - DH Lawrence (September 11, 1885 - March 2, 1930) ... 126
  - George Bernard Shaw (July 26, 1856 - November 2, 1950) 127
  - Oliver Wendell Holmes Jr. (March 8, 1841 - March 6, 1935) ... 128
  - Marie Stopes (October 15, 1880 - October 2, 1958) ... 130
  - John Harvey Kellogg (February 26, 1852 - December 14, 1943) ... 133
  - Aleister Crowley (October 12, 1875 - December 1, 1947) ... 135
- At The Core ... 141
  - The Dichotomy ... 142
  - The Shoah ... 144
  - Israel ... 153
  - Old Roots, New Shoots, Same Soil ... 159
  - Covenant ... 190
- Homo Deus – Man Is God ... 195
  - Man Merges with Machine, Transition from 20th to 21st Century ... 195
  - Human Genetics ... 200

The Birth of God Tech' 205
   Dark Intel 209
   The Conundrum 216
Human Experiments 221
   Twins 221
   Poison 224
   High Altitude 225
   Tuberculosis 228
   Phosgene 230
   Sulfanilamide, Bone, Muscle, and Joint Transplantation ... 233
   Sterilization 235
   Artificial Insemination 238
   Seawater 241
   Euthanasia 243
   Nameless Testimony 245
   Wehrmacht-Einheitskanister – (The Jerry Can) 247
   Stainless Steel 248
   The Zipper 249
   The Atomic Bomb 249
New Eugenics, The Final Solution 253
   Materials Revisited 254
   Spiritual Roots from Another Era 254
   The First Hippie Colony - Monte Verità (Mountain of Truth?) 257
From Ascona to California 267

Not So Random Questions 271
The Kings of 'Pop' Culture 273
   Aldous Huxley 273
   Timothy Leary – Psychedelic Religion: Psychology 277
   Lafayette Ronald Hubbard - Scientology 281
   Jack Parsons – Rocketeer and Thelema 284
      New Psychiatry 289
   Sigmund Freud, 1856-1939: The Father of Psychoanalysis 291
   Carl Jung: New Psychiatry / Psychoanalysis 294
   Abraham Maslow - Humanism in Psychology and Empirical Spirituality 309
   Mental Illness 313
   Medicine 317
Antipsychotics. The Problem or the Cure? 319
Population Control 327
   Save the Planet Lose the Child / Age Reduction 328
Modern Art 333
Syncretism - So What's New? 337
   Religion 337
   Music 342
      Worship Matters 342
      The HipHop Occult Culture 344
   New Age Ministry 352
      Worship Teams 352
      What Should We Say About Music Awards? 361

Preachers / Teachers and the Gifted	363
Politics	375
Too Good to Be True	379
Trans-religions	383
Tech Religions Put Down Their Roots	383
Terasem	384
The Church of Perpetual Life	385
Way of the Future Church of AI	390
The Christian Transhumanist Association	391
Evolutionary Leaders	393
Religion and The Theory of God	394
Transcendence	395
Singularity	395
Deliver Us from Transhumanism	397
The Masters of the Universe?	400
Lekh-L'kha	404
Get Yourself Out of Here	404
It's Time to Move On	406
Your Body, Your Mind, Your Choice	406
The True Vine	409
Standing In the Place of the Nations	409
Our Place of Safety	410
The Feast of Passover	412
A Salutation	415

Glossary of Terms ____ 419

Appendix ____ 421

    Eugenics Record Office, Bulletin 10A ____ 421

    Race Crossing in Jamaica ____ 423

    Hitler's Testimony Before the Court for High Treason ____ 435

    The CBC Tenets as set out in Appendix C of THE AUTHORIZED LIFE OF MARIE C. STOPES BY AYLMER MAUDE ____ 440

Introduction

"Then He said to me, "Son of man, dig into the wall"; and when I dug into the wall, there was a door.

And He said to me, "Go in, and see the wicked abominations which they are doing there." So I went in and saw, and there — every sort of creeping thing, abominable beasts, and all the idols of the house of Israel, portrayed all around on the walls. And there stood before them seventy men of the elders of the house of Israel, and in their midst stood Jaazaniah the son of Shaphan. Each man had a censer in his hand, and a thick cloud of incense went up. Then He said to me, "Son of man, have you seen what the elders of the house of Israel do in the dark, every man in the room of his idols? For they say, 'The Lord does not see us, the Lord has forsaken the land.' "

Ezekiel 8:9-12 (NKJV)

For decades scholars, philosophers, politicians, and a plethora of other influencers in society have explored the deep issues of humanity and have awakened with a headache of humongous proportions. Wars, ethnic groups against ethnic groups, famines, epidemics, poverty, inequality, global warming, economic instability, terrorism, the list goes on and on.

It is in this environment of chaos and self-worship that 'great thinkers' have spent a lifetime searching for root causes and solutions. They use nothing more than the human intellect and lean on the explorations of past thinkers as the compass for navigating the issues of the soul. As a result, we are inundated with incredible and incredulous ideas, clothed in the garb of science, technology, and spirituality.

For advanced civilisations, we have not moved on from the teachings of people like Plato, a man born in the fifth century BC, who believed that nothing in the material world is constant. To Plato, the material world is unreliable for the search for truth. In his opinion, only those who can understand the true reality behind the world of everyday experience can determine true knowledge. He gave the modern world his thoughts and methods in how to understand the human psyche (soul). Today, we call it psychology. Aristotle (a student of Plato) is numbered amongst the great teachers too. Yet, this great teacher believed that women were nothing more than deformed men, who were subordinate to men, but higher than slaves. [1]

Have we moved on as much as we think, or are we simply deceiving ourselves? Do we believe that we have 'evolved'? Unfortunately, there is little evidence for such a theory. It is to our detriment as God's creation, that we think our brilliance has

---

[1]

https://www.researchgate.net/publication/236725862_Plato_and_Aristotle_on_the_Nature_of_Women

changed the world we live in for the better. However, as we examine how wars usually begin, we uncover human self-centeredness and elitist agendas; wealth and power rocking the cradle of society with one hand while creaming off the profits with the other; ordinary people who are destroyed in the wake of such greed and prejudice, leaving behind a trail of human devastation and poverty-stricken families in the wake of their presence. People who are led to believe, through disinformation, that the solution to issues of the mind can be solved by popping a pill or engaging in repackaged eastern mysticism, such as [2]Yoga. Now, it is difficult to imagine a world without the teachings of people like Maharishi Mahesh Yogi. Entertainment on a whole has morphed into a mass evangelisation machine, with its mode of worship, indoctrination, preachers, and holy books. Hip-hop is the dominant tool for this generation, masquerading as a musical expression, but exposing its place as a new religion with its own teachings embodied in the pages of the Hip-hop bible, designed to introduce witchcraft and the occult to young people who were not attracted by the last wave of occultism preached through rock music. Mix that with the legalisation of drugs, and the promotion of prescription medication[3], made popular by the marketing of Mental Illness and you have a recipe for disaster. Here's one example of how the Bible spoke about the system that we would find ourselves in, a system that is rooted in ancient occultism and anti-Messiah sentiment:

"The light of a lamp shall not shine in you anymore, and the voice of bridegroom and bride shall not be heard in you anymore. For

---

[2] An idea that was brought from Asia to western cultures and rebranded as an exercise regime in which even atheists and humanists take part, while at the same time claiming to have no religious persuasions whatsoever. Made popular in the U.K. by The Beatles in the 1960s.
[3] Read Medication Madness by Dr Breggin.

*your merchants were the great men of the earth, for by your **sorcery*** all the nations were deceived."

Revelation 18:23 (NKJV)

*(Definition of sorcery taken from the Greek. In the Strong's concordance, 5331 **pharmakeía** (from pharmakeuō, "administer drugs") – properly, drug-related sorcery, like the practice of magical-arts, etc.)

These are just some of the areas that we have bought into without first determining the measure, the source, or the impact these toxic ingredients will have on us if consumed without reading the warning label on the bottle. It is because of this inability to be genuine seekers of objective truth, that we find ourselves lost in the maze of human pursuits and self-worship, taken advantage of by unseen, very real, dark forces, that do know the truth.

Interestingly, most modern scientists spend their time trying to prove that God does not exist, by presenting alternative theories to fill the gaps in our knowledge which The Bible (God's revealed word) once occupied. For example, the British legal system, which was developed through the writ system, was influenced by a biblical worldview, but today, it is being redefined by a humanistic worldview. The same appears to have happened with the study of the world we live in, including what is described today as science.

So, to aid the reader in understanding the rest of this book it is important to know that the Bible has been placed at its core because it has been proven to be infallible, accurate, and is the only book that tells us what is coming next without the need to consult spirits, mediums, gurus, and other such entities. So, whatever your thoughts are, they will be challenged by what you read next, but I trust that you will be courageous enough to keep reading.

Trading in The Souls of Men

*"And the merchants of the earth will weep and mourn over her, for no one buys their merchandise anymore: merchandise of gold and silver, precious stones and pearls, fine linen and purple, silk and scarlet, every kind of citron wood, every kind of object of ivory, every kind of object of most precious wood, bronze, iron, and marble; and cinnamon and incense, fragrant oil and frankincense, wine and oil, fine flour and wheat, cattle and sheep, horses and chariots, and **bodies and souls of men.**"*

Revelation 18:11-14 (NKJV)

The 21st century is celebrated for a myriad of reasons. We are said to be living longer, due to our ability to address illnesses that would have once wiped out nations, such as the 'Black Death', tuberculosis, cholera, polio, and smallpox just to mention a few. However, to the contrary, modern science has been accurately accused of introducing modern diseases or illnesses, climate change, and other global experiences. Yet we claim success in their reduction or eradication. Isn't this ironic? How is this progress?

We pride ourselves on the technological advancements made through 'modern' science and promote our achievements at every opportunity through a communication system called 'the media'. Ignoring the voices of individuals who cry 'foul play' while simultaneously and systematically saturating the airwaves with disinformation to manipulate and control the masses.

It is a fact; the world has become smaller and our appetite for self-determination has grown exponentially. Mystical, ancient ideas have filled our minds to the point that we believe we can become gods, we can transcend. Satan has been a preacher of this philosophy since the beginning of the world's history *(see the biblical account of creation in the Book of Genesis)*. Satan's first audience being Adam and Eve, the first humans; coequal, and appointed stewards of the world. Reading the biblical account, this couple had everything anyone could ever dream of. There was no lack. In comparison, the joint wealth of humanity throughout later history could not parallel with the position and influence they were given. Yet a tree, the only thing that was off limits to them, became a catalyst for their downfall and the failure of generations to follow. The symbol of trust became the symbol of destruction and distance from the only true God, YHWH.

"And the woman said to the serpent, "We may eat the fruit of the trees of the garden; but of the fruit of the tree which is in the midst of the garden, God has said, 'You shall not eat it, nor shall you touch it, lest you die.' <u>Then the serpent said to the woman, "You will not surely die. For God knows that in the day you eat of it your eyes will be opened, and you will be like God, knowing good and evil.</u>"

Genesis 2:2-5 (NKJV)

By choosing to break that trust, by tasting the fruit of the tree, they made an indelible choice. Rather than accepting an open honest relationship with all its privileges rooted in love, they chose Satan's philosophy which had not been tried, tested, or proven. Satan had not created this couple, nor did he consider their need for companionship. He had nothing to recommend himself by other than false philosophy, a dishonest agenda, and a false offer of godhood/transcendence through self-determination. Yet his influence caught their attention, gripping their imagination of 'what could be' and the possibility of transcending the human form to some other level of awareness. This one act set humanity on a course that has plagued us ever since. Every moment of every day we are sold the philosophy of becoming gods, transcending our current human form by developing a greater awareness of who we are 'without God'. As time passes, the pursuit of transcendence becomes more and more relentless, seeping into every area of our human existence, gripping our every thought and tragically ending in the same way as the first humans. A never-ending trail of disaster, destruction, and godlessness, or as the Bible describes it, Torahlessness (without Torah or God's teaching/instruction). Death.

If we were to consider the Genesis account carefully, we would identify an impostor, Satan. Like a true conman, he peddled his wares offering the 'ultimate experience' but selling nothing more than an idea, a concept, a philosophy, an experience. In today's language, it would probably sound something like, *"If you give me your soul, I will give you an experience as you have never had before. You will not find it in the biblical faith, nor in the pursuit of the biblical Messiah. You cannot understand it through reason, it isn't logical. The experience begins within you. You are a god."*

Contrary to some of the ideas that have been peddled in Gnosticism, God did not play a cruel trick on humanity, nor did He leave us without a remedy. He gave humanity the freedom to choose. The freedom to choose a limitless relationship with The Creator of the universe, the freedom to choose to rule with God over a perfectly balanced ecosystem, the freedom to raise children with foundations inclusive of the ability to engage actively in a global plan that would embrace the whole human race raising each person to the level of true equality. He also gave humanity the freedom to disobey, the freedom to pursue knowledge without God and without the benefits. After all, would you want someone to be in a relationship with you if they did not choose to be?

Adam and Eve were caught in the headlights of Satan's philosophy, mesmerised by his charismatic delivery and insightful words of perceived knowledge. We can only imagine the thoughts that raced through their hearts and minds. Maybe they went something like, "If I eat the fruit, I will become godlike...hmm?" "If I eat the fruit of this tree, maybe I will ascend to a higher level of consciousness...hmm?" "If I eat the fruit of this tree, God will never know, right?" Of course, this is only speculation but, in today's world these sorts of questions are a reality, wrapped up in blasphemous charisma, sugar-coated in sin, and swallowed heartily by the masses.

As parents to the rest of humanity, Adam and Eve were not the best examples of taking responsibility for their poor choices. This is evident when God confronted both of them about their new-found knowledge regarding nakedness; a concept that had no place in their minds before eating the fruit. They swiftly went ahead to blame someone else for their actions, displaying the first signs of degradation which would trouble humanity for centuries to come. Adam redirected the conversation with God to Eve, Eve redirected the conversation to Satan and Satan is silent in the text. Job done! Their children, Cain and Abel became the unfortunate recipients of their parents' legacy, by continuing in the family tradition and Satan's philosophy. Cain became the instigator of an atrocious crime following an internal battle with the pangs of jealousy he felt towards his brother Abel. His attitude and thoughts of self-importance drove him to distraction as he observed Abel's selfless adoration of God (YHWH) and God's acceptance of Abel's worship. As Satan breathed on the fire of jealousy in Cain's heart, this emotion eventually became uncontrollable. Overwhelmed by prejudicial imaginations and thoughts, he killed his brother in cold blood and devised a further plan on how to bury the evidence to hide the truth from his parents and even God. These were brothers naturally walking in the outworking of their parents' choices. They were brothers, yet one of them became a jealous murderer, not of a stranger, but of his flesh and blood. Sadly, this unthinkable act is now immortalised in the language of the world today, adding legitimacy to the fact that this happened. With quotations like "Raising Cain". *('To raise', as used since the 14th century, means 'to conjure up; to cause a spirit to appear by means of incantations').* So, by 'Raising Cain', one is conjuring up a spirit like Cain's to create an uproar. What a disturbing legacy.

It is only the uninformed who believe that religion is the cause of the world's atrocities. By applying simple logic, we can deduce that a difference in theology was not the cause of Abel's death. The fall of the first humans was not caused by overzealous preachers. The great depression which led to the loss of lives and future incomes, the slaughter of millions of Jews in the Holocaust, the sterilisation of innocent children in the poor neighbourhoods of America, the world wars, the abortion of the innocent were not caused by religious differences. So, what lies at the centre of the demise of humanity? It can only be **Sin**. Sin is at the root of all destructive behaviour, and it is manifest through the unrestrained actions of ordinary people. People who all have the potential to commit abominable acts when God is removed from the picture. Of course, we all know that God can be used as an excuse, but the truth is, He is and has been excluded from our plans. Besides, His teachings have been grossly misrepresented to pin the blame on an unseen God and abdicate any personal responsibility for our actions. Let's remember, it was Adam and Eve that listened to Satan and ate the fruit. Cain was the one who became filled with jealousy and killed his brother. So how does God get the blame?

In modern history, there have been millions upon millions that have suffered at the hands of others who claimed to be fulfilling a higher calling, somehow connecting their soulish cause to a just, transparent God. From the same standpoint as Cain, history has been littered with the debris of human souls whose destruction has been justified by the philosophy of Satan; *Am I my brother's keeper? God does not see. So, who cares?*

Every decade, we have witnessed and recorded the atrocities that have taken place because of this unrestrained thinking and behaviour. Not because God is in the picture but because we have removed Him from it. When Cain's act was exposed, he could not and did not deny that he had acted brutally. We, on the other hand, have elevated the act of murder to a position of acceptability and entrepreneurship, even entertainment. Children are taken from their homes and turned into trained killers to reinforce a regime. Young women are promised a better life in another country and are transported in the hope of breaking the shackles of poverty, only to discover that they have been conned, and find themselves trapped in a human trafficking ring. Government systems and legislation which is sold to the public as a model for protecting our security by helping the poor and providing an opportunity for all, reveal a dark underbelly of disinformation and manipulation. The 'have-nots' have less and the 'haves' have much, much more. Including more power, more influence, and more control over private (and public) lives. Satan has spread his demonic philosophy even in the boardrooms and classrooms of modern society, indoctrinating our future leaders through his evangelists to ensure that God isn't even a consideration in the minds of tomorrow's children. However, humanity has proven that we couldn't live without God in the garden of Eden, and it is still evident that we cannot live without Him now.

The Revelation to John in Revelation 18:11-14 NKJV makes this abundantly clear:

*"And the merchants of the earth will weep and mourn over her, for no one buys their merchandise anymore: merchandise of gold and silver, precious stones and pearls, fine linen and purple, silk and scarlet, every kind of citron wood, every kind of object of ivory, every kind of object of most precious wood, bronze, iron, and marble; and cinnamon and incense, fragrant oil and frankincense, wine and oil, fine flour and wheat, cattle and sheep, horses and chariots, and **bodies and souls of men**."*

It reveals so many things about the world and its exploits. Secular society, with all its attempts to live better and higher lives by pursuing wealth and happiness at the expense of excluding God, finds that there are disastrous consequences. Loss, exploitation, manipulation, selfishness, and even death. Global business, corrupt conglomerates, false religious movements which have thrived for decades on the back of humanity, will find themselves languishing in the dungeons of despair when the demonically enthused system collapses. The impact will be catastrophic. The food supply that was once plentiful and held its value will find no place in the global market, the precious stones and minerals which were secured in the banks of the elite will be like trading in sand, valueless.

This sounds like a fiction story, but we are reminded in history and in Genesis 47:15-17 (NKJV) that this is always possible and has happened repeatedly at key points in history. It is the natural outworking of sin and humanity's refusal to change direction and repent.

*So, when the **money failed** in the land of Egypt and in the land of Canaan, all the Egyptians came to Joseph and said, "Give us bread, for why should we die in your presence? For the **money has failed**."*

Then Joseph said, "Give your livestock, and I will give you bread for your livestock, if the money is gone." So, they brought their livestock to Joseph, and Joseph gave them bread in exchange for the horses, the flocks, the cattle of the herds, and for the donkeys. Thus, he fed them with bread in exchange for all their livestock that year.

The above scripture is a testament to the limitations of man-made trade agreements. It emphasises the fickleness of money, goods, wealth, and power. Exchange of goods for services has always been a necessity but when we forget that we are given the privilege to make wealth by The Creator, God, we slip into the mire of self-importance. We forget that the world's resources were and are for the benefit of the whole of humanity. In Egypt, God was gracious when he sent Joseph ahead to secure the future of families and nations, but the coming famine stood as a worthy reminder of who we are on planet Earth. Equally, when everything is gone that we once worshipped, the removal of these things forces us to take a long hard look in the mirror and answer the tough questions about ourselves. This can be a scary experience, but it can also be the point at which we are humbled and repentant.

In Genesis 47 the item of trade was money, then livestock in exchange for food. In Revelation 18 we have a list of other non-perishable items, items that carry value and can be traded internationally. As we all know, international trade can bring together the most unlikely candidates in an alliance which makes each party extremely rich. They do not necessarily like each other or share each other's views, but the exchange of goods for wealth means the potential for greater influence and power. As a result, towns, cities, and whole continents experience political and economic growth. Even communities are brought together by trade routes, as entrepreneurs act as middlemen for an influential political representative, marketplaces are developed in the most unlikely locations established by the exchange of goods from near or distant shores.

In the book of Revelation, something unusual is revealed by Yeshua to John about the whole matter of global trade. He provides an extensive list of 'exchange for services' items (which are a compilation of perishable and non-perishable items), then He continues to reveal to John that the merchants of the earth also trade in **bodies and the souls of men**. This is yet another manifestation of the spirit of Cain, not unique to Cain but visible in the history of world trading. As at the beginning of world history, even the presence of an all-seeing God will not and does not deter humanity from performing atrocities against other human beings.

It is imperative to note that trading in **bodies** (as written in the King James translation) is written as **'slaves'** in other translations. Introducing the word 'slaves' into the text immediately evokes a personal connection with the act. Using this text as a springboard, we are then transported through the passage of recent history to events such as:

- **The Transatlantic Slave Trade** or the **MAAFA** (a Kiswahili term that means "great calamity"). The number of African slaves continues to be debated but from the 15th – 19th Century, it is estimated that 15 to 20 million slaves were exported.

- **The Sub-Saharan** or **Arab Slave Trade.** While Europeans targeted men in West Africa, Arabs targeted women who would serve as nannies, sex slaves, and domestic slaves. However, this did not exclude the use of men, who would be castrated (preferably at a young age) to prevent the pollution of their women. Unlike the Transatlantic Slave Trade where children were born to slaves to add to the future workforce or financial investment of the slavemaster, the descendants of these slaves were reduced by the practice of castration. [4]Dr Azumah states, *"However, a minimum of 28 million Africans were enslaved in the Muslim Middle East. Since at least 80% of those captured by the Muslim slave traders were calculated to have died before reaching the slave markets, it is believed that the death toll from 14 hundred years of Arab – Muslim slave raids into Africa could have been as high as 112 million."*

There are campaigns today across the globe that fight to stop human trafficking, and rightly so, but there is something much more sinister about the connection of trade with the trading of humans that we may not at first realise. When we look at the statistics from history, we are aghast at how anyone could

---

[4] These are words taken from Dr John Azumah's video. *John Azumah holds a PhD in Islamic Studies from the University of Birmingham, UK, and is the Director for the Centre of Islamic Studies at the London School of Theology. He has previously served as a Research Fellow with the Akrofi-Christaller Institute in Ghana.* **Dr Azumah is the author of The Legacy of Arab-Islam in Africa: A Quest for Inter-Religious Dialogue** *(Oxford: Oneworld Publications, 2001)*

commit such crimes against humanity. Yet, in a very different guise, we are witnessing the largest human trafficking network the world has ever seen. It is not in the form of transporting a people group from one continent to the next as mentioned previously but, it is in a manner that will be instrumental in establishing a different type of global slave trade. A trade that will (and is as we speak) place all physical and spiritual aspects of humanity up for sale to the highest bidder. It will also place the vulnerable or unsuspecting in a place of servitude without the ability to opt out. This will not be done in secret, but in plain sight. Please consider the earlier global and regional atrocities and recognise that enslavement was never a secret affair. Also, please note, that it is impossible to see another human being as a commodity without first dehumanising them. You cannot freely enjoy the money that has made you rich without first having a perception of your brother or sister that is less than that of an animal. Ultimately, trading in the souls of men reflects the deepest form of degradation that humanity will stoop to and, sadly, it sits at the heart of society today.

Consider this, when Balak (representing the King of Moab and the King of Midian) was desperate to gain power and influence of the nation of Israel. He knew of Israel's success rate against phenomenal odds in 'man to man' warfare. He and the other kings may have assumed that Israel's success was due to a superior form of 'magic'. Whatever their thoughts, one thing was clear, to secure a victory against Israel, Balak had to resort to calling on ancient forces. This resulted in him calling on the power of the occult. He was willing to pay any price, employ any person that could do the job. He was prepared to call on Satan if it gave him power over Israel. The man for hire on this occasion was a man called Balaam who didn't come cheap (Numbers Chapter 22 – Chapter 23). We know that Balaam was unsuccessful in his exploits, but how is it conceivable that the leader of the nation, with his fellow leaders, could resort to such debased behaviour as representatives of their people.

Little has changed since and the examples given are only some of the reasons why God will judge the nations of the world. We have given ourselves to a bastion of satanic ideas that feed our destructive appetites. Continually educating ourselves in demonic theology we are well versed in evil and ignorant of the need for humility before the all-seeing God of Israel.

It is all too easy to shake our fists at heaven when we are ignorant of how God works and thinks. After all, if we can be advisors to 'The Creator', He wouldn't be God, right? We must remember that God's perspective on atrocities surpasses our calculations and finite minds. He isn't basing His information on hearsay, third-hand information, or the immediate scenario alone. This is how we judge matters when confronted by our judicial system. For example, when we consider the term **'trade in slaves and souls of men'** we at once identify with numbers to quantify the impact inflicted on society. However, we know by the revealed word of God (the Bible), that the aftermath of such acts of sin rips mercilessly through the very fabric of homes, communities, and nations. Its full impact cannot be measured in a numerical form. For instance, the removal of a man from his wife and family at once leaves an open door to other less favourable characters, it could also leave that wife and family open to banditry, kidnapping, betrayal, rape, etc. Now multiply these examples by the millions of men, women and children who were taken into slavery. Consider the calculated effect on the African continent. Travel across the waters which are laden with the lifeless remains of innocent people who died from disease, suicide, and exploitation, now cast your minds into the halls of power, the power bases of the world where the proceeds of the 'death trade' is shared between international beneficiaries. As if that were not enough, consider how we have all inherited the legacy of this degrading type of business and the Earth, intoxicated with the blood of the innocent, convulsing repeatedly with earthquakes, famines, and disease. Contrary to scientific diagnosis, the root cause of the world's deficit is sin. The adverse effect on the world's natural resources is due to the greed of man and the pillaging of gold, silver, diamonds, oil, ivory, herbs, sugar, cocoa, fruit, water, animals, people, ideas, affection. The supposed gradual depleting resources of the world are not the result of global warming, climate change, or any such ignominious ideas, but it is firmly rooted in sin. Yet, our finite minds cannot comprehend the level of wickedness that God sees, we are incapable of traversing time, past and present, to review every detail of human history accurately based on 100% fact. Our view, regardless of how well educated, is just the tip of the iceberg in comparison to God's multi-dimensional perspective. He makes this abundantly evident when providing us with a general overview of the world's condition. After all, how else could He convey a multifaceted, global condition to the simple minds of you and me? We cannot equate or relate to what God sees: if we could, He wouldn't be God.

"The LORD saw how great the wickedness of the human race had become on the earth, and that every inclination of the thoughts of the human heart was only evil all the time."

Genesis 6:5 (NIV)

The Soil – The Blood of Abel

The LORD said, "What have you done? Listen! Your brother's blood cries out to me from the ground."

Genesis 4:10 (NIV)

Soil is an incredible substance. First, the genius of YHWH formed the human body out of it and created an amazing vehicle, the likes of which has never and can never be duplicated, but also, from the same compound He was able to grow every living vegetation that humanity would ever need. We recall that before the sin of Adam and Eve the Earth remained pure and functioned in the perfect order that God had intended. However, after their sin, degradation would change the way that the earth functioned. Humanity would have to work the land and remove weeds to produce the necessary food needed for sustenance. Incredible, yet here lies the real dichotomy. The soil was created to bring forth life for our benefit, but we have used it as a place for hidden crimes. The soil hides the bodies of billions of Abels whose blood is crying out for justice, mercy, and truth. The cry is unbearable.

Soil can mean different things to different people. If you ask most people, they will probably refer to the soil being a mixture of minerals and decomposed material. To a civil engineer, the soil is loose material that isn't rock. Soil is complex, it can vary in depth, type, colour, and mineral content. Its composition is directly connected to the environment around it, past and present. You only have to take a look at farmland to see how the years of cultivation have influenced the texture of the soil used for planting crops, whereas, in other areas where the ground hasn't been worked for centuries, the texture can be different again. Local temperature, climate, man-made structures, absence of plant life, absence of water, can all influence the type of soil in any given region. It is with this understanding that we can now begin to explore the soil that provided the nutrients for a new era. An era that would begin with the sowing of a counterfeit seed using the same satanic agent who entered the Garden of Eden and planted it in the heart of the first created couple.

Do you remember the parable Yeshua (Jesus) told in the book of Matt. 13:1-9; Mark 4:1-9; Luke 8:4-8?

*Later that day large crowds of people gathered and came to Yeshua, and he told them this parable: "A sower went out to sow **his seed**. As he sowed, some fell on a footpath. First it was trampled, then the birds of the sky ate it. Some fell on rock. At first it sprouted, but then it dried out from want of moisture. Some fell among thistles. At first it sprouted, but then the thistles choked it. And some fell on good soil. It not only sprouted, it even produced grain, so that the sower saw a hundredfold return!*

"Whoever has ears to hear, let him hear!"

This parable is called 'the Parable of four soils'. [5]David Bivin and Joshua N Tilton in an article make this observation when examining the parable:

"By not revealing what the Four Soils parable was about until its dramatic conclusion Jesus drew in his audience and held their attention, making them the very thing the parable urged them to be: good listeners."

What was the dramatic conclusion that David Bivin and Joshua N Tilton are referring to? (See Matt. 13:10, 18-23; Mark 4:10, 13-20; Luke 8:9, 11-15)

Yeshua's disciples approached him and said, "What is the meaning of this parable?"

*So Yeshua replied, "The meaning of the parable is this: **the seed** represents the word of God. The scenario of the seed on the path represents those who hear God's word but do not accept it, so Satan comes and uproots it from their hearts. The scenario of the seed on the rock represents those who hear God's word and joyfully accept it, but since they have missed the point they turn away in times of testing.*

---

[5] Jerusalem Perspective article, Four Soils Parable by David N Bivin and Joshua N Tilton https://www.jerusalemperspective.com/17602/

The scenario of the seed among the thistles represents those who hear God's word and accept it, but worries, possessions and worldly pleasures choke them more and more. The scenario of the seed in the good soil represents those who hear God's word and accept it with a sincere determination to put it into practice."

The parable makes a very strong point about being a good listener but also conveys the message of having a good heart. The type of heart that keeps what one hears from the Word of God and acts upon, being careful to guard against influences that can come and take it away. The seed of God is relating to the teachings of God which are embedded in the Hebrew Scriptures. Now, in contrast, Rabbi Paul writes to Timothy about opposed teaching which he describes like this:

*The Spirit clearly says that in later times some will abandon the faith and follow deceiving spirits and things **taught by demons**. Such teachings come through hypocritical liars, whose consciences have been seared as with a hot iron. 1 Timothy 4:1,2 (NIV).*

Rabbi Paul is warning against the teaching that would attempt to turn the hearer towards another destructive teaching. So, we can conclude that if the word of God or the teaching of God is related to 'seed' for the hearers then it stands to reason that the teachings of Satan are related to a counterfeit 'seed' which Rabbi Paul describes as 'things taught by demons'. For this demonic seed to grow successfully it would require soil that has been cultivated and fed for a given period.

The Nutrients or Toxins?

We have already seen how slavery was a global business for an extraordinarily long time, and we may even have asked, why did it happen? How is it possible that the world could have engaged in this unthinkable business without stopping to consider the consequences? Well, you and I are not the first to have examined this issue.

"Then the LORD saw that the wickedness of man was great in the earth, and that every intent of the thoughts of his heart was only evil continually." Genesis 6:5 (NIV)

God's insight is recorded in such a clear manner that we struggle to refute it even in today's culture of "love and wellbeing". I would like to suggest to you that the whole business of slavery was the soil that would serve as the intoxicated ground for a false seed (false ideas) that had been held in readiness until the perfect season for its planting. Without slavery, the false ideas that would be formed from this seed could not masquerade in the guise of science, politics, education, religion, law, business, language, art, literature, history, etc. It would be distasteful to the modern palate of the masses. In other words, for this seed to grow it had to be sown in an environment that had no issue with the segregation of races, the sale, or murder of human beings (whether they were adults or unborn children). Its very success would rely on ancient teaching, expressed through the same spirit that worked through Cain, "Am I my brother's keeper?"

To prove this, I have included an article from an American newspaper called [6]'A New Slavery', taken from the September 21, 1900, edition of the Iowa State Bystander. This was an African American newspaper that made it a point to warn African Americans of the dangers of voting for the Democratic Party. Not much has changed since I fear.

Here's what it says,

[7]*"A New Slavery!" Newspaper Article, September 21, 1900*

---

[7] "A New Slavery!" Iowa State Bystander, p. 5, 21 September 1900. Courtesy of Library of Congress

A NEW SLAVERY Colored Voters, Read This and Be Warned.

HOW THE DEMOCRATS DO IT. First Take Away the Right to Vote, and Then What?

Democratic leaders in West Virginia are very solicitous of the negro vote. They profess great friendship for them. Let the negro look at what they do in Virginia, Kentucky, North Carolina, South Carolina and indeed all over the south with "Jim Crow car" laws and disenfranchisement of colored voters. Senator Tillman of South Carolina is close to Bryan and is a leader of leaders among Democrats. Here is what he said in the United States Senate on Feb. 26, 1900: "We have 125,000 negroes of voting age, and we had 100,000 whites. Beat that by honest methods. Yet you stood up here and insisted that we must give these people a 'free vote and a fair count.' They had it for eight years. *** We stuffed ballot boxes. We shot them. We are not ashamed of it. *** With that system-force, tissue ballots, etc.-we got tired ourselves. So we called a constitutional convention, and we eliminated, as I have said, all of the colored people whom we could under the fourteenth and fifteenth amendments." If the Democrats carry the legislature of West Virginia, what will happen to the colored people? *DISFRANCHISEMENT IS THE FIRST STEP INTO A NEW SLAVERY.*

This article conveys the mindset of the period it was written in. Openly racist language and action were considered normal in a supposed civilised society. Ironically, the legal system was manipulated to justify said actions, and the place of rhetoric was the US Senate, both of which were said to represent freedom and democracy: the American dream. Was this experience unique to America? Certainly not. Here is another [8]newspaper advertisement, this time in the London Daily Post, dated 13 September 1740. It is an advertisement for the sale of an 8-year-old girl, who is described as 'handy in the House and works with her needle', and a 14-year-old boy who *is able to wait at a Gentleman's Table.*' This was considered normal by the educated society of Britain as is demonstrated by the fact that even the newspaper didn't refuse to print the advert. Remember, to treat another human being as lesser than an animal, one must first dehumanise them. It is unthinkable today that your son or daughter could be advertised in such a grossly, inhumane manner, yet these newspaper cuttings demonstrate that humanity was generally accepting of such behaviour. There is a mindset here.

---

[8] Advertisement in the London Daily Post, 'Any persons disposed to buy a Negro', 1740
https://www.bl.uk/learning/images/georgian/large107332.html

In addition to this mindset, the language used in each newspaper item is quite revealing. In this advertisement the seller stated, *"any **person** disposed to buy a **Negro** boy or girl..."* the purchaser being denoted as a person, whereas the purchased was denoted as a non-person, a negro. The same occurs in the previous American newspaper when Senator Tillman states openly, *"We shot them. We are not ashamed of it."* The collective 'we' stood for a people group that considered 'them' to be non-persons. This is a natural progression of this mindset. It exposes the ignorance of the person's ignorance while using a language that is familiar to the reader. Why is this relevant? Well, this language and thinking were deeply embedded in the soil of slavery. It even influenced modern medicine and herbarium (the collection of preserved plant specimens). [9]Researchers are now discovering the connection between some of the world's largest plant collections and the slave trade voyages. This connection also includes, and is not exclusive to, the collection of slave body parts which were sent to England with the stated purpose of advancing science and medical practices. The slave ships supplied an opportunity

---

[9] A physician by trade, Sir Hans Sloane was also a collector of objects from around the world. By his death in 1753 he had collected more than 71,000 items. Sloane bequeathed his collection to the nation in his will and it became the founding collection of the British Museum.
https://www.britishmuseum.org/about-us/british-museum-story/sir-hans-sloane

to travel to these distant lands to collect unusual plant life and also to experiment on slaves who were the property of slavemasters.

In a book written by Reverend Josiah Priest, published in 1852 called [10]'*Bible Defence of Slavery; and Origin Fortunes, and History of the Negro Race,*' we gain a further snapshot into the religious mind. I use this term loosely here, as it is unfair and illogical to think true biblical faith is defined by our prejudices. So, with this in mind here are some extracts from the book:

"In presenting the following work to the American public, no apologies are offered. We live under a Government which tolerates liberty of thought and freedom of press, and in this expression of our honest views and feelings upon a subject relating to the general welfare of the country, we are but exercising a right which belongs to every American citizen."

Later he continues by saying…

The existence of free blacks in any community, whether free or slave, is universally admitted to be an evil of no minor consideration. Their removal, therefore, is a matter deeply affecting the interests and well-being of both races. Their present number and natural increase, places this beyond the reach of individual enterprise. The resources of the general government must, therefore, be brought into requisition in the removal of this, as well as any other evil of a general or national character…

The author has sought, in the oracles of God, in authentic history, and in the analogies of nature, the key to the mystery of the degradation, through the unchronicled ages of the past, of the negro race. The fact of the inferiority and consequent subordination of the black race to the white, being in accordance with the will of the

---

[10] Library of Congress catalog 'Bible Defence of Slavery; and Origin Fortunes, and History of the Negro Race' by Rev. Josiah Priest, A.M
https://hdl.handle.net/2027/loc.ark:/13960/t73t9pr9t

Supreme Ruler of the universe, is not like a mathematical problem, susceptible of absolute demonstration (Pg vii & viii)

As if this were not erroneous enough, he continues...

The great thickness and hardness of the heads of this people – the African race – is, in another respect, a singular providence in their favor, as a defense against the blows of angry masters, in a state of servitude – it being almost impossible to break their skulls even with a club.

Is this mentioned in the Bible somewhere?

The author has made the fatal mistake of looking at the Bible through the lens of his own or others' preconceptions. This is true of every false teaching where there is always an embedded element of truth. For example, the idea that a black person's skull is by divine providence designed to withstand the blows of a slavemaster is abhorrent, however, if you wrap that idea in biblical truth statements it becomes an assumed statement of 'divine' truth. The issue then becomes even more acute if the statements are made orally without the hearer doing their due diligence by listening well and questioning what they are listening to. It is well known that the Bible was used to subjugate slaves, but it is also a fact that Yahweh is not a supremacist of any kind, black or white. It is foolish to think that The Creator would denigrate His Torah (teachings) to the promotion of obviously divisive, destructive tenets.

The idea that one nation or people group is superior to another is not new either, it has been around for centuries. The use of 'experience' based evidence is also a common approach, in other words, the premise that one nation is superior to another evidenced by victory in war or that the subjugation of a class within a culture is indicative of the superiority of that culture. In both instances the evidence presented may seem overwhelmingly correct due to the numbers alone but, neither are true if other specifics cannot be answered. Such as, what do you mean superior? Are your ideas based on a biblical worldview or some other worldview? Are there racist, feminist, chauvinist, undertones to the substance of the debate? All of these and other questions make a huge difference to the answer regardless of our convictions or feelings. Finally, if God's measure of morality is absent it is wise to dismiss any such claims as spurious and even outlandish or embrace them at your peril.

By the 1800s the soil of slavery had been well tilled, the nutrients that would give much-needed sustenance to a carefully prepared seed was ready. Any moral boundaries that had restrained earlier generations had, by the 1800s, shifted so far that the meaning of caring for a fellow human being had been redefined. This insatiable appetite for the unthinkable created resistance to anything that remotely resembled biblical truth. There is no doubt that this period conditioned the way people thought about themselves and each other. These thoughts were often mixed with fear of a future that may affect their wealth, safety, and happiness; only serving to fuel the toxic business of slave trading that had gone on for centuries before. Interestingly, in contrast to Reverend Josiah Priest's biased thesis on faith and slavery, a Presbyterian preacher called Charles Finney painted a vivid picture of Christianity in America in 1857-1858. His works are also recorded in the Library of Congress should you want to undertake your examination. In his memoirs, [11]Charles Finney records the following information about the impact that the preaching of the biblical faith was having in the northern and southern parts of America:

---

[11] The direct link to Memoirs of Rev. Charles G. Finney / Written by himself. Finney, Charles G., 1792-1875 is stored in the Library of Congress but is stored digitally https://www.hathitrust.org/

The winter of 1857-1858 will be remembered as the time when a great revival prevailed throughout all the Northern states. It swept over the land with such power that for a time it was estimated that not less than fifty thousand conversions occurred in a single week. Daily prayer meetings were established throughout the length and breadth of the Northern states.

This revival is of so recent a date that I need not enlarge upon it, because it became almost universal throughout the Northern states. A divine influence seemed to pervade the whole land. Slavery seemed to shut it out from the South. The people there were in such a state of irritation, of vexation, and of committal to their peculiar institution of slavery, which had come to be assailed on every side, that the Spirit of God seemed to be grieved away from them. There seemed to be no place found for him in the hearts of the Southern people at that time. It was estimated that during this revival not less than five hundred thousand souls were converted in this country. The New York Tribune at that time published several extras, filled with accounts of the revival in different parts of the United States.

His observations are irrefutable. If the biblical message of salvation was being preached in the northern and southern parts of America, the general response should be the same, not necessarily numerically, I hasten to add. Isn't it amazing that the South was closed off to the preaching that God through ordinary people could not transform the lives there? It stands to reason that God's message will reach the heart of people who want to receive it, it also stands to reason that a counterfeit to God's message could not be sanctioned by His presence which is all about saving souls from sin. It is also obvious that in Reverend Josiah Priest's article, the use of the Bible to support racism carried no weight with anyone except those who shared his philosophy. This stands as a cautionary note for any proclaiming Bible reader, God is not here to support 'our' philosophy, He's given us the Bible to provide an insight into <u>His</u> teachings.

Hopefully, we are beginning to understand that the Bible was used as a tool alongside many other tools, to control, to divide, and conquer the innocent. Even in my youth, I have heard Bible teachers referring to '[12]the Curse of Ham' teaching, which plagued my mind every time something did not go my way or if I was treated badly. The default position was that as a black man, it will never be any different for me, my life was always going to be ruled by a series of slavemasters who were superior to me, all because of the curse of Ham. Thankfully, reading the Bible set me free from such an incredibly godless idea. However, these ideas have led many others to view Christianity as a 'white man's religion'. Of course, this is the furthest thing from the truth, especially as we understand that Christianity's real roots were embedded in Israel and not Britain, America or any other country.

Regardless of how history has tried to spray paint over real history, a careful re-examination must be undertaken. If not, we are likely to believe and promote the same erroneous falsehoods that past perpetrators successfully wholesaled to the masses.

---

[12] The 'Curse of Ham' has been around for many years and has been peddled as a biblical idea. Preached in white and black congregations, it has embedded itself into the religious world and masquerades as biblical truth. This teaching has cousins such as 'the mark of Cain' which alludes to Cain's physical skin colour change to black due to God placing 'a mark' on him. Incredulous as this all sounds, many people still believe it regardless of the poor application of the scriptures that relate to it. Reverend Josiah Priest's book picks up on these threads but only serves to reinforce the error. (See page 63 of his book 'Bible defence of slavery' – Moses, Miriam and Aaron in Numbers 12:1).

The Root System

Man vs Machine – Transition from the 18th to 19th Century (First and Second Industrial Revolution)

In a few chapters, we have traversed time in the hope that the origin of much controversy is recognised for what it is: deception. This deception is best described as the 'root system'. In other words, the organic structure from which later developed or matured ideas would run. Ideas that fed off the ground in which it was planted with never-ending possibilities to its source of nourishment and growth. It is also important to remember that as with the roots of any organic lifeform, the root system is intricately designed to prevent immediate detection. As it expands, it does so without being noticed by the person who walks over its soil, supplying organic foundations to the green shoot that would break through the surrounding surface to manifest itself at the most opportune time.

So, let us begin putting this into context. The world was going through a transition of huge proportions as it was moving into an era when humanity believed in its technological advancements. Self-determination was beginning to occupy the throne of people's hearts and the philosophy of dead men was being reintroduced into a world that needed alternative answers to the Bible. In other words, removing the perceived shackles of biblical faith in favour of a more 'me' centred approach.

Science was part of the root system that was steadily being groomed as the answer to the world's problems. It would eventually be rebranded to give credence to the whims of the human intellect, proving how man is completely self-sufficient. Science had largely explored the world to prove that God exists and is The Creator of all things, but this was to be reversed to answer the question, "How could God exist?"

It was under the banner of this pseudo-science that the theory of evolution was propelled into the public domain, drawing its newfound sustenance from the human desire for something new and relevant. If deception was the 'root system' then the theory of evolution was the seed. This theory supplied a recognisable form that encapsulated and gave legitimacy to society's historically embedded ideas about racial distinguishers. *At last, there was scientific evidence to the origin of races, the origin of man, even the reason for slavery and poverty. At last, the world would know that we were right about the superior intellect and success of the upper classes.* The climate was exactly right for the seed of evolution surpassing earlier attempts to plant this seed of an idea. Attempts that did not germinate.

Intentionally or not, Charles Darwin became the face of a new world brand that would span decades. Historians and ordinary people would grapple with his ideas and use them to their advantage, which usually meant the oppression of others. So, what began as a theory about the evolution of humans and the world, soon became much more forceful in its application. At the core of Darwinism was the idea that all organisms came from a common ancestor which experienced small genetic changes over time. This apparent process resulted in a selection of organisms that could survive and reproduce under the harshest conditions which would inevitably pass on their genes to future generations, leading to a process called 'the survival of the fittest'. Darwin initially used the animal kingdom to explore and examine how animals worked and survived, however, his ideas were eventually applied to human beings. This is where Darwinism grew from a seed into an established root system called Social Darwinism. It is under this banner of Social Darwinism that we see a progression of the 'theory of evolution' and an application that is often viewed in isolation from other world philosophies of the time. If we were to think carefully about the images that would be marketed under Social Darwinism, we would quickly see that they bore no relevance or hope to the black diaspora. The Neanderthal man is the image that most people think of when discussing evolution. However, most proponents of evolution will ignore the image of darker races being referenced as apes in the evolution picture of humanity's progression. Yet, it will still be argued that evolution is somehow the answer for all species, (including humans) and is the sure foundation for all races clearly denouncing God's existence but elevating man's superiority. It is important to note, this theory is not as 'all-embracing' of all human beings as we are led to believe, and it bears the same hallmarks as any man-centred philosophy: prejudice, domination, manipulation, and segregation, to mention just a few.

Interestingly, the mascot for this brand of philosophy, Charles Darwin, enrolled in 1825 at Edinburgh University at the age of 16 but dropped out after two years. His subject of study was medicine and not natural history or biology, as you might expect. This was probably an attempt to follow in the footsteps of his father and grandfather who both studied medicine at Edinburgh University, which at the time had a reputation for being a leader in medicine. It is difficult to understand how he made the leap from a university dropout to a global brand.

'Social Darwinism' hypothesised about many things; for example, if animals can be cross bred to create a hybrid with the best of the genetic traits, it was considered logical that this principle could also be applied to humans. In other words, if there is a process of natural selection in the animal kingdom that manifests itself in the longevity of the fittest due to genetics, then the careful choice of a physically strong and healthy male or female amongst human partners would ensure that the genetically superior, healthier traits of races would also be preserved, guaranteeing the longevity of the fittest variations in humans. Can you see where this is going? You do not have to be a [13]genius (excuse the pun) to work out how the prejudices of

---

[13] genius (n.)
late 14c., "tutelary or moral spirit" who guides and governs an individual

the past were easily embedded into such notions, giving way to the rebranding of ancient supremacist and embarrassingly unethical ideas. This also provides a clearer understanding of the thinking of wealthy business owners who gained their prosperity through a system of slavery. We can also understand why their descendants were segregated from their peers on the grounds of race and economic opportunity, continuing to pass on their wealth from generation to generation. Critically, these behaviours that directly contributed to the poverty-stricken slums in London and other areas of the world were being justified using the position of Social Darwinism as evidence. Branding it as scientific to promote a certain credibility, creating an unseen immune system that would withstand the probing questions of ordinary people whose inhumane experiences were contrary to its tenets. After all, who could disagree with Social Darwinism's conclusions when the assumption is that Social Darwinism is clearly measurable, testable, and provable?

It was not long before Social Darwinism had embedded itself in every area of the public and private sphere. It rapidly grew into a root system that mutated and attached itself to education, science, anthropometrics, religion, politics, psychology, psychiatry, sociology, biology, anatomy, mental testing, geography, genealogy, history, law, economics, biography, surgery, medicine, ethnology and finally, genetics. As it grew, it was redefining society while simultaneously gaining its nourishment and momentum from advocates in

---

through life, from Latin genius "guardian deity or spirit which watches over each person from birth; spirit, incarnation; wit, talent;" also "prophetic skill; the male spirit of a gens," originally "generative power" (or "inborn nature"), from PIE *gen(e)-yo-, from root *gene- "give birth, beget," with derivatives referring to procreation and familial and tribal groups. Sense of "characteristic disposition" of a person is from 1580s. Meaning "person of natural intelligence or talent" and that of "exalted natural mental ability" are first recorded 1640s. https://www.etymonline.com/word/genius

every area of society's professions, institutes of education and, of course, political parties. Charles Darwin's books such as, '*On the Origin of Species by Means of Natural Selection, or the Preservation of Favoured Races in the Struggle for Life*' (which is its original title) would be central to the movement while providing a platform for others to voice their own longstanding concepts in support of Charles Darwin's ideas. People such as the socialist Herbert Spencer who believed that evolution did not only apply to biological organisms but also applied to the development of human beings. He was the person responsible for coining the phrase '[14]*survival of the fittest*' in his 1864 book Principles of Biology, which he wrote after reading Charles Darwin's book '*On the Origin of Species by Means of Natural Selection, or the Preservation of Favoured Races in the Struggle for Life*'. Herbert Spencer was born April 27, 1820, Derby, Derbyshire, England— died December 8, 1903, Brighton, Sussex. He has been lauded as one of the most prominent philosophers of our time but now we are forced to ask, "What does that mean?"

It may be argued that neither Charles nor Herbert agreed with the position that others took after reading their material but, it cannot be denied that longstanding fears were reinvigorated by the theory of evolution. On the one hand, the poorer class appeared to be increasing in number, thus creating objections by the other classes to humanitarian support for the inferior, unfit, and unwanted. This was based on the misguided premise that humanitarian aid would only serve to keep the unfit around longer. Using the philosophy of the root system it was thought that only the fittest should be allowed to survive and this process should in no way be tampered with by good intentions. On the other hand, some did not think there was a problem in helping the process by aiding individuals who had

---

Herbert Spencer. (2015). In *Encyclopædia Britannica*. Retrieved from
[14] http://www.britannica.com/EBchecked/topic/559249/Herbert-Spencer

a desire to improve themselves, therefore, those individuals should be given help to do just that.

Either way, the world had now entered a new era where self-determination was king. Humanity had relinquished a duty of care to its fellow human being, while simultaneously abdicating accountability to a Creator. The resounding question was 'Why care for the weak?' With this new position, it was inevitable that fear would drive conversations on population growth in supposedly undeserving communities; it was also inevitable that there would be such an alarm amongst the upper classes who considered the sheer numbers of people in these unfit communities as a threat to other races. Communities that had not created their dilemma but were the product of global greed and hunger for personal power or pleasure. The conversations have changed little since then and we continue to see the ongoing influence of such ideas - ideas which are firmly rooted in the fear of a rapidly increasing birth rate in poor neighbourhoods and nations. The kind of fear that has been utilised by politicians to convince millions of people to pursue an independent, nationalistic culture at the exclusion of immigrants who appear to have little to offer. Immigrants (including children) who are perceived as promiscuous and predisposed to crime due to their evolutionary status.

Immigration and poverty are not new social issues but throwing off restraint during the 'Age of Enlightenment', in exchange for 'free thought', fuelled a process that grew into something that fitted comfortably into the mindset of the age. You may ask, how did we miss it? Surely, if this were true historically, it would have been taught in our education system. The truth is, the sinister presence of this unseen, dark hand was not easily identified due to the bedazzling effect of the prideful intellect, the accepted source of empowerment for many. The ability to decide one's own path and the freedom to revel in personal success under the banner of self-deserving praise due to a superior genetic makeup was all too much to resist. In many minds and institutions, including the government (which I will come to later), it all made perfect sense. This diseased thinking grew at speed in the soil of the nations, with Britain being at the head of many of the ideas. The city of Derby, UK was a focal point for industrial transformation and philosophy which is evident in its cotton mills and the philosophical society founded by Erasmus Darwin in 1783 (Charles Darwin's grandfather). Ironically, while industry was being revolutionised and people were embracing new ways of thinking, the business of slavery continued to supply the income and material for the philosophers and mill owners in the city. In other words, change was only happening for those that had the wealth and opportunity to afford it.

As the root system of Social Darwinism pushed deeper into the fabric of the human experience, others like Leonard Darwin (Charles Darwin's son) and Francis Galton (Charles Darwin's cousin) felt that Social Darwinism did not go far enough. These men and many others like them were instrumental in developing a system that would rebrand Social Darwinism and market it in the same manner as any other religious movement but diametrically opposed to the biblical worldview. It would, however, succeed in carrying the world with it to pick up where visible slavery had left off, which was easy to do considering the period in which this was happening. At the very heart of this theology was the complete and utter worship of self. Its ancestral character is found in Genesis 11:1-9, the origin of all things. Here the pursuit of godhood led to the setting up of a city and a structure[15] called Babel (which means to mix or confuse). Babel represented and conveyed supernatural connotations and goals, such as the overarching

[15] Genesis 11:4 *And they said, come let us build ourselves a city, and a tower whose top is in the heavens; let us make a name for ourselves, lest we be scattered abroad over the face of the whole earth* (NKJV)

goal to reach into the heavens to set up humanity as a self-proclaimed power. It is unfortunate and tragic that many a Christian perceives the influence of such minds to be creative and constructive, when not so long ago Yeshua's disciples were resisting such ideas and concepts as satanically infused philosophy. Ideas which entered congregations through secret conversations and manipulative individuals whose sole purpose was to infiltrate and disrupt a righteous movement set on a course of truth by The Jewish Messiah, and Rabbi, Yeshua.

As Britain led the way, the momentum of the 18th to 19th centuries was breathtaking as new inventions to supposedly improve the human experience and the world were created. The discoveries were ground-breaking, and the world was set to enter a new age with all the colours of success, success, success. At last, mankind had found the key that had eluded humanity for centuries, the key to happiness, peace, and ultimate liberation from the shackles of all external rules of conformity. This was to some, the fulfilment of ancient voices who had predicted this time of change through the application of human reasoning. This was also an opportunity for self-direction through the intervention of new concepts.

With the intellect, the challenge of improving the human experience and overcoming obstacles to doing and being what we choose, exploded in a race to be the first and the greatest.

[16]For completeness, here are some examples of the inventions that were birthed during this period:

1701   Jethro Tull invents the seed drill.

---

[16] Bellis, Mary. "Inventions and Inventors of the 18th Century. "ThoughtCo, Feb. 11, 2020, https://www.thoughtco.com/18th-century-timeline-1992474.

1709   Bartolomeo Cristofori invents the piano.

1711   Englishmen John Shore invents the tuning fork.

1712   Thomas Newcomen patents the atmospheric steam engine.

1717   Edmond Halley invents the diving bell.

1722   French C. Hopffer patents the fire extinguisher.

1724   Gabriel Fahrenheit invents the first mercury thermometer.

1733   John Kay invents the flying shuttle.

1745   E.G. Von Kleist invents the Leyden jar, the first electrical capacitor.

1752   Benjamin Franklin invents the lightning rod.

1755   Samuel Johnson publishes the first English language dictionary on April 15th after nine years of writing.

1757   John Campbell invents the sextant.

1758   Dollond invents the achromatic lens.

1761   Englishmen John Harrison invents the navigational clock, or marine chronometer, for measuring longitude.

1764   James Hargreaves invents the spinning jenny.

1767   Joseph Priestley invents carbonated water or soda water.

1768   Richard Arkwright patents the spinning frame.

1769   James Watt invents an improved steam engine.

1774   Georges Louis Lesage patents the electric telegraph.

1775   Alexander Cummings invents the flush toilet.

Jacques Perrier invents a steamship.

1776 David Bushnell invents a submarine.

1779 Samuel Crompton invents the spinning mule.

1780 Benjamin Franklin invents bifocal eyeglasses.

Gervinus of Germany invents the circular saw.

1783 Louis Sebastien demonstrates the first parachute.

Benjamin Hanks patents the self-winding clock.

The Montgolfier brothers invented the hot-air balloon.

Englishman Henry Cort invents the steel roller for steel production.

1784 Andrew Meikle invents the threshing machine.

Joseph Bramah invents the safety lock.

1785 Edmund Cartwright invents the power loom.

Claude Berthollet invents chemical bleaching.

Charles Augustus Coulomb invents the torsion balance.

Jean Pierre Blanchard invents a working parachute.

1786 John Fitch invents the steamboat.

1789 The guillotine is invented.

1790 The United States issued its first patent to William Pollard of Philadelphia for a machine that roves and spins cotton.

1791 John Barber invents the gas turbine.

Early bicycles are invented in Scotland.

1792 William Murdoch invents gaslighting.

The first ambulance arrives.

1794 Eli Whitney patents the cotton gin.

Welshman Philip Vaughan invents ball bearings.

1795 Nicolas Francois Appert invents the preserving jar of food.

1796 Edward Jenner develops the vaccination for smallpox.

1797 Amos Whittemore patents a carding machine.

A British inventor named Henry Maudslay invents the first metal or precision lathe.

1798 The first soft drink is invented.

Aloys Senefelder invents lithography.

1799 Alessandro Volta invents the battery.

Louis Robert invents the Fourdrinier Machine for sheet papermaking.

We cannot deny that lives were changed because of these inventions, nor can we assume that everything humanity created was used for evil. However, by placing these events into a historical context we begin to realise that we are witnessing a global transition of huge magnitude. A transition that would reshape everything in the human experience and understanding, while simultaneously preparing the human soul for further sinful gratification. In fact, during this period there are a series of historical layers that appear to wrestle for attention. Eventually, the tension between these layers would lead to further eruptions on a global scale, all appearing to be disconnected but very much related; in a way, opposing worlds constantly colliding in public view. The list of dates next to the inventions portrays a linear story of history, one that is easier to navigate if it were in a straight line. However, while considering a linear timeline we must also consider the layers within the timeline.

The sentiment, which was tied to the voice of racism described in earlier chapters, was closely akin to the experience of the Jewish community.

During and after the early Messianic Jewish movement of the first century, the definition of what it meant to be a disciple of Yeshua was subtly redefined. By the fourth century, influential characters of the religious and non-religious world had joined the ranks of evangelism teaching an anti-Semitic ideology. Although anti-Semitism is a term that was coined recently, its presence has been around since ancient times, practically anywhere the Jews existed. This influence of anti-Semitism has left an indelible mark on today's society. Take a moment to think about this. Consider the slavemasters that we discussed earlier who used the Bible to oppress and subjugate innocent mothers, fathers, and children. Now consider the inquisitions which were devised by Popes to maintain the State and the Roman Catholic Church's authority and religious unity. The inquisitions, which was their way of dealing with such heretics even under the pain of death. From the inquisitions came pogroms and ghettos which led to violent attacks and even the banishing of Jews from various countries[17] (no, African Americans were not the first to live in ghettos). So, wait a minute, isn't Roman Catholicism classed as Christian? Wasn't Constantine, The Emperor of Rome a Christian?

You can see the confusion that millions of people are faced with, when in fact Yeshua did not identify himself with Roman

---

[17] See The Dent Atlas of Jewish History by Martin Gilbert (From 2000 BC to present day) ISBN 0460861824. The book provides a pictorial journey of Jewish History.

Catholicism, Pentecostalism, Methodism, Anglicanism, or any other 'ism. He was born in Israel, presented to a Jewish Priest, raised by Jewish parents, studied the Hebrew Scriptures (what we disrespectfully refer to as the Old Testament), and was baptised in the presence of a Jewish Prophet. He taught from the Hebrew Scriptures and even stood against Satan using the Hebrew Scriptures. He is The Word made flesh, The Torah made flesh, and The teachings of God made flesh. He is the centre of the Apostolic writings (The New Testament - The Renewed Covenant). He is a Jew.

Tragically, today's world of biblical theology is still influenced by a similar if not exact premise that Jesus came to give us a New Testament, to deliver us from the law (Torah), Judaism. Why?

The answer is quite simple. If you can distance a person from the Hebraic expression of the biblical faith, you distance the ordinary man and woman from the richness or fullness of The Messiah. Satan knew this when he entered the Garden of Eden, and he knows that this is still true today. Tragically, we often give ourselves over to his devices by embracing anti-Jewish sentiment without appreciating that this by default is anti-Messiah. If we cannot love a Jewish person, then how can we love The Messiah, no, The Jewish Messiah. Yeshua puts it like this,

"The King will reply, 'Truly I tell you, whatever you did for one of the least of these brothers and sisters of mine, you did for me.'

"Then he will say to those on his left, 'Depart from me, you who are cursed, into the eternal fire prepared for the devil and his angels. For I was hungry and you gave me nothing to eat, I was thirsty and you gave me nothing to drink, I was a stranger and you did not invite me in, I needed clothes and you did not clothe me, I was sick and in prison and you did not look after me.'

"They also will answer, 'Lord, when did we see you hungry or thirsty or a stranger or needing clothes or sick or in prison, and did not help you?'

"He will reply, 'Truly I tell you, whatever you did not do for one of the least of these, you did not do for me.'

"Then they will go away to eternal punishment, but the righteous to eternal life."

Matthew 25:40-46 – (NIV)

Tertullian, a Christian author from Carthage in the Roman province of Africa, made this observation in his article *'Prescription Against Heresies'*, regarding a man called Cerdo, a Christian gnostic and influencer of Marcion:

[18]*"To this is added one Cerdo. He introduces two first causes, that is, two Gods-one good, the other cruel: the good being the superior; the latter, the cruel one, being the creator of the world. He repudiates the prophecies and the Law; renounces God the Creator; maintains that Christ who came was the Son of the superior God; affirms that He was not in the substance of flesh; states Him to have been only in a phantasmal shape, to have not really suffered, but undergone a quasipassion, and not to have been born of a virgin, nay, really not to have been born at all."*

Cerdo is promoting [19]Gnosticism which contradicts the biblical faith and tries to redefine who God and His son are, by

---

[18] https://ccel.org/ccel/tertullian/heretics **Prescription Against Heretics.** Read this work.
Originally printed in 1885, the ten-volume set, Ante-Nicene Fathers, brings together the work of early Christian thinkers. In particular, it brings together the writings of the early Church fathers prior to the fourth century Nicene Creed.
[19] Definition of *Gnosticism*: the thought and practice especially of various cults of late pre-Christian and early Christian centuries distinguished by the conviction that matter is evil and that emancipation comes through gnosis.

saying that the God of the Old Testament is different and distinct from the God of the New Testament. However, if you are not familiar with Gnostic teaching it would be easy to assume that Cerdo simply had another opinion on the Hebrew Scriptures. It is also easy to assume that Gnosticism was somehow birthed out of the biblical faith when it was paganism that tried to embed itself in the faith. It was Gnosticism's erroneous and blasphemous ideas that the early Apostles contended with when Gentiles came to faith. Read the letters from Rabbi Paul to the Corinthian congregation, for example. It is also important for every Christian to note that Cerdo is anti the Law (Torah) and prophets. This was later picked up and magnified by Marcion.

Marcion, obviously influenced by Cerdo's ideas, went on to dissect the biblical texts by rejecting the God of the Tanakh or Hebrew Scriptures and promoting the idea that Yeshua (Jesus) had secret knowledge (gnosis) while on the other hand accepting Rabbi Paul's writings on grace as ok. However, this did not stop him from dissecting the New Testament (The Renewed Covenant) too.

Examine his approach carefully and you will see an obvious attempt to distance the reader from anything remotely Jewish. It is partly for this reason that modern congregations embrace the idea of *'not under law but under grace'* out of context or misapply the term *'legalism'*. When either of these terms are used, it is usually in the context of being saved by the God of the New Testament (Yeshua) and being set free from the God of the Old Testament (YHWH), the lawgiver. This theology is anti-Jewish and therefore, once again, anti-Messiah and logically anti-God.

"Gnosticism." *Merriam-Webster.com Dictionary*, Merriam-Webster, https://www.merriam-webster.com/dictionary/gnosticism. Accessed 22 May. 2021.

Gnosticism through the following characters and others has given us this theology: -

- Cicero, Origen of Alexandria (185-254 AD),
- John Chrysostom (344-407 AD) and even Martyn Luther (1483-1546).

Rome was central to this anti-Jewish sentiment and continued to fuel the fire of anti-Semitism for centuries later. Also, the machine of propaganda continued to reinforce a stereotype about the Jewish person to illegally release them of their God-given responsibility to teach the gentile world about The God of Israel and His Messiah. Of course, with all such attempts, inevitably, freedoms are also removed, and other places of liberation are sort by the victims of such propaganda. As a result of this flagrant mindset, the Jewish community were almost erased from the pages of history during the 1800-1900s and no-one seemed to notice.

The Evangelists

"Men of Athens, I perceive that in all things you are very religious; for as I was passing through and considering the objects of your worship, I even found an altar with this inscription: TO THE UNKNOWN GOD.

Acts 17:22 (Last Part) – 23

The seed and the root system find their origin in evolution or Darwinism, a new movement, but what would follow is the appearance of green shoots. Shoots that began breaking through the soil from which the blood of the innocent continually cried, the soil that had given this green shoot and its root system full protection and anonymity until an appointed time. However, we cannot continue our exploration of this complex subject without first pausing to review some of the foundational members who can only be described as the evangelists, preachers, and apostles of this movement. These are ministers who were baptised and ordained to establish this new religion, not by a Holy God or through the inspiration of His Holy Spirit, I hasten to add, but through the intervention of another kind of spirit. Enthused with a drive to reform the world and baptised by evil these individuals aid the newly forming plant by watering and feeding it with the substance of unwitting worshippers from every nation, tribe, and tongue. Intoxicating it with the blood of the innocent while it and the surrounding ground cry out mercilessly for more souls, more worship, more blood.

Many other individuals played a role in the growth of this new religion but as with any movement, some play a more prominent role than others. It would be impossible to examine all of the proponents involved in this book alone but what can be said is that they were all inspired by the same spirit and manifested the same characteristics. Messianic believers of the first century described them as follows:

*"For such **false apostles** as these are deceitful workers disguising themselves as apostles of Messiah. And no wonder: for [20]Satan disguises himself as an angel of light. Therefore it is not great*

[20] It is no surprise that Satan is connected with disguising himself as an angel of light as another name is 'Lucifer' which means "light bringing or light bearer" and is from the Latin lux "light" and ferre "to bring" https://www.etymonline.com/word/lucifer

*if his servants also are **disguised as servants/ministers** of righteousness: whose end will be according to their works."*

II Corinthians 11:13,14 – (ONM)

*"Beware of **false prophets**, who come to you in sheep's clothing, but inwardly they are ravenous wolves."*

Matthew 7:15 – (NKJV)

*"But there were also **false prophets** among the people, even as there will be **false teachers** among you, who will secretly bring in destructive heresies, even denying the Lord who bought them, and bring on themselves swift destruction."*

2 Peter 2:1 – (NKJV)

Let's not forget, the biblical faith stands alone in stark opposition to Satan's realm. A realm that relies upon confusion, violence, chaos, and any debased means necessary to execute its goals.

With that said, here is a cautionary note that should not slip the reader's attention. The instances referred to in the following pages could be brushed off as conspiracy theories - a term that was created to divert the enquirer away from the truth, but it is good practice to approach any subject by giving the benefit of doubt to the speaker. Only then can what has been said be verified or contradicted by the hearer.

In this chapter, a selection of persons will be mentioned along with additional references to words and/or phrases coined by the individual. Though brief, their thoughts and credentials will speak for themselves later so take notes if necessary and keep them alongside the book. Be a discerning reader. Let's begin.

Francis Galton

Quote:

[21]*"The improvement of our stock seems to me one of the highest objects that we can reasonably attempt."(Page 50)*

The founder of eugenics and the cousin of Charles Darwin was born in Birmingham, UK on February 16th, 1822 (you will probably have noticed by now that the Darwin family and relatives play a significant role in transforming the face of British society). According to the records of the United Grand Lodge of England, it was in February 1844 that Galton became a freemason at the Scientific lodge, held at the Red Lion Inn in Cambridge, progressing through the three masonic degrees:

Apprentice, 5 February 1844; Fellow Craft, 11 March 1844; Master Mason, 13 May 1844.

Francis Galton read the works of his cousin Charles and was so impressed he concluded that the evolution theory did not go far enough. If the question at the heart of the survival of the fittest was *'Why care for the weak?'*, the question for Francis Galton's hypothesis was, *'Could not the human race be improved?'* Francis Galton would be instrumental in navigating evolution further down the road of racial science, a pseudo-science like many others that used evolution to authenticate the notion of

---

[21] EUGENICS: ITS DEFINITION, SCOPE AND AIMS by FRANCIS GALTON, D.C.L.; Sc.D.; F.R.S. Read before the Sociological Society at a Meeting in the School of Economics and Political Science (London University), on May 16th, 1904. Professor KARL PEARSON, F.R.S., in the chair.

inferior and superior races. A quote from his article *'Eugenics: Its Definition, Scope and Aims'* states,

> *"Out of the hundreds and thousands of species that have been tamed, very few indeed are fertile when their liberty is restricted and their struggles for livelihood are abolished; those which are so and are otherwise useful to man becoming domesticated. There is perhaps some connection between this obscure action and the disappearance of most savage races when brought into contact with high civilisation, though there are other and well-known concomitant causes. But while most barbarous races disappear, some, like the negro, do not. It may therefore be expected that types of our race will be found to exist which can be highly civilised without losing fertility; nay, they may become more fertile under artificial conditions, as is the case with many domestic animals." (Page 48)*

It is this constant interweaving of supposed deep philosophical thought with racial tones that confuse the modern reader. Of course, in the period these ideas were posited it would not generate shock in some quarters, for the reasons we have mentioned in previous chapters. Nonetheless, the idea that science can be racist is a consideration we all have to conclude with the affirmative.

In 1865 Francis Galton published his first article in [22]Macmillan's Magazine. It was entitled *"Hereditary Talent and Character"*. It reveals his early thoughts which set the tone for his quest to improve the human race. His focus was on the intellect and how this could be passed from generation to generation. Francis Galton states:

> *"The power of man over animal life, in producing whatever varieties of form he pleases, is enormously great. It would seem as*

---

[22] https://galton.org/essays/1860-1869/galton-1865-macmillan-hereditary-talent.html Part I, *Macmillan's Magazine*, vol. 12, 1865 pp. 157-166.

though the physical structure of future generations was almost as plastic as clay, under the control of the breeder's will. It is my desire to show, more pointedly than - so far as I am aware - has been attempted before, that mental qualities are equally under control." (Page 157)

This may seem like a plausible position to take but as the article progresses, some disturbing language and comparisons are revealed.

He writes,

(Hereditary Talent and Character - Second Paper)

"Still more strongly marked than these, are the typical features and characters of different races of men. The Mongolians, Jews, Negroes, Gipsies, and American Indians; severally propagate their kinds; and each kind differs in character and intellect, as well as in colour and shape, from the other four. They, and a vast number of other races, form a class of instances worthy of close investigation, in which peculiarities of character are invariably transmitted from the parents to the offspring." (Page 320)

"Here, then, is a well-marked type of character, that formerly prevailed over a large part of the globe, with which other equally marked types of character in other regions are strongly contrasted. Take, for instance, the typical **West African Negro**. He is more unlike the **Red man** in his mind than in his body. Their characters are almost opposite, one to the other. **The Red man has great patience, great reticence, great dignity, and no passion; the Negro has strong impulsive passions, and neither patience, reticence, nor dignity. He is warm-hearted, loving towards his master's children, and idolised by the children in return. He is eminently gregarious, for he is always jabbering, quarrelling, tom-tom-ing, or dancing. He is remarkably domestic, and he is endowed with such constitutional vigour, and is so prolific, that his race is irrepressible.**

The Hindu, the Arab, the Mongol, the Teuton, and very many more, have each of them their peculiar characters. We have not space to analyse them on this occasion; **but, whatever they are, they are transmitted, generation after generation, as truly as their physical forms."** *(Page 321)*

In the second part of the article, he dives into specific people groups to highlight their differences and his observations. He refers to them in a manner that appears to be scientific. However, an intelligent person could not agree. Could they?

"In strength, agility, and other physical qualities, Darwin's law of natural selection acts with unimpassioned, merciless severity. The weakly die in the battle for life; the stronger and more capable individuals are alone permitted to survive, and to bequeath their constitutional vigour to future generations. ***Is there any corresponding rule in respect to moral character? I believe there is, and I have already hinted at it when speaking of the American Indians.*** *I am prepared to maintain that its action, by insuring a certain fundamental unity in the quality of the affections, enables men and the higher order of animals to sympathise in some degree with each other, and also, that this law forms the broad basis of our religious sentiments." (Page 323)*

His conclusion is based on an assumption. An assumption that one race is superior in intellect to another. A premise that would sit at the heart of everything he would write about and act upon later. He believes that intelligence along with other characteristics is hereditary as is *tom-tom-ing* and *jabbering*. In his final paragraph (as with a few others) we see the connection between his philosophy and Charles Darwin's. The article is a continuation of the same idea, presented in a myriad of ways.

He concludes the whole article with a reference to the origin of man and the original sin (which is a reference to the book of Genesis in the Bible).

"The sense of original sin would show, according to my theory, not that man was fallen from a high estate, but that he was rapidly rising from a low one. It would therefore confirm the conclusion that has been arrived at by every independent line of ethnological research - that our forefathers were utter savages from the beginning; and, that, after myriads of years of barbarism, our race has but very recently grown to be civilized and religious." (Page 327)

The ideas conveyed in his first and second article are a complete reversal of the Bible's concept of sin and the high estate of the first human beings. However, this should not be surprising as we have already seen that the soil for these ideas is firmly rooted in slavery. The seed is Darwinism and now its manifestation as a green shoot is supported by an invisible yet actively present root system.

It is important to note that it wasn't until 1869 that Francis Galton published 'Hereditary Genius' where he expanded on some of the ideas mentioned in these articles. His premise was that mental and physical attributes were passed within descendants and that 'genius' was a high-level ability that an individual was born with due to their family stock. So, in his world, it was important to have parents who were intellectually adept to produce a child that would be born with a superior intellect. An idea that gained prominence and is still embedded in the thinking and language of society today. When we want to applaud the impressive work of a bright child, we make statements like, *'It's all in the genes...'*, *'he/she must have got it from parent A or B'*.

Consider this, the word 'genius' originated in Rome and is from the Latin verb 'gignere' meaning 'to give birth or bring forth'. The Romans believed that every individual had a spirit that guided them through life and was part of them from birth. So, when a person demonstrated exceptional aptitude in a given activity or area, they were called a 'genius' because of the spirit that manifested these attributes through them. If we were to compare the Roman and Galton idea without knowing the origin of the information, it would be easy to assume that they came from the same source. This wouldn't be far from accurate, as Francis Galton and other new thinkers borrowed from dead men's brains, rebranding Hellenistic philosophy as science (see earlier chapters).

The wise writer of Ecclesiastes in the Bible states:

All things are full of labor; Man cannot express it. The eye is not satisfied with seeing, Nor the ear filled with hearing. That which has been is what will be, That which is done is what will be done, And there is nothing new under the sun. Is there anything of which it may be said, "See, this is new"? It has already been in ancient times before us.

Ecclesiastes 1:8-10 (NKJV)

The Galton Institute and its Eugenics Past

Interestingly, the organisation which was The Galton Institute (renamed Adelphi Genetics Forum) rejects outright the theoretical basis and practice of coercive eugenics, which it regards as having no place in modern life. [23] *"Galton's idea of 'eugenics' was based on concepts and hypotheses that served to create artificial hierarchies and division between peoples of different class, ethnicity and culture. The Galton Institute wishes to state clearly and unequivocally that it deplores these outmoded and discredited ideas, which should play no part in society today."*

---

[23] *The Galton Institute rejects the eugenic past –*

https://adelphigenetics.org/history/eugenic-past/

It has been over 100 years of suffering, humiliation, and manipulation since organisations like this were founded. Its objectives were clear then, so has anything changed?

Phrases and words coined by Francis Galton

Eugenics

The term 'eugenics' was coined by Francis Galton in 1883. It is a word that is derived from the Greek 'eu-genes' which means 'well-born' or 'good birth'.

As mentioned previously, the ideas and concepts of evolution and eugenics were not new. They were simply borrowed from people like Plato who referenced such ideas in his article *'The Republic of Plato*[24]*'*. Francis Galton believed that eugenics should be embraced by society as a religion. Here is an extract from his article 'Eugenics, Its Definition, Scope and Aims':

[25]*Persistence in setting forth the national importance of Eugenics. There are three stages to be passed through.* **Firstly** *it must be made familiar as an academic question, until its exact importance has been understood and accepted as a fact;* **Secondly** *it must be recognised as a subject whose practical development deserves serious consideration; and* **Thirdly** <u>*it must be introduced into the national conscience, like a new religion*</u>*. It has, indeed, strong claims to become an orthodox religious tenet of the future, for Eugenics co-operate with the workings of Nature by securing that humanity shall be represented*

---

[24] https://archive.org/details/in.ernet.dli.2015.149151
[25] Francis Galton. *"Eugenics, Its Definition, Scope and Aims." Sociological Papers.* London, 1905.
https://journals.sagepub.com/doi/pdf/10.1177/0038026104SP100104

by the fittest races. What Nature does blindly, slowly, and ruthlessly, man may do providently, quickly, and kindly.

In 1926 this sentiment was repeated by the President of the American Eugenics Society.

Quote:

"The eugenic movement, therefore, cannot be a short campaign like many political or social movements. It is, rather, like the founding and development of Christianity, something to be handed on from age to age."

As with Darwinism, Eugenics soon became Social Eugenics as Francis Galton (and others) encouraged the perceived intellectually superior, healthy individuals to have children to improve the human stock to outdo the lesser intelligent, unhealthy gene pool. The natural progression led to ways of discouraging or reducing the birth rate of the unfit members of society.

By definition, Eugenics is a religion, its beliefs and goals are laid out in [26]*A Eugenics Catechism, American Eugenics Society, Inc. 1926*. It worships the intellect by placing it firmly on the throne of our hearts and crowning it as 'wisdom'. This leaves us with a poignant question. So, if Eugenics is a religion, what does that make Darwinism?

Nature and Nurture

In 1874 Francis Galton popularized the phrase "nature and nurture" with the publication of *'English Men of Science: Their*

---

[26] *Vermont Eugenics: A Documentary History. This document is: A Eugenics Catechism, American Eugenics Society, Inc. 1926.*
http://www.uvm.edu/~eugenics/primarydocs/oraesec000026.xml

Nature and Nurture'. Such terminology has become the foundation for current discussions on human development as though the idea of successful progress in life can be summed up in an intellectual framework. In other words, does the environment play a significant part in a person's success in life (nurture) or is a genetic predisposition (nature), passed on from parents to a child the reason for success? Francis Galton believed the latter. However, once again the idea of nature vs nurture originated in Greek philosophy. Greek philosophers such as Plato favoured nature and others like Aristotle favoured nurture.

Julian Sorell Huxley

Was born on 22 June 1887 and was the grandson of [27]Thomas Henry Huxley, Darwin's bulldog, as he was named due to his forceful defence of Charles Darwin and evolution. This is reflected in a letter from Thomas Henry Huxley to Charles Darwin, 23 November 1859.

[28]*I finished your book yesterday. . . Since I read Von Baer's Essays nine years ago no work on Natural History Science I have met with has made so great an impression on me & I do most heartily thank you for the great store of new views you have given me. . .As for your doctrines, I am prepared to go to the Stake if requisite. . .I trust you will not allow yourself to be in any way disgusted or annoyed by the considerable abuse & misrepresentation which unless I greatly mistake is in store for you. . . And as to the curs which will bark and yelp – you must recollect that some of your friends at any rate are endowed with an amount of combativeness which (though you have often &*

---

[27] In 1869 Thomas Henry Huxley coined the term agnosticism (from Greek agnōstos, "unknowable")
[28] https://ucmp.berkeley.edu/history/thuxley.html

justly rebuked it) may stand you in good stead -- I am sharpening up my claws and beak in readiness

The Huxley family shared an obvious affinity with the Darwin family and were largely responsible for the distribution of the theory of evolution. As families of intellectuals, they were given opportunities that resulted in positions of great influence. Of course, they used this to the fullest and set a course to change the world with a new brand of theology. It is with this understanding that the role of Julian S Huxley draws particular interest as he was a humanist, evolutionary biologist, eugenicist, and internationalist who occupied several influential positions and received awards and accolades for his work. These include, but are not exclusive to:

- President of the British Eugenics Society (1959 - 1962)
- The First President of the Humanist Society
- First Director-General of UNESCO (1946 - 1948)
- An evolutionary biologist (which is the study of the evolutionary process that produced a variety of life forms on Earth)
- A founding member of the World Wildlife Fund
- Knighted in 1958
- Awarded the Laskar Foundation (in the category of Planned Parenthood)

From his credentials, we see a theme unfolding. A humanist who believes in eugenics and the evolutionary process of humanity who wins an award in the category of Planned Parenthood (birth control/abortion/sterilization) is given the position of First Director-General of UNESCO, the United Nations Educational, Scientific and Cultural Organisation. An international body that was responsible for educating the world. Is this a coincidence? By no means. By simply reading the booklet, *'UNESCO: Its Purpose and Its Philosophy', by Julian Huxley* it is obvious that Julian S Huxley uses this platform to amplify a very clear agenda that was intended to change the way the world thought. Within the pages of this booklet, he boldly includes the tenets of this new global religion. Of course, the common man may never have heard of this literature or been made aware of its presence, but its influence would be seen and felt by everyone.

He clearly outlines the direction of UNESCO:

[29]*'Thus the general philosophy of Unesco should, it seems, be a scientific world humanism, global in extent and evolutionary in background.' (Page 8)*

In his discourse, he touches on the issue of equality, which lifts the reader to a place of feeling included but then all such feelings are soon dashed when the reader lights upon statements such as:

'...indeed, the principle of equality of opportunity must be amended to read 'equality of opportunity with the limits of aptitude.' Thus it is a fact, however disagreeable, that considerable percentage of the population is not capable of profiting from higher education; to this point we shall return later. It is equally a fact that a considerable percentage of young men have to be rejected for military service on the grounds of physical weakness or mental instability, and that these grounds are often genetic in origin.' (page 20)

'At the moment, it is probable that the indirect effect of civilisation is dysgenic instead of eugenic; and in any case it seems likely that the dead weight of genetic stupidity, physical weakness, mental instability, and disease-proneness, which already exist in the human species, will prove too great a burden for real progress to be achieved. Thus even though it is quite true that any radical eugenic policy will be for many years politically and psychologically

---

[29] UNESCO: Its Purpose and Its Philosophy by Julian Huxley. (Preparatory commission of the United Nations Educational Scientific and Cultural Organisation 1946)

impossible, it will be important for Unesco to see that the eugenic problem is examined with the greatest care, and that the public mind is informed of the issues at stake so that much that now is unthinkable may at least become thinkable.' (Page 21)

Julian Huxley saw there would be challenges to educating the world in the things of humanism, evolutionary biology, eugenics. So, in the second chapter, he sets out a programme on how his vision could be achieved. Once again for brevity, I will refer to such areas of interest in short:

• **Mass Campaigns for Education:** *'Thus mass campaigns against illiteracy and for a common fundamental education must form part of Unesco's programme.' (Page 17)*

• **Human Values: Philosophy and The Humanities**: *'Unesco must accordingly promote the study of philosophy as an aid in the clarification of values, for the benefit of mankind in general. It must also do so in order to have its own clearly thought-out scale of values to guide it in its own operations, both positively in what it should undertake or assist, and negatively in what it should avoid or discourage. Here it will be guided by the philosophy of evolutionary humanism which I adumbrated in my first chapter. Such a philosophy is scientific in that it constantly refers back to the facts of existence.' (Page 39)*

• **The Social Sciences**: *'The social sciences are almost coterminous with the study of man. At any rate, since social life based upon self-reproducing tradition is the distinguishing feature of man, they can claim to be dealing with the essential features of the human sector of the evolutionary process.' (Page 44)*

• **The Creative Arts**: *'The field of the arts includes music; painting; sculpture and the other visual arts; ballet and dance;*

creative writing, from poetry and drama to the novel and the critical essay; architecture and the film, in so far as arts; and all the applications of art, from interior decoration to industrial design.' (Page 48)

- **Libraries, Museums and Other Cultural Institutions:** *'We conclude by amplifying the point from which we started-that libraries and museums and kindred establishments have the double function of conserving and making available the world's heritage, both cultural and scientific, both human and natural. These two functions are sometimes referred to rather baldly as storage and preservation on the one hand, public exhibition and use on the other.' (Page 57-58)*

- **Mass Media:** *'In the first Article of its Constitution, Unesco is expressly instructed to pursue its aims and objects by means of the media of mass communication-the somewhat cumbrous title (commonly abbreviated to "Mass Media") proposed for agencies, such as the radio, the cinema and the popular press, which are capable of the mass dissemination of word or image.' (Page 58)*

"Taking the techniques of persuasion and information and true propaganda that we have learnt to apply nationally in war, and deliberately bending them to the international tasks of peace, if necessary utilising them, as Lenin envisaged, to "overcome the resistance of millions" to desirable change. Using drama to reveal reality and art as the method by which, in Sir Stephen Tallent's words, "truth becomes impressive and living principle of action," and aiming to produce that concerted effort which, to quote Grierson once more, needs a background of faith and a sense of destiny. This must be a mass philosophy, a mass creed, and it can never be achieved without the use of the media of mass communication. Unesco, in the press of its detailed work, must never forget this enormous fact." (Page 60)

Huxley's vision for UNESCO and its programmes were considered, targeted and executed with the support of like-minded individuals. Ironically, UNESCO has successfully accessed communities around the world that have no idea of its origins or its agenda. These communities exist in other cultures, poor, diseased and without opportunity. Yet UNESCO continues to be seen as a world educator and humanitarian organisation. Borrowing the words of Jeremiah the prophet, *'Can an Ethiopian change his skin or a leopard its spots? Neither can you do good who are accustomed to doing evil.'* (Jeremiah 13:23, 24- NIV)

*UNESCO is only one of 17 specialised agencies of the United Nations; the United Nations being formed in 1945 following the Second World War. For your information and perusal, the names of all the [30]specialised agencies to date are:

- FAO: Food and Agriculture Organization of the United Nations
- ICAO: International Civil Aviation Organization
- IFAD: International Fund for Agricultural Development
- ILO: International Labour Organization
- IMF: International Monetary Fund
- IMO: International Maritime Organization
- ITU: International Telecommunication Union
- *UNESCO: United Nations Educational, Scientific and Cultural Organization

---

[30] https://ask.un.org/faq/140935 **UN specialized agencies** are international organizations that coordinate their work with the United Nations through negotiated agreements.

- UNIDO: United Nations Industrial Development Organization
- UNWTO: World Tourism Organization
- UPU: Universal Postal Union
- WHO: World Health Organization
- WIPO: World Intellectual Property Organization
- WMO: World Meteorological Organization
- World Bank Group
    - IBRD: International Bank for Reconstruction and Development
    - IDA: International Development Association
    - IFC: International Finance Corporation

Exploring the influencers within the UN's special agencies would require another book. However, be it accurate to say that at the leadership level of the agencies you will discover individuals of the same or similar mindset as Julian Huxley. Does this mean that we have witnessed the biggest hoax in living history? I'll let you decide.

Phrases and words coined by Julian S Huxley

Transhumanism

Here are some extracts from Julian Huxley's book [31]'New Bottles for New Wine' (1957), where the term was first used:

The human species can, if it wishes, transcend itself — not just sporadically, an individual here in one way, an individual there in another way, but in its entirety, as humanity. We need a name for this new belief. Perhaps transhumanism will serve: man remaining man, but transcending himself, by realizing new possibilities of and for his human nature. (Page 21)

*"I believe in **transhumanism**": once there are enough people who can truly say that, the human species will be on the threshold of a new kind of existence, as different from ours as ours is from that of Pekin man. It will at last be consciously fulfilling its real destiny. (Page 21)*

Transhumanism is the merging of the human body with technology to enhance the human body to become 'superhuman'. Once again, this is not purely a concept or an idea as we may first assume, it is a religion.

Charles Davenport

Quote

[32]"*Shall we not rather take the steps that scientific study dictates as necessary to dry up the springs that feed the torrent of defective and degenerate protoplasm?"*

---

[31] Huxley, Julian. (1968). Transhumanism. Journal of Humanistic Psychology - J HUM PSYCHOL. 8. 73-76. 10.1177/002216786800800107.
[32] Davenport, C. B. (1910). Report of Committee on Eugenics. Journal of Heredity, 1(2), 126-129.

[33]*"I believe in the selection of immigrants so that our national germplasm is not adulterated with traits of social maladjustment."*

The undisputed leader of Eugenics in America, born 1 June 1866 in Stamford, Connecticut, USA. He received a doctorate in Zoology at Harvard University in 1892 where he taught until 1899 while securing funds to create the Station for the Experimental Study of Evolution which later became the Department of Genetics at the Carnegie Institution of Washington. He left Harvard University to join the University of Chicago as a curator of the zoological museum from 1901 to 1904. In 1904 he became the director of **Cold Spring Harbor Laboratory** which is where he founded the [34]**Eugenics Record Office** in 1910. It was here that an archive of thousands of family histories was compiled to study and promote Eugenics. Within the **Eugenics Record Office, Bulletin No 10A** there are very clear statements about the motives, methods and agenda behind the establishment. Ironically, the committee were vigilant at documenting their thoughts on paper, making it easy for any researcher to reach reliable conclusions. In the opening statement on the front cover, we have the following:

"Report of the Committee to Study and to Report on the Best Practical Means of Cutting Off the Defective Germ-Plasm in the American Population. By Harry H. Laughlin, Secretary of the Committee."

This is followed by a selected paragraph and diagram in the report.

---

[33] NAS Biographical Memoir of Charles Benedict Davenport by Oscar Riddle
[34] Haunted Files is a project of the Asian/Pacific/American Initiative at NYU. Here, the Eugenics Record Office is reimagined:
https://apa.nyu.edu/hauntedfiles/

[35]*In those wherein heredity is demonstrated to be the prime factor, the control of heredity should be the means used by society in controlling the qualities so determined. It is the business of eugenics to seek out such instances and to develop a practical method of control.*

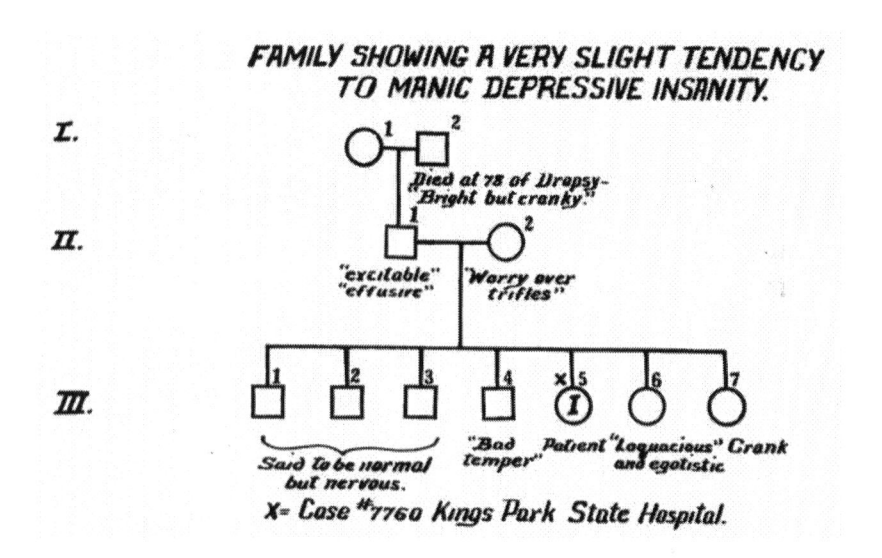

FAMILY SHOWING A VERY SLIGHT TENDENCY TO MANIC DEPRESSIVE INSANITY.

I. ○¹—□²
       Died at 78 of Dropsy-Bright but cranky.

II. □¹ ○²
    "excitable" "Worry over
    "effusive"   trifles"

III. □¹ □² □³ □⁴ ⊗⁵ ○⁶ ○⁷
     _____/   "Bad   Patient "Loquacious" Crank
     Said to be normal temper"   and egotistic
     but nervous.

X = Case #7760 Kings Park State Hospital.

As if that were not enough, here is an extract from page 45 titled *"Suggested Remedies"* which is self-explanatory in outlining the organisation's plan of attack. It reads as follows:

In a study of this sort it is proper carefully to consider each of the several different remedies which have been proposed or suggested or which appear as possibly efficacious for purging from the blood of the race the innately defective strains described in the previous chapter. The following list is a catalogue of such agencies.

1. Life segregation (or segregation during the reproductive period).

---

[35] Extract from Eugenics Record Office, Bulletin NO. 10 A page 40. The diagram is taken from page 38.

2. *Sterilization.*

3. *Restrictive marriage laws and customs.*

4. *Eugenical education of the public and of prospective marriage mates.*

5. *Systems of matings purporting to remove defective traits.*

6. *General environmental betterment.*

7. *Polygamy.*

9. *Neo-Malthusianism.*

10. *Laissez-faire.*

Davenport was involved with the **American Breeders Society** (now called the **American Genetics Society**), in particular the Eugenics Committee, which is a sub-group of the American Breeders Society. As you have probably gathered, Davenport was a puritan of Eugenics, a true disciple. His obsession with Eugenics is probably the main reason he became a leader of the movement in the USA.

One of his written works is called [36]*'Heredity in Relation to Eugenics' 1911* where he defines what Eugenics is:

"Eugenics is the science of the improvement of the human race by better breeding or, as the late Sir Francis Galton expressed it: — ''The science which deals with all influences that improve the inborn qualities of a race." The eugenical standpoint is that of the agriculturalist who, while recognizing the value of culture, believes that permanent advance is to be made only by securing the best ''blood." Man is an organism — an animal; and the laws of improvement of corn and of race horses hold true for him also. Unless

---

[36] This may be viewed on the Internet Archive
https://archive.org/details/heredityinrelati00dave/page/n9/mode/2up

people accept this simple truth and let it influence marriage selection human progress will cease." (Page 1)

This all falls in line with his contemporaries and makes the point that man is an organism, an **animal** to whom the laws of improvement apply. The selection of one's partner for marriage being of utmost importance to the protection of the 'good gene'. The idea of a biologically superior individual crossing with an inferior individual comes across as repugnant to Davenport as in his world a deficient gene is the reason for alcoholism, drug abuse, crime, and mental retardation, etc.

Davenport is not remembered for coining a phrase or word that became a major factor in future developments, but he did undertake a study which was called [37]*'Race Crossing in Jamaica',* which was intended to demonstrate the deteriorating consequences of race crossing. His companion in this pseudo-scientific research was an anthropologist called Morris Steggerda. Localities and institutions where the adult population was studied and measurements taken include: Mico College, Shortwood Training College, Gordon Town, Glengoffe, Brownsville and Emboma, Seaford Town, Grand Cayman Island, Fire Department, Kingston, Police Depot, Kingston, General Penitentiary, Kingston, Kingston Whites, City Creche, Kingston. (*In the **appendix** you will see a copy of the contents page which is so thorough that it provides a snapshot of the eugenics application of its theology, some of which will be explored in the next chapter*).

In the opening paragraph of the introduction, he states:

---

[37] 'Race Crossing' - This exercise was also undertaken in Britan in 1919 by Professor Fleure and his assistant Rachel Fleming. Wilson, R. (September 13, 2013). Race crossing project (Britain). Retrieved May 21, 2021, from http://eugenicsarchive.ca

"In March, 1926, the Carnegie Institution of Washington accepted a gift from a gentleman who expressed his interest in the problem of race crossing, with special reference to its significance for the future of any country containing a mixed population. The work was undertaken by the Department of Genetics, Carnegie Institution of Washington. The first step was to organize an advisory committee; and the following persons eventually associated themselves as such committee: W. V. Bingham, C. B. Davenport, E. L. Thorndike, Clark Wissler."

To obtain accurate results regarding the hereditary differences between the Black, Brown (mixed race) and White groups they would employ several tests, one of which is called the *'Knox Moron Test'*. Now Dr Knox apparently made major contributions to 'intelligence testing' using the methods he created to screen immigrants for mental deficiencies. I wonder if he was ever tested…?

I'll let Davenport explain how this works:

"This test was designed by Dr H.A. Knox (1914), and was listed as a ten-year-old test (Plate 19, Fig.1). The procedure and the method of scoring used in this work are as follows:

The blocks were removed from the form board and two placed on either side of it. The board opening (a) was turned toward the individual. The subject was asked to fit the blocks into the cavity of the board as quickly as possible.

The errors which occurred while placing the blocks into the board were not recorded, but only the time taken to complete the performance. As soon as the test was completed the board was emptied and turned so that the board opening (a) was on the opposite side from that of the first trial. This was done generally quite unobserved by the subject, who was asked to place the blocks again, to see if he could complete the placing in less time than the first trial. If the first trial was completed by accident or chance, it generally took longer for the second attempt" (Page 40)

The point of this research was to obtain data from the 'brown' which would demonstrate the disharmonious relationship between the 'black' and 'white'. In other words, data that reflected mental incompetencies or deficiencies. 'Surprisingly', their research did not reveal or corroborate any of their assumptions.

It is fair to say the results were thrown out as unscientific.

Clarence Gamble

[38]*"To date less than 2,000 insane and mentally defective North Carolinians have been sterilized under the existing law — a figure that represents less than one out of every 41 of the State's estimated mentally unfit. This means that for every one man or woman who has been sterilized, there are 40 others who can continue to pour defective genes into the State's blood stream to pollute and degrade future generations."*

If you are familiar with the American multinational company Procter and Gamble, you will know that it specialises in consumer products related to health and personal care. Founded in 1837 by William Procter and James Gamble, the partnership saw their sales reach $1 million by 1859, which is equivalent to circa $27,818,125 million or £114,846,627 million in 2021.

Clarence Gamble was the grandson of James Gamble, a co-founder of Procter and Gamble and was born into one of the

---

[38] Reprinted from BETTER HEALTH, the Magazine of the NORTH CAROLINA SOCIAL HYGIENE SOCIETY, October, 1947. BETTER HUMAN BEINGS TOMORROW by CLARENCE J. GAMBLE, M. D. http://deadlymedicine.weebly.com/uploads/4/6/0/2/46023165/maga_dr.. pdf

wealthiest families in America with a company brand that still resonates with consumers today. He was born in Cincinnati in 1894 and graduated from Princeton University in 1914 and Harvard Medical School in 1920. He began his residency at Massachusetts General Hospital and in 1923 secured an apprenticeship with Alfred Newton Richards, in the Department of Pharmacology. However, before he could begin, his father David Berry Gamble died which disrupted the start of his apprenticeship.

Later, Clarence Gamble inherited the Procter and Gamble fortune to which were tied a condition of contributing 10% to charities, which seemed to become a driving force to his later pursuits. He was the wealthiest eugenicist amongst them all.

He founded the Pathfinder Fund in 1957 which became a dominant and effective organisation throughout the world, but in particular in underdeveloped countries. What we miss here is the reason an organisation like Pathfinder would target underdeveloped communities. The purpose of this organisation was to introduce birth control in the populations it worked in. Birth control was marketed as a way for women to take control of their own body, but for the eugenicists this was simply another way to reduce births amongst the unfit. Enter 'population control.'

Gamble became one of the first American individuals to fund the activities of the kind provided by the Pathfinder Fund and continued to [39]provide financial support for its activities for at least 10 years after its creation. In 1965 the Pathfinder funds would go from $250,000 into the millions following the death of Clarence Gamble in 1966. This increase would be due to a new

---

[39] Pathfinder International Annual Report 1992, p. 5

funder, [40]the United States Agency for International Development (USAID), who climbed on board to ensure the effective future of Pathfinder. The USAID's current website provides a [41]family planning programme timeline confirming the dates mentioned above and more. Here are some extracts from their table of events:

Pre 1965

- After passing the Foreign Assistance Act in 1961, Congress authorizes research on family planning and population issues, including the provision of family planning information to couples who request it.

1963

- Addressing the World Food Congress, President Kennedy recognizes that rapid population growth in under-developed countries has become a serious concern. It is *"too often the highest where hunger is the most prevalent."*

1965

- President Johnson declares that he will *"seek new ways to use our knowledge to help deal with the explosion in world population and the growing scarcity of world resources."*

---

[40] Randy Engel, "The International Population Control Machine and the Pathfinder Fund," International Review of Natural Family Planning, Vol. V. No. l, Spring 198l, reprinted in booklet form by the Human Life Center (Collegeville, Minnesota), p. 16. The author is indebted to Mrs. Engel and her original research on Gamble and the Pathfinder Fund for much of the information contained in this article.
[41] USAID FAMILY PLANNING PROGRAM TIMELINE: BEFORE 1965 TO THE PRESENT
https://www.usaid.gov/global-health/health-areas/family-planning/usaid-family-planning-program-timeline-1965-present

- The USAID population and reproductive program begins.
- The U.S. Government adopts a plan to reduce birth rates in developing countries through its War on Hunger and investments in family planning programs.

1966

- Congress amends the Food For Peace Act to authorize USAID to use funds to manufacture and distribute medical supplies, including **contraceptives**.

1968

- With strong bipartisan support, Congress allots foreign assistance for family planning.
- USAID makes its first purchase of contraceptives for distribution in developing countries.

1969

- President Nixon describes population growth as *"one of the most serious challenges to human destiny in the last third of this century."*
- The Office of Population is established to provide leadership, initiative, coordination, technical guidance, and assistance in developing and conducting population/family planning activities.

At the end of 1969

- USAID takes a leadership role in providing condoms and contraceptives to developing countries.

The motivation for moving into countries that were growing in population was rooted in a eugenics ideology. Once it had taken root as the answer to the world's ills, it then became easy to establish legislation to support what appeared to be humanitarian programmes. The solution wasn't the introduction of food programmes or local training to enable communities to become self-sufficient. These programmes, with the introduction of birth control were the package. In other words, we give you food as long as you accept birth control measures.

The Pathfinder Fund changed its name in 1991 to Pathfinder International.

Gamble was also a founding member of the Human Betterment League of North Carolina in 1947, which later became the Human Genetics League in 1988 but was later disbanded. This organisation was connected to atrocious cases of sterilization.

Pathfinder Distance Themselves from Clarence Gamble

On the 7th of April, 2021 the organisation which Clarence Gamble founded and funded, and which expressed the eugenics religion, made a statement to distance themselves from his beliefs:

[42]*"We sought to understand his personal views more fully so that we could determine how best to address his legacy, and that of the full organization, going forward.*

That review has confirmed Gamble's undeniable involvement in the practice of eugenics through the first half of the twentieth century and coinciding with the founding of Pathfinder. Into the 1960s, his racially biased and unscientific beliefs clearly influenced his work in

---

[42] A note about our founder Dr Clarence Gamble
https://www.pathfinder.org/news/a-note-about-our-founder/

the U.S. and other countries and were manifest in his efforts to limit or reduce birthrates in certain communities, regardless of whether or not the people in those communities expressed consent with his methods. Though Gamble died in 1966, the influence of his beliefs could be traced in Pathfinder's work into the 1970s, generally under the banner of "population control," a euphemism adopted by governments and family planning organizations at the time."

Although, as with Charles Davenport, Gamble did not coin a phrase or word, he too used his influence to promote the eugenics agenda in a way that is still evident today. His thoughts on eugenics and the financial clout he acquired were the keys that opened the door to the sterilization of both men and women, mostly poor and mainly from ethnic extraction. He also worked on projects with the following preacher, Margaret Sanger.

Margaret Higgins Sanger

Margaret was the face of eugenics. She was to the Eugenics movement what Charles Darwin was to evolution.

Quote:

[43]*"Eugenics without birth control seems to us a house builded* [sic] *upon the sands. It is at the mercy of the rising stream of the unfit."*

Born as Margaret Louise Higgins 14 September 1879 in New York. Her father was Michael Hennesey Higgins, a

---

[43] Margaret Sanger, "Birth Control and Racial Betterment," Feb 1919. Published article. Source: Birth Control Review, Feb. 1919, Library of Congress Microfilm 131:0099

stonemason and her mother was Anne Purcell Higgins, a devout Catholic Irish-American. Margaret was one of eleven children.

Amongst all of the individuals we have mentioned so far, Margaret Sanger seems to stand out for very different reasons from the others. She is an intelligent, unrelenting strategist who has not come from an intellectual family heritage but somehow manages to pioneer a new path for the eugenics religion. She is articulate, charismatic, single-minded and resolute in what she believes; attributes which point to a 'driven' person. Where did this all come from? How was she not deterred from her chosen path? The answer is in her early observations of her parents and the family home. Not only did she come from a large family that struggled to get by, but at nineteen years of age she witnessed her mother's deterioration and eventual death due to tuberculosis, to which she identified her mother's frequent pregnancies as the root cause of her early death. Her father was also a figure of blame due to his inability to provide for his family and lack of care due to drinking and his radical views which alienated him and his family from the wider community. Her mother had eleven children and seven miscarriages (18 births) during her lifetime, dying at the age of 50. This experience set the tone for her future life and mission but unfortunately, as with any individual who carries a feeling of helplessness and anger, the potential for destructive behaviour (of themselves and others) is magnified. For Margaret, she would spend the rest of her life running to escape the fate of her mother while viewing other families through the eyes of her childhood loss. Consumed by powerlessness Margaret Sanger burned with a mission and a message enthused with deathlike tenors of racism. Her perspective on families would also be firmly rooted in the idea of large families being doomed to poverty, illness, and destructive behaviour, in contrast to smaller families where the opposite is assumed. She states:

[44]*"A marriage license shall in itself give husband and wife only the right to a common household and not the right to parenthood."*

Some interesting facts:

- In 1912 Margaret began writing a newspaper column called *"What Every Girl Should Know."*
- In 1914 she started a feminist publication called "The Woman Rebel." This was published during the Comstock Laws which prohibited such publications as they were classed as 'obscene and immoral materials.' This landed Sanger in trouble with the law facing a possible five-year sentence in prison, so she fled to England where she worked in the women's movement and acquired additional information on forms of birth control. It was here that Margaret Sanger and Marie Stopes (who we will expand on later) would cross paths.
- Separated from her husband who she later divorced, Margaret Sanger delved into the world of free love and had affairs with Havelock Ellis and HG Wells.
- Margaret Sanger is the founder of the birth control movement in America and opened the first birth control clinic in 1916 in Brownsville, Brooklyn.
- Five years after her first clinic was opened, in 1921 she founded the **American Birth Control League** (ABCL) which was one of the organisations that made up the **Birth Control Federation of America** (BCFA) in 1942. She also founded the Clinical Research Bureau (CRB) in 1923 which functioned under the umbrella of the ABCL.
- Margaret organised the first World Population Conference in Geneva in 1927.
- A 1952 letter shows Margaret Sanger was on the American Advisory Board of the 'Euthanasia Society of America.'

[44] Margaret Sanger, "America Needs a Code for Babies," Article 3, 27 Mar 1934.

- She was first president of the International Planned Parenthood Federation, which was founded in 1953.

Sanger created the **Negro Project** in 1939, which was implemented by the **Birth Control Federation of America** (BCFA) which later became the **Planned Parenthood Federation of America**. Its purpose was to bring birth control and forms of contraceptives into the black community using education and black operated clinics. After three years it failed and had to close its doors in 1942. Ironically in the same year on 10 December, Margaret Sanger wrote a letter to Clarence Gamble which many believe was related to the Negro Project. The extract reads as follows:

[45]*"to employ a full time Negro physician. It seems to me from my experience where I have been in North Carolina, Georgia, Tennessee and Texas, that while the colored Negroes have great respect for white doctors they can get closer to their own members and more or less lay their cards on the table which means their ignorance, superstitions and doubts. They do not do this with the white people and if we can train the Negro doctor at the Clinic he can go among them with enthusiasm and with knowledge, which, I believe, will have far-reaching results among the colored people. His work in my opinion should be entirely with the Negro profession and the nurses, hospital, social workers, as well as the County's white doctors. His success will depend upon his personality and his training by us.*

The ministers [sic] work is also important and also he should be trained, perhaps by the Federation as to our ideals and the goal that we hope to reach. **We do not want word to go out that we want to exterminate the Negro population and the minister is the man who can straighten out that idea if it ever occurs to any of their more rebellious members."**

---

[45] Sanger, Margaret, 1879-1966, "Letter from Margaret Sanger to Dr C.J. Gamble, December 10, 1939.," *Smith Libraries Exhibits*, accessed May 26, 2021, https://libex.smith.edu/omeka/items/show/495.

There is no doubt that she recruited church ministers and any other person she could influence to preach the message of birth control. Her presence at KKK meetings reinforces the idea that there were no limits to what she would do to get this message across about the unwanted contingent of black, poor, and disabled individuals.

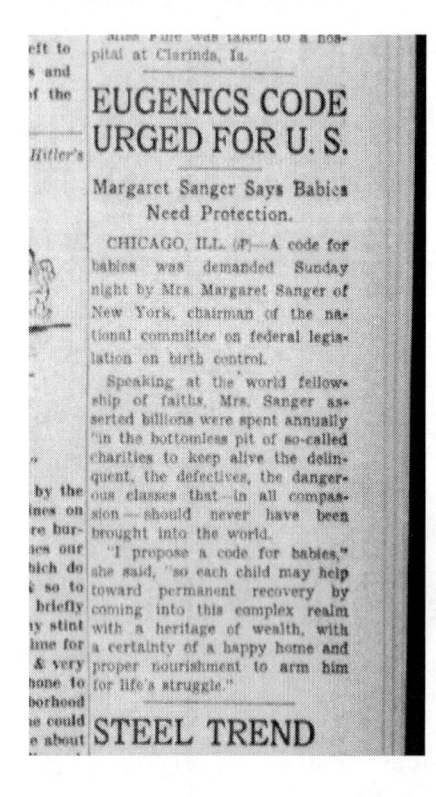

However, there are clear divisions on Margaret Sanger's intentions when it came to the issue of race. In one corner she is viewed as the determined feminist trying to liberate women giving them a choice over their bodies. On the other hand, she is deemed a racist whose goal was to target poor ethnic groups and reduce their birth rate. Is it possible to resolve this? Could it be that we have got her all wrong and she was simply acting in a manner that was considered normal in her day? Well, here is a newspaper article. What do you think?

EUGENICS CODE URGED FOR U. S.

Margaret Sanger Says Babies Need Protection.

CHICAGO, ILL. (P) — A code for babies was demanded Sunday night by Mrs. Margaret Sanger of New York, chairman of the national committee on federal legislation on birth control.

Speaking at the world fellowship of faiths, Mrs. Sanger asserted billions were spent annually "in the bottomless pit of so-called charities to keep alive the delinquent, the defectives, the dangerous classes that—in all compassion—should never have been brought into the world.

"I propose a code for babies," she said, "so each child may help toward permanent recovery by coming into this complex realm with a heritage of wealth, with a certainty of a happy home and proper nourishment to arm him for life's struggle."

STEEL TREND

Also, in The United States vs Margaret Sanger case in 1914 she was accused of using the mail to 'incite murder and assassination'. Let's see if the following extract from the document produced by the Commission on Industrial Relations, 1912 sheds any light on the discourse:

[46]"Another case of The United States v. Margaret H. Sanger. Margaret Sanger was the author of the articles in the New York Call, to which I have already referred, and which were excluded from the mails. After she became the editor of a little paper called the 'Woman Rebel, No Gods, No Masters', in its issue for July 1914, she published an article entitled *'A defense of assassination'*, by Herbert A. Thorpe. This article reads as follows:

It is generally agreed that lower forms of life must give place to higher types, and when the pioneer of civilization makes his way into the forest, he must of necessity destroy the man -killing animals living therein. Exterminating warfare is also waged against the savage members of the human race wherever they oppose the establishment of conditions necessary for the development of the more highly organized types. Of course, where improvement by instruction and subsequent cooperation is possible, this extreme of annihilation need not be practiced, but unless it can be shown that there is room enough on earth for both savage and civilized, the savage must go."

We could continue to mention other quotations that point to her mindset, but this court case is sufficient in many ways. It highlights other influences that we haven't explored yet such as her admiration of Thomas Malthus who anonymously published an essay called "An Essay on the Principle of Population" in 1798. Of course, this was another theory in which he outlines the connection between population growth and the resources of the Earth to sustain the population. It is, therefore, interesting that later advocates built off Thomas Malthus's ideas to further the goals of eugenics.

Now as with any emotive subject, we always default to defending what is important to us, personally. Objectivity and reason are rare in light of such intense, invested emotions. There is only one way to get to the truth and that is by removing

---

[46] Senate Documents, 64th congress, session 1, vol. 29, page 10891

Margaret Sanger from her iconic pedestal and reminding ourselves that she is a person like any other. Now begin your examination again, place her life back into the context of the time, her history and her beliefs. In addition, examine carefully her companions and partners turning the pages of their own words, now combine those words as one book, one voice, one religion.

Planned Parenthood Remove Margaret Sanger's Name

On the 24th July 2020 Planned Parenthood North Central released the following statement regarding Margaret Sanger:

[47]*"As a health care organization with over 100 years of history, Planned Parenthood provides crucial health services and we also acknowledge that some of our current work was built on a harmful past. Our founder, Margaret Sanger, perpetuated a number of problematic beliefs and actions. We want to be very clear that we vehemently denounce her ideology that certain people – specifically people of color, people with low incomes, and people with disabilities – should be prevented from having children. This repugnant belief runs directly counter to our organization's current mission of supporting every person in choosing when and whether to become a parent."*

Planned Parenthood, by their admission, confirmed that Margaret Sanger's ideology was a eugenicist worldview, therefore racist, totalitarian ideology. Her name will be removed from their building in an attempt to distance themselves from her legacy. This pattern of attempting to distance the organisation from its founder/s will become a familiar pattern

---

[47] Statement about Margaret Sanger and Planned Parenthood's mission **For Immediate Release:** July 24, 2020

as the religion of eugenics continues to manifest itself on the wings of white supremacy, caste structures and other ignominious expressions around the world.

Phrases and words coined by Margaret Sanger

Birth Control

Sanger coined the term 'birth control' and used every skill to bring the idea to the masses. Her ultimate desire was to create a 'magic' pill that would act as a contraceptive.

Dear reader, to view Charles Darwin, Francis Galton, Julian Huxley, Clarence Gamble, and Margaret Sanger in complete isolation of each other descends any sensible discussion into an ostrich-like point of view, the equivalent of burying one's head in the ground of dark confusion, oblivious to the bigger picture and degrading divine consideration to the debased place of self-indulgence and satisfaction. God looks down once again to witness an evil conglomerate, bent on burying the body of truth and 'Raising Cain'.

As we slide down the slippery slope of timeless degradation, we now add to the baseless question of "Am I my brother's keeper?" and we ask, "Are we our children's, keeper?"

The Hidden Tree

'For in Him we live and move and have our being,' as also some of your own poets have said, 'For we are also the offspring'

Aratus, Phaenomena 5

since we are offspring of God, we ought not to think that the divine is like gold or silver or stone, a mark of skill, ***or thought of man.***

Acts 17:28-29 (ONM)

Every organisation requires a means of identifying itself to an audience that may not be familiar with its product, purpose, or direction. This is usually in the form of imagery, which today we call a 'logo'.

A logo is an identifier, sometimes abstract and other times obvious depending on the message the company or organisation wants to convey. The eugenics movement is no different in this regard, as in 1921 the Eugenics Society decided to use the emblem of a tree as their logo in the [48]Second International Congress of Eugenics. It was placed on certificates and awarded to individuals for their contribution to the eugenics exhibition.

LIKE A TREE EUGENICS DRAWS ITS MATERIALS FROM MANY SOURCES AND ORGANIZES THEM INTO AN HARMONIOUS ENTITY.

---

[48] Taken from the booklet – The Second International Exhibition of Eugenics 22 September – 22 October 1921, by Harry H Laughlin

This organic form with its mass of roots mimics the idea of 'The Tree of Life' in a caricature-like manner, branding eugenics as the answer to the future of the human race. Its appearance, healthy yet conspicuous, draws the viewer closer as it subtly imparts a new sense of individuated morality. The observer is invited to explore the text at its base and root system until an almost trancelike state disarms them of a true sense of reality. The world grows dim, the gaze grows stronger and an ancient familiar voice whispers, 'You shall not surely die.' At the sound of this voice, the trance is broken and a sense of historical reality enters. With this reality the realisation is that this tree is not just symbolic of the year 1921 when it was introduced but it also represents an ancient past and an advancing future. One that would be exclusive, elusive, and even more destructive.

It is the origins of this historic conundrum that Rabbi Paul recognises as he waits for his companions in Athens (the largest city of Greece, the home to Plato's Academy and Aristotle's Lyceum). The Bible records,

'Now while Paul waited for them at Athens, his spirit was provoked within him when he saw that the city was given over to idols.'

Acts 17:16, (NKJV)

Making use of the time, Rabbi Paul held discussions in the synagogues and taught in the marketplace day after day with people who were passing through (Acts 17:16 - 32). This included Epicurean and Stoic philosophers (the two main schools of philosophy). When engaging with Rabbi Paul, the philosophers realised that he was teaching something that they had never heard before, something that didn't sit comfortably with their philosophy on life and their pursuit of 'happiness'. So, they took him to the High Council, the *Aero Pago*. At which point he explains that he perceives they are religious having examined their objects of worship and having discovered an altar that was engraved 'TO THE UNKNOWN GOD'. He continued to express the truth about this God that they did not know, but worshipped with ignorance of heart. This God who created the world and everything in it, the Only One who is Lord over the heavens and the earth and who does not live in sanctuaries made by human hands, needing nothing yet giving life and breath to everything. Through one human making nations of humans to settle upon the face of the earth after He determined fixed times and boundaries of their habitations. The God who is waiting to see if they would seek after tokens of Him. Paul then states *"and truly He is not far from any one of us"* (Acts 17:27-Last Part)

In infinite wisdom, he draws from the Athenian's poets

'For in Him we live and move and have our being,' as also some of your own poets have said, 'For we are also the offspring'

Aratus, Phaenomena 5

So, since we are offspring of God, we ought not to think that the divine is like gold or silver or stone, a mark of skill, or thought of man.

Acts 17:28-29 (ONM)

This still doesn't make complete sense until we understand the context in which Rabbi Paul found himself. [49]Athens had experienced an epidemic that had swept through the land around 430 BC. Physicians had no experience with the kind of illness that they were facing and its impact would affect the wealthy as well as the wider community. [50]Thucydides

---

[49] Mark, J. J. (2020, April 01). Thucydides on the Plague of Athens: Text & Commentary. World History Encyclopedia. Retrieved from https://www.worldhistory.org/article/1535/thucydides-on-the-plague-of-athens-text--commentar

[50] The Plague of Athens killed tens of thousands, but its cause remains a mystery.
Killing nearly a third of the population, an epidemic ripped through Athens in 430 B.C. Historic accounts and new technology are helping identify the

recorded that anyone infected would die within seven to nine days. In the end, it is estimated that 75,000 – 100,000 lives were taken, approximately a third of the population.

The sheer speed and magnitude with which this disease spread through the population caused them to believe that they had angered the gods somehow. The problem was that Athenians worshipped many gods, so which one should they appease? The answer was to build [51]altars to all the gods they could think of including 'THE UNKNOWN GOD', The God of Israel. It was the altars and the inscription that provided evidence of what had happened and also indicated what was important to its worshippers. We will bow to any god that fits the bill.

As with these altars, the symbol of the tree represents many things but importantly reveals the heart of its inventors and much, much more. It tells us what we need to know about the religion of its worshippers, it exposes the stages of an agenda that originates in the ancient past and stretches far into the future. Without paying attention to this modern yet ancient symbol it is almost impossible to understand or connect the multiplicity of dots that expose the truth about its aims, goals and purposes. So far,

1. We have established the seed of Darwinism as the delivery and root system embedded in the soil of slavery (including its mindset and terminology).

true culprit. https://www.nationalgeographic.co.uk/history-and-civilisation/2021/05/the-plague-of-athens-killed-tens-of-thousands-but-its-cause-remains-a-mystery

[51] Benjamin, Anna S. "The Altars of Hadrian in Athens and Hadrian's Panhellenic Program." Hesperia: The Journal of the American School of Classical Studies at Athens 32, no. 1 (1963): 57-86. Accessed June 4, 2021. doi:10.2307/147351.

2. We have also proven that eugenics is the plant that breaks through the soil and grows into an organic form rooted firmly in Darwinism.
3. Finally, we have established that this plant form represents a religious movement. Remember the words of Francis Galton?

"...*it must be introduced into the national conscience, like a new religion*"

The phrase that is at its root and energises the root system states, "*Like a tree eugenics draws its materials from many sources and organises them into an harmonious entity.*" This telling statement points to a uniformed, organised, camouflaged object which like a tree draws its materials from many sources, but what materials?

Secondly, the phrase on either side of the tree's trunk, "*Eugenics is the self-direction of human evolution.*" can be summed up in a simple word, "self-determination." A word which is reinforced by a bold "*Eugenics*" stamp of approval.

To summarise, this is a tree that is symbolic of a belief system. A system that did and will continue to draw its substance from any and every area of the human experience to feed its parasitic appetite, ensuring that it achieves its future evolution through the implementation of self-determination practices. These practices will not be introduced in one series but in a progressive manner through stages of perceived human evolution. To understand this better, we must examine some of the materials it refers to within its root system. For the sake of brevity, we will deliberately select a sample of the materials used.

The Materials

Racial Laws | Racial Politics

Psychology | Psychiatry

If you search Google under the words 'psychology' and 'psychiatry', terms that relate to the human experience, you will find that they are portrayed as synonymous with the word 'scientific'. Unfortunately, for most people, the quest to understand the purpose and meaning of psychology and psychiatry pretty much ends with a Google search. The question of whether these terms reflect scientific approaches to understanding humanity is assumed to be a fact and considered to be the only basis on which we can understand the human race. However, as we have already seen, this can lead to all kinds of problems that are not easy to resolve or unravel — ultimately resulting in blind trust which leads us to wrongly assume that experts with academic credentials, scientific papers and awards behind them are indeed experts. The trail of unresolved issues surrounding these experts and the multiplicity of unanswered questions demonstrates otherwise.

Here are a few definitions regarding the origin of the word Psychology:

[52] *The word psychology was formed by combining the Greek psychē (meaning "breath, principle of life, life, soul,") with -logia (which comes from the Greek logos, meaning "speech, word, reason"). An early use appears in Nicholas Culpeper's mid-17th century*

---

[52] "psychology" *Merriam-Webster Dictionary*, https://www.merriam-webster.com/dictionary/psychology. Accessed 10 Jun. 2021.

translation of Simeon Partliz's *A New Method of Physick, in which it is stated that "Psychologie is the knowledg of the Soul*.[sic]"

Psychology also (*as with all the other ideas we have seen so far*) takes its lead from Greece, in its definition and application. It was the study of the soul, and it was and is a branch of philosophy that attempts to understand what makes humans tick. Early proponents of this study of the soul theorised about the location of the mind, the character, life, death, emotions and how all these elements of the human being work. Of course, there were no definitive answers applicable to the human condition, so intellectualism directed students to look within for the answers, introspection. In light of this, Psychology was not and is not, by any means a science by any stretch of the imagination. Here is a brief dialogue which was written by Plato, a student of Socrates (Greek philosophers). It revolves around the issue of the soul which Psychology claims to have the answers to. It goes like this:

[53]"*Then the soul is more like to the unseen, and the body to the seen?*

That is most certain, Socrates. And were we not saying long ago that the soul when using the body as an instrument of perception, that is to say, when using the sense of sight or hearing or some other sense (for the meaning of perceiving through the body is perceiving through the senses) — were we not saying that the soul too is then dragged by the body into the region of the changeable, and wanders and is confused; the world spins round her, and she is like a drunkard when under their influence?

Very true.

---

[53] Plato. *The Apology, Phædo and Crito*, trans. by Benjamin Jowett. Vol. II, Part 1. The Harvard Classics. New York: P.F. Collier & Son, 1909–14; Bartleby.com, 2001. https://www.bartleby.com/lit-hub/hc/the-apology-phaedo-and-crito/

But when returning into herself she reflects; then she passes into the realm of purity, and eternity, and immortality, and unchangeableness, which are her kindred, and with them she ever lives, when she is by herself and is not let or hindered; then she ceases from her erring ways, and being in communion with the unchanging is unchanging. And this state of the soul is called wisdom?

That is well and truly said, Socrates, he replied.

Now if you understand that...? To think that we draw our knowledge from discussions like this is incredible, to say the least. So how did Psychology make its mark? How did it become an accepted norm amongst apparently intelligent, superior thinkers?

As with evolution and eugenics, psychology needed to be considered scientific for it to be taken seriously, therefore, it had to be branded as such.

Wilhelm Wundt was the first to call himself a psychologist and in 1879 he founded a psychological laboratory in Leipzig, Germany. Many applaud Wilhelm Wundt's psychology for successfully making the transition from the arena of philosophy into science, but did he distance it from its philosophical roots? On the contrary.

Psychologists, like psychotherapists and psychiatrists, masqueraded as experts in the mind/soul, and *'human behaviour'* was the measuring line for their ideas. Some would debate that these great individuals have a vast array of studies of human behaviour and have a greater understanding of human make-up now than they ever did. The problem with these notions is that after hundreds of years they still cannot answer fundamental questions about human beings using the theories of 'psychology'. There isn't a 'psychological' datum to work from regardless of their passionate assumptions, which is why there is a myriad of different opinions for one human action, ultimately leaving the psychologists to resort to guesswork as to the reasons behind that action. They do not have a consistent measure of what they cannot see: the mind, the soul, the character, emotions, and the innate ability to reason. If they did have such information, their input would be refined over time and the results would be consistent and not speculative.

Here are some comments of these learned practitioners who share their academic knowledge with the rest of us mere mortals:

Let's begin with Samuel A Cartwright with his lecture on Drapetomania. Take it away Sam:

[54]*"In noticing a disease not heretofore classed among the long list of maladies that man is subject to, it, was necessary to have a new term to express it. The cause, in the most of cases, that induces the negro to run away from service, is as much a disease of the mind as any other species of mental alienation, and much more curable, as a general role...*

Before negroes run away, unless they are frightened or panic-struck, they become sulky and dissatisfied. The cause of this sulkiness and dissatisfaction should be inquired into and removed, or they are apt to run away or fall into the negro consumption."

Really Sam? I know people like that: sulking, frightened and always wanting to run away from everything, so what is your recommended cure for such a malady and what is the scientific definition for such a cure?

Sam: *"When sulky and dissatisfied without cause, the experience of those on the line and elsewhere was decidedly in favor of*

---

[54] THE NEW ORLEANS MEDICAL AND SURGICAL JOURNAL MAY 1851 PART FIRST, ORIGINAL COMMUNICATIONS: 1.-Report On The Diseases And Physical. Peculiarities Of The Negro Race. By Samuel A. Cartwright, M.D. Chairman Of The Committee Appointed By The Medical Association Of Louisiana To Report On The Above Subject.

whipping them out of it, as a preventive measure against absconding or other bad conduct. It was called whipping the devil out of them."

Well, that's not exactly what I had in mind Sam, but you're the expert. Maybe Benjamin Rush might have a perspective that is a little more useful? Come on in Benj, I hear that in 1797 you derived some amazing insight which astounded your scientific friends. Also, I hear they call you the father of American psychiatry, leader of the enlightenment, a signatory to the United States Declaration of Independence and an abolitionist?

Benjamin: [55]*Dr Smith in his elegant and ingenious essay upon the variety of color and figure in the Human Species has derived it from four causes, climate, diet, state of society, and disease. I admit the Doctor's facts, reasoning as far as he has extended them, in fullest manner. I shall only add to them a few observations which are intended to prove that the color and figure of that part of our fellow creatures who are known by the epithet of negroes are derived from a modification of the disease, which is known by the name leprosy.*

Ok...so if the colour issue is a disease, is there a cure for blackness?

Benjamin: *In Henry Moss the color was first discharged from the skin in those places, on which there was most pressure from clothing, and most attrition from labor, as on the trunk of his body, and on his fingers. The black color was probably occasioned by the absorption of the coloring matter of the rete mucosum, or perhaps of the rete mucosum itself, for pressure and friction it is well known aid the absorbing action of the lymphatics in every part of the body. It is from the latter cause, that the palms of the hands of negro women who*

---

[55] Schomburg Center for Research in Black Culture, Manuscripts, Archives and Rare Books Division, The New York Public Library. "Observations intended to favour a supposition that the black color (as it is called) of the Negroes is derived from the leprosy" The New York Public Library Digital Collections. 1760 - 1813. https://digitalcollections.nypl.org/items/ac54c7c0-1628-0134-e13b-00505686a51c

spend their lives at a washing tub, are generally as fair as the palms of the hands in labouring white people.

Depletion, whether by bleeding, purging, or abstinence has been often observed to lessen the black color in negroes. The effects of the above remedies in curing the common leprosy, satisfy me that they might be used with advantage in that state of leprosy which I conceive to exist in the skin of the negroes.

A similar change in the color of the negroes, though of a more temporary nature, has often been observed in them from the influence of fear.

Hmm, something about Benjamin's ideas seems a little off, don't you think? Yet, there is no end to articles written that venerate him as a leading figure. The real concern is that Samuel Cartwright and Benjamin Rush are not exceptions. They, along with many others, have shaped the way that we think and behave, and we fail to challenge the authenticity or origin of their thought. This begs us to ask the question, 'who is conning who?'

It's also important to note that the terms psychologist and psychiatrist are often used without any understanding of their differences (not that this adds any credibility to their philosophy). In the modern world, put simply, a psychologist is not classed as a 'medical doctor' and cannot prescribe medication whereas a Psychiatrist is a 'medical doctor' and can prescribe medication with psychotherapy if required. Both professions use the Diagnostic and Statistical Manual of Mental Disorders (DSM) produced by the American Psychiatric Association and the International Classification of Diseases and Related Health Problems (ICD).

These manuals are not definitive markers for a condition; how could they be if they are only a collection of opinions from the 'experts'. These experts have developed their opinions over years by describing different distresses and publishing them in what I can only describe as a book of opinions.

Psychotherapy

Measuring these mental distresses is as old as some of the ideas postured in previous chapters. The problem is that modern proponents have rebranded and led the general population to believe that their knowledge was acquired through universities and institutes that promote objective learning.

Let's explore some of the methods that were used in the founding days of Psychotherapy: -

- **Phrenology**

The term phrenology is derived from Ancient Greek for 'mind' and 'knowledge'.

This approach believes that it is possible to determine the individual's character, intellectual capacity, and brain function by studying the skull shape, size, and bumps. Somehow, it was thought that the skull provided valuable information which could be read and interpreted by the initiated. [56]Franz Joseph Gall created this system of measurement in the early 1790s in Vienna, which later became a popular approach to precede important life choices.

- **Physiognomy**

This is not far removed from phrenology in that a study of the face is meant to reveal the person's character. The face is said to be divided into parts which in turn reflect human character traits, emotions, ideas, passions, and volition. Ironically,

---

[56] On the functions of the brain and of each of its parts: with observations on the possibility of determining the instincts, propensities, and talents, or the moral and intellectual dispositions of men and animals, by the configuration of the brain and head, by Gall, F. J. (Franz Josef), 1758-1828; Lewis, Winslow, 1799-1875, translator.

Physiognomy is experiencing a renaissance in the 21st century through facial recognition technology. A Swiss pastor called [57]Johann Kasper Lavater became the leading voice in this abstract notion.

- **Mesmerism**

Another description for Mesmerism is 'animal magnetism', sound familiar? The German doctor **Franz Anton Mesmer** was the originator of the term 'mesmerism'. He practised in Austria and developed the idea that every living or animate object had an invisible, yet universal 'fluid' or 'energy' running through it. This substance is often referred to as the 'aura', however, he called this force 'mesmerism' a magnetic field. He believed that people only became ill or experienced psychological problems when this magnetic field was out of balance. This idea and the practice of the mesmerist or magnetiser as they were called, is similar to, if not the same as [58]Reiki, [59]kinesiology, energy healing, [60]and chakra balancing. Referred to as 'hypnotists' today, it is more accurate to use the original description of 'magnetist'.

- **Spiritism**

There are attempts to make a distinction between spiritism and spiritualism similar to practitioners in the world of the occult who make a distinction between black and white witchcraft. In

---

[57] Essays on physiognomy, calculated to extend the knowledge and the love of mankind.
by Lavater, Johann Kaspar, 1741-1801. n 80046189; Moore, C., Rev
[58] Originating in Japan, reiki is the practice of spiritual healing. The word Reiki come from the Japanese words Rei (universal life) and ki (energy).
[59] Kinesiology proports to balance your body's energy system through gentle pressure on strategic parts of the body. It is based on the eastern meridian chart which apparently maps the energy path through the body and is used in acupuncture and other 'wellbeing' practices. https://hk-uk.co.uk/what-is-health-kinesiology/
[60] Originating in India, chakra balancing is believed to be the restoration of an even flow of energy through the chakra system.

essence, these are non-arguments as one definition or practice springs from and directly relates to the other. So, Spiritism (which is a branch of occultism) is another philosophy that delves into exploring the spirit world, desiring to understand how the unseen realm works. Through this 'understanding', individuals that are experiencing tormenting voices and physical illness sadly rely upon these practitioners who attempt to use their knowledge to release the tormented individual from their invisible prison. How? By the laying on of hands, i.e., moving the hands across the problematic areas inches above the body transmitting what they call 'divine energy'. Ironically, they are also known to give the patient 'blessed water' to drink which is energised by the laying on of hands. Engaging in a form of prayer this interaction between the energy, the healer and the patient takes place.

- **'Mental healing'/'Positive visualisation'**

These are ideas that are rooted in mesmerism and owe their prominence to a man called Phineas Parkhurst Quimby. It is suggested that Quimby came to embrace Mesmerism following his own experience of illness and after listening to a lecture on Mesmerism by Charles Poyen St. Sauveur, a French disciple of Franz Anton Mesmer. Whichever way his progression into mesmerism occurred, one thing is certain. He is considered to be the father of 'New Thought', a movement that includes Christian Science, Religious Science and Unity.

Quimby believed in the invisible fluid (magnetism) as Franz Anton Mesmer did, but he also believed that thoughts could interrupt the flow of the fluid. Of course, based on the premise of Mesmer, if this happens, illnesses and other psychological mind issues can manifest. His influence gave rise to an idea that brought to the forefront 'mind power'. In other words, if you think it, it will happen. An idea that has infiltrated Christian circles for many years.

Amongst his patients was a lady called Mary Baker Eddy (formally known as Mary Patterson) who he treated for emotional and physical illnesses. She later formed the Christian Scientist Association later known as the Church of Christ, Scientist.

The Unity School of Christianity was started after Myrtle Fillmore read a book by Mary Baker Eddy called *'Science and Health with a Key to Scriptures'* She, like others before her, believed that illness was a figment of the imagination.

Included in this list of mind science advocates are the brothers Ernest and Fenwicke Holmes. Fenwicke assisted his brother Ernest Holmes in founding the Institute of Religious Science and Philosophy, in Los Angeles in 1927, which became the Church of Religious Science in 1953, and is currently recognised as the Center for Spiritual Living.. Once again, this idea that we are set free when we have attained their form of truth resonates in their response to the human experience.

An emphasis on an apparently 'scientific' approach to knowing God and His teachings through meditation is reflected in Ernest's book 'Science of Mind'.

These ideas are all about knowing yourself by invoking an approach that is borrowed from a world of supernatural occult practices. We continue to evidence these practices in religions such as [61]Theosophy, which is made up of any number of

---

[61] Melton, J. Gordon. "Theosophy." Encyclopedia Britannica, April 27, 2020. https://www.britannica.com/topic/theosophy.
The term theosophy, derived from the Greek theos ("god") and sophia ("wisdom"), is generally understood to mean "divine wisdom." Forms of this doctrine were held in antiquity by the Manichaeans, an Iranian dualist sect, and in the Middle Ages by two groups of dualist heretics, the Bogomils in Bulgaria and the Byzantine Empire and the Cathari in southern France and Italy. In modern times, theosophical views have been held by Rosicrucians

philosophies that postulate that there is a deeper spiritual reality that can be achieved through spiritual ecstasy, intuition, meditation, revelation or transcending human consciousness. This ancient idea was also popularised by modern proponents such as Helena Blavatsky, Henry Steel Olcott and William Quan Judge who fused eastern philosophy and religious concepts with western mysticism, Neoplatonism, and Kabbalah; which included but is not exclusive to communicating with the spirit world. In other words, they embraced and taught occult spirituality.

Theosophy, like many other spiritual movements, influenced and drew people from around the world, establishing its esoteric arm of the society in London in 1888. It is no secret that this section of society practised occultism as its members pursued a higher level of consciousness. Notwithstanding, it is possible to draw a chronological line connecting the founders with earlier thinkers as instruments in the root system of Eugenics. This is not an accident or coincidence.

Sadly, these practices are ever-present in churches across the globe. Masquerading as evidence of a holy connection with God, preachers are duping congregations with their new (yet old) found knowledge that claims the status of superiority to that of the disciples of Yeshua (Jesus) and even Yeshua himself. In blasphemous disguise, this manifestation of knowledge is misappropriated as a 'word of knowledge' followed closely by the 'laying on of hands' which to the inexperienced and naive would appear to be the power of God demonstrating healing and deliverance. This is not, however, to detract from the true work of the Holy Spirit and the gifts of The Holy Spirit which

---

and by speculative Freemasons. The international New Age movement of the 1970s and '80s originated among independent theosophical groups in the United Kingdom.

are authenticated by God's word, the Holy Bible. Now, before you close the book, this is exactly the type of opposition that the early Apostles were contending with. The letter of Rabbi Paul to Timothy states:

Their teaching will spread like gangrene. Among them are Hymenaeus and Philetus, who have departed from the truth. They say that the resurrection has already taken place, and they destroy the faith of some. Nevertheless, God's solid foundation stands firm, sealed with this inscription: "The Lord knows those who are his," and, "Everyone who confesses the name of the Lord must turn away from wickedness." II Timothy 2:17-19 NKJV

"The Spirit clearly says that in later times some will abandon the faith and follow deceiving spirits and things taught by demons." I Timothy 4:1 NKJV

"Just as Jannes and Jambres opposed Moses, so also these teachers oppose the truth. They are men of depraved minds, who, as far as the faith is concerned, are rejected. But they will not get very far because, as in the case of those men, their folly will be clear to everyone." II Timothy 3:8, 9 NKJV

Mental Testing | Racial Testing

As we move forward in this discourse, we begin to understand that the material to achieve the growth of this tree is endless. Within the structure of its model is the strategic focus on every aspect of the individual with intelligence being the core which in turn overshadows numerous elements. As with other distinguishers, the measure of human intelligence becomes a tool to categorise and ostracise people from each other. As time went on, institutes would be established on the grounds of the results and opportunities, or the medical treatment of an individual would be authorised based on the results of such tests. Once again Francis Galton was strategic in pioneering the measuring of human intelligence, as a founder of the eugenics movement it should come as no surprise that its application would be expanded.

From this eugenicist position, the Intelligence Quotient would play a vital role in the categorising of individuals based on human intellect. The (IQ) test was created in France in 1905 by physician Théodore Simon and psychologist Alfred Binet. It began as an intelligence index to categorise small groups of special needs children and eventually developed into the IQ test. Binet used an approach that gauged a child's development by the performance of other children that could accomplish similar tasks. For example, if a 20-year-old could only achieve the same activities as an average 6-year-old then that individual would be categorised as mentally deficient. Hence the mental age of that individual would be equivalent to a 6-year-old.

Although they may not have intended to create a standardised approach that would be used widely, they did create something that provided additional material to the eugenics movement.

During the development of the tests, there were definitions and criteria which had to be established. These tests were also employed for different reasons i.e., to measure mental deficiency.

It will come as no surprise that in my later school years, the IQ test was used to decide our level of intelligence. This placed my peers and me into hierarchical school year groups according to our intellectual capabilities ranging from lower to upper bands, as they called it. Tragically, this relegated some of us to a school experience that offered little choice for the future by taking away hope, replacing it with disillusionment and resulting in truancy and little or no education for many. The education system blamed the parents while the real cause hid behind a system that had been in the making for centuries. This is not to say that parents are free from the responsibility of raising their children, on the contrary, if the mechanism in which children spend most of their time is biased against them, why would anyone expect a different outcome from the one I have just described?

Psychometric Testing and Sociology

Although the idea of psychometric testing has been posited for some time, it is through Francis Galton that its application would become common in modern society. [62]It is said that the birthplace of psychometric testing as a "science" was in Cambridge between 1886 and 1889. The first laboratory was set up at the University of Cambridge by James McKeen Cattell. Cattell was an American who undertook and completed his PhD entitled 'Psychometric Investigations'. He completed this with Wundt at Leipzig (see earlier section on Wundt). His connections with Wundt and Francis Galton would inevitably lead to a fusion of ideas that would result in a testing mechanism (psychometric testing), created by combining a pseudo-science (psychophysics) with mathematics. So, in essence, he took anthropometrics (rooted in the eugenics philosophy), combined it with mathematics and developed an accurate system of measurement?? Does one plus one make five or two? It was through the efforts of Cattell in conjunction with James Ward, a Fellow of Trinity College, that the world's first laboratory on the psychometric study was established, located within the Cavendish laboratory. This laboratory was to become influential in the science world, giving place to people like:

[62] https://www.psychometrics.cam.ac.uk/about-us/our-history/first-psychometric-laboratory

[63]**Lord Rayleigh (John William Strutt)** for his investigations of the densities of the most important gases and his discovery of argon in connection with these studies. **Ernest Rutherford** was awarded for the splitting of the atom and **James Watson** and **Francis Crick** for the discovery of the double-helix structure of DNA. Unfortunately, the discovery of this opened up a huge narrative for the eugenics movement. In the presentation speech for the Nobel Prize for the discovery of the Structure of DNA, this narrative was established:

[64]*"The discovery of the three-dimensional molecular structure of the deoxyribonucleic acid - DNA - is of great importance because it outlines the possibilities for an understanding in its finest details of the molecular configuration, which dictates the general and individual properties of living matter. DNA is* **the substance which is the carrier of heredity in higher organisms.***"*

I hasten to add that we have already seen how 'evangelists' like Francis Galton, Charles Davenport and others were able to foist their strange yet culturally acceptable ideas on the wider society. Yet, the development of psychometric testing grew to become a globally accepted scientific method, simply by distancing its image from its obvious eugenics roots.

On Francis Galton's team at the Anthropological Institute was John Venn best known for the Venn diagram which is also used the world over. Venn was the secretary of the Anthropological Institute but is credited with having carried out tests on 1450 Cambridge University undergraduates using Francis Galton's techniques. The focus of the tests was on 'physical attributes' and 'intellectual characteristics'. His results?

---

[63] https://www.nobelprize.org/prizes/physics/1904/strutt/facts/
[64] (Engström, 1962, as cited in Award Ceremony Speech, 1964, para. 4).

[65]*"We find then that, in regard to all the ordinary elements of health and strength, there does not seem to be the slightest difference between one class of our students."*

At this juncture, it is important to note that psychometric testing in its early form is directly related to the religious system of eugenics. Its recent derivation is a brand that has a more sophisticated, insidious image and which was used by later proponents to open up the human mind to unfounded measures with unsettling results. This by no means gives it any more credibility than it had at the outset.

The University of Cambridge is also home to its eugenics society. Its founding chairman was Roger Fisher who gave a short talk and produced a paper which is entitled as follows:

CAMBRIDGE UNIVERSITY EUGENICS SOCIETY

Paper on "Heredity" (comparing methods of Biometry and Mendelism) read by Mr R.A. Fisher, Caius, (Chairman of Committee) at Second Undergraduate meeting of the Society in Mr C.E. Shelley's rooms, C. New Court, Trinity College, on Friday, November 10th 1911, at 8:30 p.m.

Within its introduction, Roger Fisher states:

I have almost entirely devoted myself to the two lines of modern research which are of particular interest in Eugenics, that is to Biometrics and Mendelism, and perhaps experts and professions will forgive the absence of the more complicated details in both branches.

---

[65] Journal of the Anthropological Institute 18 : 401-19
https://galton.org/criticism/10-14-02/venn-1889-j-anthro-cambridge-anthropometry.pdf (Page 149) Also located at
https://galton.org/anthropologist.htm
Year 1889 Dyrbye, L. (n.d.). Nobel Prize awarded for the Discovery of the Structure of DNA.

We could labour his ideas on hereditary traits and the need for dominant traits to be given the chance to increase amongst the superior classes, but this would avert attention from the more important issues. RA Fisher is another character that is usually defended by his followers due to his contribution to science, but it is impossible to ignore the longstanding effect that his 'contribution' has made on society as a whole. You see, RA Fisher is credited with proposing the introduction of a family allowance scheme that would be proportional to parental income. He is recorded as an avid supporter and promoter of family allowances. Indeed, this resulted in crossing paths with other campaigners and politicians such as Eleanor Florence Rathbone and William Beveridge.

It is understood that Fisher did not campaign for family allowance because of Eleanor Florence or his contemporaries, but it was his eugenics religiosity that fuelled his motivation for family allowances. If it had been implemented using his model, the poorer class of society would receive a lesser allowance (based on a percentage of their income) than their wealthier counterparts, who would receive a greater portion due to a much higher income. Basically, it would have been a hierarchical benefits system that would stimulate an upper level of society to produce more children with the bonus of being able to fund their education, clothing etc. Although Fisher was not successful in securing his version of the benefits system, it did form the foundation for the later model promoted by William Beveridge.

On the face of it this seems like a generous undertaking, as with all of the eugenics philanthropic endeavours, but behind the open hand of financial assistance lay a plan that had a very specific purpose. It is evident that communications between Fisher and Beveridge did not lead to the implementation of this model, but how could it be possible when parliamentarians had to approve of such a scheme? The welfare system that William Beveridge introduced has been credited with providing a means of income for a struggling society, but there is still something problematic about this. William Beveridge was also involved with the eugenics society and as it is obvious to any human being, dissociation from an ideology does not mean that it will not influence your decision-making in policy and other areas of life. This influence is evident in the system of benefits which on the one hand appears to provide an advantage to the poor while on the other hand making it impossible for the financially dependent to break out of the benefits system without securing a profession that can provide an equal or better income to the collective family benefit. For many, this means a lack of education and lack of opportunity resulting in a form of solitary confinement. The benefits system maintains a level of class that no other system can. It reinforces one of the eugenics tenets, *"if you cannot afford to have children then don't."*

There has been a lot of speculation about William Beveridge, some taking the position that he was completely objective and did not allow eugenics ideas to influence the policy. However, numerous articles counter this position. Is there a conclusive answer?

In the Eugenics Societies Annual Report of 1942 – 1943, page 23.[66] an extract reads as follows:

__Family Allowances-__ Sir William Beveridge, in his report, recommended a flat-rate scheme of family allowances, beginning with the second child, payable to families in all income groups. In his Galton lecture, Sir William made it clear that it was in his view not only possible but desirable that graded family allowance schemes, applicable to families in the higher income groups, be administered concurrently

---

[66] Annual report, 1942-3. Eugen Rev. 1943 Apr;35(1):22-4. PMID: 21260440; PMCID: PMC2986098.

with his flat-rate scheme. The graded family allowance has long been advocated by the Society, and has been espoused since the publication of the Beveridge report by the Family Endowment Society, to which a grant of £250 has been made.

Interestingly, a gentleman by the name of Dennis Sewell wrote about William Beveridge in his book [67]'The Political Gene' which reads as follows:

Page -93-

On the day the House of Commons met to debate the Beveridge Report in 1943, its author slipped out of the gallery early in the evening to address a meeting of the Eugenics Society at the Mansion House. Beveridge thanked his audience for the part they had played in developing the idea of child allowance - a key element of his proposals. His report, he was keen to reassure them, was eugenic in intent and would prove so in effect. Some of those present, though, were sceptical. The idea of child allowances had been developed within the society with the twin aims of encouraging the educated professional classes to have more children than they currently did and, at the same time, to limit the number of children born to poor households. For both effects to be properly stimulated, the allowance needed to be graded: middle-class parents receiving more generous payments than working-class parents. Many eugenicists believed that the reason the middle class had so few children was that they were being taxed so highly to support a vast number of feckless degenerates they limited the size of their own families as a necessary economy.

Page -94-

Home Secretary had that very day signalled that the government planned a flat rate of child allowance. But Beveridge, alluding to the problem of an overall declining birth rate, argued that even the flat rate

---

[67] The Political Gene : How Darwin's Ideas Changed Politics, By Dennis Sewell 2009 - 9780330427449
033042744X

would be eugenic. Nevertheless, he held out hope for the purists. 'Sir William made it clear that it was in his view not only possible but desirable that graded family allowance schemes, applicable to families in the higher income brackets, be administered concurrently with his flat rate scheme,' reported the Eugenics Review."

Middle to upper-class families who were taxed more heavily due to their income would limit the number of children they had. The family allowance scheme would stimulate them to have more children in conjunction with a eugenics narrative. The other classes just couldn't compete. To conclude this part of our discourse, it would be unfair to make all these statements without allowing William Beveridge to defend himself. So here are his words from his report on 'The Problem of the Unemployed', 1909. Pay particular attention to the last sentence:

[68]*Every place in free industry, carrying with it the rights of citizenship-civil liberty, political power, fatherhood, conduct of one's own life and government of a family--should be, so to speak, a "whole" place involving substantially full employment and average earnings up to a definite minimum. Those men who through general defects are unable to fill such a "whole" place in industry, are to be recognised as "unemployable." They must become the acknowledged dependents of the state, removed from free industry and maintained adequately in public institutions, but with the complete and permanent loss of all citizen rights-including not only the franchise but civil freedom and fatherhood.*

Education

[68] 1. Beveridge WH. The Problem of the Unemployed. The Sociological Review. 1906;sp3(1):323-341. doi:10.1177/0038026106SP300130

The education of society at large needed to be undertaken in a manner that highlighted the problem of the degenerate human being. To do so would require a perceived logical and scientific approach sometimes employing the use of statistics and on other occasions using the media to drive home a point. As Julian Huxley and others openly dialogued, influencing institutes globally in a way that appeals to men and women of all ages was imperative.

Although we have touched on some of the organisational vehicles for the dissemination of this education let us briefly visit the British Eugenics Society.

British Eugenics Society

The British Eugenics Society, as it was named in 1926, was formerly known as the Eugenics Education Society from 1907. It was founded by Francis Galton, and it attracted middle-class professionals from across the British society of the day. Keeping it in the family tradition, Leonard Darwin became its president following the death of Francis Galton.

This small organisation had big goals and used its societal influence to the maximum. Not settling for the position as a societal idea but pushing for societal change from the home to the place of work, the Eugenics Society manoeuvred its way into strategic places of power and systematically led the world down a very slippery slope into the intellectual abyss.

In 1913 the Eugenics Society was actively involved in the drafting of the Mental Deficiency Act, demonstrating their influence on the powerbase of modern society. To show how eugenics played its role in governing the laws, below is an extract from the legislation which was debated in the House of

Commons in 1913. The bold text draws your attention to the terminology used to define the individuals that would come under the Act:

[69]***Clause 2*** *— (Circumstances Rendering Defectives Subject To Be Dealt With)*

(1) A person who is a defective may be dealt with under this Act by being sent to or placed in an institution for defectives or placed under guardianship —

*(a) at the instance of his parent or guardian, if he is an **idiot** or **imbecile**, or at the instance of his parent if he is under the age of twenty-one; or*

(b) if in addition to being a defective he is a person —

*(i) who is found **neglected, abandoned**, or **without visible means of support**, or **cruelly treated**; or*

*(ii) who is found **guilty of any criminal offence**, or who is ordered or **found liable to be ordered to be sent to a certified industrial school**;*

*(iii) who is **undergoing imprisonment** (except imprisonment under civil process), or **penal servitude**, or is undergoing detention **in a place of detention by order of a Court**, or in a reformatory or industrial school, or in an inebriate reformatory or who is detained in an institution for lunatics or a criminal lunatic asylum; or*

*(iv) who **is an habitual drunkard** within the meaning of the Inebriates Acts, 1879 to 1900; or*

---

[69] Mental Deficiency Bill, Volume 56: debated on Wednesday 13 August 1913 https://hansard.parliament.uk/Commons/1913-08-13/debates/f519b693-16aa-4e19-bdb9-64edf52255c5/MentalDeficiencyBill

(v) in whose case such notice has been given by the local education authority as is hereinafter in this Section mentioned; or

(vi) who is in receipt of poor relief at the time of giving birth to an illegitimate child or when pregnant of such child.

(2) Notice shall, subject to regulations made by the Board of Education, to be laid before Parliament as hereinafter provided, be given by the local education authority to the local authority under this Act in the case of all defective children over the age of seven –

(a) who have been ascertained to be incapable by reason of mental defect of receiving benefit or further benefit in special schools or classes, or who cannot be instructed in a special school or class without detriment to the interests of the other children, or for whom the Board of Education certify that no suitable special school or class is available;

(b) who on or before attaining the age of sixteen are about to be withdrawn or discharged from a. special school or class, and in whose case the local education authority are of opinion that it would be to their benefit that they should be sent to an institution or placed under guardianship.

<u>Lords Amendments:</u> –

In Sub-section (1), paragraph (a), after the word "if" ["if he is under the age of twenty-one"], insert the words "though not an idiot or imbecile."

In Sub-section (2), paragraph (a), leave out the words "no suitable special school or class is available," and insert thereof the words, "there are special circumstances which render it desirable that they should be dealt with under this Act by way of supervision or guardianship."

<u>Lords Amendments agreed to.</u>

The Mental Deficiency Act 1913 was popular amongst the eugenicists of the day, motivating policy changes that we now understand to be against specific people groups. This was due to a fear of the 'feebleminded' or the 'unfit' degrading the human gene pool by the overpopulation of their defective class and a lower birth rate amongst the reducing number of the elite. However, as we have seen (and will continue to see), this fear, although not unique to Britain, had its roots firmly grounded in British thinking and British politics. During the debate on the implementation of the Act there were only three people who objected to it.

Now it is difficult to speak of individuals in ways that would be considered unpatriotic, but we need to look into the eyes of history with honesty and objectivity. Remember that no one is above reproach when it comes to the issue of sin. A condition that plagues humanity's soul without mercy and seeps into the thoughts of God's creation daily, pressuring and tempting the unsuspecting vulnerable person to be complicit with the most ignominious crimes.

Preceding the 1913 Bill, the British Royal Commission on the Care and Control of the Feeble-Minded was set up by the government in which Winston Churchill was a cabinet minister. What is a Royal Commission? It's an official enquiry which is meant to be a formal, public, and independent enquiry initiated by the government to investigate illegal activity or failures. The commission is expected to be an objective, independent investigation that draws together evidence and witnesses to determine a satisfactory outcome. It is these investigations and their findings that gave credence to the legislation that would follow. Following the Royal Commission (of which there is nothing Royal) came a list of recommended measures that were deemed to be the answer to an ever-growing problem. These would include measures that Winston Churchill was in favour of, and he made his thoughts on the matter quite clear. Page 34 of the report recommended,

"...*segregation on moral grounds rather than those on mental grounds which affect the whole management of different classes of mentally defective persons.*".

This would mean that mental defectives could be locked away for life. This report, made of eight volumes, also recommended to government sterilisation as well as institutionalisation. Of course, this would be in the interest of the community at large?? How could there be a eugenics agenda behind this? To resolve the questions, here is a quotation from Winston Churchill, who was a eugenics advocate and honorary vice-president for the eugenics society.

He is quoted saying to his cousin Ivor:

[70]"*The improvement of the British breed is my aim in life.*"

As unpalatable as it may seem, whether he embraced eugenics philosophy in brief or for life is an irrelevant debate to have. The individuals who would later be kept in confinement due to the 1913 Bill and other such legislation would not have the luxury of opinion or debate. The law would be forger of their future existence and lifestyle. So, with positions of influence come great responsibilities and unfortunately, in this regard, Winston Churchill's influence could have yielded an even more catastrophic outcome. His preference for the sterilisation of the 'mentally unfit' was rejected in favour of incarceration in British asylums while in Canada and America sterilisation was embraced, setting the stage for atrocities of unimaginable

[70] Gilbert, M. (2009). Churchill and Eugenics. The Churchill Centre. Retrieved from https://winstonchurchill.org/publications/finest-hour-extras/churchill-and-eugenics-1/

proportions for many, many years to come. To place all of this in context, the Mental Deficiency Act 1913 was not repealed until the Macmillan British government in 1959. The effects of the Act continue to affect British society even today.

Economics

An overlooked element of the root system is economics, the root that provides financial stability to the maturing, religious tree. Without it, there is almost no point in the existence of the remaining strands in this organic structure. Where there is money there is power, greed and self-glorification. The beneficiaries are rarely the families that have laboured in the heat of the day, but those that hold the purse strings and make decisions that only impact the pocket of the ordinary person.

The structure is always hierarchical with room at the top for one. The imagery of such a structure ironically always forms the shape of a pyramid. Hence, the apt term 'pyramid scheme', is a model of doing business that exploits the desperation of millions of people while the originator gets rich quickly and then disappears with pockets laden with gold. Meanwhile, the remaining victims continue to work tirelessly to recruit more people to this leech-worthy scheme in the hope that they will increase their coffers through the manipulation and desperation of others.

The use of a pyramid is not a coincidence, but its visual form represents everything that Satan's kingdom is. No, the all-seeing eye on the American dollar bill isn't where this is going but feel free to include this in our dialogue. This is about the world's system of finance, the accepted approach to raising a business, the methods of management (if you can call it that), and the approach to creating opportunities for personal, financial growth or 'getting rich quick'. Mysteriously, whichever model you look at in the secular world of business and finance, they all seem to reflect a hierarchical, top down, Ponzi scheme image.

A Ponzi scheme is a form of fraud that offers investors a huge return on their investment, always based on a great opportunity or idea intentionally fabricated by the con artist. Once committed, the investors are subtly manipulated to part with their cash, only to discover that the pot of gold at the end of the rainbow was a fantasy. Sadly, the scheme always ends the same, the investors lose their investment, and the con artist becomes wealthy overnight. Keep in mind that there was only ever enough room at the top for one person; everyone else played a role in making that person rich. Driven by greed, trying to outdo someone else or simply attempting to elevate themselves to become super-rich, the persons lower down the pyramid are not discerning of an unseen force that keeps them just where they are needed to make the whole thing work.

In the early 1900s, not only did the British Royal Commission produce a report on the Care and Control of the Feeble-Minded, but they also produced what was called, the [71]**'Minority Report'** which was focused on the Poor Laws and was led by Beatrice and Sidney Webb. On the outside, this all looked like an attempt to make great strides in social reform, but is that all it was?

At the centre of the enquiry were the two main subjects of:

1. The Poor Law
2. Methods of meeting distress outside the Poor Law

---

[71] https://www.spectator.co.uk/article/how-eugenics-poisoned-the-welfare-state

Both are relevant considerations for anyone in an era where there is poverty due to societal inequalities, but central to this scheme, sorry, enquiry were two key figures, Beatrice and Sidney Webb. They were active members of the Fabian Society, which later became a founding organisation of the Labour Representation Committee in 1900 and therefore, became a root from which the present day Labour Party grew. Interestingly, Sidney and Beatrice also co-founded the London School of Economics.

Beatrice and Sidney are unusual characters, as their legacy has been eulogised in the north aisle of the nave of Westminster Abbey where their ashes were laid, marked by a small memorial stone. This couple, along with characters like Winston Churchill, represented a collective in society whose focus was not on improving the state of the poor but was fixated on saving, improving and securing the British human gene pool. Their contributions were motivated by the eugenics religion, doggedly determined to employ measures that would apply the eugenics tenet. How? Through government policy, a legal framework. Driven to write, preach and teach about this idea of change that was believed to be the only way to secure Britain's future may be distasteful to some and unbelievable to others, but it existed nonetheless, shaping the British experience in a manner that many are still trapped by today. As demonstrated earlier, addressing the issue of the poor and unemployed required a strategy that would provide an answer to the most elite questions, which asked, how are we going to prevent the poor, degenerate families and individuals from increasing and outpopulating the more progressive, intelligent members of British society?

As ardent eugenicists, this couple used their influence to set the tone for future events. For the most part, the Minority Report remained an unread document to most people but to the custodians of British history, it would be recited as the birthplace of the Welfare State. The Minority Report is the bedrock of the welfare system which was later developed by William Beveridge. Indeed, it was Sidney and Beatrice Webb, hardline eugenicists, that introduced William Beveridge to Winston Churchill and the rest, as they say, is history.

Once again, for the sake of completeness, an extract from the [72]'Eugenics and the Poor Law – The Minority Report', by Sidney Webb is included:

The existing Poor Law operates almost exclusively as an anti-eugenic influence; notably in the laxity of its provision for feeble-minded maternity, in the opportunities for undesirable acquaintanceship afforded by the General Mixed Workhouse, in its inability to search out defectives and wastrels who do not apply for relief, and in its failure to provide any practical alternative to the Outdoor Relief now afforded to tens of thousands of feeble-minded or physically defective parents. (Page 233)

But the inference from these facts is not, as some persons seem to imagine, that we had better make no public provision at all. The policy of " Laisser faire " is, necessarily, to a eugenist the worst of all policies, because it implies the definite abandonment of intelligently purposeful selection. Even if we were agreed that the rigorous selection of the " state of nature " were the sort of selection best suited to the needs of a modern highly civilised community, it would not be practicable or possible to let that " natural " selection take its course. If for a moment we, as a nation, forswore our humanitarian principles, and decided to abolish collective provision for the weak and the unfit, there would, inevitably follow an outburst of the most sentimental private charity. It is characteristic of such charity that it not only neglects all eugenic principles, but that in so far as it has any discrimination it often discriminates the wrong way. That is to say, it tends to maintain, without any possibility of segregation, exactly the

---

[72] An extended précis of a lecture delivered to the Eugenics Society at Denison House, Vauxhall Bridge Road, S.W., December 15th, 1909.

worst, i.e., the weakest, the most afflicted, and therefore the most appealing, cases. (Pages 234-235)

Genetics

In the earlier chapters, we have laid the foundation for the ideas behind genetics as it was perceived by its supporters. With the technology we have today alongside the glamour of science it is easy to say, "but genetics is true". We must, however, remember that the advocates of eugenics were not of a scientific mindset. On the contrary, genetics in this tree was firmly embedded in the beliefs of eugenics which is prejudicial at the very least.

Genetics here served to supply a large playing field for theories that were as unfounded as the hypothesis that we are all different in character, intelligence, and social standing due to the genetic makeup of our family genetic heritage. Refusing to accept that a person's experience, environment, or living conditions influences the final determination of a person's character. In other words, a perfect measuring line had been created that was believed to be suitable for gauging all things human. This invented datum of pseudo perfection used the platform of genetics to its advantage requiring nothing more than repetition to demonstrate its authenticity or accuracy.

> [73]*The desire to be filled his mind*
> *As he focused intently on the measuring line*
> *Yes, the measuring line*
> *You know, the words of a man that says you can be*
> *Yes, you can*
> *Yes, you can*

---

[73] Poem by the author Valton Brown referencing a school experience in verse.

With little hearts stirring around the room
Excited at the prospect of becoming a ... soon
No boundaries, no fear of what may ensue
But dreaming, yes dreaming of paths they'll pursue

With visions of the future captivating their minds
The possibilities, opportunities, clearly defined
One by one, they answer the call
A nurse, a doctor, a policeman too
"But you boy, what about you?"
"A fireman!" he shouted with infinite pride
No boundaries, no fear, just the measuring line
You know, the words of a man
That says you can be
Yes, you can
Yes, you can
"I know he means me"

With eyes opened wide
He sat up in his chair
Just waiting to hear the voice of...
Despair was the sound that replaced the glad tones
In a young beating heart of a child yet unknown
"You'll never be that" came the cutting reply
"You'll never be that" was the measuring line
You know the words of a man that says, "You'll never be,
You'll never be,"
I know he means me

Truth is the only measuring line for any concept that we care to employ. It is truth that provides every human being with the safe knowledge that there are boundaries to every aspect of the human experience. Now the philosophical position will ask

"What is truth?" and will try to outline ideas about it using the human mind as the standard, but we all know that everyone has their own opinion on what is right and what is wrong. So, we very quickly discover that truth must be set as the datum by someone, somewhere. It isn't an abstract thought or feeling but a necessary, tangible evidential measuring line for all of us.

Now before you sign off and before we get to the reason for making these points, if you know anything about the crucifixion of The Messiah Yeshua you may remember a man called Pontius Pilate. A man who was the fifth governor of the Roman province of Judea. He served under Emperor Tiberius from around 26 to 37 AD and is said to be the bloodiest and most anti-Semitic of all the Roman proconsuls who ever ran Judea. It is this man that the Samaritans reported to Vitellius, the legate of Syria, after he attacked them on [74]Mount Gerizim and after which he was ordered back to Rome to stand trial for cruelty and oppression.

Pilate was a man who represented the Roman justice system, a man who had the power to execute a person without the need for further approval, who now faced accusations presented to him against a Jewish Rabbi. A Rabbi who had never taken a life but was only guilty of saving them. At this pseudo trial Pilate came face to face with the truth about the truth as evidenced in this dialogue with Yeshua.

Pilate therefore said to Him, "Are You a king then?"

Jesus answered, "You say rightly that I am a king. For this cause I was born, and for this cause I have come into the world, that I should bear witness to the truth. Everyone who is of the truth hears My voice."

---

[74] Britannica, The Editors of Encyclopaedia. "Pontius Pilate". Encyclopedia Britannica, 15 Jun. 2021, https://www.britannica.com/biography/Pontius-Pilate. Accessed 14 May 2022.

Pilate said to Him, "What is truth?" And when he had said this, he went out again to the Jews, and said to them, "I find no fault in Him at all.

John 18:37 – 38 (NKJV)

Pilate cannot and does not declare Yeshua guilty of a crime and only sentences Him to death on the request of the audience The same Yeshua who said, *"… I am the Way, the Truth, and the Life; no man cometh unto the Father, but by Me. (John 14:6 NKJV)*

Yeshua is stating clearly that truth is a person, not a concept and He is truth.

....

It comes as no surprise that the Pontius Pilate of genetics formed the basis for abuses and acts of injustice that would mould the experience of many innocent parties. Its maladministration would be forced by the hands of a mob whose appetite had acquired the taste for anything but the truth. Through its use, communities would experience disadvantage in opportunity, manifesting itself even in the design and location of the most important place for any family, their homes. Tailored to their apparent inferior needs and strategically placed to reinforce the separation between the superior and inferior.

Apostles of Apostasy

Remember Julian Huxley's words from his UNESCO manifesto? Here is a reminder.

"Taking the techniques of persuasion and information and true propaganda that we have learnt to apply nationally in war, and deliberately bending them to the international tasks of peace, if necessary utilising them, as Lenin envisaged, to "overcome the resistance of millions" to desirable change. Using drama to reveal reality and art as the method by which, in Sir Stephen Tallent's words, "truth becomes impressive and living principle of action,"

It would at first seem that his vision of the future had a certain degree of fantasy attached to it, and yet year after year there was a progression that brought this fantasy into reality. Through the most unlikely candidates in modern history, his vision of the future and implementation would be established, preaching with a fervency and passion that would put most preachers to shame. The message of their kingdom becomes ever present while the blood of the Abels continues to cry out for justice and mercy.

These preachers and disciples of this movement share the same foundation as the Evangelists of the new era, guided by an unseen hand which remains in the shadows, pulling the strings, manipulating the scenery and clouding the mind of reason. In every image or symbol where the person behind the hand is portrayed, his true identity is hidden in obscurity, an image which stands in stark contrast to the God of the Bible who is unafraid to make himself known to the truth seeker.

Unsurprisingly, in this unholy movement symbolised by the tree, is a united voice embodied in individuals who occupy the most prominent places in society that are both influential and personally beneficial. Their ideas are often hidden behind the white noise of the media and collective voices of their adorers, and it is easy to surmise that these are elitist with an elitist agenda (even though this may be true), but there is always a presence behind the advocates of such plans, the unseen hand. Nevertheless, their mission trips and campaigns mark the landscape of time and country making it almost impossible for their audience to avoid becoming captive.

So here is a selected list of names accompanied by their thoughts in their own words. What do you think?

DH Lawrence (September 11, 1885 - March 2, 1930)
Writer, poet.

"If I had my way, I would build a lethal chamber as big as the Crystal Palace, with a military band playing softly, and a Cinematograph working brightly; then I'd go out in the back streets and main streets and bring them in, all the sick, the halt, and the maimed; I would lead them gently, and they would smile me a weary thanks; and the band would softly bubble out the 'Hallelujah Chorus'."

(Quote by DH Lawrence in a letter to Blanche Jennings, October 9, 1908).

Ironically, DH Lawrence is regarded as one of the most influential writers of the 20th century. Although this may be the case in literary circles, in other circles DH Lawrence held some rather unsavoury ideas which most people would find abhorrent today. However, in a twisted, almost predictive manner we see the manifestation of these ideas in Europe during Nazism.

George Bernard Shaw (July 26, 1856 - November 2, 1950) Playwright, activist, critic

[75]"*We should find ourselves committed to killing a great many people whom we now leave living, and to leave living a great many people whom we at present kill. We should have to get rid of all ideas about capital punishment ...*

A part of eugenic politics would finally land us in an extensive use of the lethal chamber. A great many people would have to be put out of existence simply because it wastes other people's time to look after them."

Another quotation from GB Shaw is as follows:

[76]"*The moment we face it frankly we are driven to the conclusion that the community has a right to put a price on the right to live in it ... If people are fit to live, let them live under decent human conditions. If they are not fit to live, kill them in a decent human way. Is it any wonder that some of us are driven to prescribe the lethal chamber as the solution for the hard cases which are at present made the excuse for dragging all the other cases down to their level, and the only solution that will create a sense of full social responsibility in modern populations?*"

George Bernard Shaw, an influencer of western culture through the arts and a Nobel prize winner for literature, openly declares his views which align with DH Lawrence's ideas.

---

[75] George Bernard Shaw, Lecture to the Eugenics Education Society, Reported in The Daily Express, March 4, 1910.
[76] George Bernard Shaw, Prefaces (London: Constable and Co., 1934), p. 296.

Oliver Wendell Holmes Jr. (March 8, 1841 - March 6, 1935)
An American jurist, legal scholar, and an associate justice of the Supreme Court of the United States

"An Act of Virginia, approved March 20, 1924, recites that the health of the patient and the welfare of society may be promoted in certain cases by the sterilization of mental defectives, under careful safeguard, &c.; that the sterilization may be effected in males by vasectomy and in females by salpingectomy, without serious pain or substantial danger to life; that the Commonwealth is supporting in various institutions many defective persons who, if now discharged, would become a menace, but, if incapable of procreating, might be discharged with safety and become self-supporting with benefit to themselves and to society, and that experience has shown that heredity plays an important part in the transmission of insanity, imbecility, &c. The statute then enacts that, whenever the superintendent of certain institutions, including the above-named State Colony, shall be of opinion that it is for the best interests of the patients and of society that an inmate under his care should be sexually sterilized, he may have the operation performed upon any patient afflicted with hereditary forms of insanity, imbecility, &c., on complying with the very careful provisions by which the act protects the patients from possible abuse.

[...]

We have seen more than once that the public welfare may call upon the best citizens for their lives. It would be strange if it could not call upon those who already sap the strength of the State for these lesser sacrifices, often not felt to be such by those concerned, in order to prevent our being swamped with incompetence. It is better for all the world if, instead of waiting to execute degenerate offspring for crime or to let them starve for their imbecility, society can prevent those who are manifestly unfit from continuing their kind. The principle that sustains compulsory vaccination is broad enough to cover cutting the Fallopian tubes. Three generations of imbeciles are enough."

... Judgment affirmed.

(His words in the 1927 case Buck vs. Bell decision)

Oliver Wendell Holmes Sr. was an intellectual, the Dean of Harvard Medical School, poet, and apparent father of the supreme court. Notably recognised as the originator of the term 'Boston Brahmin', a term used to describe a wealthy group of families. Oliver Wendell wrote a series of articles which were compiled to create the novel Elsie Venner. Chapter 1, titled, [77]*'The Brahmin Caste of New England'* opens with:

"There is, however, in New England, an aristocracy, if you choose to call it so, which has a greater character of permanence. It has grown to be a caste – not in any odious sense – but, by the repetition of the same influences, generation after generation, it has acquired a distinct organization and physiognomy which not to recognise is mere stupidity, and not to be willing to describe would show a distrust of the good nature and intelligence of our readers who like to have us see all we can and tell all we see." (pages 2-3)

He is said to be the most cited and influential supreme court justice in history. It is interesting that he was also one of the first Americans to promote eugenics, and who began a form of eugenics that would provide a platform in institutions like Harvard, for others of like mind, [78]Charles Davenport being one of those individuals.

---

[77] Britannica, The Editors of Encyclopaedia. "Brahmin". Encyclopedia Britannica, 26 Jul. 2016, https://www.britannica.com/art/Brahmin. Accessed 6 August 2022.
[78] See section on Evangelists, Charles Davenport

Marie Stopes (October 15, 1880 - October 2, 1958)
Pioneer, reformer and campaigner for women's rights

Marie Stopes is venerated as a campaigner for women's rights and family planning. However, as noble as these pursuits may appear they detract from the motivation that weaves itself into both popular perceptions.

Marie Stopes came from an affluent family which gave her the commodity that most could not afford, time. Time to explore her ideas (including the outlandish ideas) and time to implement them. To put it bluntly, Marie Stopes was to Britain what Margaret Sanger was to America. Her drive to influence family planning and the rights of women was rooted in her passion for eugenics. Rarely mentioned is that her belief in eugenics began long before her interest in birth control and it was her belief in eugenics that led to her founding the Society for Constructive Birth Control and Racial Progress (CBC). *(Its main tenets are referenced in the appendix).*

In her own words, she writes in her book *'Radiant Motherhood, A Book for Those Who are Creating the Future,'*

"A second and almost greater danger is not a simple ignorance, but the inborn incapacity which lies in the vast and ever increasing stock of degenerate, feeble-minded and unbalanced who are now in our midst and who devastate social customs. These populate most rapidly, these tend proportionately to increase, and these are like the parasite upon the healthy tree sapping its vitality. These produce less than they consume and are able only to flourish and reproduce so long as the healthier produce food for them ; but by ever weakening the human stock, in the end they will succumb with the fine structure which they have destroyed."

The Voluntary Parenthood League (an organisation that was in direct competition with Margaret Sanger's American

Birth Control League but would later merge with it) recorded a [79]Town Hall meeting in the USA, 27th October 1921. Marie Stopes would be the main speaker as the President of the Society of Constructive Birth Control and Racial Progress. Mr Norman Hapgood calls the meeting to order at 8:30pm and opens with a revealing set of statements that bring to the forefront other individuals who were also avid followers of the same ideology,

"Ladies and gentlemen, my first task tonight is a pleasant one. I have to read to you messages from three of the best known literary men of England. If we had in the United States to secure an expression of opinion on a subject that had considerable delicacy, that aroused a considerable amount of uninformed opposition, I am not at all sure that we would be able to secure names as distinguished as these. I think we may say that the nation to which our distinguished visitor belongs has had for one of its choicest assets throughout its history a sense of obligation in the intelligent class to show courage, to show intellectual leadership.

Of the three kinds of courage: physical courage, moral courage and intellectual courage, it is possible that the rarest of the three is intellectual courage. First, I will read a message from Havelock Ellis:

"I have followed the Birth Control Movement in America for many years and with much sympathetic interest, so that I am very pleased to hear of these great public meetings which you and Mrs. Margaret Sanger are holding in New York this year. Such meetings are convincing testimony to the progress which has been made and an encouraging promise for the future. I congratulate the League on the presence of Dr. Marie C. Stopes, whose name is so well known for her work in the cause of sex education in the widest sense, and who will

---

[79] Verbatim report of the Town Hall Meeting under the auspices of the Voluntary Parenthood League at which Dr Marie C. Stopes, of London was chief speaker: October 27, 1921
by Stopes, Marie Carmichael, 1880-1958; Dennett, Mary Ware, 1872-1947; Hapgood, Norman, 1868-1937; Voluntary Parenthood League (N.Y.)

long be remembered in connection with the establishment of the first birth control clinic in this country.

With all good wishes, Sincerely Yours, Havelock Ellis."

The next is from Edward Carpenter:

"Dear Mrs. Dennett:

I am glad to hear that Dr. Marie Stopes is to speak in New York on the 27th of October in connection with the Voluntary Parenthood League. Birth control is one of the most important movements of the present day, and you could not have a better and more authoritative speaker on it than Dr. Stopes."

The last is from a man who is influencing world thought today in the mass probably more than any other writer alive - from H. G. Wells:

"Dear Mrs. Dennett:

I regret very much that I shall miss your interesting meeting. I am a very great admirer of the outspoken courage of Dr. Marie Stopes and of the useful work she is doing in the propaganda of reasonable sexual knowledge. Our hopes of a civilized life for all rest entirely on the possibly of sane birth control.

Very sincerely yours, H. G. Wells.

Following her research on Marie Stopes, June Rose describes Stopes in her book, [80]*Marie Stopes and the Sexual Revolution'*,

"To our ears, in the aftermath of Hitler, there is something blood- chilling in her fearless quest for excellence, sacrificing ordinary humanity on the altar of The Race. But at the time, the notion of

---

[80] Marie Stopes and the sexual revolution by Rose, June 1926

suppressing weaker members of the next generation, reducing the need for institutions such as prisons and hospitals, and relieving the burden on taxpayers was immensely attractive to many members of the wealthier classes. Since wartime recruitment had drawn attention to the large numbers of physically lowgrade 'C3' people in the population, they could no longer be ignored and, rather than improve general standards of health, housing and hygiene, a preferred solution was sterilization or birth control. Marie was singular only in the zeal and lucidity with which she expressed those ideas. She even went so far as to personally hound the deaf and dumb father of four deaf children who had appealed for help to get his son admitted to the Royal School for Deaf and Dumb Children at Margate for irresponsibly 'bringing more misery into the world."

Marie Stopes once again demonstrates the insidious manner in which this ideology uses the idea of 'caring' while systematically destroying the lives of innocent individuals in the process. Needless to say, once again it is impossible to be a believer, or preacher of the eugenics religion without also being anti-Semitic. To see the presence of such organisations in cultures across the globe, apparently serving poor communities, causes one to ask, 'Who are the real carers of our children?'

Today MSI Reproductive Choices is the modern face of her organisation founded in 1976 following the near closure of the Marie Stopes clinic. As with other organisations, Marie Stopes International has followed suit by trying to distance itself from Marie Stopes' eugenics beliefs.

John Harvey Kellogg (February 26, 1852 - December 14, 1943)
Doctor, Nutritionist, and Inventor of Cornflakes

[81]"*Long before the race reaches the state of universal incompetency, the impending danger will be appreciated, the cause sought for and eliminated, and, through eugenics and euthenics, the mental soundness of the race will be saved.*"

John Harvey Kellogg embraced the idea that races should not mix, and that the future of the races is dependent on a lifestyle of good diet, no alcohol and no smoking. As a vegetarian and a former member of the Seventh-day Adventists (which he broke away from in 1907), he went on to hold firm views about the place of eugenics in the role of society. However, his view on segregation seems to be at odds with his Battle Creek Sanitarium which did not have segregation between races. Also, he and his wife fostered 42 children of various races, this may have been due to their belief that environment could change hereditary tendencies.

His position on the sterilisation of the defectives and his role on the Michigan Health Board led the way to legislation being passed under the Public Act 34: 1913. Under this legislation, it is estimated that 3800 people were involuntarily sterilised. An Act which wasn't repealed until 1974.

In addition to his activity in influencing law he also worked with Charles Davenport, and Irving Fisher to host the first Race Betterment Conference in 1914 and together set up the Race Betterment Foundation. A foundation which would encourage people of better stock to breed and protect the superior race.

The invention of the world-famous Kellogg's Cornflakes has the most bizarre origins. John Kellogg believed that onanism was the cause of many different illnesses; at least 39. Here's where Kellogg's Cornflakes comes in. John Kellogg believed

---

[81] Kellogg, JH (1913). Relation of Public Health to Race Degeneracy. The American Journal of Public Health, p. 656.

that by eating bland and healthy foods one would control sexual desires and passions. One such food was Kellogg's Cornflakes, a cereal that established Kellogg's business and brand even though it had no sugar and was truly bland.

While it is believed that John Kellogg and his Battle Creek Sanitarium were the epicentre of eugenics in America, it is true that Kellogg and others pretty much had a free hand in the state of Michigan, turning the state into one out of four states that had the largest number of sterilisations.

Aleister Crowley (October 12, 1875 - December 1, 1947) English occultist, ceremonial magician, poet, painter, novelist, and mountaineer

"The key of joy is disobedience."

"Do what thou wilt shall be the whole of the law."

Wherever you turn these days, you cannot mention evil influences or individuals without citing the name of Aleister Crowley. A name which will usually be at the top of the list, not just amongst young adults, as may be assumed, but all age groups. What is it about him and why mention him here? Well, this section is incomplete without referencing some of his connections in the hidden world of associates, networks, and philosophies. It is through this man that things take a sinister turn, one that is too easily dismissed as nonsense or religious fanaticism.

To emphasise his significance and to prove that these are not words of a crank, Aleister Crowley was held in such high regard in Britain that in 2002 he is recorded in a BBC poll as the

73rd greatest Britain. This is following William Booth, who established the Salvation Army at 71st position and preceding Bob Geldof who was the lead singer of the 1970s Irish rock band the Boomtown Rats at 75th place.

Crowley's father was Edward Alexander Crowley, who was the heir to a brewing fortune. His father was initially a Quaker who converted to become a member of The Plymouth Brethren (exclusive). His mother was Emily Bertha Bishop who also converted to The Plymouth Brethren when they married. Aleister Crowley on the other hand disliked his mother and had an aversion to Christianity in any form at a very young age. Described as 'the Beast' by his mother, Aleister would later wear the name with pride.

Aleister was another (like Marie Stopes) who acquired wealth from a family inheritance and who was free to pursue any interest that caught his imagination. Sadly, his interest was eventually directed toward occultism beginning with the 'Hermetic Order of the Golden Dawn', a secret order which was more commonly known as Golden Dawn. The Golden Dawn has its roots in [82]Rosicrucianism, which is a global brotherhood whose teachings are a mixture of occultism and pretty much any other esoteric beliefs including but not exclusive to Gnosticism,

---

[82] Rosicrucian, member of a worldwide brotherhood claiming to possess esoteric wisdom handed down from ancient times. The name derives from the order's symbol, a rose on a cross, which is similar to the family coat of arms of Martin Luther. Rosicrucian teachings are a combination of occultism and other religious beliefs and practices, including Hermeticism, Jewish mysticism, and Christian Gnosticism. The central feature of Rosicrucianism is the belief that its members possess secret wisdom that was handed down to them from ancient times.
Melton, J. Gordon. "Rosicrucian". Encyclopedia Britannica, 7 Sep. 2022, https://www.britannica.com/topic/Rosicrucians. Accessed 9 September 2022.

and mysticism. It claims to have ancient secret wisdom that has been handed down from one generation to the next.

Aleister Crowley was drawn to the philosophy of this secret order. His interest would not stop at the exploration of the occult as a follower, but he would go on to develop his form of occultism. A form that is still in vogue today.

The catalyst for this took place in 1904 while on a honeymoon in Egypt with his wife Rose Crowley where he recorded his three-day encounters (through channelling) with an entity he referred to as Aiwass, the messenger of [83]Horus.

[84]*"The Voice of Aiwass came apparently from over my left shoulder, from the furthest corner of the room. It seemed to echo itself in my physical heart in a very strange manner, hard to describe. I have noticed a similar phenomenon when I have been waiting for a message fraught with great hope or dread. The voice was passionately poured, as if Aiwass were alert about the time-limit ... The voice was of deep timbre, musical and expressive, its tones solemn, voluptuous, tender, fierce or aught else as suited the moods of the message. Not bass – perhaps a rich tenor or baritone. The English was free of either native or foreign accent, perfectly pure of local or caste mannerisms, thus startling and even uncanny at first hearing. I had a strong impression that the speaker was actually in the corner where he seemed to be, in a body of "fine matter," transparent as a veil of gauze, or a cloud of incense-smoke. He seemed to be a tall, dark man in his thirties, well-knit, active and strong, with the face of a savage king, and eyes veiled lest their gaze should destroy what they saw. The dress was not Arab; it suggested Assyria or Persia, but very vaguely. I took little note of it, for to me at that time Aiwass was an "angel" such as I had often seen in visions, a being purely astral."*

---

[83] Britannica, The Editors of Encyclopaedia. "Horus". Encyclopedia Britannica, 22 Aug. 2022, https://www.britannica.com/topic/Horus. Accessed 17 September 2022.
[84] The Equinox of the Gods, Chapter 7

Through this encounter, Aiwass claimed that Aleister Crowley would be the prophet of the New Age of Horus. An age, according to Crowley, that would supersede the era of patriarchal religions and usher in an age of self-determination or self-sovereignty through the law, *'Do what thou wilt'*.

Needless to say, but necessary, Rabbi Paul (as a true Apostle) cautioned the early followers of The Messiah against such false apostles, centuries before Aleister Crowley came on the scene. Rabbi Paul was familiar with this kind of individual and did not hold back in speaking out against them and their encounters. A message that we do well to remind ourselves of.

He states,

But what I do, I will also continue to do, that I may cut off the opportunity from those who desire an opportunity to be regarded just as we are in the things of which they boast. For such are false apostles, deceitful workers, transforming themselves into apostles of Christ. And no wonder! For Satan himself transforms himself into an angel of light. Therefore it is no great thing if his ministers also transform themselves into ministers of righteousness, whose end will be according to their works.

2 Corinthians 11:12-15 – (NKJV)

Rabbi Paul addresses accurately a deception that was attracting the attention of new believers in Yeshua. A most powerful and attractive possibility for the power-hungry and misguided pursuant of any kind of philosophy. We must also note that where there is a Crowley there is a disciple in training, there is a community of believers, a congregational order, all of whom live and work in this world like you and me.

Crowley recorded the encounters in poetry form in his book called 'The Book of the Law'. He said that this book was dictated to him by Aiwass. The book became the accepted scripture for the Ordo Templi Orientis or the O.T.O., a secret society or mystical group of German origin, which still draws membership from the world of entertainment and other spheres of influence today. It is in this 'Book of the Law' that the teaching *"do what thou wilt shall be the whole of the law"* comes from, although its origins can be traced back many years before Aleister Crowley. Eventually, Aleister would go on to establish his version of the order called 'Thelema.'

Although at first, this might seem to have little relevance to anything other than a man who held the strangest ideas and a passion for equally debased pursuits, it is worth noting that many similar characters in other areas within the root system are also venerated for spearheading a new religion or form of spirituality, founded on encounters with entities. No, these entities are not 'aliens', these are disembodied beings which the Bible refers to as demons. On each occasion where such an encounter is recorded the individuals are often worshipped as a 'religious leader' or 'global celebrity' due to their acquired knowledge or enlightenment on all things supernatural. There is also something quite telling that becomes evident during the outset of their journey or sometime later, and that is their disdain for the Bible, The God of The Bible, and of course, Israel.

Aleister Crowley is one such example. Crowley being an apostle of this dark movement, was commissioned to draw as many souls as possible into the religion's mirky grasp.

It is duly noted that although he drew some popularity during his life, Crowley was more popular after his death. Actors, musicians, and famous and infamous characters purchased his books and applied his teachings without fear of the consequences. Time could be spent on writing about this man alone, but the information is sufficient to drive home the necessary point about the world that he and others sought to establish.

It is at this juncture that the narrative of the new era of disciples takes a subtle yet vitally important turn. As we focus on Aleister Crowley the lens must pan out a sufficient distance to provide a clear overview of his influence on his contemporaries. By doing so we also witness the emergence of a new root of philosophy shooting out of the tree's complex root system

There were other contemporaries of Aleister Crowley that worshipped and drew from the same root system, using their influence to promote the eugenics religion. People such as Bertrand Russell (18 May 1872 – 2 February 1970), a mathematician, writer, logician, philosopher, and Nobel Prize recipient for literature in 1950. A man whose grandfather, John Russell, served as Prime minister twice and was given the noble position of the 1st Earl Russell by Queen Victoria. Also, [85]John Maynard Keynes, a British economist who was considered to be one of the most influential in this area and whose ideas would shape the government's approach to the economy. His book 'General Theory of Employment, Interest, and Money' (1936) was used by President Franklin D Roosevelt during the great depression. However, he also served as director of the Eugenics Society and advocated eugenics as the way forward even though he had passed through the Second World War and was aware of its atrocities. Later we will see how these connections unfold in a gripping, yet unbelievable way but let us pause here for a moment and refocus the lens to inspect the issue that sits at the core of all of these and other events.

---

[85] Kurbegovic, C. (2013, September 14). Keynes, John Maynard. Retrieved September 13, 2022, from https://eugenicsarchive.ca

At The Core

*And the King will answer and say to them, 'Assuredly, I say to you, inasmuch as you did it to one of the least of these **My brethren**, you did it to Me.*

"Then they also will answer Him, saying, 'Lord, when did we see You hungry or thirsty or a stranger or naked or sick or in prison, and did not minister to You?'

Then He will answer them, saying, 'Assuredly, I say to you, inasmuch as you did not do it to one of the least of these, you did not do it to Me.'

Matthew 25:40, 44, 45 (Part) (NKJV)

The Dichotomy

Various versions of history have informed the minds of billions of children and adults worldwide, however, there are tensions within the historical narrative that are not easily ratified. The expression of what is purported to be advancement wrestles with the reality of human tragedy and depravity at a level that is difficult to process. This is no less the case with the next subject embedded in this complex organic ecosystem. However, I would ask you to guard your heart before proceeding as the intention here is not emotive but simply a compilation of statements and observations that are designed to navigate you to a safe landing place. Equally, it stands as a reminder that good intentions and sweeping policies have never stopped a single human being from performing selfish acts of unkindness and indifference against another human being. We all too often speak highly of our human potential but are easily offended when God in His infinite wisdom and vision performs His unbiased examination of our grandiose claims. Without revocation, His examination of us often arrives at a very different conclusion,

"The heart is deceitful above all things, And desperately wicked; Who can know it? I, the Lord, search the heart, I test the mind, Even to give every man according to his ways, According to the fruit of his doings.

"As a partridge that broods but does not hatch, So is he who gets riches, but not by right; It will leave him in the midst of his days, And at his end he will be a fool." Jeremiah 17:8-10 (NKJV)

To derive such clarity without emotional influence or bias, cannot be found in simple logic or intellectualism, as neither of these provides sufficient objectivity to warrant anyone's complete trust (as we have already seen). This pure vision is only resident in and through The Messiah and His Holy Spirit, without which we cannot honestly navigate the emotional and personal desires of the heart. The heart, that secret hiding place that only we and God see. A place resident to a multiplicity of terrains and vacillating landscapes that if allowed to, deceives us into believing that the terrain of our heart is unique.

As obvious as this seems, this is a truth that evades us in our quest to know and respond to the cumulative facts. First of all, we ask *'What is truth?'* to which our own heart responds *'Anything you consider it to be'* a premise which once again defaults to the human intellect for answers and not the God of the Bible, our Creator. In many cases, the enormity of the internal conflict rooted in such an opinion results in driving us deeper into searching out philosophers, gurus and spiritual experiences in the outside hope that we will light upon a conclusive resolution. This approach is posited as new in this era but has been an approach popularised since the beginning of time. Unfortunately, it has led and continues to lead many to react with clearly divided opinions. Some will say *'the world is full of wickedness'* while others retort, *'things are not so bad, it's all about your perspective on life, we are generally good people.'*

Regrettably, it is this tension between the truth of who we are and the reality of human interventions that leaves us dumbfounded. With all our legislation on human rights and the ongoing interventions of agents of change, we repeatedly witness the uncomfortable truth hidden behind the veil of deceit, a truth that reminds us that humanity has an eternal problem. To deflect the problem unto God is to be nothing less than dishonest and defamatory against the only one who restrains us from the opportunity to do much, much worse. As Rabbi Paul aptly put it *"Indeed, let God be true but every man a liar."*

PART Romans 3:4 (NKJV)

The Shoah

Justice is turned back, and righteousness stands afar off; For truth is fallen in the street, And equity cannot enter. So truth fails, And he who departs from evil makes himself a prey.

Isaiah 59:14, 15 (NKJV)

As we circumnavigate the history of this Eugenics tree, juxtaposing between persons, events and places, we find that this unnatural, organic edifice developed by the British and taken forward largely by the Americans begins to take on a presence that overarches anything that the world had witnessed before. This thriving yet toxic force (which once grew in the shade) now arises from obscurity, from amongst people in the nations and begins to spread its potency, its greatest toxicity alighting in the most unlikely place. Germany.

Its origins appear ambiguous, its impact indelible and its reach rapidly spreading like [86]knotweed throughout Europe, uprooting every moral and ethical boundary it lighted upon while releasing mind-bending toxins to anyone who participated in its fruit. To some, this remains an event that is recorded alongside a host of other historical events, to an erroneous few it never happened. Yet, its origin, purpose and residue are not a mystery but a stark, sad revelation of a long history. Like the slave trade before it, the statistics on the number of people that died become a debating point, often to the detriment of the main issue which is, this event should never have happened. However, if we are determined to resign this event to the annals of time as just another occurrence, or an event just like any other atrocity we do a disservice to the victims and we align ourselves as co-conspirators with the

---

[86] One of the most aggressive weeds that is capable of weakening building foundations and ultimately property damage that can be costly to rectify.

individuals involved in this climactic manifestation of a crime against humanity.

The Shoah (Holocaust) was the largest, systematic eugenics programme of our time and Nazi Germany was the instrument that accepted the eugenics mantle. Eugenics, a religion that had been employed by the west but through the vehicle of Nazism would be taken to a new level. Led by an apostle of eugenics (Adolf Hitler) who received the tenets of the new denominational religion while in prison (recorded in his book Mein Kampf). Rising to power through incremental stages, baptised by evil, free to take advantage of a world that had been in preparation for this offshoot religion called the Third [87]Reich.

From the Garden of Eden to the transatlantic/sub-Saharan slave owners, to the evangelists of eugenics, the [88]Third Reich would demonstrate to the world that something else had arrived. The Third Reich was presumed to be the successor to the early modern 'Holy Roman Empire' of 800 to 1806 (the First Reich) and then the German Empire of 1871 to 1918 (the Second Reich). Nevertheless, there were a series of connected incidents that led up to the establishment of this Third Reich which also contributed to Hitler's rise to power; it isn't a coincidence that the Third Reich rose on the back of the Great Depression of 1929 when Germany, along with other nations, was plunged into an economic disaster which in turn paved the way for extreme world views.

---

[87] Ray, Michael. "Why Was Nazi Germany Called the Third Reich?". Encyclopedia Britannica, Invalid Date, https://www.britannica.com/story/why-was-nazi-germany-called-the-third-reich. Accessed 2 July 2022.
[88] Britannica, The Editors of Encyclopaedia. "Third Reich". *Encyclopedia Britannica*, 9 Jan. 2020, https://www.britannica.com/place/Third-Reich. Accessed 8 January 2022.

It was in 1924, five years before the Great Depression when Hitler began writing Mein Kampf in Landsberg prison after being convicted of treason against the German republic (the German government at the time) in November 1923. As the fledgling leader of the Nazi Party, Hitler, and his collaborators had hoped to spark a revolution by marching on Berlin. His effort to seize power from the German Government was infamously called The Beer Hall Putsch (also known as the Munich Putsch). It ended in complete failure and cost the lives of over a dozen of Hitler's supporters. After this failed attempt which culminated in his conviction, his 24-day trial became the epicentre for his evangelistic campaign. What should have been a trial and a life-threatening conviction somehow became a pulpit for Hitler to preach the tenets of Nazism to a captive audience. An audience that had never been exposed to a demonically inspired preacher before. Yes, this is possible. Let me digress a little to explain. In the account of Luke in the book of Acts 8, an earlier historical incident is recorded that reflect similar characteristics as were seen in Germany.

But there was a certain man called Simon, who previously practiced sorcery in the city and astonished the people of Samaria, claiming that he was someone great, to whom they all gave heed, from the least to the greatest, saying, "This man is the great power of God." And they heeded him because he had astonished them with his sorceries for a long time. (Acts 9:9-11 NKJV)

Simon was worshipped as a god and was believed to be a man who obtained his power by some divine ordination. The emphasis is on his ability to influence anyone that heard him, from the least to the greatest. His charisma surpassed many of the preachers today who rely upon slick marketing campaigns and exorbitantly expensive media streams to gain popularity. Simon had no such luxuries, yet his influence was undeniable, having practised the dark arts amongst these people for a long time and unchallenged. Every man, woman, and child were exposed to his powerful demonstrations and that caused astonishment and misplaced veneration, leading them to blindly follow his every command due to his assumed superior understanding and demonstration of power.

And when Philip came down to the city of Samaria he proclaimed the Messiah to them. And the crowds paid attention to those things which were spoken by Philip. Of one mind in this, they listened and saw the signs which he was doing. For then many of them had unclean spirits and they, unclean spirits, were coming out shouting in a loud voice, and many paralytics and lame were being healed and there was much joy in that city. (Acts 8:5 -8 ONM)

Following the persecution of those that came to believe in the Jewish Messiah, Yeshua, Philip went to Samaria and preached the message of his Messiah's kingdom. Philip's arrival was received in a manner that was diametrically opposed to the world of Simon the sorcerer:

- Philip was not the focus of attention.
- He pointed people, to The Messiah.
- Joy was the ultimate response to being set free.
- A complete renunciation of occult practices was a natural outworking of the community's newfound freedom.
- Money was not involved.
- It was not a business transaction between the powerful and the powerless.

However, Simon, for the first time in his life, was to witness a greater manifestation of power, the type of power that put him out of business. His response would be to become a follower, a disciple of The Messiah engaging in a baptism like everyone else, to demonstrate his allegiance to this new leader The Messiah, Yeshua (Jesus). At first, his actions appear genuine but his closeness to Philip and his observation of another kind of power only served to reveal his true intentions. As we read,

"And when Simon saw that through the laying on of the apostles' hands the Holy Spirit was given, he offered them money, saying, "Give me this power also, that anyone on whom I lay hands may receive the Holy Spirit."

But Peter said to him, "Your money perish with you, because you thought that the gift of God could be purchased with money! You have neither part nor portion in this matter, for your heart is not right in the sight of God. Repent therefore of this your wickedness, and pray God if perhaps the thought of your heart may be forgiven you. For I see that you are poisoned by bitterness and bound by iniquity." (Acts 8:14-23 NKJV)

Simon was still hungry for a platform of influence over other people. His desire for greatness had not abated but he was looking for another business opportunity. Thankfully, this unholy act amongst Holy people was detected and will always be detected sooner or later, therefore, it is incumbent on us to understand that the power Simon was initially enthused by, in his earlier practice of the dark arts, is the same power that inspired Hitler and there was nothing Holy about it. Hence the reason for astonishment when audiences listened to this once fumbling stature of a man (Hitler). A man who somehow morphed into this charismatic preacher whose words metamorphosed into bitter, poisonous syllables catapulting themselves into the heart of people across all age groups. Piercing the impenetrable walls of the prison, grabbing the attention of inmates and guards alike then sweeping across the nation of Germany and the world on the crest of media waves instantly swaying beliefs and opinions.

His trial was the perfect opportunity to begin his campaign with Satan as his financial backer and spiritual advisor. Preaching satanic theology for 24 days virtually unrestricted, mesmerizing a variety of people, some of whom had been waiting for someone to present a cause and solution to their plight. A person of demonstrative power, a vision of pseudo-heroism and apparent compassion for German suffering. Hitler was to this transition similar to what Charles Darwin was during the industrial revolution, a perfect candidate for the next wave of global change.

[i89]Here are extracts from the court transcript,

FRANKFURTER ZEITUNG

1st Morning Edition

26 Sept. 1931

HITLER'S TESTIMONY BEFORE THE COURT FOR HIGH TREASON

The witness, Adolf Hitler testified that he was born on 20 April 1889 in Braunau on the Inn, without citizenship...

President: *You have been invited to testify at the request of Dr. Frank to give evidence that the NSDAP is striving to attain its goal by purely legal means, does not intend to take violent action against the Constitution or Government neither encourages its members or supporters to violent action against Constitution or Government or even to prepare for this, even in 1923. I ask you to describe in brief outline the EVOLUTION OF 'THE NAZI PARTY*

Hitler: *I fought on the Westfront as soldier in the fall of 1918. At that time I already saw the collapse coming. This resulted because all political organizations were suffering from the same sickness. There*

---

[89] Hitler's Testimony Before the Court for High Treason from Frankfurter Zeitung. 1st Morning Edition, 26 September 1931. Translation of Extract of Document 2512-PS / Office of U.S. Chief of Counsel.
Courtesy of Cornell University Law Library, Donovan Nuremberg Trials Collection https://digital.library.cornell.edu/collections/nuremberg

are in general three phenomena which always reappear at such times, when the country is declining and which have slowly disintegrated the German people also. The non-utilization of our own national strength brought about by the general international attitude.

Moving on further into the latter part of the court's recorded transcript, Hitler continues as follows:

Hitler: *The German National People's Party is an opposition party just as we are. But the German National People's Party is a reform party. The Nazi movement sees as the core of the State, that which is summed up in the term "people" (Volk). Therefore we cannot be compared with other Parties. But it cannot therefore be said, because we used other methods - therefore by force - Our propaganda is the spiritual revolutionizing of the German people. This change is at least as gigantic as that brought about by the Marxist ideology. It is a completely new world. Our movement has no need of force. The time will come when the German nation will get to know our ideas. Then 35 million Germans will stand behind me. Whether we take over the Government today or form an opposition is immaterial to us. The next election will increase the number of Nazis in the Reichstag from 107 - 200. There will come a time when people will be glad that there is such a movement, the members of which are now trembling before the Court. Our opponents are interested in representing our movement as anti-state because they know our goal is to be attained by legal means. Nevertheless they realize that our movement must lead to a complete change of State.*

President: *What relation does this bear to the so-called* 'THIRD REICH?

Hitler: *We honor the memory of the old German Empire, we have fought for it. But this State had an inner weakness from the very beginning. Out of it came the present Germany.*

It is the embodiment of Democracy and Internationalism. This second State wants tolerance the German people no men behind, who will defend their rights before the world. We hope, therefore, for a new Reich in which all institutions - beginning with the organisation of the State itself down to those which serve to maintain the national life (Volkstums) - will lead the people towards a splendid future. It 1s only natural that this Third Reich will quarrel with the decadent forces of today. Consequently, the attempts by our opponents to designate our methods as illegal and to attribute to us a trend which we do not have. He who maintains that isolated quotations are proof of a point of view, which he cannot construe from regulations and Party orders, will find a thousand possibilities for this. I have in our movement countless millions of people, whose hearts bleed for Germany. These young men, themselves fighters, are pushed about, come before the Court, although they had only the best intentions. They are struck down and hounded by the "red" mobs. That these people make statements, which are not in accordance with the spirit of the movement, is understandable because of their youth...

CERTIFICATE OF TRANSLATION

OF EXTRACT OF DOCUMENT

NO. 2512-PS

17TH November 1945

I, EVELYN GLAZIER, P/O, W.R.N.S., 37371, hereby certify that I om thoroughly conversant with the English and German languages; and that the above is a true and correct translation of Extract of Document 2512-PS

Hitler's preaching during these days concluded in a trend of religion that would embrace and eventually implement everything that the dark ministers of eugenics were responsible for propagating. People such as Francis Galton, Margaret Higgins Sanger, Julian Sorell Huxley, Charles Davenport, Clarence Gamble, Leonard Darwin, Marie Stopes, Helen Keller, George Bernard Shaw, Sidney and Beatrice Webb, Bertrand Russell, HG Wells, Winston Churchill, William Beveridge, John Harvey Kellogg: a brief list which should include the multiple slavemasters, business tycoons, landowners, cotton manufacturers, inventors, doctors, lawyers, estate owners, philosophers, psychiatrists and an infinite number of others who boldly proclaimed racist, anti-Semitic bellicosity mixed with a heavy dose of elitist separatism.

The impact of Hitler's preaching was clear. His prison sentence was reduced from a five-year sentence to approximately nine months due to his rising popularity. To put this into context, the Third Reich was the official Nazi designation for the regime in Germany from January 1933 to May 1945, 12 years. From 1925 to 1945, its membership handbook (Mein Kampf) sold over 12 million copies and was translated into over a dozen languages including a braille edition.

The result of this religious agenda is estimated to have taken the lives of six million Jews. This made up 2/3rds of the Jewish population in Europe, which was approximately 9.5 million. It equated to (based on the number of 6 million) approximately 1369 murders per day for 12 years if we were to spread the number of deaths evenly across this time frame. Of course, the fact that there were no averages in the daily death rate makes the picture of this monstrous campaign even more disturbing. In comparison to the natural deaths in South Africa in 2019, from a population of 60 million South Africa's numbers came to approximately 1500 deaths per day (based on 9.4 deaths per 1000).

These comparisons help to gauge the magnitude of this event and the intensity with which pain and suffering were inflicted, but it only tells a small part of the story. The slaughter of millions of innocent citizens destined to their fate by the vehicle of humanistic philosophy and the religion of eugenics, is dismissed as simply an atrocity, featured in multiple documentaries as social history and denied by a few as fiction. Yet the Holocaust or Shoah remains the single most horrific event that has indelibly marked the world's landscape since the transatlantic and Sub-Saharan slave trade. Why?

Israel

And the king will answer and say to them, 'assuredly, I say to you, inasmuch as you did it to one of the least of these my brethren, you did it to me.'

Matthew 25:40

The paradoxical question of the modern era is 'Does God exist?' A question that implies that He has somehow reneged on His covenants and His concern for humanity. This proposition would include His overarching responsibility and concern for Israel, a community whose origin and right to exist have coexisted with the ever-present threat of annihilation. Not only during this century but since their very inception, when they were known as a small family in the Middle East before their founding as a nation; and even before that when a covenant was made between God (YHWH) and Abraham. The God whose character did not and does not concur with any other caricatures of Him that we may attempt to peddle as authentic. No, this is the God who was in the Garden with the first humans when they chose the path of self-determination over a perfect relationship of trust and longevity. This is the same God who covered their nakedness even though they had freely listened and followed the burning voice of Satan over and above the proven voice of their creator. This is the same God who did not allow this act to deter Him from establishing a long-term covenant with Abraham, Isaac, and Jacob (later called Israel). A covenant that would not be conditional upon their obedience or the obedience of their descendants. No, this covenant was incumbent because of one thing and one thing only, "In the beginning 'God'..." (Genesis 1:1 - First Part - NKJV)

It was (and is) God's original thought to introduce us into His world and not the other way around. A world where He lavishly placed upon humanity the gifts of life, freedom, and companionship, a world that did not dream of Utopia but was the epitome of it.

The account of Genesis opened with this bold statement "In the beginning 'God'..." A statement which later became the stumbling block to the power-hungry, non-religious and religious globalists alike. A statement that provides the simple understanding that God's world is not mechanical, elitist, opportunist or exploitative. It is a world that provides a constant, simple, transparent reminder that He is God and there is none other. Of course, such declarations come ready branded with a huge red bull's eye and an open invitation to strike it if you can, using any instrument of your choice. Really, anything, and before we credit ourselves with being the first to question God's existence let's think again. In the Hebrew Scriptures, woven into its rich tapestry is a profound recognition in the writings:

"The fool has said in his heart, "There is no God. They are corrupt, They have done abominable works,

There is none who does good."

Psalm 14:1

So why do we get all bent out of shape over this one fact, trying to usurp God's function and throne without either the capability or intellectual capacity to tie our shoelaces, never mind fulfilling the criteria of universal leadership? If it were permitted, which of our global leaders and influencers would you trust to sit on God's throne? No, the ancient world had no problem embracing forms of spirituality, god concepts, and mystical and philosophical contexts. So, in light of this, the psalmist in Psalm 14:1 understood that the heart of the fool makes a ridiculous proposition, *'There is no God.'* Equally, it was not a statement or opinion that was directed at some random force of nature or power in the sky that we endlessly dialogue about, but it was pointed squarely at The God of Israel (YHWH).

These individuals who say in their heart *"there is no God"* are described as corrupt, people who have done abominable things and none who does good. Later in the same text, there are further revelations about their character and attitude:

"Have all the workers of iniquity no knowledge, Who eat up my people as they eat bread, And do not call on the Lord?"

Psalm 14:4

While claiming the God of Israel does not exist, they exploit the ordinary people who would otherwise have continued their lives without the devastation inflicted upon them. Did God see? Of course, and a day of judgment, of justice, was coming for the foolish thinker. They just didn't want to see it or admit it.

It is this understanding of justice and unconditional covenant that sheds a bright light on Yeshua's (Jesus) exposition in Matthew 25:40. The Rabbi, The Jewish Messiah reminds the listener of a longstanding attitude and outcome. He describes when the ultimate administration of justice will take place,

"When the Son of Man comes in His glory, and all the holy angels with Him, then He will sit on the throne of His glory."

and then Yeshua makes an important point, *"...all the nations will be gathered before Him, and He will separate them one from another, as a shepherd divides his sheep from the goats.* (Verse 31)

This one event has global and eternal ramifications. There is no get-out and no excuses so it's imperative that we understand what was wrong so that we can put it right now.

It is common to use this text to encourage humanitarian works, acts of kindness and equality for all, but is this the focus.? After all, there is an emphasis on **'the nations'** as opposed to the individual. It isn't until later in the discourse that we are introduced to this provocative picture of separation between the sheep and the goats. The sheep being invited by The King in verses 34-36:

"Come, you blessed of My Father, inherit the kingdom prepared for you from the foundation of the world: for I was hungry and you gave Me food; I was thirsty and you gave Me drink; I was a stranger and you took Me in; I was naked and you clothed Me; I was sick and you visited Me; I was in prison and you came to Me."

At this juncture the righteous step forward from the crowd asking, *"Lord, when did we see You hungry and feed You, or thirsty and give You drink? When did we see You a stranger and take You in, or naked and clothe You? Or when did we see You sick, or in prison, and come to You?"*

The King's response is telling, *"Assuredly, I say to you, inasmuch as you did it to one of the least of these My brethren, you did it to Me."*

The remaining 'goats' make an attempt to appeal on the grounds of ignorance which is obviously perceived and not actual ignorance. The response to them was corporate and final, *"Assuredly, I say to you, inasmuch as you did not do it to one of the least of these, you did not do it to Me.'*

So why is it important to grasp this teaching and what is its relevance?

Well firstly, Yeshua makes the point (as did the Psalmist) that 'God sees', 'God exists' and will administer justice on **their** behalf.

Secondly, the people referred to in both texts are placed centre stage as objects of abuse and yet they remain important to God and He promises to vindicate them. Finally, Yeshua (Jesus) refers to them as family, His family. Being born Jewish, working with his father Joseph building homes for his community in Israel, going to synagogue and the temple at the appointed feast times in the year, celebrating the weekly Shabbat reading the Hebrew Scriptures, defending the broken, healing the sick, feeding and restoring the lost, Yeshua let us all know who these people (his family) were and are.

These twelve Jesus sent out and commanded them, saying: "Do not go into the way of the Gentiles, and do not enter a city of the Samaritans. But go rather to the lost sheep of the house of Israel. And as you go, preach, saying, 'The kingdom of heaven is at hand.'

Matthew 10:5-7 (NKJV)

I suggest to you that 'these people' referred to in Matthew 25 are the same people mentioned in Psalm 14:1 and 4 who are exploited by those who said in their heart "There is no God". A victimised yet victorious people whose experience would become synonymous with words like ethnic cleansing, genocide, and anti-Semitism. A people to whom Rabbi Paul states:

"For I am not ashamed of the Gospel, because it is the power of God for salvation for everyone who believes, Jewish first and then the Greek." Romans 1:16 - ONM)

To the Jew first. What an incredible yet controversial proposition. To some, Israel is a political argument centred on the issue of land acquisition and misdemeanours against other nations. On the other hand, some perceive Israel as a religious representation of all the things that are opposed to things biblical (*under the law and not under grace...* and all that), both camps missing the point completely.

God chose a people whom he knew nations would lambast, despise, and politically manoeuvre and yet their existence would also be tantamount to independence, a land, an irrevocable covenant between them and the God of Israel. God positioned them in the centre of the world, allowing them to be surrounded by endless possibilities of aggression. Placing on public record a caution to all nations,

"...inasmuch as you did it to one of the least of these My brethren, you did it to Me."

It, therefore, stands to reason that if one has a problem with the Jewish community on the grounds of identity then by default one has a problem with The Jewish Messiah. An attitude that is described today as anti-Semitism. God calls it the spirit of anti-Messiah or antichrist. The same spirit that was opposed to the work of creation in Genesis, the same spirit that attempted to annihilate Israel in Egypt, the same spirit that was the administrator of the crucifixion, the same spirit that attempted to wipe out a nation in the Shoah and the same spirit that fills the earth today.

Old Roots, New Shoots, Same Soil

So, what of the soil that has been central to the early development of evolution, eugenics and the like. What specific role (if any) did it play in the rise of Nazi Germany, keeping in mind that the earlier chapters explain the soil of slavery, its mindset and language?

We know that Hitler's effort to eliminate the Jews used psychiatry as the doorway or vehicle to the development of death camps but, there is something slightly elusive in the story in the lead up to the implementation of such actions. What is missing? The key to answering this question resides in the pages of the book 'Mein Kampf', the foundational teachings of The Third Reich.

Hitler wrote, "The Jews were responsible for bringing Negroes into the Rhineland, with the ultimate idea of bastardising the white race which they hate and thus lowering its cultural and political level so that the Jew might dominate."

Notice how he uses the presence of black people in Germany to add credence to the insidious idea of a Jewish conspiracy to take over Germany. In his effort to persuade a naive audience of the dangers of becoming friends with such people or intermarrying with them, he remonstrated that the blood of Germans will be contaminated until the German race becomes inferior and eventually dominated by the Jewish race as a result. This idea of a Jewish conspiracy is poured out on the soil of slavery, reviving its colonial and eugenic racial hatred. It is this racism that provides the real substance for Hitler to begin establishing an empire, it is this deep-seated darkness of the soul that creates the perfect growing ground for a regime that would target the Jews. Without it, there would be little if any opportunity to direct attention to the Jewish question of existence, which on the face of it is a racial issue.

This may seem a little far-fetched but, if considered carefully makes perfect sense. During this era, the representation of 'dark skin' was equated with the lowest, unintelligent human form in society. This idea of inferiority made identification of such people easy to distinguish from other races and therefore, easy to demonise. This also goes some way to explain how such a small number of black people present in Germany could be considered a threat to the purity of the German race. Approximately 2,000 black people were living in Germany at the time of Hitler's rise to power.

There is a twist to this story though. It isn't usually mentioned that Germany had colonies in Africa and other territories which were unified in the early 1870s under chancellor Otto von Bismarck but, by 1915 they had lost control of the colonies to Great Britain, France and Japan. It wasn't until the end of WWI that Great Britain, France and Japan officially stripped Germany of the colonies at the Treaty of Versailles, which was signed on June 28, 1919, and took force on January 10, 1920. In between the lines of this account hides a not so obvious story that goes some way to understanding Hitler's rant in his writings.

Let's travel back to 1901 when a renowned German geographer called Friedrich Ratzel coined the phrase *Lebensraum* (living space). He believed that a nation had to be self-sufficient and have its territory and resources to avoid external threats to its survival, a view held by others at the time. Ratzel was also an admirer of Charles Darwin's work on 'The Origin of the Species' so unsurprisingly he (and others) applied *Lebensraum* to nation states. This led him to believe that the overpopulation of Germany could be improved by establishing colonies in Europe, a region that was believed by some to be the lost land of Germany. The idea of superior races during colonialism was indelible in nationalistic minds across the globe long before Darwinism. However, as explained earlier, Darwinism became the seed that gave form and legitimacy to unthinkable acts, under the banner of 'survival of the fittest'.

From the 1890s to the 1940s the term *Lebensraum* was used to describe the early German concept of colonialism which formed part of their philosophy and politics. This idea of creating more living space was also laced with the idea of being superior to other nations and having a 'mystical right' to fulfil their destiny as a race. Whatever our thoughts on the application of the term, the philosophy of *Lebensraum* is unequivocally racial, we only have to review its application to arrive at this conclusion. For example, between 1904 and 1908, during the period when Africa was colonised by Germany, there were the Nama and Herero people who lived under German colonial rule. Within 20 years Germany had occupied all their land; they also owned 50% of the Herero people's cattle. This led to the inevitable collective efforts of indigenous people to fight for their land and cattle which were central to their economy and survival. The response was outrage, and the result was the annihilation of 80% of the Nama and Herero people, placing the rest in concentration camps. Of course, those that survived suffered hunger or thirst. During this period of occupation, some prisoners were required to skin the heads of other human beings like an animal so that German scientists could use the skulls for eugenics research.

What you have just read is a brief description of the first recorded genocide! Historians are now calling this 'The Forgotten Genocide'.

[90]*"The German atrocities against the Herero and Nama were not unique; similar attacks were made by British settlers against Aboriginal Tasmanians in Australia in the nineteenth century and by American settlers against the Yuki in California around the turn of the twentieth century. Contemporary historians call these episodes – in which an imperialist country intentionally tries to annihilate an Indigenous people in order to control their land and resources – frontier genocide."*

[90] Facing History and Ourselves, "Imperialism, Conquest, and Mass Murder," last updated November 7, 2017.

Now let's jump forward again to the First World War. This was a war during which African soldiers were amongst the ranks of the German army and later settled in Germany. France, however, had 20,000 black soldiers in their ranks who were posted with the French troops to the Rhineland as part of the treaty at the end of World War I. Of course, some of the soldiers had relationships with German women giving birth to mixed race children, the presence of which created a fear of a future mixed race. By 1920 there were estimated to be between 600-800 mixed race children in the Rhineland. In 1937 (under the 1933 Law for the Prevention of Hereditarily Diseased Offspring) these Rhineland children were targeted for sterilisation leading to 385 operations. This provided perfect ammunition for Hitler's promotion of conspiracies and the need for racial purity.

Psychiatry and The Final Solution

Sadly, the masses, are overly impressed by university degrees, awards, and charisma. It is almost impossible to attribute and recognise a person's God-given ability without first spending endless hours smashing societal branding and hierarchical titles, tailored to make a person easy to quantify and categorise. Ironically, in today's world, you may be the worst doctor in the area of medicine but with a PHD, you are unquestionably an expert. Where's the evidence?

No, this isn't a rant against titles and academia, but it is an important observation of a mindset that gives credence to many things that should otherwise be easy to identify and reject from the outset. Unfortunately, we make ourselves prey by embracing everything this mindset offers.

For example, under the guise of psychiatry, the study of the mind and human behaviour hijacked centre stage along with other ancient beliefs. It fitted perfectly into a world that was waiting for measures that would confirm what the intellectuals already thought they knew about the disrespectfully named feeble-minded or insane. Once the ancient philosophy of such preachers took hold it was easy to introduce the Psychiatrist with an encyclopedia of 'mental diseases'. I use the term disease loosely as the disease of the mind implies that you are ill; equivalent to someone who has a physical growth or infection that can be observed under the microscope. 'Disease of the mind' is a deliberately misleading definition and is used to legitimise the diagnosis of the psychiatrist's handbook. This is not to say that one cannot experience some form of trauma of the mind, as this is the experience of all human beings who, for example, lose a loved one or have witnessed horrific events, but it is important to clarify the narrative embedded in the world of psychiatry, an industry which had to find a way to redefine the human experience to fit it into a humanistic, diagnostic framework.

In Germany, this narrative took on a twist that remained buried in history for many years, with a few individuals courageous enough to exhume the body of evidence and introduce it into the public domain. Thankfully, we can now speak about the real area of influence used as a preparation ground for the slaughter of millions of innocent people. Thankfully, we can now speak of the role of psychiatry (a prominent root in the eugenics tree), which has set the benchmark for healthcare as defined by the purported great thinkers of the time. It is in the arena of healthcare that we discover the amalgamation of most (if not all) of the religious subheadings or tenets found in the root system. A mechanism of healthcare that was not about extending or preserving life but removing the defective, degenerate gene pool and their carriers. The originator of modern euthanasia programs should be described as 'Deathcare'.

During this period, human experimentation on all age groups was considered normal and acceptable behaviour and it continued under the guise of white coats and stethoscopes in the heart of German society. Once again revealing the true face of this religious system which has conned us into believing it had the individual's health and wellbeing at heart.

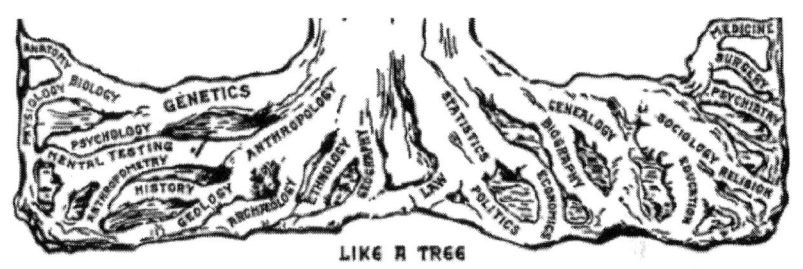

LIKE A TREE
EUGENICS DRAWS ITS MATERIALS FROM MANY SOURCES AND ORGANIZES THEM INTO AN HARMONIOUS ENTITY.

Long before the killing of millions of Jews in gas chambers, the eugenics religion was present in societal thinking, forging a specific sleeper mentality that would be activated at a later appointed time.

Under the umbrella of psychiatry, eugenics also began its programme with the slaughter of millions of disabled children. Children who were deemed 'unfit' to live or exist in society. As experienced and witnessed with any cult, its activity escalated in number and drew in numerous adults causing the numbers to skyrocket during the spread of Nazism across Europe. It is important to note, however, that supposed mercy killings were taking place in five of Germany's psychiatric killing centres: Hartheim, Hadamar, Sonnenstein, Grafeneck, Brandenburg, and Bernburg before the establishment of the Third Reich.

It was under the self-propelled belief of psychiatry that an atmosphere of death was created that utilised the legal system of its day. Its emissaries created and implemented training programmes and administration processes, including the approval of government specialists to administer death to an unsuspecting individual, supported by the falsification of paperwork which often described some other cause of death to families or relatives. In addition, the process of death by specially tailored scientific diets and the cremation of the bodies in the estimated 400 crematoria continued well after the Second World War was over, even though the extermination camps had been captured and decommissioned by allied troops. This is important to remember and not lose sight of, as the historical context of the environment for such atrocities and its beliefs were in development long before Hitler took the world stage.

Psychiatry presented a face that was accepted as completely trustworthy, the face of a medical specialist, the kind of specialist that has been trained by other professionals in the care and protection of other human beings. Of course, it would be difficult to see how this could happen in today's world, right? Yet nationalistic pride and the greater good of the fatherland took precedence over the longevity of human life; a doctrine that continues to manifest itself across nations today. It is astonishing to discover that these were educated people who were strategising and planning the death of innocent women, children, fathers, people who were comfortable experimenting with efficient ways of killing their 'Abel', their family. In the end, not requiring government support to continue the homicide once the war was concluded, but driven on by a religious belief that the weak must die.

How could this be allowed in a civilised society? Where was the conscience and body of outrage one may ask? History is silent.

Here is an extract from an article on the subject of psychiatry's role in the holocaust.

[91]*Eventually, 250 000 to 300 000 patients were murdered throughout Europe according to the Allied estimate at the Nuremberg Doctors' Trial [5], p. 66).*

By the end of the war, some of Germany's large psychiatric facilities were empty. Hitler's views on the unofficial continuation of the euthanasia program are not known. In *A Sign for Cain*, psychiatrist Fredric Wertham lays the blame for psychiatry's activities fully at the feet of the profession:

The tragedy is that the psychiatrists did not have to have an order. They acted on their own. They were not carrying out a death sentence pronounced by someone else. They were the legislators who laid down the rules for deciding who was to die; they were the administrators who worked out the procedures, provided the patients and places, and decided the methods of killing; they pronounced a sentence of life or death in every individual case; they were the executioners who carried out or - without being coerced to do so - surrendered their patients to be killed in other institutions; they supervised and often watched the slow deaths. (p. 161)

We now know that the death camps, gas chambers, hospitals, the network of delivery systems, accounting and methods of execution had their origins firmly embedded in the inventions of psychiatry. It is under the guise of psychiatry that families and patients were taken advantage of. It was behind this dangerous falsification of 'medical practice' that 'the weak' were weeded out from society and eventually placed into the hands of 'trained professionals' whose only professional occupation was that of their father 'Cain', murdering their brother. Of course, it is easy to sit in an armchair and make such sweeping statements, but the truth is that these practitioners

---

[91] International Journal of Risk and Safety in Medicine 4:133-148, 1993. Adapted from a paper delivered at "Medical Science Without Compassion" in Cologne, Germany and published in the conference proceedings.

were ordinary people like you and me. Perhaps people had no idea that they had the potential to take another life, but this is where the real caution lies. If we do not pay attention to God-given requirements on how we are to live, our pride and intellect will always lead to ruin in one way or another. We will eventually lean the other way believing that we can make God decisions, such as who should live and who should die.

The only way to keep all of what we do in its correct context is to first understand that if God did not exist, the Jewish nation would have become a story that was told, just like the Babylonian empire, the Persian empire, the Greek empire, the Roman empire and all the other kingdoms that have come and gone. Not to mention the tribes and civilisations that have left behind their empty monuments, temples and lush islands once established in honour of a multitude of other gods and beliefs. Even in the most evil of desires, God allows us to choose our path but as He did with Job, He places a boundary around the extent of suffering, even at the risk of being accused of indifference, not caring and even not existing. After all, how can an all-seeing God not intervene at a time of such horrific suffering? A question that should be rephrased to ask, how can a self-sufficient culture with such high moral and spiritual ideals not protect their fellow human being instead of behaving like Cain?

Thankfully, Nazism's 'Final Solution' failed and the image of eugenics collapsed with it, suffering embarrassment along the way in various arenas. For example, in sports James Cleveland, more commonly known as Jesse Owens, won four gold medals in the 1936 Summer Olympics in Berlin, openly exposing the false Aryan supremacy idea. However, Jesse Owens is the only name most people remember for the embarrassment he caused Germany during those games, but Jesse Owens was one of many who upset Hitler and the regime during the 1936 Olympics.

Alongside Jesse were nine other black Olympians who also won medals.

Ralph Metcalfe, who ran the 4 x 100 metre relay with Owens won a gold medal. Metcalfe also won a silver medal (coming second to Owens) in the 100 metre sprint. Matthew MacKenzie "Mack" Robinson won a silver medal taking second place to Owens in the 200 metres. Ironically, he did manage to do this in style by breaking the Olympic record in the process.

Cornelius "Corny" Johnson won a gold medal in the high jump. Dave Albritton (David Donald Albritton) came second to Corny Johnson in the same event winning a silver medal. Archie Williams won the 400 metres, James "Jimmy" LuValle won bronze in the 400 metres, John Woodruff won the 800 metres, Frederick "Fritz" Pollard won bronze in the 100 metre hurdles and Jackie Wilson won silver in bantamweight boxing. You may not know but black female athletes also shook the athletics stage in Berlin. Tidye Pickett became the first black woman to compete in the Olympic Games. Tragically, she fell and injured herself in the semi-finals and of course, Louise Stokes who was also part of a phenomenal team sadly just missed out on running for the team in the Olympics. Eighteen black athletes represented the USA in the 1936 Olympics.

However, before we restate a history that venerates the obvious successes of the few black representatives, there is another story that also deserves recognition. The story of the Jewish athletes on the American team, [92]Marty Glickman and Sam Stoller. These two men had prepared and secured a place on the American team and were set to run in the 4 x 400m relay with their teammates Foy Draper and Frank Wykoff.

On the day of the event, Jesse Owens and Ralph Metcalfe were brought in to replace Marty Glickman and Sam Stoller, making them the only two American athletes who did not compete after arriving in Berlin. Ironically, their two teammates, Foy Draper and Frank Wykoff remained on the relay team and celebrated their easy victory alongside Owens and Metcalfe. The reasons for this action have been shrouded in noise diverting the attention away from the real issue. However, the track and field sportsman Marty Glickman

---

[92] Marty Glickman and Sam Stoller, members of the United States track team, train on board the USS Manhattan, on their way to the 11th Summer Olympic Games in Berlin. US Holocaust Memorial Museum, courtesy of Marty Glickman

(who went on to become an outstanding sports presenter) aptly exposed the events in his book '[93]The Fastest Kid on the Block'. He States,

"We worked out together in the days leading up to our relay, which was scheduled for the last two track-and-field days of the Olympics. There's little doubt that Owens and Metcalfe were faster than the rest of us. But Wykoff, Draper, [Stoller], and I were all about even. I would say that if the four of us ran three races against each other, there could well have been three different orders of finish. But Wykoff, [Stoller], and I invariably beat Draper..."

He continues,

"Owens and Metcalfe did not do any stick-passing because there was no expectation that they would run in the relay. They never touched a baton until they actually ran in the 4 by 100-meters heat."

What Marty describes is the lead up to what should have been straightforward participation of athlete against athlete. However, the twist in the day of the event is described as follows,

"We gathered at about 9am in a small room in the Olympic Village. My recollection of that meeting is so vivid that I can still recall where each of us sat. There were a couple of beds in the room. Owens sat across from me. I sat on the edge of a bed. Sam was a few feet to my left. To his left was Cromwell in an armchair, and then Robertson standing near the door, Draper and Wykoff sprawled on the other bed. Mack Robinson was to my right, slightly behind me, and Metcalfe was alongside Robinson.

With a grim face Robertson said he'd been told the Germans were hiding their best sprinters, saving them for the 400-meter relay to upset

---

[93] The Fastest Kid on the Block : the Marty Glickman story, By Glickman, Marty, 1917-2001
Publisher: Syracuse University Press; Revised edition (September 1, 1999)
Language: English ISBN-10 : 0815605749, ISBN-13: 978-0815605744

the heavily favored American team. Therefore, Stoller and I were to be replaced by Owens and Metcalfe. Draper and Wykoff, Cromwell's two USC runners, would stay on the relay squad.

There was stunned silence in the room. This came out of the blue to me. I was shocked and angry. Being young and brash, I said, "Coach, there's no reason to believe the Germans are any kind of threat to the relay. To be a world-class sprinter, you have to compete in world-class competition."

... Late on Sunday afternoon, after we won the 400-meter relay by the huge margin, I was walking across the Olympic Village grounds when I heard my name called. It was Robertson, hobbling toward me with the aid of his cane. We looked at each other, He said, "Marty, I've made a terrible mistake. Please forgive me."

I was self-conscious and rather abashed at the hurt look in his eyes, I mumbled something about the team winning, then we both turned and walked away.

I have come to feel over the years that anti-Semitism was a motivating factor at the time. My thinking centers very much on Brundage. He was quite a piece of work: a tactless and arrogant man who alienated people needlessly...

When he came back from his pre-Olympics inspection trip of Germany in 1935 and declared that the Nazis didn't discriminate against Jewish athletes, he took offense at those who questioned his faith in the German officials who had been friends. He called criticism of him "Jewish propaganda." He said, "Certain Jews must now understand that they cannot use these Games as a weapon in their boycott against the Nazis." He intimated that those who opposed participation in the Games were Jews or Communists. Yet Judge Jeremiah T. Mahoney, the leading boycott advocate, was a Roman Catholic.

This travesty of a decision to drop two Jewish athletes from running in the Olympics exposed the deeper roots of anti-Semitism. Roots that were endemic in an age of Nazism that was pervading Germany and other nations around the globe. It is idealistic to believe that any nation had clean hands when it came to Nazism and its totalitarian agenda. There were (and there still are) influential figures in society that support the ideas of Hitler and the Third Reich, maybe not always as overt defenders but as believers in its tenets. To bring balance to the narrative in this section, allow me to include a list of those that did compete in the Olympics who went on to win medals in the battle of the races.

Samuel Balter - United States: Basketball, gold

Gyorgy Brody - Hungary: Water Polo, gold

Miklos Sarkany - Hungary: Water Polo, gold

Karoly Karpati - Hungary: Freestyle Wrestling, gold

Endre Kabos - Hungary: Individual Sabre, gold. Team Sabre, gold

Irving Maretzky - Canada: Basketball, silver

Gerard Blitz - Belgium: Water Polo, bronze

Ibolya K. Csak - Hungary: High Jump, gold

Robert Fein - Austria: Weightlifting, gold

Helene Mayer- Germany: Individual Foil, silver

Ellen Preis - Austria: Individual Foil, bronze

Ilona Schacherer-Elek - Hungary: Individual Foil, gold

Jadwiga Wajs - Poland: Discus Throw, silver

However, in light of these victories and the obvious ludicrous beliefs that the Third Reich represented it would be unwise to think that the religion itself had disappeared. On the contrary, the following years of this burdensome tree would experience further growth, spreading its roots deeper into Europe and the rest of the world, eventually taking us all by surprise.

Companies, Charities and Eugenics

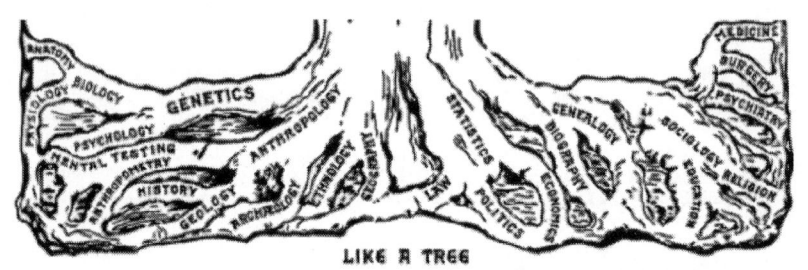

LIKE A TREE EUGENICS DRAWS ITS MATERIALS FROM MANY SOURCES AND ORGANIZES THEM INTO AN HARMONIOUS ENTITY.

It is easy to forget that the eugenics religion draws its materials from many sources and organises them into a harmonious entity (as the motto at its roots states). It is also easy to forget that the rise of the denominational offshoot of Nazism presented a platform for many individuals and companies to benefit from the Holocaust. This is a notion that is difficult to comprehend in our self-proclaimed 'tolerant, civilised' society, but many of these individuals and companies still exist today and it would be remiss to omit them from this dialogue. Some were founded on principles related to the experimentation on the mind, body, and soul of the human through the doorway of psychiatry, while others gained their longevity through opportunities created by Nazi ideology. As with slavery, this reality is a very difficult pill to swallow and a provocative area of discussion. However, it must be mentioned nonetheless.

It is also difficult to understand the context of such activity when considering the disturbing, unacceptable response of onlookers. People who were not always isolated from the grim realities of the Nazi regime but who were willing to support it with skills and resources, aiding its growth. Of course, there were those who through fear of death complied with Nazi demands but, as with any other nation, there had to be a focal point of belief by the general populace, and there had to be a decision regarding the future appearance of the nation amongst the nations, and there could not be a place of neutrality for anyone.

So how was this expressed on the ground? How did businesses, charities and churches face the challenge of a rising power that demanded allegiance? Well, some withstood Hitler and his regime by doing what they could to save lives, by disrupting the movement and even by bringing an end to the regime itself. Many, on the other hand, agreed with the vilest message of hatred that Europe had seen in modern history, from ordinary working people to politicians and royals. Tragically, out of this environment of separatism and elitism came an opportunity for some and guaranteed death for others.

Some organisations in the historical hall of shame placed their faith in a philosophy that degraded humans and treated them below the level of animals. A philosophy that manipulated, dominated, segregated and ultimately took the lives of millions of innocents to feed its growth. The results of such shameful philosophy can never fully be realised or quantified within the pages of a single book but to aid understanding, a brief list of companies (including charities) has been listed below, all of whom profited in some way from the Nazi belief, the religion of eugenics, and some of which have since changed their names maybe to veneer over the war years of the organisation's financial origins. Also listed are the camps where they were able to obtain the labour to develop their projects in support of the regime. Some of the names you may recognise, others you may not.

Company names appear in capital letters.

* denotes the name of the Camp, followed by the name of the town or location where the work was done.

ADLER SA
Natzwiller-Struthof*
Frankfurt-Am-Main

AEG (Allgemeine Elektricitäts-Gesellschaft AG) (German for 'General electricity company')
Stutthof*
Thorn-Torun
Riga-Kaiserwald*

ASTRA
Flossenbürg*
Chemnitz

AUTO-UNION
Flossenbürg*
Hohenstein-Ernstthal
Zschopau
Zwickau

BMW
Buchenwald and Dora-Mittelbau*
Abteroda
Eisenach-Thür
Dachau*
Ellach
Blaichach

Kaufbeuren
Lochhausen
Moosach
Natzwiller-Struthof*
Geisenheim
Papenburg*
Rastdorf-am-Werlte
Sachsenhausen*
Königs Wusterhausen

MESSERSCHMITT
Dachau*
Asbach-Bäumerheim
Augsburg
Augsburg-Pfersee
Burgau
Durach-Kottern
Fischen
Gablingen
Horgau-Pfersee
Kaufering
Moosach
Flossenbürg*
Johanngeorgenstadt
Mauthausen*
Camp Central

METALL UNION
Auschwitz-Oswiecim
Camp Central

OPTA RADIO
Flossenbürg*
Wolkenburg

OPTIQUE IENA
Buchenwald and Dora-Mittelbau*
Weimar-Fischtenheim
PHOTO AGFA
Dachau*
Munich
PUCH
Mauthausen*
Graz
RHEINMETALL BORSIG AG
Buchenwald and Dora Mittelbau*
Dusseldorf

SHELL
Neuengamme*
Hamburg
Geilenburgh

SCHNEIDER
Buchenwald and Dora-Mittelbau*
Leipzig-Lindenthal
Meuselwitz
Raucha

DAIMLER BENZ
Schirmeck (on the Rhine)*
Haslach

DORNIER
Dachau*
Aufkirch-Kaufbeuren
Kaufering
Trutskirch-Tutzing

ERLA
Buchenwald and Dora-Mittelbau*
Thekla/Leipzig
Leipzig-Lindenthal
Flossenbürg*
Mulchen-Psankt-Micheln

FORD
Buchenwald and Dora-Mittelbau*
Cologne Ford-Werke

GOLDSCHMITT
Gross-Rosen*
Langenbielau-Bielawa

HEINKEL
Buchenwald and Dora – Mittelbau*
Gandersheim
Mauthausen*
Wien-Schwechat
Natzwiller-Struthof (at the Rhine)*
Zuffenhausen
Ravensbrück*
Barth/Ostsee
Berlin-Schönefeld*
Rostock-Marienehe*
Schwarzenforst*
Sachsenhausen*
Oranienburg

IG FARBEN INDUSTRIES
Auschwitz-Oswiecim*
Camp Central
Buchenwald and Dora-Mittelbau*
Wolfen-Bitterfeld

Gross-Rosen*
Waldenburg

After World War II, G Farber

JUNKER
Buchenwald and Dora-Mittelbau*
Aschersleben
Halberstadt
Tarthun

KRUPP
Buchenwald and Dora-Mittelbau*
Essen
Gross-Rosen*
Langenbielau-Bielawa
Markstädt-Laskowitz
Flossenbürg*
Nuremberg
Ravensbrück*
Camp Central
Furstenberg*
Neubrandenburg*

OLVAY
Buchenwald and Dora-Mittelbau*
Bernburg

STEYR
Mauthausen*
Aflens
Steyr-Münichholz
Radom*

TELEFUNKEN (A subsidiary of AEG)
Gross-Rosen*
Langenbielau-Bielawa

VALENTIN
Neuengamme*
Bremen-Farge

VISTRA
Buchenwald and Dora-Mittelbau*
Wolfen-Bitterfeld

VOLKSWAGEN
Neuengamme*
Fallersleben
Wolfsburg

ZEISS-IKON
Flossenbürg*
Dresden

ZEITZ
Buchenwald and Dora-Mittelbau*
Gleina "Willy"

ZEPPELIN
Dachau*
Friedrichshafen

For the sake of brevity, the following companies/organisations have been extracted from the list so that your attention can be drawn to some important details. They may not all have used free labour during the Holocaust, but they did profit or contribute to the eugenics cause in some way that brought obvious financial benefits. Others believed in the doctrine of eugenics and implemented these beliefs through their organisations, ideas which provided a platform for eugenics beyond the Shoah.

BAYER HealthCare Pharmaceuticals, Inc.
One of the companies of IG Farben, listed previously, manufactured the 'Zyklon B' gas used in the gas chambers. They were also responsible for the design of the birth control pill 'Yaz'. Yaz birth control pills were approved by the FDA (US Food and Drug Administration) in 2006, the drug's use was extended to the treatment of acne. That's right, acne.

It is important to understand that when a drug is invented, it will have a patent that runs for some years, preventing other drug companies from copying and selling a similar product. Once the patent has run out, other companies are allowed to sell identical versions of the original, brand drug. This can lead to cheaper copies of the patented drug. By law the generic or 'copy' drug must be identical or equivalent to the original drug and therefore, it will have the same side effects as the original.

Copies of the Yaz pill, referred to as 'generic Yaz' birth control pills were created and named Gianvi, approved by the FDA in 2010 and 'Loryna' approved by the FDA in 2011. These drugs have been linked to damage to health and as a result claims have been submitted in court on behalf of women who suffered health problems.

Ironically, the company's first and best-known product was the Aspirin, which was designed by a Jewish man, [94]Arthur Eichengrün but credit was given to Felix Hoffman, an Aryan. This latter position is still recorded in a document produced and

---

[94] Eichengrün A. 50 Jahre Aspirin. Pharmazie. 1949; 4:582–584.
Bayer-Archiv. 271/2.1 Personal data on Eichengrün. Dr A. Eichengrün, Aspirin, KZ Theresienstadt. 1944:2. Cited by Sneader,5.

available on Bayer's website entitled 'The Bayer Story 1863-1988'. Felix Hoffman is credited with the discovery of Aspirin on page 139. However, it was Arthur Eichengrün's job at Bayer to identify new products as head of the pharmaceutical division. Felix Hoffmann (1868-1946), a chemist, worked for Eichengrün and also Heinrich Dreser (1860-1924), the head of the pharmacology section (responsible for clinical trials) [95]

The controversy which surrounds these claims is due to several factors. Factors which were explored in a book titled *Eurekas and Euphorias: The Oxford book of scientific anecdotes by Gratzer, W. B. (Walter Bruno)* and outlined in a British Medical Journal paper by Sneader, W. *"The discovery of aspirin: a reappraisal."* [96]In his paper Sneader arrives at the following conclusion:

- Everything that Eichengrün claimed in his 1949 published account of the discovery of Aspirin was compatible with the chronology of events.
- Eichengrün's statement that Dreser set acetylsalicylic aside for 18 months has never been challenged.
- Hoffmann lived until 1946 without publishing his own account of the discovery of Aspirin.
- Hoffman also repeatedly spoke of Dreser setting the drug aside.
- The account of the discovery first appeared in 1934 as a footnote in a history of chemical engineering written by Albrecht Schmidt, a chemist who had recently retired from IG Farbenindustrie—the organisation into which F Bayer & Co had been incorporated in 1925.

---

[95] Desborough, M.J.R. and Keeling, D.M. (2017), The aspirin story – from willow to wonder drug. British Journal of Haematology, 177: 674-683. https://onlinelibrary.wiley.com/doi/10.1111/bjh.14520
[96] Sneader, W. "The discovery of aspirin: a reappraisal." BMJ (Clinical research ed.) vol. 321,7276 (2000): 1591-4. doi:10.1136/bmj.321.7276.1591

- The unreliability produced in the footnote in 1934 must be balanced against Eichengrün's 1949 paper.
- The most reasonable conclusion is that Arthur Eichengrün was telling the truth when he wrote that acetylsalicylic acid was synthesised under his direction and that the drug would not have been introduced in 1899 without his intervention.
- The analysis of relevant archival and published material supports Arthur Eichengrün's claims.

Arthur had a long list of patents under his name while at Bayer, but he left to set up his own laboratory which created a list of revolutionary inventions which include: Cellon, a flame resistant plastic which replaced Celluloid and was used in pilots' goggles, windshields and gas masks, and Cellulose Acetate, a fire-resistant substitute applied to aircraft wings to make them water-resistant. Eichengrün eventually opened a factory to manufacture cellulose acetate products but in the process pioneered injection moulding.

Eichengrün was eventually forced to sell his shares to Germans of Aryan descent and was finally forced to sell the company completely. For a while, he lived in freedom at home while continuing his experiments but was eventually arrested and charged for not including the name 'Israel' when writing to a Reich official. In May 1944 Eichengrün was deported to Theresienstadt concentration camp and died shortly after his release at the age of 82.

After the war, some employees of Bayer appeared in the IG Farben trials.[97] Lawsuits against Bayer by former concentration camp prisoners brought the world's attention to

---

[97] United States Holocaust Memorial Museum. "SUBSEQUENT NUREMBERG PROCEEDINGS, CASE #6, THE IG FARBEN CASE." https://encyclopedia.ushmm.org/content/en/article/bayer#responsibility-and-reparations-2.

the depravity of human experimentation which Bayer undertook in collaboration with people like Dr Josef Mengele.

Bayer is now one of the largest pharmaceutical companies in the world.

SIEMENS
Auschwitz-Oswiecim*
Bobrek
Trostberg

As the German labour force decreased due to being drafted into the military, Siemens was faced with the issue of increasing its labour force to service the increasing demand for armaments. Siemens' slave labour force was used to construct the gas chambers they would be killed in.

The [98] Aryanisation Programme helped to further Siemens' growth through connections with the SS via its Director, Rudolph Bingel, and Heinrich Himmler. Himmler was one of Hitler's loyal followers and fanatics who was a mystic and occultist.

In more recent years, Siemens' application for the use of 'Zyklon' to promote new household products in a patent (including gas ovens) caused an obvious uproar. The obvious outcome was a withdrawal of the application and an apology.

---

[98] United States Holocaust Memorial Museum. "Aryanization" Collections Highlights.
https://encyclopedia.ushmm.org/content/en/article/aryanization#voluntary-aryanization-0 Accessed on 30 July 2022.

Coca-Cola – (Drink)
Made drinks for the Americans during the war. However, the German arm of Coca-Cola ran out of syrup, so Coca-Cola created a special drink for the Nazis, called 'Fanta'. Fanta is one of the leading four brands of Coca-Cola to date. Brazil is the largest consumer in the world.

Allianz – (Insurance)
This company, along with others, sold fire, liability and accident insurance to the Nazi SS units that operated the concentration camps, including, but not exclusive to, the covering of supplies, and buildings. Leading up to the Holocaust Jewish families purchased various types of insurance policies to protect their assets and futures. However, after World War II the survivors and their families were denied, any rights provided under the policies and were prevented from redeeming the value of their policies.

In total, the amounts owed to Holocaust survivors by insurance companies such as Allianz of Germany are estimated at $25 billion in total with over $2 billion being owed by Allianz at the time of publication.

Information on the survivors and their current fight for justice can be found at www.hsf-usa.org.

The Full Committee Hearing, Holocaust-Era Insurance Claims, Tuesday, September 17th, 2019.
https://www.judiciary.senate.gov/

In 2019 the company's annual revenue was $37.27 billion.

Mind – (Health)
Originally known as 'The National Association for Mental Health (NAMH). It was made up of three voluntary groups, two of which were part of the 'social hygiene movement' and advocated eugenics and sterilisation. The two groups were:

- The Central Association for Mental Welfare (CAMW) (1913)
- National Council for Mental Hygiene (NCMH) (1922)

The only group that was not part of the social hygiene movement was the Child Guidance Council (CGC).

Its growth coincided with the development of the Welfare State and continues to be a leading organisation in the treatment of the mind.

Please note, in the area of charities, woven into each narrative is a perception of care and a broken system of care. The puzzle is only unravelled when one understands the subtle changes in terminology without which one would assume that 'mental health' has always existed as a legitimate term from the beginning of time. Therefore, it is assumed that the specific term 'mental illness' must have existed for as long. However, the diagnoses developed and included in manuals such as the DSM (Diagnostic and Statistical Manual of Mental Disorders) targeted human experiences such as sadness. Sadness is one of those emotions that is reclassified in society's language as 'depression'.

Before the introduction of the classifications into the manual, there was no scientific evidence underwriting the diagnoses listed in its pages, with only a small number having any biological roots such, as Alzheimer's, which are known as 'organic disorders'. To support the authenticity of the manual of diagnosis, scientists were employed to provide the research into such disorders, hence providing a veneer of credibility to the disorders listed. The fact that the research was carried out <u>after</u> manuals like this had already been in use for years should sound warning bells. Especially when you consider the Hypocritic..., apologies, Hippocratic oath that governs medical doctors. Doctors who practice real medicine, who strive to understand the ailment and track its origin back to the cells, organs, or some other part of the human anatomy. Can you imagine walking into a doctor's surgery, sitting in front of your doctor with a splitting headache and they take one look at you and say,

"Good morning Mr Brown, I can see that you are in desperate need of an operation for that foot problem of yours. No, no, I know what you're going to say. How could I have known that? Well, you see we have been given this new manual that tells us all that we need to know about your condition, and I could tell by the way you were holding your head that you had an obvious issue with your foot.

Also, the way that you are looking at me right now suggests that there may be some other underlying condition which we will need to examine further. Thank you for coming in and please pass this document to the receptionist on your way out. Goodbye."

Do you get the point?

To highlight the issue further, can you answer this question? "What would a psychiatrist or a medical professional do with the following incident recorded by the Physician, Doctor [99]Luke in Luke 8:29-35 (NKJV)?

"Then they sailed to the country of the Gadarenes, which is opposite Galilee. And when He stepped out on the land, there met Him a certain man from the city who had demons for a long time. And he wore no clothes, nor did he live in a house but in the tombs. When he saw Jesus, he cried out, fell down before Him, and with a loud voice said, "What have I to do with You, Jesus, Son of the Most High God? I beg You, do not torment me!" For He had commanded the unclean

---

[99] Luke the beloved physician and Demas greet you.

spirit to come out of the man. For it had often seized him, and he was kept under guard, bound with chains and shackles; and he broke the bonds and was driven by the demon into the wilderness.

Jesus asked him, saying, "What is your name?"

And he said, "Legion," because many demons had entered him. And they begged Him that He would not command them to go out into the abyss.

Now a herd of many swine was feeding there on the mountain. So they begged Him that He would permit them to enter them. And He permitted them. Then the demons went out of the man and entered the swine, and the herd ran violently down the steep place into the lake and drowned.

When those who fed them saw what had happened, they fled and told it in the city and in the country. Then they went out to see what had happened, and came to Jesus, and found the man from whom the demons had departed, sitting at the feet of Jesus, clothed and in his right mind. And they were afraid."

How many disorders would this man have had if he were present in today's world? More importantly, would he ever have been cured under the banner of Mental Health or would he become another casualty of a eugenics philosophy which relegates such individuals to the category of mentally deficient with the promise of medication for life?

Audi
Famous for its four interlocking rings, Audi was founded in 1909 by August Horch. Audi formed one of four companies i.e., DKW, Horch, Wanderer and of course, Audi, which merged on 29 June 1932 to form The Auto Union AG. Each ring represents one of the arms of the business.

A report commissioned by Audi investigated the actions of former colleagues and revealed the shocking truth that at least 20,000 slave labourers had been used. The report also included the company's "moral responsibility" for the deaths of 4500 people from the Flossenbürg concentration camp in 1944/1945.

The founder of the Auto Union, Richard Bruhn, who was a member of the National Socialist Party held close ties with the Nazi elite and had plans to expand his slave labour force before Hitler's defeat.

Audi is worth over $17.18 billion today.

Covenant

In this collection of historical narratives and connections that seem to span continents, there is a huge question that is beating on the door of opportunity for our attention. Who would stage such an elaborate scheme to annihilate the Jews from history?

This question has two important propositions rooted in it:

Firstly: Everything you have read to date is part of a plan.

In other words, if everything to date is simply a series of coincidences then I'm Barack Obama.

Secondly: The target is the Jew first.

Meaning that the plan is intended to remove a people group from the pages of history, then all other groups that did not fit the profile of 'good seed' according to the philosophy of the religious tree. This is why during the Shoah (and before) propaganda was designed to demonise the Jews. The language used placed the Jews at the heart of the problem while taking advantage of all streams to rid the nation of all other unwanted groups of people. However, we must understand that this is the position of the planner, this is an expression of his anger and his mindset which believes human life means nothing.

Finally: Someone has a goal.

Remember behind every design there is a designer. That includes the experiences that we are living in, real time. We choose to engage with one idea or another, we choose to listen to the voices that entice us to run with the crowd, to agree with falsifications, to exploit the vulnerable and execute the innocent. All the things that God instructed Israel not to engage in when He elevated them from family status to national status at Mount Sinai. How did He do this? Through covenant.

An interesting and poignant fact is that the word 'covenant' is mentioned at least 292 times in the King James Bible, making it a pretty important word. Indeed, a covenant was and is important to the God of Israel. It is the reason that Satan will do anything in his power to eradicate the power or presence of a covenant. He understands that if he is successful, he achieves what no other person has ever been able to achieve, and that is, to prove God to be incapable of keeping the covenant.

This covenant was ratified by the blood of The Suffering Servant in Isaiah 53:10-12 (NKJV),

Yet it pleased the Lord to bruise Him; He has put Him to grief. When You make His soul an offering for sin, He shall see His seed, He shall prolong His days, And the pleasure of the Lord shall prosper in His hand.

He shall see the labor of His soul, and be satisfied. By His knowledge My righteous Servant shall justify many, For He shall bear their iniquities. Therefore I will divide Him a portion with the great, and He shall divide the spoil with the strong, because He poured out

His soul unto death, And He was numbered with the transgressors, And He bore the sin of many,

And made intercession for the transgressors.

We must also note that the centre of the covenant that God made with Abraham, Isaac and Jacob relates to a land, a people and a place which stands as a timepiece to the rest of the world. We can read further expressions of God's heart in the book of Isaiah:

"Yet hear now, O Jacob My servant, And Israel whom I have chosen. Thus says the Lord who made you and formed you from the womb, who will help you: 'Fear not, O Jacob My servant; And you, Jeshurun, whom I have chosen.

For I will pour water on him who is thirsty, And floods on the dry ground; I will pour My Spirit on your descendants, And My blessing on your offspring; They will spring up among the grass like willows by the watercourses.'

One will say, 'I am the Lord's'; Another will call himself by the name of Jacob; Another will write with his hand, 'The Lord's,' And name himself by the name of Israel. "Thus says the Lord, the King of Israel, And his Redeemer, the Lord of hosts: 'I am the First and I am the Last; Besides Me there is no God.

And who can proclaim as I do? Then let him declare it and set it in order for Me, Since I appointed the ancient people. And the things that are coming and shall come, Let them show these to them.

Do not fear, nor be afraid; Have I not told you from that time, and declared it? You are My witnesses. Is there a God besides Me? Indeed there is no other Rock; I know not one.' "

Isaiah 44:1 – 8 (NKJV)

There have been many attempts, spanning centuries, to unravel the plan of God, to somehow expose His perceived inability to keep covenant; and yet a covenant made on a mountain in the desert, outside of the architectural institutes of the world, still stands. How amazing is that! To date, it has never been threatened with disaster, has never been shaken by any human government or intervention and will continue to stand as a daily reminder that everything connected to it will play out as He has promised. We see this when we understand the detail of what we read. For example, and in true God like fashion, what should have been the total annihilation of a people during a condensed period of persecution was overruled by God's promises under which the plan of annihilation became the place of fulfilment.

> Who has heard such a thing?
> Who has seen such things?
> Shall the earth be made to give birth in one day?
> Or shall a nation be born at once?
> For as soon as Zion was in labor,
> She gave birth to her children.
>
> Isaiah 66:8 (NKJV)

Following the huge loss of life and persecution thrust onto the Jews, their struggles continued well beyond the Holocaust. However, in 1968 a nation was born in a day as revealed by God to Isaiah.

Against all odds, the establishment of a homeland for the Jewish people was realised and people from around the world have been returning to Israel ever since. Of course, this great gift would come with great responsibility for the custodians of God's land and Torah, but that discussion is for another day.

Homo Deus – Man Is God

Man Merges with Machine, Transition from 20th to 21st Century (Third and Fourth Industrial Revolution)

But these, like natural brute beasts made to be caught and destroyed, speak evil of the things they do not understand, and will utterly perish in their own corruption, and will receive the wages of unrighteousness, as those who count it pleasure to carouse in the daytime.

2 Peter 2:12 – 13 (NKJV)

At this juncture, we stand in the centre of another global transition in a similar vein to the last. A transition that goes hand in hand with an explosion of purported new ideas and inventions. Yet the foundation for all that would come after it was already established many years before. How? Through the actions and influence of the earlier evangelistic eugenic movement.

The world was entering a period which some may describe as a form of 'black awakening', in other words, a form of revival that was opposite to a Holy, biblical revival. With this new move would arise a new wave of ministers, key figures who would enter the public arena as vanguards of the future, this time gaining more ground and embedding the philosophy even deeper in the public mind.

As always, a form of chaos had to take centre stage to create a distraction and a traumatic atmosphere of such magnitude that would engulf the minds of the swaying victims and onlookers alike. To achieve its goals, it had to employ the illusion and use of sleight of hand by directing the viewers' attention to one hand of historical events while subtly crafting the next stage of progression with the other hand. This may be an oversimplification of the matter as, once again, there are layers and overlapping timelines that constantly ebb and flow throughout this period. However, this was without doubt another huge global transition that catapulted society into an existence that no single individual could have envisaged.

It was through the devastating experience of the First and Second World Wars that a shift mirroring the industrial revolution took place in global politics, health, justice, religion, and all other areas of societal influences. These events brought the global value system under the microscope of truth and the findings were not pretty. It revealed the hearts of nations and exposed the destructive nature of humanistic philosophy that reigned supreme across societies. As always, the aftermath of such a revelation temporarily shocked some into action, people who would dedicate themselves to searching out the reasons for the obvious evils that pervaded the public conscience. However, what remained constant is that on this grand platform in the 20th century, the truth of a godless philosophy was exposed for what it was, reminding the world that it had witnessed the public outworking and application of the tenets of 'humanistic' religion.

The trail of devastation and the disquieting of communities everywhere supplied the backdrop to a modern, intelligent, civilised world that would never be the same again. Never again would a human being be able to look into the mirror of transparency and honestly say that we are inherently good. The body of evidence weighted against us, embodied in the Holocaust, magnified by the covenant of God would perpetually retort, [100]"*for all have sinned and fall short of the glory of God,*"

However, with all the devastation the hand of God remained a constant source of salvation and restoration before, during and after such events, weaving His tapestry of global visitations that would save lives and restore a broken covenant. The kind of visitations we commonly refer to as 'revivals' during which God would visit the most unlikely places to fellowship with the most unlikely people. People who bowed the knee before an extraordinary God. The God of Israel.

Nothing could avert His plan or break His promise, not even the rise of an anti-messianic global force that threatened the very existence of the world and the nation God had

---

[100] Romans 3:23 (NKJV)

created[101]. A force whose goal was to annihilate the very Ambassadors to the world who were commissioned to teach the [102]gentiles about a creator the gentiles never knew and most certainly did not worship. About the divine edict given to Israel (The nation of ambassadors), God said,

"But you shall be named the priests of the LORD, They shall call you the servants of our God."

Isaiah 61:6. (NKJV)

And if that were not enough, this edict is also reiterated by Yeshua the Messiah when speaking to His Jewish disciples, Mark records,

Later He appeared to the eleven as they sat at the table; and He rebuked their unbelief and hardness of heart, because they did not believe those who had seen Him after He had risen. And He said to them, **"Go into all the world and preach the gospel to every creature. He who believes and is baptized will be saved; but he who does not believe will be condemned.** *And these signs will follow those who believe: In My name they will cast out demons; they will speak with new tongues; they will take up serpents; and if they drink anything deadly, it will by no means hurt them; they will lay hands on the sick, and they will recover."* Mark 16:14 (NKJV)

---

[101] And who *is* like Your people, like Israel, the one nation on the earth whom God went to redeem for Himself as a people, to make for Himself a name—and to do for Yourself great and awesome deeds for Your land—before Your people whom You redeemed for Yourself from Egypt, the nations, and their gods? (II Samuel 7:23 (NKJV)

[102] Gentile, person who is not Jewish. The word stems from the Hebrew term goy, which means a "nation," and was applied both to the Hebrews and to any other nation. The plural, goyim, especially with the definite article, ha-goyim, "the nations," meant nations of the world that were not Hebrew. Britannica, The Editors of Encyclopaedia. "Gentile". Encyclopedia Britannica, 3 Jun. 2021, https://www.britannica.com/topic/Gentile. Accessed 8 October 2022.

This divine commission can never be destroyed because the person that made it cannot be manipulated, bribed, or broken. As we see in the following example:

Then Jesus, being filled with the Holy Spirit, returned from the Jordan and was led by the Spirit into the wilderness, being tempted for forty days by the devil. And in those days He ate nothing, and afterward, when they had ended, He was hungry.

And the devil said to Him, "If You are the Son of God, command this stone to become bread."

But Jesus answered him, saying, "It is written, 'Man shall not live by bread alone, but by every word of God.'"

Then the devil, taking Him up on a high mountain, showed Him all the kingdoms of the world in a moment of time. And the devil said to Him, "All this authority I will give You, and their glory; for this has been delivered to me, and I give it to whomever I wish. Therefore, if You will worship before me, all will be Yours."

And Jesus answered and said to him, "Get behind Me, Satan! For it is written, 'You shall worship the Lord your God, and Him only you shall serve.'"

Then he brought Him to Jerusalem, set Him on the pinnacle of the temple, and said to Him, "If You are the Son of God, throw Yourself down from here. For it is written: 'He shall give His angels charge over you, To keep you,' and, 'In their hands they shall bear you up, Lest you dash your foot against a stone.'"

And Jesus answered and said to him, "It has been said, 'You shall not tempt the Lord your God.'"

Now when the devil had ended every temptation, he departed from Him until an opportune time

Luke 4:1 – 13 (NKJV)

Now before we applaud and breathe a sigh of relief, the story doesn't end there. As the visible face of eugenics became unfashionable in the public realm and its public image became soiled and unpopular, the tree and its root system remained intact. How? It was the toxicity of this period which acted as added sustenance to this tree, enabling it to thrive in the harshest, darkest, environmental conditions. This is the reason that its presence remained active and unrelenting. So how can it have been out of vogue and yet flourish in the public forum when its public image had been so obviously tainted? The answer is that it went through a rebranding of its nature and image, whilst also taking advantage of everything developed during the wars, including the atrocities inflicted on every man woman and child during the holocaust. Remember, this system ..."*draws its materials from many sources..*"

In addition, it took past definitions coined by earlier evangelists, and turned them into something that was seemingly more palatable for the society it found itself in. Of course, its recipients wouldn't necessarily notice its presence and influence, except for its victims, the people who had seen its work first hand or that were affected by its work indirectly.

Human Genetics

The rebrand would require a new name for the movement, one that would open the door to a world of new possibilities. Appearing different but simply continuing the work of eugenics, drawing its materials from many sources and organising them into a harmonious entity. This would happen under the new name of Human Genetics or as I prefer, New Eugenics (Newgenics).

As with most rebranding exercises, little changed. The symbol of a tree remained, the root system remained, and the spirit of the movement continued. However, the phylogenetic tree or the tree of life, the type of tree drawn by Charles Darwin in one of his notebooks which is used today to depict family lineage, seemed to gain more relevance.

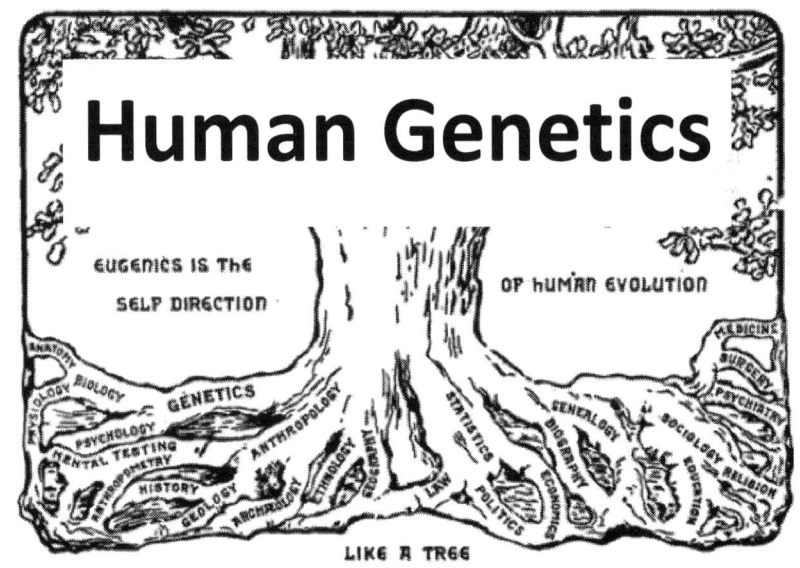

Human Genetics

EUGENICS IS THE SELF DIRECTION OF HUMAN EVOLUTION

LIKE A TREE EUGENICS DRAWS ITS MATERIALS FROM MANY SOURCES AND ORGANIZES THEM INTO AN HARMONIOUS ENTITY.

We have seen how immigration laws were introduced to prevent the flow of the unwanted into a country and how sterilisation in large numbers was used to prevent the growth of numbers amongst the poor. Neither of these approaches could resolve the core issue of the 'genetically', predisposed individuals who were classified as criminals, feeble-minded or other. No, the eugenics movement had to upgrade its beliefs, it had to ensure that they were more relevant than ever before. So, the rebrand gave acceptance to a growing idea and in a way was more invasive than its early form.

Focusing on the 'genome' meant that no one would escape the clutches of this insidious system if proven to have a gene of a specific type or hereditary origin. Delving into the gene at a biological level gave much more credence to the movement. However, there was something about this which created somewhat of a conflict for eugenicists. If it were true, that an unwanted trait such as feeble-mindedness or poverty was genetic then it was also true that these problems could never be eradicated. Why? Firstly, the genetic composition of a human being includes numerous genes and scientists soon discovered that criminality, intelligence, and other human traits were not transmitted from generation to generation. The issues were simply too complex to explain away with the hereditary theory. Of course, this removed any notion that a person is predisposed to follow a family experience or tradition due to their genetic makeup. Therefore, all the measures that were implemented to remove the unfit using social programmes and government legislation were pointless. This also meant that the idea of 'Nature versus Nurture' was an error, as there are many factors that influence the lifestyle choices of all humans, and they were not genetic.

It is with this realisation that the philosophy should have waned but instead it went on from strength to strength, influencing everything that would exist in the human experience. Largely, without most people realising it or wanting to accept it. In some ways, this movement didn't have to prove anything, it simply had to continue repeating the rhetoric of past centuries using human genetics as its new mantra.

The sphere of influence was now well proven and growing rapidly. The hereditary model remained embedded aided by genetics, undermining the fabric of society and replacing truth with some other form of measuring line. This time the revolution would be a technological one, a season of new inventions that is described as - 'God Tech'.

The Birth of God Tech'

"Bringing things we once prayed for or only imagined into the real world"

A direct quotation taken from a personal email received from financial experts and the financial benefits of investing in technology that is transforming the human body.

We have always accepted that God is the one that gives man the ability to create, invent and explore the world around us, supporting such notions by listing the names of famous and influential figures in the world of science. However, in the world of religion and philosophy, technology may be considered neither a good nor evil thing but simply a vehicle, one whose effect on our world is determined by who uses it and how it is used. For the most part, one could debate that these perspectives are true and carry plausible evidence to support them but, as always, we must review them in the light of God's word. To do otherwise leads us back to the influence of emotionalism and potentially fantasy, neither of which should govern what we think and how we live. While doing so, we will be reminded that we are constantly surrounded by messages that demand our attention and allegiance, subtly redefining what we think about morality, truth, the world and even God.

To understand where we are in the world of progressive inventions, travel back with me to the year 2016. A year when my established perspective on technology, science and religion was to be shaken to the core by an experience that was unexpected and was certainly without any attempt on my part to seek out. Let me explain. One day in 2016, while checking through my emails the subject line of some of the messages in my inbox caught my attention. Their titles caused me to think that the content was rather strange and out of context to anything that I had subscribed to or connected to, theologically or otherwise. The obvious thought was that they were spam emails that had managed to get past my computer's software, but on closer scrutiny, the email addresses that they came from were from sources that I recognised. Little did I know that they were to reveal a hidden side to a narrative I did not know existed, yet one that continued to forge the path towards the ultimate revelation of 'the hidden tree'. After choosing to follow this path, subject matter like this would repeatedly discover me (instead of me discovering it), reminding me of the numerous times that it is recorded by the Prophets in the Hebrew scriptures *"and the word of the Lord came unto me saying."* A phrase and experience that highlights to the recipient that humanity is truly ignorant without God revealing to us what He knows. Do not misunderstand, I am not claiming to be a prophet but simply an explorer ignorant of the world around me awaken by the words of someone greater and wiser.

It is foolish to believe that we know more and can or have discovered more than God, especially as we compare our finite lives of a few years to the eternal existence of God who is the complete embodiment of wisdom and history. No, He wins the competition for having the most insight and collective knowledge – more than any human being that has ever existed.

Ironically, embedded in one of the emails was a hyperlink to a video which I repeatedly tried to open, only to discover that a transcript was to be found in its place. Initially, I thought it was a glitch with my computer, so I made several attempts to find a workaround or a solution to the root cause of the problem.

After several frustrating attempts, I gave up on trying to solve the problem, at which point it slowly dawned on me that I had in my possession a 'written document' in the form of a transcript that I could copy and read at my leisure. What initially seemed to be a frustration turned out to be way more useful than the video I was trying to access. Isn't that just the way that Yeshua works, gently nudging us to stop and listen?

The other surprising element was that the emails came from financial advisors who I subscribed to due to my interest in the economy and its relevance to global developments. This added to my initial curiosity as I flicked through the content, wondering, when did financial advisors begin promoting religious material. The pages were full of overt anti-God sentiment while simultaneously purporting to have humanity's answer to becoming godlike while getting rich in the process:

The front page reads like this,

Now, in 2016, we have reached a NEW stage of human evolution.

This is the dawn of

Homo – Deus

The Epoch of the Man-God.

I couldn't believe my eyes, what was this about? What does this have to do with finance? Included on the front page was a reference to the Darwinian theory of evolution but as we will see later, the evolution of man would not be without humanity's assistance; Social Darwinism through technology.

Here are the stages referenced in the transcript:

Stage 1: Two million BC – Homo Habilis (Able Man)

Stage 2: 498,000 BC – Homo Erectus (Upright Man)

Stage 3: 250,000 – Homo Sapiens (Wise Man)

Stage 4: In 2016 – Homo Deus (Man God)

As if this were not outlandish enough, the opening page took the reader on a secular history lesson of how civilisation has farmed to feed itself, how it has created vaccines to defeat diseases, built machines to do the work of 100 men, linked the world with great networks of energy and communication, etc. It eventually crescendos into a cacophony of irreverence with the words, *"Now we have cracked The God Code..."*

This is the point at which the Genesis event in the Garden of Eden rushed back into my mind. This derisive declaration of godhood revealed that the desire to be godlike was still alive and well in the sinful nature of man today. Not only have we not learned from past mistakes, but we have also arrogantly set our faces to build on our errors with an added drive to surpass God himself. This brings with it the consolidation of everything that we have seen in the ancient hidden systems of worship all in the name of *'becoming like gods'*

Here are a few quotations taken from the transcript,

- *"Now the God Code has been cracked...there are no limits to our powers..."*
- *"...this new era of 'God Technology' has handed mankind the ability to heal itself on an entirely new level..."*
- *"Bringing things we once prayed for or only ever imagined into the real world."*
- *"As Tom Hugland of The Foundation for Fighting Blindness says: It used to be a religious miracle, but now it's a scientific miracle."*
- *"The era of Homo sapiens is coming to a close. We have massively accelerated evolution."*
- *"This is not just a new wave of technology. It is the next stage in the evolution of human life on earth."*

Even when I read these statements and accompanying pages, I was still thinking this had to be a joke. There was no way that people held these ideas and believed that it was possible to evolve through technology, did they? Yet with all of the wrestling with similar questions, I could not ignore what I was reading. So, the logical conclusions were, if this is part of a new religious identity then there had to be an identifiable source behind it all. As God speaks to men and women regarding the welfare and safety of humanity then there had to be the opposite contender who was unleashing a new phase of human identity that would be popular and inclusive at all levels, yet deeply destructive and insidious to say the least.

So where did these and other people get their information from?

Dark Intel[103]

For we do not wrestle against flesh and blood, but against principalities, against powers, against the rulers of the darkness of this age, against spiritual hosts of wickedness in the heavenly places. Ephesians 6:12 (NKJV)

Is everything around us good or is it evil, can we tell? The Bible sweeps away our notion of good and evil and exposes the face of deceptive personalities that would have us believe they were somehow honest and full of integrity.

Through the letters of individuals like Rabbi Paul, in the letter to the congregation at Ephesus, we are led through an exposition of the world and its powerbase, a world that inflicts untold damage on the very existence of innocent and sometimes

---

[103] Short form of intelligence: secret information, for example about another country's government, an enemy group, or criminal activities.

naive bystanders. In a truly inspired manner, Paul grabs the listeners' attention with commanding, powerful words that were imparted to him through the Holy Spirit. The Holy Spirit... you ask? Yes, The Holy Spirit. Not an energy, force, or mystical entity but the guiding, creative presence of Hashem (God).

Rabbi Paul was raised with the Torah (*Teachings*) from a child and in his adulthood found himself wrestling with its truths. By the time we light upon the letter to the congregation in Ephesus, he is speaking boldly to an audience that may otherwise have continued in ignorance over the matter of evil influences in this world. In his letter to the congregation in Ephesus, he describes the form and character of an enemy that every follower of Messiah will wrestle with. Also, his description leaves no room for speculation about the seat of power in the ensuing battle. Yet he does not begin with the description of the wrestle but begins with a call to immediate action to the believer,

"From now on, you must right away become strong in the Lord and in the power of His strength." Ephesians 6:10 (ONM)

His wise counsel continues with the imperative, *"You must continually be clothed with the full armour of God to enable you to stand against the strategies of the devil:"* Ephesians 6:11 (ONM)

As a warrior who contended for many years, standing against the floodtide of darkness, in the power of God's might, Rabbi Paul ensures that younger, inexperienced combatants are fully aware of the place of struggle and the identity of their real enemy. His descriptive, revealing letter points to the power behind the powerbase of this world. However, The God of Israel is still sovereign, ruling over all, there is no mistaking this and Paul outlines this at the beginning of his discourse with his brethren:

"And because of this, since I heard of your faith in the Lord Yeshua and your love for all the saints, I have not ceased giving thanks concerning you, making mention of you in my prayers, in order that the God of our Lord Yeshua Messiah, the Father of glory, would have given you a spirit of wisdom and revelation for your knowledge of Him, that the eyes of your heart have been enlightened; for you to have known what is the hope of His inheritance, the riches His glory, of His inheritance for the saints, and which exceeds the greatness of His power in us, those who believe, according to the working of the might of His strength. **Which He worked in Messiah when He raised Him from the dead and He seated Him on His right hand in the heavenlies far above every rule and authority and power and dominion, and then He was named above every name, not only in this age, but also in the one that is coming: and He made all things subject under His feet and gave Him authority over everyone in the congregation, which is His body, the extension of the One Who fills everything in every way.**" *Ephesians 1:15-23 (ONM)*

There is a hierarchical, global power which is joined with *"spiritual forces of wickedness in the heavenlies"* whose presence and agenda will strive to dominate this world and its occupants for all eternity and at any cost. In every age, this powerbase is heard, seen, and felt in plain sight and yet in gullibility we deny the existence of God by the allure of entities we describe as 'aliens'; we bow the knee at altars of fraternities, recite spiritual incantations without a thought. These entities are evidenced in global architecture, in ancient structures built using methods we cannot comprehend, feats of engineering that we cannot replicate and materials that are beyond our capabilities to reproduce.

So, we all agree that there is a designer behind every design and an author behind every power structure, but we consistently fail to ask the important question. Who is the designer? This is the reason for Rabbi Paul's instruction to the congregation in Ephesus; he understood that anything that makes our life easier, or that resolves a physical or emotional problem should not be automatically assumed as having its origin in God. Incredible as it seems, he understood that we are prone to make decisions about who and what to follow based on personal benefit and emotional experience alone i.e., *if it feels right let's do it or if helps my immediate emotional or financial position, what's the harm?* An attitude that makes us vulnerable to the [104]father of lies and susceptible to manipulative tactics designed to lead us to consume what seems good in our eyes but ultimately does us (and others) serious harm.

Paul states,

"Therefore, I say this, and I bear witness in the Lord, that you no longer walk as the heathens walk in the futility of their minds, since they have been darkened by being in their understanding, because they have been alienated from the life of God through the ignorance which is in them, because of the insensibility of their hearts, who, when they became callous, gave themselves over to licentiousness in practice of every impurity, with a desire to have more. But you did not learn Messiah in this way, if you really heard about Him and were taught by Him, just as truth is in Yeshua, you laid aside the old man, according to your former behaviour, in accordance with the destruction of your deceitful desires, then to have been renewed in the spirit of your mind and to have put on the new man, the one which has been created corresponding to God in the righteousness and holiness of the truth." (Ephesians 4:17-24 (ONM)

The assumptions that are popular in today's world and within the false guidance of *'do what thou wilt'* may appeal to some but, we are reminded in earlier chapters that there is a false

---

[104] You are of your father the devil, and the desires of your father you want to do. He was a murderer from the beginning, and does not stand in the truth, because there is no truth in him. When he speaks a lie, he speaks from his own resources, for he is a liar and the father of it. (John 8:44 NKJV)

representation of truth; visually good things are not always from good people or righteous sources.

What does all this have to do with dark intel? Well, when Yeshua was teaching an audience about His kingdom, He made a statement that resonates with the points that will be highlighted in this section. He says,

"For false christs and false prophets will rise and show signs and wonders to deceive, if possible, even the elect. But take heed; see, I have told you all things beforehand." Mark 13:21-23 (NKJV)

Interestingly, Yeshua makes no distinction about the origin or religious persuasion of such 'false messiahs' or 'false prophets' here, He simply states that they will rise. With them will be the ability to gain followers by using visually impactful means (supernatural or otherwise) that give them a sense of credibility and authenticity that elevates them as unique in the world of normal human beings. Also note, that to be a false messiah and/or [105]false prophet one does not have to be connected to the biblical faith in any way. No, this kind of person in simple terms is the embodiment of a false voice with false promises or broken promises to the recipient as the penultimate reward and destruction as the last. Typically, an anti-Messiah figure that is inspired by a spirit that is against The Messiah and that will stop at nothing and use any means to win your vote and gain your favour.

As the followers of Yeshua, are moved and inspired by The Holy Spirit, the 'false messiahs and prophets' receive their intel and inspiration from another source. The information shared with them can only be described as 'Dark Intel'. A term

---

[105] Then the Lord said to me, "The prophets are prophesying lies in my name. I have not sent them or appointed them or spoken to them. They are prophesying to you false visions, divinations, idolatries and the delusions of their own minds. Jeremiah 14:14 (NIV)

referring to information that is imparted to an individual that has not acquired it through everyday thinking or human intellect but has derived it from another source opposed to The God of the Holy Scriptures and His Son Yeshua The Messiah. This became clearer as I read the material in the 2016 transcript as there was no doubt that my conclusions about many things had to be redefined. Here is a summary of my conclusions.

1. Not all **inventions** are God inspired.
2. Not all **innovation** is God centred.
3. Some believe humanity can evolve.
4. Many believe technology is the key, or that '**Science is salvation.**'
5. There is an ultimate goal.

However, if these conclusions, and others like them, are true there must be evidence of 'dark intel' and its influence somewhere, but to discover its handiwork we are obliged to look into the shadowy places once again. Those places which are rarely explored, veiled by a form of obscurity which is aided by our blind belief that [106]'the end justifies the means'.

Here's how Yeshua describes those places and our affinity to them,

"This is the verdict: Light has come into the world, but people loved darkness instead of light because their deeds were evil. Everyone who does evil hates the light, and will not come into the light for fear that their deeds will be exposed. But whoever lives by the truth comes

---

[106] Used to say that a desired result is so good or important that any method, even a morally bad one, may be used to achieve it.
They believe that the end justifies the means and will do anything to get their candidate elected. "The end justifies the means." Merriam-Webster.com Dictionary, Merriam-Webster, https://www.merriam-webster.com/dictionary/the%20end%20justifies%20the%20means. Accessed 12 Nov. 2022.

into the light, so that it may be seen plainly that what they have done has been done in the sight of God." (John 3:19-21 (NIV)

Ironically, this extract is from a conversation between Yeshua and an educated, upstanding Rabbi called Nicodemus and not a debased cult leader. (*You can read about Nicodemus in John chapter 3 in the Bible*). It is evident from their discourse that Nicodemus, a leading member of the community, had little understanding of this darkness that Yeshua was speaking about, yet by his repeated visits to Yeshua, without drawing attention to himself, he was challenged by the clarity and purity of Yeshua's words. Words that could not be refuted by this leading, educated, Torah teaching, religious man. A man who shared the same Hebrew Scriptures and religious background as Yeshua, yet Yeshua's teachings penetrated Nicodemus' heart and mind in a way that nothing else had. The words shone brightly, leaping out of the pages of the Torah made flesh [107](Yeshua) to impact Nicodemus' heart, exposing the hidden things by bringing them into the light.

We must consider that Nicodemus' ignorance is a picture of most people's perspective on the darkness in this world. The kind of darkness which leaves us (like him) clueless as to why human beings are naturally drawn to it and influenced by it. In this context 'Dark Intel' takes advantage of this love of the darkness, and it is this combination of 'Dark Intel' and 'god Tech' that has formed an unholy alliance which is central to the new frontier in the world of inventions and religious persuasions which is transitioning us from the 20th century and into the 21st century. Similarly, when the light is shone into the dark crevices of this alliance it exposes our questionable claims of ethical and moral advancement.

---

[107] And the Word became flesh and dwelt among us, and we beheld His glory, the glory as of the only begotten of the Father, full of grace and truth. John 1:14 NKJV

Importantly, it is from this darkness that the Third Reich's dream of an Aryan race was birthed. A dream that was more of a nightmare which embraced human experimentation in stark contrast to the backdrop of the popular image of the German intelligentsia. We would do well to accept the caution of this observation, after all, which one of us can honestly say that we are immune from performing the most atrocious acts due to our superior intellect or education? To be confident in this way is folly.

Also, this was not the first time that such an event had taken place but, on this occasion, there was something different to its scale, impact and importance. This global event was the point at which darkness of global magnitude was released. It was beyond human comprehension yet foundational to later derivations of science, art, politics, and other cultural behaviours. Including, the early seed of *'god tech'* which in essence is the enhancement or replacement of the human body or its parts. All under the guise of saving or extending lives, but whose life and for what purpose?

Strangely, the cataclysmic effect of such an event makes no sense to the ordinary person and it cannot be explained in any rational manner, hence, leaving a void for all kinds of speculative thoughts and theories.

The Conundrum

There are so many justifications which are used to support our pursuit of individual and collective advancement; in fact, our thirst for complete autonomy as human beings has left us with what can only be described as 'eternal problems'. Deceiving ourselves we press ahead in the blind belief that we'll work it out on our own, doggedly searching for ways of resolving obvious issues such as ageing, disease, trauma, equality and ultimately, peace. So, to believe that we are godlike with the capability of resolving age old problems using archaic means *(which we define as technological advancement)* is a fallacy. If we were so successful, the resulting passages would not be necessary to articulate in any form whatsoever. Nevertheless, there is a paramount need for us to consider carefully the past and future objectives in light of such stark realities and truisms.

So, when considering the rise of this racist offshoot of eugenics, Nazism, one would think that nation states would distance themselves from anything devised by this regime, including their technological claims. However, to the contrary and, sadly, current information shows that this was rarely the position and the debates as to why still roll on. We know this because the data obtained from Nazi human experimentation during the Holocaust, for example, was not discarded and we have since discovered that even scientists or doctors that were involved in these immoral experiments were integrated into the nations that were once the judge and jury of the perpetrators of these crimes. According to the declassified documents stored by the US National Archives, 1500 German scientists were taken to the US under [108]Operation Paperclip, which included Walter Schreiber, who was instrumental in human experimentation in the camps. The release of these documents was due to the Nazi War Crimes Disclosure Act, Approved on October 8, 1998. Paradoxically, Britain also engaged in a similar pursuit, in conjunction with the US, via what was called 'Operation Matchbox' under which 127 scientists are said to have been

---

[108] Freedom of Information Act Electronic Reading Room.
Visit https://www.cia.gov/readingroom/ and search for Operation Paperclip.
https://www.archives.gov/
Records of the Secretary of Defense (RG 330). Foreign Scientist Case Files 1945-1958 (Entry A1-1B) Boxes 1-186 location: 230/86/46/5

transported to Australia during a period when Germans were barred from entering the country.

Since then, the substitution of morality with ethics has created a chasm of understanding that continues to be filled with human reasoning, mainly arguing for the benefits of past human experiments data. Yet, in stark contrast in a preceding step to protect lesser species, the Cruelty to Animals Act of 1835 was passed in the UK parliament to prevent the mistreatment of cattle, while the Nazis Animal Protection Act of 1933 began its policy to secure the lives of animals. Yet in 1941 the transition to the mass genocide of Jews began, officially placing animal life above the sanctity of human life.

It is difficult to understand the motivation behind the pain inflicted without fully realising the source of the whole matter, the pursuit of which has led to countless books and hypotheses often leaving us none the wiser. It is even more difficult to understand how any of the documented discoveries during this period of human experimentation could ever be used to further modern society in any way, shape, or form. This includes the use of the intellect behind such atrocities that were perpetrated by other nations. However, while reflecting on all these points and questions, key characters and events provide more understanding than any bystander's words could ever achieve.

So, what follows are accounts which give us a brief insight into the mindset in Germany during the Second World War. The accounts that are listed will go some way to evidencing the five-point conclusions mentioned earlier but are by no means exhaustive.

Each heading points to a specific area of experimentation carried out on innocent people, from children to adults, male and female. Remember, the areas of human experimentation are central to the aim of creating an Aryan race and achieving global dominance. Pay close attention to the headings, which are still referenced today in scientific journals, media headlines and other outlets. Is this a coincidence? I suggest not as without much thought or hesitation, our attention is still focused on the 'breakthroughs' while choosing to ignore the origin of an idea's inception and its original purpose.

The accounts are drawn from various sources such as eyewitness accounts and extracts from the Nuremberg Trials. Remember,

1. Not all inventions are God inspired.
2. Not all innovation is God centred.
3. Some believe humanity can evolve.
4. Many believe technology is the key, or that 'Science is salvation.'
5. There is an ultimate goal.

Human Experiments

Twins

[109]*Transcript for NMT 1: Medical Case - Page 980 - 981 (1945 - 1946)*

"*Finally it must be said, that from a total number of 40 cases there are 1 positive case and 4 positive cases with certain reservations, contrary to 35 failures of which 10 ended fatally.*

"*The experiments in Dachau are being continued.*

"*Besides the hitherto existing program special attention is directed to research of twin cases in similar conditions, of which one will receive an allopathical, the second a bio-chemical treatment.*

"*(1. marginal note: read: [Ravensbrück] 3-9-1942 signature: K. Gebhardt).*"

Here we find the Defendant Gebhardt fully cognizant of the work being conducted at Dachau on phlegmon experiments.

"*2. In the concentration camp of Auschwitz three typical cases of sepsis, which developed from phlegmons, were treated - according to prescription - with Potassium phosphoricum D 4. In none of these cases a therapeutical influence on the progress of the disease could be observed. All 3 cases ended fatally.*

---

[109] Harvard Law School Library. Nuremberg Trials Project: A Digital Document Collection, https://nuremberg.law.harvard.edu. Accessed 4 November 2022

"*The experiments are being continued.*

(Signature) Grawitz" If the Tribunal please, we will now pass on to the next document as this document is self-explanatory and seems to need no comment.

The next document is Document NO-408 which the Prosecution offers in evidence as Prosecution Exhibit 250. This is a letter from one Theodor Laue, former Senator SS [Standartenführer]. This Theodor Laue would seem to be the same [Standartenführer]. Laue who is given in the testimony of the Witness Stoerr on Page 578 of the Transcript as a visitor at Dachau in the late summer or fall of 1943 at which time Laue inspected the surgical department, inspected the phlegmon wounds and seems to have given orders with respect to treatment.

[110] *Eyewitness account by Eva Herskovits entitled 'Experiences of Twin Sisters in the Camps'.*

Dear Family Karol

Maybe you can imagine how happy we were when we received your lovely telegram yesterday. We have already written a telegram and an airmail letter to Grete but haven't received a response yet. It was addressed to: Victoria Memorial.- You were asking about Ruth's illness. Well, I don't want to skip anything, so I would like to report in sequence. I will just write briefly and only of the main things. Details next time. - As you know we were deported to Theresienstadt in July 43. We were previously two weeks in the prison of Hanover. We were the last Jews from the town. Nine people. We rode in a cattle wagon to Theresienstadt. We had comparatively "fair" luggage. Bedclothes, mattresses, clothes and a bit of tableware. When we arrived, we were received by Czech gendarmes. Luggage was searched and robbed by

---

[110]Eyewitness account by Eva Herskovits entitled 'Experiences of Twin Sisters in the Camps'
https://www.testifyingtothetruth.co.uk/viewer/metadata/105726/1/
Reproduced by permission of the Wiener Holocaust Library.

Jewish people. Meanwhile, they brought us to an old, ruined house. We spent the summer in this house in the stiflingly hot attic. Ruth and I lived in the youth centre during the winter. Father and mother lived in the same house but downstairs. In the first couple of months we had additional food from home. Then mother sold bedclothes for bread. We left the ghetto every day and did farm work. We exchanged vegetables which we smuggled into the ghetto for bread also. Of the parcels from Lisbon we received only three. In May 44 we arrived, as part of a transport of 7500 people, in Auschwitz. 65 people with a lot of luggage in one cattle wagon. Old people. 170 people dead because of the transport. We had to leave the luggage. They brought us to a family camp containing only people from Theresienstadt. That means: The transports from Theresienstadt were given preferential treatment. 1. Men and women in one camp. 2. The arriving transports were not selected at the station (I'll write about this later) 3. They didn't shave our hair, just cut it up to the ears. They tattooed us the next day. A number on the left arm.- These 2 months were the most horrible of our lives. We were starving. At half 10 we got a half litre of water soup, which really could only be eaten by those people who were not able to stand anymore because of hunger. Soon they gave us the daily bread ration. 1 kg. bread for 4 – 5 people. But very often the bread was mouldy. In addition to that, a tiny piece of margarine, ham, or a spoon of jam. This was the whole of our food. A woman was able to survive with it but a man couldn't. Everyone suffered, starving and then starving themselves further for the sake of others. The picture of the camp street: men with poor clothing and bald heads towed heavy stones, followed by men with bludgeons. The bludgeons struck constantly on their poor limbs. Behind the barracks lay a lot of dead bodies, people who died daily from typhus. Nobody cared for them as long [as] they were still alive. All of this is framed with barbed wire as far as the eye can see. It's loaded with electricity. Behind the wire other camps. As far as you can see: one big hell, a concentration camp nobody had seen the like of before. What can I say? When we see each other, I will tell you everything. Just one thing: the SS camp doctor did research on twins for amusement. What he has done with us is unbelievable. A hundred times over we were examined, measured, weighed. How much blood was drawn off? They brought us in a car to Auschwitz to take photos (We were in Birkenau). They didn't forget to do x-rays. For all these efforts we got an extra portion of soup. That was very welcomed, so we could help father and mother. - Now I want to write something about the "selection", then you will understand the following better.- They unloaded every transport with Jews on it. Men to the right, women to the left. In the middle stood the commandant and the camp doctor.

Poison

[111]Transcript for NMT 1: Medical Case – Page 23

A sort of rough pattern is apparent on the face of the Indictment. Experiment concerning high altitude, the effect of cold, and the potability of processed [salt] water have an obvious relation to aeronautical and naval combat and rescue problem[s]. The mustard gas and phosphorous burn experiments, as well as those relating to healing value of sulfanilimide for wounds, can be related to air-raid and battle field medical problems. It is well known that malaria, epidemic jaundice, and typhus (spotted fever) were among the principal diseases which had to be [combatted] by the German armed forces and by German authorities in occupied territories.

To some degree, the therapeutic pattern outlined above is undoubtedly a valid one, and explains why the Wehrmacht, and especially the German Air Forces, participated in these experiments. Fanatically bent upon conquest, utterly ruthless as to the means or instruments to be used in achieving victory, and callous to the sufferings of people whom they regarded as inferior, the German

---

[111] Harvard Law School Library. Nuremberg Trials Project: A Digital Document Collection, https://nuremberg.law.harvard.edu. Accessed 4 November 2022

militarist[s] were willing to gather whatever scientific fruit these experiments might yield.

But our proof will show that a quite different and even more sinister objective runs like a red thread through these hideous researches. We will show them in some instances, the true object of these experiments was not how to rescue or to cure, but how to destroy and kill. The sterilization experiments were, it is clear, purely destructive in purpose. The prisoners at Buchenwald who were shot with poisoned bullets were not guinea pigs to test an antidote for the poison; their murderers really wanted to know how quickly the poison would kill. This destructive objective is not superficially as apparent in the other experiments, but we will show that it was often there.

Mankind has not heretofore felt the need of a word to denominate the science of how [most] rapidly to kill prisoners and subjugated people in large numbers. The case and these defendants have created this gruesome question for the lexicographer. For the moment, we will christen this macabre science "thanatology", the science of producing death. The thanatological knowledge, derived in part from these experiments, supplied the techniques for genocide, a policy of the Third Reich exemplified in the "[euthanasia]" program and in the widespread slaughter of Jews, gypsies, Poles and Russians. This policy of mass extermination could not have been so effectively carried out without the active participation of German medical scientists.

High Altitude

[112]*Transcript for NMT 1: Medical Case – Page 24 -25*

The experiments known as "high altitude" or "low pressure" experiments were carried out at the Dachau concentration camp in

[112] Harvard Law School Library. Nuremberg Trials Project: A Digital Document Collection, https://nuremberg.law.harvard.edu. Accessed 4 November 2022

1942. According to the proof, the original proposal that such experiments be carried out on human beings originated in the spring of 1941 with a Dr. Sigmund Rascher. Rascher was at that time a captain in the medical service of the German Air Force, and also held officer [rank] in the SS. He is believed now to be dead.

The origin of the idea is revealed in a letter which Rascher wrote to Himmler in May 1941 at which time Rascher was taking a course in aviation medicine at a German Air Force Headquarters in Munich. According to the letter, this course included researches into high altitude flying and "considerable regret was expressed at the fact that no tests with human material had yet been possible for us, as such experiments are very dangerous and nobody volunteers for them."

Rascher, in this letter, went on to ask Himmler to put human subjects at his disposal and baldly stated that the experiments might result in death to the subject but that the tests theretofore made with monkeys had not been satisfactory.

Rascher's letter was answered by Himmler's adjutant, the defendant, Rudolf Brandt, who informed Rascher that:

"Prisoners will, of course, gladly be made available for the high flight researches."

Subsequently, Rascher wrote directly to Rudolf Brandt asking for permission to carry out the experiments at the Dachau concentration camp, and he mentioned that the German Air Force had provided "a movable pressure chamber" in which the experiments might be made. Plans for carrying out the experiments were developed at a conference late in 1941 or early in 1942 attended by Dr. Rascher and by the defendants Weltz, Romberg, and Ruff, all of whom were members of the German Air Force medical service. The tests themselves were carried out in the spring and summer of 1942, using the pressure chamber which the German Air Force had [provided]. The victims were locked in the low pressure chamber, which was an airtight balllike [sic] compartment, and then the pressure in the chamber was altered to simulate the atmospheric conditions prevailing at extremely high *altitudes. The pressure in the chamber could be varied with great rapidity, which permitted the defendants to duplicate the atmospheric conditions which an aviator might encounter in falling great distances through space without a parachute and without oxygen.*

The reports, conclusions, and comments on these experiments, which were introduced here and carefully recorded, demonstrate complete disregard for human life and callousness to suffering and pain. These documents reveal at one and the same time the medical results of the experiments, and the degradation of the physicians who performed them. The first report by Rascher was made in April, 1942, and contains a description of the effect of the low pressure chamber on a 37-year old Jew. I quote:

"The third experiment of this type took such an extra-ordinary course that I called an SS physician of the camp as witness, since I had worked on these experiments all by myself. It was a continuous experiment without oxygen at a height of 12 km conducted on a 37-year old Jew in good general condition. Breathing continued up to 30 minutes. After 4 minutes the experimental subject began to perspire and wiggle his head, after 5 minutes cramps occurred, between 6 and 10 minutes breathing increased in speed and the experimental subject became unconscious; from 11 to 30 minutes breathing slowed down to three breaths per minute, finally stopping altogether.

"Severest cyanosis developed in between and foam appeared at the mouth.

"At five minute intervals electrocardiograms from 3 leads were written. After breathing had stopped Ekg (electrocardiogram) was continuously written until the action of the heart had come to a complete standstill. About 1/2 hour after breathing had stopped, dissection was started."

Tuberculosis

[113]*Transcript for NMT 1: Medical Case – Page 142 -144*

"I, Kurt Blome, being duly sworn, depose and state:

1. I was born on 31 January 1894 in Bielefeld, Germany. In 1912 I was graduated from Dortmund and studied medicine at Goetlingen [sic]. In 1914 my studies were interrupted by World War I, but I returned to my medical studies in 1919 and finished them at the Rostock University in 1920. During the war I served in the Medical Corps of the German Army. The highest rank I attained was that of a Lieutenants [sic].

2. From 1920 until 1924 I was an assistant on the medical faculty at Rostock University. From 1924 until 1934 I engaged in the private practice of medicine in Rostock.

3. [I] joined the NSDAP in 1931 and later held a rank of SA Medical [Gruppenführer]. In 1943 I was awarded the Golden Party Badge.

4. After several years of private practice I was called to Berlin in 1934 by Dr. Gerhard Wagner, Reich Health Leader where I was active as adjutant in the Central Office of the German Red Cross.

In 1935 I began my main task, namely to organize the German Medical Education 1 System.

5. In 1934, in conjunction with in duties as adjutant in the Main [Office] of the German Red Cross, I was also appointed business manager of the Reich Physicians Association. I held this position until the end of the war.

---

[113] Harvard Law School Library. Nuremberg Trials Project: A Digital Document Collection, https://nuremberg.law.harvard.edu. Accessed 4 November 2022

6. In 1938 I became President of the Bureau of the Academy for International Medical Education. In 1939 I became deputy to Dr. Leonardo Conti, [Reichsgesundheitsführer] or Reich Health Leader and successor to Dr. Wagner. I represented Dr. Conti in his capacities as:

a) Leader of the Reichs Physicians Association.

b) Nominally as head of the Main Office for Public Health of the Party.

c) Nominally as leader of the National Socialist Physicians Association.

7. From about 1941 until the end of the war I was a member of the Reich Research Council. In 1943 I was appointed Plenipotentiary for Cancer Research which was allied with the research Commission for Protection against [Biological] warfare. I held these positions until I was taken prisoner by the Americans (signed) KURT BLOME It is apparent from reading this Affidavit that Blome was an ardent Nazi from an early period.

As no [sic] states, one of his main tasks was to organize the German medical educational system. This afforded him the opportunity to inculcate in such young medical students as the Defendant, Hoven, the perverted doctrine that the ill-conceived love of thy neighbor has to disappear, especially in relation to inferior or asocial creatures. Such doctrines were taught at the [Führer] School of the German, physicians at [Alt Rehse] in Mecklenburg which was organized by the Defendant, Blome. Attendance at this school became compulsory and had to be attended for several weeks annually for five year periods. Certainly it is not strange to find a man of such beliefs associated with the extermination of peoples afflicted with tuberculosis and so-called mental illnesses.

It should also be noted that Blome was business manager of the Reichs Physicians Association and that he represented Conti in his capacity as the [Führer] of this Association.

All physicians in Germany except those on military duty were subordinate to the leader [of] the Reichs Physicians Association.

Is it not clear that a man with the influential position of Blome could have done much to prevent the criminal activities of the German physicians and scientists about which this case is concerned. The Prosecution will prove that it was not lack of knowledge of these experiments which explains the inertia of Blome. Indeed, the proof will show that he actively participated in several experiments, not to mention the unspeakable extermination of persons afflicted with tuberculosis. His activities in the field of biological warfare under the cover name "Cancer Research" will also be brought to the attention of the Tribunal.

Phosgene

[114]*Transcript for NMT 1: Medical Case – Page 2630, 3400 - 3402*

Tell the Tribunal what "phosgene" is, witness.

A Phosgene is a chemical warfare agent in gas form which can be used in gas form.

Q What was the Professor Bickenbach doing with the research station at [Natzweiler]?

A He had been given animals at Natzweiler and had conducted his animal experiments there. There was obviously a tense relationship between him and Hirt so that he wanted to disassociate himself from the group there. He asked me to help him and I did help him then to establish this laboratory which was independent of Natzweiler. It was near Strassburg [sic]. And there he wanted to resume his phosgene

---

[114] Harvard Law School Library. Nuremberg Trials Project: A Digital Document Collection, https://nuremberg.law.harvard.edu. Accessed 4 November 2022

experiments and ha [sic] didn't begin to work -- later his work was broken off through the war conditions; about in September...

Herr Professor, I think you will probably now appreciate the significance of Report Number 4 where it is stated that they were carrying out a test with a certain drug on a Russian prisoner of war; and I assume you have now read Report Number 7. For purposes of the record I will now read this report. It is stamped: "Top Secret (military); 3 copies; 3rd copy."

"To the [Führer]'s General Plenipotentiary for [Sanitation] and Health Matters Surgeon - General Prof. Dr. BRAUDT, Berlin Ziegelstrasse 5/9, Surgical Clinic at the University.

7th Report:

On the protective effect of hoxamethylentetramin [sic] for phosgene poison. Experiments were carried out on 40 prisoners on the prophylactic effect of hexamethylentetramin [sic] in cases of phosgene poisoning.

12 [of] those were protected orally, 20 intravenously and 8 were used as controls.

The method:

The chamber has a capacity of 20 cbm. In experiment I to XIV the chamber was given a coat of paint which had a strong deteriorating effect on phosgene. This decrease in concentration was measured after experiment IX. The curves are shown on chart I.

The heaviest decrease measured was taken as basis for the calculations of the average concentration for experiment I to XI. In experiments XII to XV, the initial concentration and its decrease were measured separated in each case. In the tables II and III Co stands for the quantity of phosgene infused into the chamber in mg/cbm, cm for the calculated average concentration, t for the time of reaction. Cm was measured as an arithmetic medium from 5 to 7 and calculated on the curve values obtained through interpolation.

B. *The experimental subjects were throughout persons of middle age, almost all in a weak and underfed Condition. On principle, the healthier were used as control, only control number 39 (J. Rei) and the orally protected experimental subject No. 37 (A. Rei) had a localized cirrhotic productive tuberculosis of the lungs. With the others, no pulmonary disease could be found. In the first experiments up to 6g hexamethylentetramin were given orally, later despite the much higher concentrations 0.06 g/kg body weight, orally as well as intravenously.*

Results: The intravenously protected experimental subjects, without exception, all survived the phosgene [poisoning] with a c.t. of 207 to 5400. There were no symptoms of pulmonary edema after intravenous protection, even with a c.t. of 2970. Only experiment no. 10 with a c.t. of 3960 caused pulmonary edema of the first degree, which was overcome without any therapy; and in experiment no. XIV the intravenous protection was penetrated to an extent as to cause pulmonary edema of the 3rd degree, which however was overcome by oxygen inhalation. The experimental subject recovered.

All control subjects fell ill. With a c.t. of 768 and 1180 a first degree pulmonary edema resulted which was overcome. With a c.t. of 227, one control subject died, the second contracted a second degree pulmonary edema but recovered.

A c.t. of 5400 killed one control subject after hours; the other after 14 hours.

After oral protection; a c.t. of 247 to 768 was suffered without any edema, even when the protective solution of hexamethylentetramin [sic] was drunk only 2/3 minutes before the inhalation of the phosgene. 2 control subjects showed a marked edema with a c.t. of 768. With a c.t. of 1485 one protects subject fell seriously ill with a second degree edema; a second subject like wise protected; having breathed the same phosgenic air, was unaffected. The cause of this striking difference must be sought in the different resorption of the hexamethylentetramine [sic] on the one hand and in the different reaction and the different volume of respiration of the experimental subjects on the other hand. Even a c.t. of 2275 resulted in only a slight pulmonary edema in an orally protected test subject, whereas one control subject died after 4 hours, and a second contracted a second degree pulmonary edema. The oral protection was penetrated by a c.t. of 5400. The protected test subject died; as did the two control subjects.

Sulfanilamide, Bone, Muscle, and Joint Transplantation

[115]*Transcript for NMT 1: Medical Case – Page 32 -34*

E and F. [Ravensbrück] Experiments concerning Sulfanilimade [sic] and Other Drugs; Bone, Muscle, and Nerve Regeneration and Bone Transplantation.

The experiments conducted principally on the female inmates of [Ravensbrück] Concentration Camp were perhaps the most barbaric of all. These concerned bone, muscle, and nerve regeneration and bone transplantation, and experiments with sulfanilimide [sic] and other drugs. They were carried out by the defendants Fischer and Oberhauser under the direction of the defendant Gebhardt.

In one set of experiments, incisions were made in the legs of several of the camp inmates for the purpose of simulating battle-caused infections. A bacterial culture, or fragments of wood shavings, or tiny pieces of glass were forced into the wound. After several days, the wounds were treated with sulfanilimade [sic]. Grawitz, the head of the SS Medical Service, visited [Ravensbrück] and received a report on these experiments directly from the defendant Fischer. Grawitz thereupon directed that the wounds inflicted on the subjects should be even more severe so that conditions more completely similar to these prevailing at the front lines would be more completely simulated.

[115] Harvard Law School Library. Nuremberg Trials Project: A Digital Document Collection, https://nuremberg.law.harvard.edu. Accessed 4 November 2022

Bullet wounds were simulated on the subjects by trying off the blood vessel at both ends of the incision. A gangrene-producing culture was then placed in the wounds. Severe infection resulted within twenty-four hours. Operations were then performed on the infected area and the wound was treated with sulfanilamide. In each of the many sulfanilamide experiments, some of the subjects were wounded and infected but were not given sulfanilimade [sic], so as to compare their reactions with those who received treatment.

Bone transplantation from one person to another and the regeneration of nerves, muscles, and bones were also tried out on the women at [Ravensbrück]. The defendant Gebhardt personally ordered that bone transplantation experiments be carried out, and in one case the scapula of an inmate at [Ravensbrück] was removed and taken to Hohenlychen Hospital and there transplanted. We will show that the defendants did not even have any substantial scientific objective. These experiments were senseless, sadistic, and utterly savage.

The defendant Oberhauser's duties at [Ravensbrück] in connection with the experiments were to select young and healthy inmates for the experiments, to be present at all of the surgical operations, and to give the experimental subjects post-operative care. We will show that this care consisted chiefly of utter neglect of nursing requirements, and cruel and abusive treatment of the miserable victims.

Other experiments in this category were conducted at Dachau to discover a method of bringing about coagulation of the blood. Concentration camp inmates were actually fired upon, or were injured in some other fashion in order to cause something similar to a battlefield wound. These wounds were then treated with a drug known as polygal in order to test its capacity to coagulate the blood. Several inmates were killed. Sulfanilimide [sic] was also administered to some and withheld from other inmates who had been infected with the pus from a phlegmon-diseased person. Blood poisoning generally ensued. After infection, the victims were left untreated for three or four days, after which various drugs were administered experimentally or experimental surgical operations were performed. Polish Catholic priests were used for those tests. Many died and others became invalids.

As a result of all of these senseless and barbaric experiments, the defendants are responsible for manifold murders and untold cruelty and torture.

Sterilization

[116] *Anonymous eyewitness account entitled 'Sterilisation of Jewish Wives in Mixed Marriages'.*

My wife and I were arrested at gunpoint on the night of [illegible] Rosh Hashanah (29 September 1943). At the time, we were living with the Jews that were left in a ghetto in the east of Amsterdam, having been forced to move there a few months previously.

Once all of our fellow sufferers had been rounded up, we were transported to "Westerbork" concentration camp. The camp was overcrowded to the point of being inhumane and twice a week 1035 prisoners were transferred to Auschwitz and other extermination camps.

In the barracks, the bunks were three high and I was sleeping at the very top. And because I'm not a professional climber, I had broken several ribs after a few days and had to be taken away to the sick bay.

One day, the Jewish doctor working in the sick bay came to me to pass on an order from the "Sturmbannführer", Dr Meyer. I was to sterilise Jewish women living in Amsterdam who were in mixed marriages. (The doctors who had been assigned the task previously had

---

[116] Anonymous eyewitness account entitled 'Sterilisation of Jewish Wives in Mixed Marriages'.
https://www.testifyingtothetruth.co.uk/viewer/metadata/105539/1/
Reproduced by permission of the Wiener Holocaust Library.

experienced a number of failed attempts with fatal consequences so now "they" needed a decent surgeon!)

Disgusted, I refused to accept the task. But, as you can imagine, this request affected me deeply and I was terrified because to me there seemed to be no doubt that my refusal would mean certain death for myself and my wife. An indeterminate period of trying to come up with ways to escape ensued.

After a while, the Senior Doctor returned to pass on the order in a more threatening way, bringing the consequences of my refusal to life for me this time.

As my wife was in the jaundice barracks, it was extremely difficult to contact her and it was only possible to do so in great secrecy through intermediaries. In the meantime, I had been suffering from a severe bout of dysentery, so I was horribly emaciated and in great distress. I was then summoned by the "Oberstabsführer". I told him that I wanted to try to assuage my misgivings if he would be able to give me and my wife (who I would have needed as a surgical assistant) a few days off in Amsterdam so we could regain our strength.

Dr Meyer, who had been backed into a corner by his orders "from above" and who was possibly also influenced slightly by my pitiful appearance, suddenly arranged a three-day "recuperation break" in the middle of November. We left the concentration camp at 04:30 in the morning, under the watchful eye of the guards and with the Jewish star affixed to our tattered clothing.

Our closest friends (the news had naturally spread through the camp like it was part of a whispering campaign) all cried as they were convinced they were watching us go to our death.

But fate had a different path for us. We were dropped off at the train station in the small town of Assen and we waited there with our scruffy rucksacks, looking haggard and malnourished, and stinking strongly of cheap disinfectant. My wife, who had just suffered from severe angina, was so exhausted that she could barely drag herself along. She could not cope with the people around us gawking at us (a mixture of concealed compassion on the part of the Dutch citizens and cold hatred from the Nazis) and she had a breakdown. She desperately wanted to go back to the concentration camp. It took a great deal of effort to eventually manage to push her onto the train that had just arrived.

Where on earth were we supposed to head in Amsterdam now?! We were afraid that if we tried to hide with close friends straight away, "they" would put some of our fellow sufferers in Westerbork on the transport out of revenge. So we tackled the complicated and dangerous web involved in officially reporting back to the SA doctor and Nazi authorities, before "going underground" with some Swiss friends of ours.

The sterilisation was due to start three days later, with four Jewish women having been booked in for the first day and everything having already been prepared at the hospital. That morning, at 08:00 on the dot, the SA Senior Doctor arrived with his team, ready to attend the first sterilisation. Everyone was just waiting for the surgeon – but I had disappeared off the face of the earth.

After waiting a while, they sent someone over to the address we had provided and the woman there said (as agreed!) that we had not come back for the past two days. She told them that we had just left a note thanking her for the one night that had allowed us to sleep in a bed together again and that, after reading the letter, she had assumed that we must have both done something to ourselves. In actual fact, that woman (Ms. von Sassen) really didn't know where we had managed to find refuge (with great difficulty and effort).

The "Sturmbannführer" Dr Meyer was furious! The sterilisation planned as a tragedy ended up being a great comedy in that it was an absolute sham, which any decent Dutch citizen would have secretly found amusing.

But, of course, an offshoot of this was our persecution, which started as our pictures were flagged up and the Gestapo began their search for us.

Artificial Insemination

[117] *Eyewitness account by Jiri Beranovska entitled 'Testimony in the Criminal Proceedings against the late Prof. Carl Clauberg'.*

The witness was duly informed of his right to refuse to testify under Section 108 of the Penal Code and of the importance of a testimony from the point of view of the general interest and the consequences of a false statement under Section 109 of the Penal Code; as well as the possibility of a correction of the record in accordance with his statement under Section 112 of the Penal Code.

One day in March 1941 I arrived as a prisoner in the Auschwitz concentration camp. I worked in various groups and went into the "Department for Installations" in 1943. As a result of this I had freedom of movement and free access throughout the camp because there were installations everywhere and from time to time repairs were needed everywhere. I also had access to the quarters of the SS, and even to the private apartments of the SS officers. As I naturally also had access to the rooms where medical experiments were carried out, I had the opportunity to observe the experiments using X-ray which were performed on men and women by Dr. Schumann in Block No.25 in Auschwitz-Birkenau. After I had recovered from catching typhoid fever, I discovered that the experiments were now taking place in Block No.10 in Auschwitz, right in the central camp. Once again, I and the

---

[117] Eyewitness account by Jiri Beranovska entitled 'Testimony in the Criminal Proceedings against the late Prof. Carl Clauberg'.
https://www.testifyingtothetruth.co.uk/viewer/metadata/105983/1/
Reproduced by permission of the Wiener Holocaust Library.

other members of the "Department for Installations" were able to go anywhere we were needed. In 1944 I was transferred to Birkenau camp. As before, during the course of my work I went to every corner of the camp.

In my view, Block No.25, where Dr. Schumann did his experiments, would normally be able to hold around twenty women. A certain number of women, whose ovaries had been X-rayed for the experiments, were returned to the work groups in the camp after several experiments, and to be honest usually in such a condition that they very quickly lost the capacity to work and as a result were sent to the gas chambers. A given number of women remained in Block No.25, however, for longer experiments.

I met Sylvia Friedmann who worked as a nurse in this Block at that time. I had the opportunity to verify for myself that these experiments were actually being carried out in that Block. X-ray equipment particularly requires permanent water-cooling. We of the "Department for Installations", including me, had carried out the water installation, but we did so in such a way as to cause as many problems as possible during the X-ray sessions. Problems were caused by freezing for example and in other cases when groups of women or men had already been prepared for the experiments and we then had to be called in order to fix the water installation of the X-ray apparatus. This way we were able to see for ourselves the preparations involved in these experiments.

After my recovery from typhoid fever, I participated in the installation work in Block No.10 and therefore also saw the organisation and preparation of the operating theatre in that Block. I knew the Polish doctor Dr Döring who later defected to the Germans. Initially he was a prisoner in Auschwitz, later, in 1944, he was freed as a result of joining the Germans. This doctor, who I got to know, had not sent me to be cared for in the Block for epidemic typhus when I had typhoid - this was because in this Block the prisoners were not cared for at all, but were assembled for onward transport to the gas chambers. I then learned from this doctor that in Block No.10 experiments were to be carried out on humans. I also met Dr. Clauberg during this preparation period in Block No.10. We knew Dr. Clauberg personally, knew his name, and I was able to observe that he was in charge of the preparations for these experiments. In Block No.10 the windows [were] boarded up with wood so that you could see neither out of the Block nor into the Block. There was only a narrow strip of window visible at the top. In this way, the Block was cut off from the rest of the camp, also from the courtyard between Blocks 10 and 11. This block held the prisoners who had been sentenced to death by the camp Gestapo. They were also executed in this courtyard. Block No.10 was also kept locked and was only opened when a bell was rung. Only Dr. Clauberg and Dr Döring had access to this Block. Apart from them, we workmen were able to get inside in order to carry out necessary repairs, but were always accompanied by the SS. Neither the nurses nor the women on whom the experiments were conducted were allowed to leave the Block, unless it was to fetch food - and when they did this they were accompanied by the SS both on the way out and the way back.

I would like to stress that the women on whom the experiments were performed here had had all freedom of movement outside their Block removed. At no point did they go to the so-called roll-call in which all other prisoners in the concentration camp had to participate in order to be counted. This was to enable [the] camp administrators to check whether any of the prisoners had been moved or whether something else had happened to them, in other words to check whether the situation on the ground corresponded to the concentration camp records.

Dr. Clauberg carried out his first operations with the help of Dr Döring in Block No.20, opposite Block No.10, before the latter's operating room was ready. The operations involved removing one ovary from one group of women and both ovaries from another group. Artificial insemination experiments were also performed. The experiments had a dreadful effect on the women which I was able to see for myself - it was enough for Dr. Clauberg or an assistant just to walk into the Block: the women intended for the experiments immediately started crying and screaming terribly. It was clear to see how frightened they were of the experiments. After these experiments, which Dr. Clauberg performed, some women went into a decline, I know that others died after them. I can't give you a figure as to how many because the bodies were removed during the night and taken over to the crematorium. The block contained between four hundred and six hundred women. In Block No.10 there were already long-term experiments going on and the women were not replaced, but a fixed group of a greater number of women was retained for long-term experiments. Proof that the concentration camp administrators very much wanted to keep these experiments secret can been seen in the fact that even when the whole camp was evacuated, the women from Block No.10 were kept isolated from all the other prisoners. I know that when the camp was liquidated there were only around 150 women in Block No.10, which means that the others had been taken away as corpses. As I have already mentioned, the bodies were always taken away at night so I never directly witnessed the removal of the dead. I can't say for certain whether any other experiments were conducted in Block No.10. I am also not in a position to know whether women from this block were taken back to Birkenau to be gassed after the experiments. If I go by the rumours which circulated round the camp, however, I could not rule out that this happened in some cases.

From what I've been told, Sylvia Friedman, Eta Gutman and Katarina Singer can provide you with the most accurate picture. They were in direct contact with Dr Clauberg's work.

Read, approved, signed.

Seawater

[118]*Transcript for NMT 1: Medical Case – Page 34 - 35*

[118] Harvard Law School Library. Nuremberg Trials Project: A Digital Document Collection, https://nuremberg.law.harvard.edu. Accessed 4 November 2022

For the seawater experiments we return to Dachau. They were conducted in 1944 at the behest of the German Air Force and the German Navy in order to develop a method of rendering seawater drinkable.

Meetings to discuss this problem were held in May 1944, attended by representatives of the Luftwaffe, the Navy, and I.G. Farben. The defendants Becker-Freyseng and Schaefer were among the participants. It was agreed to conduct a series of experiments in which the subjects, fed only with ship-wreck emergency rations, would be divided into four groups. One group would receive no water at all; the second would drink ordinary seawater; the third would drink seawater processed by the so called "Berka" method, which concealed the taste but did not alter the saline content; the fourth would drink seawater treated so as to remove the salt.

Since it was expected that the subjects would die, or, at least, suffer severe impairment of health, it was decided at the meeting in May 1944 that only persons furnished by Himmler could be used. Thereafter in June 1944 the defendant Schroeder set the program in motion by writing to Himmler and I quote form his letter:

"Earlier you made it possible for the Luftwaffe to settle urgent medical matters through experiments on human beings. Today I again stand before a decision, which, after numerous experiments on animals and also on voluntary human subjects, demands final resolution: The Luftwaffe has simultaneously developed two methods for making seawater drinkable. The one method, developed by a Medical Officer, removes the salt from the seawater and transforms it into real drinking water; the second method, suggested by an engineer, only removes the unpleasant taste from the seawater. The latter method, in contrast to the first, requires no critical raw material. From the medical point of view this method must be viewed critically, as the administration of concentrated salt solutions can produce severe symptoms of poisoning.

"As the experiments on human beings could thus far only be carried out for a period of four days, and as practical demands require

a remedy for those who are in distress at sea up to 12 days, appropriate experiments are necessary.

"Required are 40 healthy test subjects, who must be available for 4 whole weeks. As it is known from previous experiments, that necessary laboratories exist in the concentration camp Dachau, this camp would be very suitable.

"Due to the enormous importance which a solution of this question has for soldiers of the Luftwaffe and Navy who have become shipwrecked, I would be [greatly] obliged to you, my dear Reich Minister, if you would decide to comply with my request."

Himmler passed this letter to Grawitz who consulted Gebhardt and other SS officials. A typical and nauseating Nazi discussion of racial question ensued.

One SS man suggested using quarantined prisoners and Jews; another suggested Gypsies. Grawitz doubted that experiments on Gypsies would yield results which were scientifically applicable to Germans. Himmler finally directed that Gypsies be used with three others as a check.

The tests were actually begun in July 1944. The defendant Beiglbeck supervised the experiments, in the course of which the Gypsy subjects underwent terrible suffering, became delirious or developed convulsions, and some died.

Euthanasia

[119]*Letter from chief of institution for feeble-minded in Stetten to Reich Minister of justice Dr Frank, September 6 1940.*

---

[119] Dunn, M. D. (Ed.). (95, April 25). Remember.org - The Holocaust History - A People's and Survivors' History. Retrieved February 28, 2022, from remember.org

[ToWC, Vol. I, p. 854]

Dear Reich Minister,

The measure being taken at present with mental patients of all kinds have caused a complete lack of confidence in justice among large groups of people. Without the consent of relatives and guardians, such patients are being transferred to different institutions.

After a short time they are notified that the person concerned has died of some disease...If the state really wants to carry out the extermination of these or at least of some mental patients, shouldn't a law be promulgated, which can be justified before the people – a law that would give everyone the assurance of careful examination as to whether he is due to die or entitled to live and which would also give the relatives a chance to be heard, in a similar way, as provided by the law for the prevention of Hereditarily affected Progeny?

Letter from *[Reichsführer]-SS* Himmler to *SS-[Oberführer]* Brack, 19 December 1940.

[ToWC, Vol. I, p. 856]

Dear Brack,

I hear there is great excitement on the Alb because of the Grafeneck Institution. The population recognizes the gray automobiles of the SS and think they know what is going on at the constantly smoking crematory. What happens there is a secret and yet is no longer one.

Thus the worst feeling has arisen there, and in my opinion there remains only one thing, to discontinue the use of the institution in this place and in any event disseminate information in a clever and sensible manner by showing motion pictures on the subject of inherited and mental diseases in just that locality. May I ask for a report as to how the difficult problem is solved?

Nameless Testimony

[120]*Ms. M, Age 73*

Place of Persecution: Auschwitz - Dates: June 1944 – May 1945.

"I suffered immense pain and cruelty from the experiments. They were inhuman, but because of them I survived. As bad as the experiments were without them I would not be here today to write this ... Now that I am emotionally a lot stronger I would like to describe a little more details about my horrible experiments which no matter how hard I am trying I never get over it as long as I live. I was born November 23, 1930. I was about five weeks in Auschwitz alone, separated from my family, my parents, two sisters and two brothers when Dr. Mengele pulled me out of a queue as we were on the way from the c-lager [camp] to the gas chamber. I was the only one picked that day personally by Mengele and his assistant. They took me to his [laboratory], where I met other children. They were screaming from pain. Black and blue bodies covered with blood. I collapsed from horror and terror and fainted. A bucket of cold water was thrown on me to revive me. As soon as I stood up I was whipped with a leather whip which broke my flesh, then I was told the whipping was a sample of what I would receive if I did not follow instructions and orders. I was used as a guinea pig for medical experiments. I was never ever given painkillers or [anaesthetics]. Every day I suffered excruciating pain. I was injected with drugs and chemicals. My body most of the time was connected to tubes which inserted some drugs in to my body. Many days I was tied up for hours. Some days they made cuts in to my body and left the wounds open for them to study. Most of the time there nothing to eat. Every day my body was numb with pain. There was no

---

[120] Personal Statements From Victims of Nazi Medical Experiments
https://www.claimscon.org/about/history/closed-programs/medical-experiments/personal-statements-from-victims/

more skin left on my body for them to put injections or tubes ... One day we woke up and the place was empty. We were left with open infected wounds and no food. We all were half dead with no energy or life left in us. [One] day ... Russian soldiers tried to shake me to see if I was [alive] or dead. They felt a tiny beat in my heart and quickly picked me up and took me to a hospital."

The archives are full of accounts like the ones you have read, and I am sure many more stories have not been recorded. Yet here we are, trying to process what we have heard from the mouth of eyewitnesses and Nuremberg trial information.

Unlike the previous historical transition, the discoveries are catapulted into the public domain during this specific period. It is here that we witness an embracing of the darkness to achieve advancement for a nation at the expense of everything and everyone else. It is here that the victims become incidental when the goal is world domination.

Staying true to its core values, the followers of this global religion dedicate themselves to advancement at any cost. This blind determination resulted in an explosion that affected everyone, directly and indirectly setting the tone for generations to come, opening new frontiers while actively destroying the very fabric which kept this world safe.

Unlike in the past, for the first time in modern history, the followers of social Darwinism and social eugenics had the tools to implement social changes through the intervention and application of technology. Physical tools which placed the power of change in the hands of the descendants of Cain who were determined to rise above the boundaries of humanity's limitations in complete defiance of the One who made them. Who could have guessed that the theory of evolution would lead to eugenics and that eugenics would lead to the final solution? Who could have envisaged the continued, ongoing exploitation and murder of the innocent Abels? Thankfully, Yeshua did and

He continues to observe our choices waiting for the appointed day to say categorically and finally, it is enough.

Interwoven into the timeframe of these harrowing accounts and events are the stories of people who were behind the scenes assisting the world's transition into a new era. An era that embraced all the tenets of the past religion but wholeheartedly embraced the new brand of human genetics. With this drive came a new voice and new opportunities to change the way that society at large thought and behaved. Through 'Dark intel' and the drive to implement 'god tech' their beliefs would eventually become mainstream, gaining popularity in the secular and religious world. A bridge between the old and new voices would be formed creating a collection of soundbites that would generate a very powerful movement, breaking through all of the usual barriers, modernising itself in a way that placed it in virtually every home across the nations.

So, who were the voices that carried on the age-old tradition of the religion's predecessors? What kind of people were capable of connecting the old voices and bringing them into the 21st century without massive public resistance? To answer these and other questions we are required to apply the same mode of exploration to the final phases of this journey. Beginning with the next generation of inventions and inventors.

To give you some idea of the other inventions developed during this period here are some examples, beginning with the less ominous.

Wehrmacht-Einheitskanister – (The Jerry Can)

Designed in Germany in 1937 by Müller Engineering, using the designs of their chief engineer Vinzenz Grünvogel.

The Third Reich (like other nations) realised that the transportation of fuel was easily achieved by tankers, pipelines and the like. However, they also realised that their troops had to be fast-moving, making the issue of getting fuel to troops quickly pivotal to success. No one had created a reliable method for transporting smaller quantities to the troops quickly. To resolve this problem the Third Reich's weapons office sent out a tender for a fuel container. The design criteria were:

- It had to be light.
- A soldier should be able to carry two full cans or four empty ones.
- It had to be easy to store and must retain the liquid inside.

The final design outstripped anything that was being used by other countries. It had three handles which made it comfortable to carry for an individual (two or four at a time) but also made it easy to pass down the line from soldier to soldier. It was constructed from two pieces of steel with one weld down the middle creating a unit which was robust and less likely to leak. The form of the jerrycan allowed for a pocket of air inside enabling it to be used in water as a buoyant object if the need should arise. Its notable indentations on the sides allow the container to expand or contract without splitting the container and therefore, retain its function in hot or cold climates. The list of product design benefits goes on and on. Yet it was the war that was the inspiration behind its development.

Stainless Steel

Leading up to world war one, the British military had alighted upon a recurring problem with their guns due to the wear of the inside of the barrels after repetitive use. In 1913, Harry Brearley is said to have been the first to develop 'stainless' steel which was created by adding chromium to steel. The introduction of this new metal transformed the metallurgy[121] world.

Sheffield was known for its armament production from the latter part of the 19th century to the early part of the 20th century. This included the export of stainless steel to other parts of the world such as the US, Canada, and Japan.

The Zipper
U.S. Patent No. 1,219,881

Gideon Sundback, a Swedish immigrant to the US was brought in by Whitcomb Judson to resolve a reliability problem for a shoe latch that he had created. A latch that was based on a patent of 1851 by Elias Howe for an automatic continuous clothing closure. Whitcomb Judson set up the 'Universal Fastener Company' and Sundback became its head designer.

Sundback succeeded in creating a zipper and completed the machinery and process for its production, going on to manufacture zippers for the US military. They added the zipper to the clothes and boots for their forces, however, as with most inventions during this timeframe, the zipper was embraced and added to a variety of civilian wear.

The Atomic Bomb

---

[121] **Metallurgy**, Art and science of extracting metals from their ores and modifying the metals for use. Metallurgy usually refers to commercial rather than laboratory methods. It also concerns the chemical, physical, and atomic properties and structures of metals and the principles by which metals are combined to form alloys.

Reinvigorated by a desire to remain in front, each nation promoted its agenda in the belief that there can only be one superpower on the face of the Earth. Notwithstanding, the legacy of trial and error of recent history would not abate the thirst for the role of the supreme ruler of the world and the universe. There was nothing that would abate striving for its ancestral dream of becoming gods, not even the loss of innocent lives. Tragically, this race for greatness brought with it the threat of global dominance by the tenets of the Nazi regime which was itself rooted in the spirituality of ancient mysticism, reborn through the seed of evolution which then matured into eugenics and finally human genetics.

The threat of world dominance was real as Hitler harnessed technology (through research and development) and thrust it into the public domain through cult like propaganda (spirituality). The combination of both opened the way to creating weapons of mass destruction in a condensed period. One of those inventions was the atomic bomb. It has come to light in recent years that Nazi Germany was close to creating the world's first super weapon and had they succeeded, world history would have been rewritten to reflect the storyline of a dystopian novel. Yet on the 28th December 1942, President Roosevelt approved the formation of the Manhattan Project to create a collaboration between scientists to advance the research on the atomic bomb. The scientists were made up of homegrown US citizens but also scientists who escaped from the Nazi regime in Europe. The Manhattan Project was formed after the Japanese attack on Pearl Harbour on 7th December 1941, a surprise attack that triggered America's entry into World War II.

To head up this team of researchers a man called Robert Oppenheimer was selected by Lieutenant General Leslie Richard Groves Jr, who recognised Oppenheimer's acute mind and ability to rally people of various personalities and skills. Oppenheimer would later be filled with regret due to his involvement in the creation of a new type of weapon. Equally, he would be discarded by the institution that inaugurated him into this role due to his questioning concerns about the safety and regulation of such power.

With the goal set and the motivation to be the first, the Manhattan Project became a cohesive force of discovery and innovation. Although described as the father of the atomic bomb, Oppenheimer was part of a bigger plan, one which he later regretted along with Einstein, Leo Szilard, and others. The research development which was a culmination of all these minds and their findings before and during the Manhattan Project succeeded in producing and testing the first atomic bomb. On July 16, 1945, the first atomic bomb was detonated in the desert of Alamogordo, Mexico and became what we know as the Trinity Test.

On 6th August 1945, the same year, President Harry Truman gave the order to drop the atomic bomb on Hiroshima and to do the same again on the 9th of August on Nagasaki. On the 14th of August Japan surrendered, marking the end of the Second World War.

The most powerful weapon of mass destruction ever created was deployed immediately killing approx. [122]140,000 people in Hiroshima and 74,000 in Nagasaki, not to mention the thousands that would die later.

It is here that we witness the outworking of humanity's handiwork moulded by the hands of self-determination and self-gratification. Decades of news articles, scientific papers, and human experimentation, immersed in various forms of spirituality, exploitation and misinformation culminating in a vision of the future that is still unfolding in our lifetime. No longer historical events but daily reminders of the present future

[122] (These numbers vary between sources)

accompanied by the increasing volume of humanistic religiosity. Still, the cries of the suffering are drowned out by the deafening noise of hypocrisy. The kind that uses racial laws, racial politics, psychology, psychiatry, mental testing, psychometric testing, education, economics, genetics, and racial health to further its goal. In each cataclysmic, historical event we get a glimpse of the hidden desire which rages in the heart of man, indicators of a desire that will always look beyond wealth and global dominance, a desire that repeatedly reminds us that the world isn't enough.

Within a decade this insatiable appetite has been the vehicle for all manner of things, which will eventually be brought together to conclude a longstanding question. Who will be God?

New Eugenics, The Final Solution

Then the governor said, "Why, what evil has He done?" But they cried out all the more, saying, "Let Him be crucified!"

'When Pilate saw that he could not prevail at all, but rather that a tumult was rising, he took water and washed his hands before the multitude, saying, "I am innocent of the blood of this just Person. You see to it."

Matthew 27:23-25 (NKJV)

Materials Revisited

Our observations are now directed at the new shoots and old roots of this weathered, ancient tree. Supported by a growing, ambiguous, and complex root system, purposed to accomplish its work of providing a groundswell of philosophical sustenance to its parasitic trunk, while breaking through the desecrated soil in which it had been entombed. Above ground, the towering branches and immovable, aged stem bask in its grandeur impersonating the 'Tree of Life'; offering food for anyone who passes its abundant branches ladened down by the weight of its hapless fruit. It cannot be denied, its form is beautiful to behold, but to the discerning, its true character is plain to see.

Spiritual Roots from Another Era

[123] *A culture is a particular society or civilization, especially considered in relation to its beliefs, way of life, or art*

In the 20th century, there were simply thousands of inventions released into the public domain, their point of origin tracing back to the global conflicts of WWI and WWII from 1914 to 1945. One of the exceptions happened in 1928 when Alexander Fleming accidentally discovered penicillin due to a fungus that grew in a discarded Petri dish. The fungus (penicillin) later became a widely used antibiotic that saved millions of lives. Following penicillin's initial discovery, the people involved in its further development included Dr Florey, his employee biochemist Dr Ernst Chain and Dr Heatley, who

---

[123] Collins COBUILD Advanced Learner's Dictionary.

was also a biochemist. Dr Florey discovered Alexander Fleming's paper on the subject and worked with his colleagues at developing the medicine with a small amount of UK funding. Their first volunteer was Albert Alexander, a 43-year-old policeman who began to recover after being administered the drug. Unfortunately, their supply ran out after five days and they struggled to reproduce sufficient amounts of penicillin to treat Alexander, who later died. However, having demonstrated that the medicine worked without harm to the patient, Howard Florey managed to obtain America's support in the upscaling of manufacture for the drug at a time when WWII was in desperate need of such medicine for the wounded. Without WWII and the intervention of America, the medicine may not have been accessible to large numbers of personnel during the Second World War and would not have gone down in history as the medicine that changed the world. This noble accolade cannot be applied to some of its counterparts or its relative inventions. However, it would be incorrect to assume that mechanical or technological inventions for a physical war were the only type of inventions during this period. In complete unison with these inventions and developments during and after the war (as with any other timeframe) the battle for the mind gained equal momentum and fervour. The observation of the millions of people decimated by the world wars, ideologies, philosophies, and resultant economic displacement reveals this. The fatherless children, the dislodged and broken families, and a traumatised and lost generation searching for the meaning of life.

With all the national pride that each country paraded through their media channels and on the streets, the fallout from these wars was a generation of disillusioned young men and women that would come of age. This generation is labelled the 'Baby Boomers', children born from 1946 to 1964 who seemed to burst onto the global scene like an explosion, disrupting its equilibrium. Millions of young adults rebelled against the status quo while in many cases pursuing personal expression, consciousness, and peace through various forms of spirituality and ritual cleansings, following the lead of a new type of thinker. As a generality, this generation accumulated a net worth which surpassed other generations. At the time of writing this book the 'baby boomers' would be in their 70s or probably just coming to the end of their working life. Here is a chart that provides a visual graphic of the baby boomer generation's position related to war and the crossing over of other generations. If what we are told is true, the 'baby boomers' are the second largest age group behind their children, 'the millennials'.

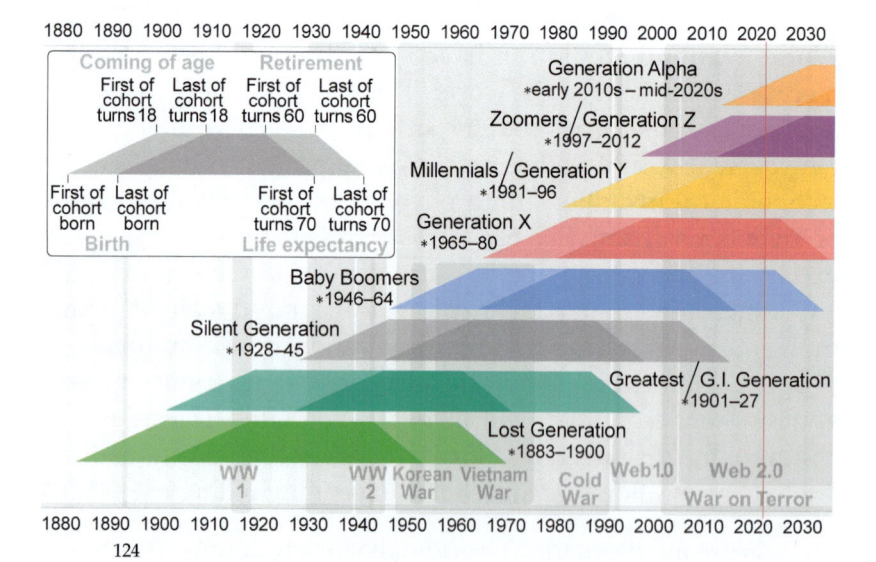

The 'baby boomers' set the tone for the next generation and the generations to follow, fixed on their goal of self-determination but determined to prove that humanity had the

[124] Cmglee, CC BY-SA 4.0 https://creativecommons.org/licenses/by-sa/4.0, via Wikimedia Commons

answer hidden within. All it required was more research, more education and more mind-bending enlightenment. Really?

The birth of a new culture was in progress, a movement that would choose its own leaders, its own voices, its self-gratifying means of expression and lifestyle. A lifestyle that would generationally throw off the restrictions of the past authoritative figures, be they governments or parents. However, the influences of the world wars would not be absent from their experience as they would be exposed to the popular forms of psychiatry such as psychoanalysis [125](popular in the US at the time). The emotional fallout from WWII would also lead to the rise of the Freudian movement which collectively paved the way for the unexpected mind experience of the 1960s, progressing to the mystical 'Age of Aquarius' in the 1970s that would usher in a New Age movement forever changing the social landscape of the world, including the faith community. But, have we missed a vital piece of information in this historical chain of events? Maybe...

The First [126]Hippie Colony - Monte Verità (Mountain of Truth?)

---

[125] **psy·cho·analy·sis** [ˌsʌɪkəʊəˈnalɪsɪs] Noun: a system of psychological theory and therapy that aims to treat mental conditions by investigating the interaction of conscious and unconscious elements in the mind and bringing repressed fears and conflicts into the conscious mind by techniques such as dream interpretation and free association. synonyms: psychotherapy, analysis

[126] **hippie**, also spelled **hippy**, member, during the 1960s and 1970s, of a countercultural movement that rejected the mores of mainstream American life. The movement originated on college campuses in the United States,

Before the 1900s Lake Maggiore, where Monte Verità is located, became an appealing location to intellectuals from various countries. The southern Swiss town of Locarno being the region that attracted foreign nationals who secured residencies turning it into a popular location for all types of anarchists, revolutionaries, theosophists, artists, writers, and various other characters. This settlement happened over time, paving the way for a later addition of the Monte Verità settlement project.

In 1889 the politician and theosophist Alfredo Pioda, Franz Hartmann, and Countess Constance Wachtmeister were planning to build a [127]Theosophist Monastery called "Fraternitas" which did not happen. However, this isn't where the story ends.

In 1986 a book was published by Martin Green entitled *'Mountain of Truth: The Counterculture Begins, Ascona, 1900-1920'*.

although it spread to other countries, including Canada and Britain. The name derived from "hip," a term applied to the Beats of the 1950s, such as Allen Ginsberg and Jack Kerouac, who were generally considered to be the precursors of hippies. Although the movement arose in part as opposition to U.S. involvement in the Vietnam War (1955–75), hippies were often not directly engaged in politics, as opposed to their activist counterparts known as "Yippies" (Youth International Party). Britannica, The Editors of Encyclopaedia. "hippie". Encyclopedia Britannica, 19 Oct. 2022, https://www.britannica.com/topic/hippie. Accessed 4 February 2023.
[127] **Occult movement originating in the 19th century with roots that can be traced to ancient Gnosticism and Neoplatonism.** The term theosophy, derived from the Greek theos ("god") and sophia ("wisdom"), is generally understood to mean "divine wisdom." Forms of this doctrine were held in antiquity by the Manichaeans, an Iranian dualist sect, and in the Middle Ages by two groups of dualist heretics, the Bogomils in Bulgaria and the Byzantine Empire and the Cathari in southern France and Italy. In modern times, theosophical views have been held by Rosicrucians and by speculative Freemasons. **The international New Age movement of the 1970s and '80s originated among independent theosophical groups in the United Kingdom.** Melton, J. Gordon. "theosophy". Encyclopedia Britannica, 30 Dec. 2022, https://www.britannica.com/topic/theosophy. Accessed 29 January 2023.

He directs our attention to Ascona, a municipality in the district of Locarno in the canton of Ticino in Switzerland. In the introduction of his book, Green makes what seems to be a 'matter of fact' statement almost as though he were writing a novel. He says,

"*This is the story of Ascona, a small Swiss-lake village, at the beginning of this century, where some remarkable people came together, and some remarkable ideas were developed, and some remarkable life-experiments were attempted...*"

So, okay, some remarkable people, ideas and life experiments were attempted in Ascona, but this isn't unusual as this could be said about thousands of places. What is the significance of Ascona? He continues,

"*The feminism, pacifism, and psychoanalysis we now know all took an imprint from these people. So did Dada, Surrealism, Modern Dance, and much modern fiction. Some of the famous names involved are Hermann Hesse, D. H. Lawrence, Franz Kafka, Isadora Duncan, Rudolf Laban, Carl Gustav Jung; but there are also other, newer names, which deserve fame.*"

Now, wait a minute. Did he just mention the name, DH Lawrence? The writer that said,

"*If I had my way, I would build a lethal chamber as big as the Crystal Palace, with a military band playing softly, and a Cinematograph working brightly; then I'd go out in the back streets and main streets and bring them in, all the sick, the halt, and the maimed; I would lead them gently, and they would smile me a weary thanks; and the band would softly bubble out the 'Hallelujah Chorus'.*"

You've got my attention, tell me more. He continues,

"*At the end of the nineteenth century, intellectual Europe became preoccupied with the problem of its own unhappiness, malaise, or to use Freud's word, 'Unbehagen'. The favorites of this rich and powerful civilization the economically and educationally privileged, the most intelligent and imaginative felt themselves to be more unhappy than more primitive peoples. The people who most felt the crisis were the Germans, the inhabitants of Germany, but also the speakers of German all over Europe who were moving faster than other peoples to grasp the glittering prizes of progress."*

Not only does the narrative of people like DH Lawrence make a regular appearance in the most unusual places but what seem to be disconnected incidents gradually reveal the complete opposite.

Green builds on this picture of unhappiness amongst the intellectuals and economically privileged describing an environment which mirrors the emotions of the 1960s. This search for happiness led to the formation of a retreat in Ascona called 'Monte Verità (Mountain of Truth)'. For some, the only way to address the issues facing modern civilisation was to withdraw from it and establish a [128]monastic way of living, in reality, a form of rebellion was emerging and with it the rebellious representatives of future societal professions. Monte Verità was such a place, starting as a sanatorium of sorts embracing nudism, vegetarianism (vegan nutrition), sustainability, sexual reform, religious reform, sun-worship and alternative lifestyles. The 'earth culture' or 'earth religion' was central to Monte Verità, long before its use as a holiday resort for golf players and the like. Converging on this place with its long-standing history of paganism and ritual sites, it was here that the modern counter-culture and Lebensreform ("life-reform") was born.

---

[128] Monasticism, also referred to as monachism, or monkhood, is a religious way of life in which one renounces worldly pursuits to devote oneself fully to spiritual work. https://en.wikipedia.org/wiki/Monasticism

From 1900 to 1920, as Green points out, Monte Verità became the centre of cultural operations that changed all aspects of the creative and political world of thought. During this period and on into the modern 21st century the influence of the arts, politics, medicine, and many other areas in all their spiritual forms were impacted by the experiences of individuals that visited here bringing into reality the vision of Julian Huxley in his UNESCO manifesto. The root system would now be revealed in its full religious form, unashamedly promoting its new expression through an immersion of occult knowledge. Could this be an exaggeration? Theodor Reuss didn't think so when he set up the "Anational Grand Lodge and Mystic Temple" of [129]O.T.O. (Ordo Templi Orientis) and the Hermetic Brotherhood of Light headquarters in the Swiss village of Monte Verità. So who was Theodor Reuss? He was the head of the Ordo Templi Orientis (a new form of Freemasonry) who travelled to Monte Verità through the sponsorship of Henri Oedenkoven and Ida Hofmann, founders of Monte Verità. On August 15-25, 1917 at Monte Verità he held a conference for the O.T.O. It was called,

---

[129] A ritual magic organization founded in Germany around 1904. The order found its inspiration in the medieval Knights Templar, who were suppressed through most of Europe in the fourteenth century. Among the charges made against the order were that they practiced various forms of illicit sex, specifically sodomy and bestiality. Through the nineteenth century a number of groups had emerged in both France and Germany claiming to carry on the Templar tradition. However, this order seems to have originated out of a Masonic group founded by Karl Keller and Theodor Reuss and chartered in 1902 by English Mason John Yarker. They began publishing a magazine, Oriflamme, in which the first mention of the OTO occurred. There was mention that the order possessed the key of all hermetic and Masonic secrets (i.e., sex magic).
"Ordo Templi Orientis (OTO)." Encyclopedia of Occultism and Parapsychology. . Encyclopedia.com. 16 Jan. 2023
<https://www.encyclopedia.com>.

"Anational Congress for Organizing the Reconstruction of Society on Practical Cooperative Lines"

The manifesto is clear in its intention to regroup and set right the world under the banner of the Hermetic Brotherhood of Light by inviting men and women from all nations to join its ranks in changing a war-torn world. How? Well as he puts it in the manifesto,

"The peoples must be reminded and brought to realize that mankind as a whole, has, and can have but one aim which is the advancement of Humanity itself..."

He continues,

"This may be achieved by establishing Brotherhood Colonies on cooperative bases all over the world, aside from all capitalist societies and enterprises.

New ethics, a new religion, a new social order based on the principle of cooperation of All, and on the common possession of the soil and the means of production by All and on true freedom (under strictest self) control in all must become the guiding lights and landmarks of these new colonies and settlements.

There should be no more waiting until the mass of the peoples might be ready to accept this form of society."

Now before we are tempted to cry conspiracy theory again, we must understand that these individuals are part of a religious movement which is the occult. These are not people of fiction whose characters and intentions are works of fantasy; they believe what they are doing. In the manifesto booklet, there is an open invitation to Masons of all denominations, Theosophists, Mystics and members of the O.T.O. to be part of this meeting to freely enjoy the lectures, 'services', and not to forget, a *'representation of Aleister Crowley's Mystic Poem ...The Ship'.*

Once again, the name Aleister Crowley appears and four years later Aleister Crowley became the successor to Theodor Reuss as the Outer Head of the order.

It may cause you to raise an eyebrow or two if you were to know their names, so here is a sample:

Alexej von Jawlensky: A Russian expressionist artist who was expelled from Germany in 1914.

Arthur Segal

August Bebel

Carl Gustav Jung: Psychologist.

DH Lawrence: Writer, poet.

Else Lasker-Schüler

El Lissitzky

Erich Mühsam, who declared Ascona "the Republic of the Homeless"

Franz Kafka

Franziska Gräfin zu Reventlow

Hans Arp (better known as Jean Arp): German sculptor, abstract artist, Dadaist and poet.

Hans Richter

Hugo Ball

Hermann Hesse

Isadora Duncan: American dancer, considered one of the greatest influences on modern dance. Her free form, which excluded the use of pointe shoes and tutus, drew its influence from various sources including the clothing styles of Greece. She is said to have held a summer school at Monte Verità every year from 1913-1918.

Karl Kautsky: German philosopher, politician, economist and theoretician of Marxism.

Marianne von Werefkin: Russian painter who is considered to be the most significant of expressionist artists.

Mary Wigman: German dancer and choreographer, who studied 'the eurhythmics of Émile Jaques-Dalcroze' in his school in Hellerau. She is described as an expressionist dance therapist who moved to Monte Verità as a pupil of Rudolf von Laban.

Her solo performance, the Dance of the Witch (Hexentanz), became her signature and she is considered to be a pioneer of free and modern dance (without Pointe shoes).

Otto Braun: German politician and a leading member of the Weimar Republic.

Lenin

Trotsky

Otto Gross: Planned a "School for the liberation of humanity" and was also a student of Freud. He also influenced Carl Jung.

Rudolf von Laban: Hungarian choreographer and dancer whose teachings on dance sit at the root of modern dance and including classical ballet. He is the inventor of 'labanotation' a method of notation of movement.

Prince Peter Kropotkin: Russian anarchist, and revolutionary of noble birth. In 1874 he was arrested and imprisoned in the Peter and Paul Fortress for subversive political activity but in 1876 was moved to St Petersburg where he managed to escape. Noted in Martin Green's book as a visitor to Ascona, *(Mountain of Truth: The Counterculture Begins, Ascona, 1900-1920, pp. 2, 3).*

"The anarchist Kropotkin, a spokesman for these enthusiasts, said in his 1880 pamphlet Spirit of Revolt:

There are periods of human society when revolution becomes an imperative necessity, when it proclaims itself an inevitable. . . . The need for a new life becomes apparent. The code of established morality, that which governs the greater number of people in their daily life, no longer seems sufficient. . . . those who long for the triumph of justice . . . perceive the necessity of a revolutionary whirlwind which will sweep away all this rottenness, revive sluggish hearts with its breath. . . . Weary of these wars, weary of the miseries which they cause, society rushes to seek a new organization.

And, as Roger Baldwin noted about Kropotkin, this change was not merely political but included "all social relations — marriage, education, the treatment of crime, the function of law, the basis of morality." Kropotkin was one of the people who came to Ascona in the period from 1900 to 1920."

Raphael Friedeberg: Anarchist doctor.

From Ascona to California

"California has been chosen as the cradle of the coming race, that race which shall fulfill for the world the idea not of competition but of cooperation, not of strife but of brotherly love, not of selfishness but of service. Here remote from the turmoil and tribulation which attends the bringing forth of the new age, fearless of famine and of cold, this land offers a broad bosom to mother the children of the future."

Southern California became the home to prominent individuals who had embraced the Ascona philosophy and who were in search of a new culture through the establishment of a global religion or movement.

Pasadena, California would also be the birthplace of NASA's Jet Propulsion Laboratory through the contributions of a young man by the name of Jack Parsons, and his friends. It would become the place that other recognisable figures would visit or migrate to, joining the millions who would be eager to be part of this new culture.

California was an important place in the minds of theosophists and has been influential throughout the globe. In New York in 1975, after the deaths of the founders Helena Blavatsky, Henry Steel Olcott and William Q Judge, the next generation of theosophists would turn their attention to establishing a presence in California. This was no accident, as they firmly believed that the next stage of human evolution would begin in this location. This is the reason for the founding of the Theosophical Society in southern California, they believed that theosophy would be the answer to civilisation as a whole.

Here is an observation from Richard Noll's book, *'The Jung Cult: Origins of a Charismatic Movement'*,

> [130]*"...during the period of Annie Besant's leadership following the death of Blavatsky in 1891, the Theosophical movement directly involved hundreds of thousands, if not peripherally millions, of individuals. Prominent among these were poets Lord Tennyson and W. B. Yeats; the young Mahatma Gandhi; the Goethe scholar, spiritualist medium, and founder (in 1913) of the rival occultist tradition Anthroposophy, Rudolph Steiner; and Thomas Edison, who was busy in the 1890s trying to invent a phonograph-like device to speak to the spirit world. (The Theosophical Society continues to thrive today, but with nowhere near the widespread cultural influence it wielded circa 1900).*

At the centre were the teachings of Helena Blavatsky, who believed in an evolutionary **'root race theory'**, a form of salvation that transitions the *'on earth race'* through seven stages of spiritual and physical evolution in a form of reincarnation. Blavatsky seems to combine the spiritual ascendence with a physical presence to describe the beginning and ultimate position of humans, concerning lost continents such as Atlantis.

1st root race - Astral/Etheric – (Did not have physical bodies)
2nd root race - Hyperboreans
3rd root race - Lemurians
4th root race - Atlanteans
5th root race - Aryans – Under development
6th root race - Yet to appear
7th root race - Final Stage - Yet to appear

At this juncture, it is also pointless dialoguing about the possible influence of such teachings on people such as Hitler, as it should be clear by now that one only has to connect

---

[130] 'The Jung Cult, Origins of a Charismatic Movement', page 65

themselves to a strand of this root system to potentially become infected by the whole. Hitler was no different from anyone else in this regard. Helena Blavatsky was simply one of many who ventured down a road of inner discovery to be enthused by a form of religion (occultism) that was and is the dark atmosphere of the world in which this ancient tree has gained an advantage over human souls. Rabbi Paul makes quite a strong statement about this kind of exploration and the proponents of this brand of religion in his letter to Timothy,

"Now the Spirit expressly says that in latter times some will depart from the faith, giving heed to deceiving spirits and doctrines of demons," I Timothy 4:1 (NKJV)

He was not careful in raising Timothy's awareness of such activity and makes this a point of warning on more than one occasion in other letters too.

So, in Helena Blavatsky's mind, and the minds of her followers, the answer to the world's problems and the ultimate destiny of humankind was not to be found in an external expansion but more of an internal one, a journey of looking within. As you may already realise, this seems to be a theme of all the connections within this network. Helena Blavatsky, like other prominent figures in this network, or should I say maze of individuals, refers to meeting with a spirit guide. In her case, she began her 'spiritual' journey at a very young age beginning with the discovery of her great-grandfather's library of occult books. Years later while in London, at the young age of 20, Helena had an encounter with someone she called Mahatma Morya, a Rajput initiate (*Mahatma is known as 'M' amongst theosophists and is credited with inspiring the founder of Theosophy*). It was this entity that told her the work that she would do but it also guided her with apparent 'Ancient Wisdom'. This wasn't the first time though, as she had earlier encounters with this entity from a child.

Why is this so important to know? What we know as the counterculture, which pervaded all industries with a new kind of lifestyle based on Ascona teaching and occult practices, is foundational to hippie modernism and the advent of self-worship and self-awareness in the 21st century. This could not have been possible without first having willing participants whose professions, emptiness and disillusionment brought them into every sphere of society with the dream of a utopia. Behind the human facades of dark intel would be the supplier of new thoughts, and new expressions necessary for the propelling of souls down the road of self-destruction, while leaning on the sharpened crutch of self-healing, self-love, free love, positive thinking, positive affirmation, name it and claim it, east meets west religious fusions and many other culturally approved practices. The world would never be the same again, driven along by the idea that man is yet to evolve further and there is a way that we can achieve the ultimate goal of the superiority of mind, position and global stature that humanity claims to deserve, beginning with how we think. Or at least that's what some believed.

Thankfully, and by divine edict, there was the counter to the counter-culture movement which has been extracted from its historical context, potentially robbing the world of the visible dynamism of an unseen yet ever present God. During the same period of hedonistic revellings of madmen, manifestations of God's love and mercy broke into the experience of the culture in the form of what we have labelled 'revivals'. However, these were not moves of God to establish a denominational super group, but the focus of these visitations was the saving of young and unborn souls during a period of world changing events at every level of society. Without this, millions would have been swept away in the arms of wars and spiritual deceptions that would leave the world bereft of the devastating, unrelenting appetite for sin. No, God through His Son responded to the need of humanity by inviting a new generation to the Genesis experience of the first humans. An invitation that didn't come without its dangers as each person would be privileged to meet and dine with their creator in open view of supernatural threats of devilish proportions instigated by the accuser of the creator and the created. Yet throughout the 20th century, California would witness a move that has been described as the Azusa Street Revival of 1906 onwards and even later in the form of The Jesus movement of the 1960s.

Not So Random Questions

Guess who made the following statements, and what was their profession?

A.   *"An end to the pretence, and lying hypocrisy of Christianity. An end to the servile virtues, and superstitious restrictions. An end to the slave morality. An end to prudery and shame, to guilt and sin, for these are of the only evil under the sun, that is fear. An end to all authority that is not based on courage and manhood, to the authority of lying priests, conniving judges, blackmailing police, and an end to the servile flattery and cajolery of minds, the coronations of mediocrities, the ascension of dolts."*

B.   *"The brain is the key, the brain is the source, the brain is God. Everything that humans do is neuroecology."*

C.   *"One does not become enlightened by imagining figures of light, but by making the darkness conscious. The latter procedure, however, is disagreeable and therefore not popular."*

D.   *A positive self image and healthy self esteem is based on approval, acceptance and recognition from others; but also upon actual accomplishments, achievements and success upon the realistic self confidence which ensues.*

Don't worry if you cannot guess, all will be revealed in this chapter.

The Kings of 'Pop' Culture

Aldous Huxley

[131]*"Despots have always found it necessary to supplement force by political or religious propaganda. In this sense the pen is mightier than the sword. But mightier than either the pen or the sword is the pill. In mental hospitals it has been found that chemical restraint is far more effective than strait jackets or psychiatry. The dictatorships of tomorrow will deprive men of their freedom, but will give them in exchange a happiness none the less real, as a subjective experience, for being chemically induced."*

English writer and philosopher Aldous Huxley was born in Godalming, Surrey on 26 July 1894 into the Huxley family. His father was Leonard Huxley, his brother was Julian Huxley, and his grandfather was Thomas Huxley (The Bulldog). Aldous is a curious character who in many ways is less charismatic than his counterparts such as Leary, yet his influence runs through literature and the occulture movement. In fact, before Timothy Leary came to the fore as an LSD advocate, Aldous Huxley had been experimenting with mescaline in 1953 and LSD in 1955. His experiences which preceded those of Leary were documented in his books.

His writings became a theme for the occulture of the 1960s, technically placing him at the head of the movement. For

---

[131] The Doors of Perception & Heaven and Hell by Huxley, Aldous, 1894-1963 ISBN 978-0-06-172907-2 (Page 12)

example, his science fiction dystopian novel published in 1932, *'Brave New World',* which brought him public acclaim is set in London in the year AD 2540. It presents an image of a world where psychological control is created through scientifically determined conditioning, eventually resulting in a caste system and state control. Approximately 30 years after writing the book and following the Second World War, he appears to change his position on the imminency of totalitarianism from being in the distant future to only around the corner.

[132]*"There will be, in the next generation or so, a pharmacological method of making people love their servitude, and producing dictatorship without tears, so to speak, producing a kind of painless concentration camp for entire societies, so that people will in fact have their liberties taken away from them, but will rather enjoy it, because they will be distracted from any desire to rebel by propaganda or brainwashing, or brainwashing enhanced by pharmacological methods. And this seems to be the final revolution."*

However, it was later when he used the drug [133]mescaline, introduced to him by the infamous Aleister Crowley when he recorded his experiences in the book, *'The Doors of Perception'* published in 1954, followed by another essay *'Heaven and Hell.'* The earlier book became popular amongst hippies, musicians, artists etc in the 1960s, setting the tone for drug experimentation. Its title was based on a phrase from a book written by William

---

[132] (Aldous Huxley, Tavistock Group, California Medical School, 1961)
[133] Mescaline (3,4,5-trimethoxyphenethylamine), mainly found in the Peyote cactus (Lophophora williamsii), is one of the oldest known hallucinogenic agents that influence human and animal behaviour, but its psychoactive mechanisms remain poorly understood.

Dinis-Oliveira RJ, Pereira CL, da Silva DD. Pharmacokinetic and Pharmacodynamic Aspects of Peyote and Mescaline: Clinical and Forensic Repercussions. Curr Mol Pharmacol. 2019;12(3):184-194. doi: 10.2174/1874467211666181010154139. PMID: 30318013; PMCID: PMC6864602.

Blake in 1790, *"Marriage of heaven and hell."* As quoted by William Blake who was an influential English writer and poet,

[134]*"If the doors of perception were cleansed everything would appear to man as it is, infinite. For man has closed himself up, till he sees all things through narrow chinks of his cavern."*

With these and other books, lectures and interviews, Aldous Huxley repeats a message that has been repeated so many times that it is almost impossible not to know what's coming next. He joins the crowd of voices in preaching the possibilities of an elevated human form, a form that can be improved upon by experimenting with the mind to take us beyond any prescribed, physical, moral, or spiritual boundaries. How? Through a new revolution as Aldous presented in his lecture, 'The Ultimate Revolution' on 20 March 1962.

"a housemate years ago remarked after reading Milton's Paradise Lost, He Says "And beer does more than Milton can to justify God's ways to man" (laughter). And beer is of course, an extremely crude drug compared to these ones. And you can certainly say that some of the psychic energizers and the new hallucinants could do incomparably more than Milton and all the Theologicians combined could possibly do to make the terrifying mystery of our existence seem more tolerable than it does. And here I think one has an enormous area in which the ultimate revolution could function very well indeed, an area in which a great deal of control could be used by not through terror, but by making life seem much more enjoyable than it normally does. Enjoyable to the point, where as I said before, Human beings come to love a state of things by which any reasonable and decent human standard they ought not to love and this I think is perfectly possible."

---

[134] Marriage of Heaven and Hell, by William Blake, 1906 (p. 26)

DH Lawrence, one of the Apostles of apostasy, introduced the mystic teachings of Monte Verità to Huxley, [135]Gerald Heard and Christopher Isherwood. Gerald Heard also trialled mescaline in 1954 and later tried LSD, agreeing with Aldous Huxley's proposition that the mind can be enhanced by the "proper" use of these drugs. Not an idea that I'd recommend though. Heard introduced Bill Wilson to LSD in 1956 under Sydney Cohen's guidance (a Californian psychiatrist). Christopher Isherwood, however, was a British – American novelist, playwright, screenwriter, autobiographer and had interests in [136]Vedanta philosophy. Gerald Heard and Christopher Isherwood were initiated by Swami Prabhavananda and shared their ideas and experiences with Aldous Huxley who eventually became a Vedantist being given the opportunity to write the introduction to the translation of the Bhagavad Gita.

As Huxley's health deteriorated, his wife Laura read from Timothy Leary's manual (which is extracted from the Tibetan Book of the Dead), finally performing his final request to administer LSD as part of an assisted death.

There is so much more that could be said about this man and his colleagues, but this will need to be part of a future discourse. It is safe to say that they were steeped in the pursuit of a lifestyle and religious persuasion that informed Huxley's ideas around a caste system and the earth culture. His family heritage played a large part in developing his ideas and, of course, his brother Julian Huxley reflected the pursuit that this family was obviously engaged in. The pursuit of a better world.

---

[135] Henry FitzGerald Heard, commonly called Gerald Heard, was a British-born American historian, science writer, public lecturer, educator, and philosopher. He wrote many articles and over 35 books.
[136] Hindu-centred philosophy and meditation.

Timothy Leary – Psychedelic Religion: Psychology

[137] *"Seven million people I turned on, and only one hundred thousand have come by to thank me."*

Born Timothy Francis Leary (October 22, 1920 – May 31, 1996), Leary was raised in a Catholic household to Timothy "Tote" Leary who was a Lieutenant in the US Army, and an alcoholic. His mother was Abigail Ferris and as Leary states, she was always disappointed in him.

In Leary's book *'Flashbacks: An Autobiography. A Personal and Cultural History of an Era'*, he describes his father as follows,

[138]*"I stood at the top of the stairs. Below, Mother was sobbing on the phone. Grandfather had passed away. Where was Tote? Disappeared on a three-day bender. Uncles were dispatched to country clubs, saloons, and downtown bars to locate the prodigal son and sober him up for the funeral, which turned out to be a noisy family reunion with the elegant Boston Learys.*

Then came the great day, the reading of Grandfather's will. I was playing my special brand of solitary baseball in front of the house. Tote rushed out of a taxi, which stayed at the curb with its motor running. He stopped on his way in to hand me, his only son and heir, a hundred dollar bill, then walked rapidly into the house where he told Abigail the bad news. The estate was depleted: the stock market crash, the years of mismanagement, the large loans to Uncle Arthur's boutiques, the large loans to Tote, now called in, left just a few thousand dollars. Tote handed Abigail a thousand, announced his plan to go to New York on business and jumped back in the cab.

---

[138] Flashbacks: An Autobiography. A Personal and Cultural History of an Era, by Leary, Timothy, 1920-1996.

By midnight, after getting royally drunk at the Astor Bar, Tote had been rolled of every last cent of the inheritance he had anticipated for forty-five years. I did not see my father again for twenty-three years.

What pride! Tote never returned to his hometown, never faced the burghers he had once looked down on with pity. He just disappeared."

Timothy was 13 years of age when his father abandoned them.

Leary is described in many ways including 'The High Priest of LSD' of the 1960s. He received his PhD at Berkeley University and lectured as a Harvard Academic in Psychology where he set up the 'Harvard Psilocybin Project' with Richard Alpert. One of the founding board members of the project was English writer and Philosopher, Aldous Huxley (*the grandson of Charles Darwin's 'Bulldog' Thomas Henry Huxley and the brother of Julian Huxley – see chapter 'The Evangelists'*). This is an interesting connection, especially as the Huxley family, along with other influential figures, play a strategic role in forming and theorising about the future for humans, much of which helped to create the foundation for later societal experiences.

At the time this project was established drugs like Psilocybin and LSD (Acid) were not illegal and so were administered to volunteers at the university in the hope of documenting the effects of the drug on human consciousness. Volunteers for the programme would be made up of psychology students, prisoners, artists, and Aldous Huxley plus others. Leary believed that the researcher had to be in the same state of mind as the subject to fully appreciate what the individual was experiencing. Of course, as the programme progressed, complaints from some students were brought to the attention of the university, stating that they were being pressured to participate in taking psychedelic drugs. This is contested on both sides of the debate but what is true is that psychedelic drugs gained popularity due to the influence of Timothy Leary. President Richard Nixon called him "The most dangerous man in America."

Leary subsequently became the poster personality for the use of LSD amongst millions of young adults, and also became the surrogate father to a generation who were looking for an alternative to what the US and other nation states had to offer. So, from the moment Leary first tried the psilocybin mushroom to well into the 1960s the level of drug use amongst young adults reached such levels that it continued to attract the attention of the government and other influential individuals. With this came the eventual prohibition of psychedelic drugs. In his attempts to maintain the legal use of drugs, he produced a leaflet called *'Start Your Own Religion'* in which he uses the popular Leary statement, *"Turn on, tune in, drop out."* But what did this slogan mean? Leary explains how it came about,

[139]*"One morning, while I was ruminating in the shower about what kind of slogan would succinctly summarize the tactics for increasing intelligence, six words came to mind. Dripping wet, with towel around my waist, I walked to the study and wrote down this phrase: "Turn On, Tune In, Drop Out."*

Turn On meant go within to activate your neural and genetic equipment. Become sensitive to the many and various levels of consciousness and the specific triggers that engage them. Drugs were one way to accomplish this end.

Tune In meant interact harmoniously with the world around you – externalize, materialize, express your new internal perspectives.

Drop Out suggested an active, selective, graceful process of detachment from involuntary or unconscious commitments. Drop Out

---

[139] Flashbacks: An Autobiography. A Personal and Cultural History of an Era, by Leary, Timothy, 1920-1996 (p. 253)

meant self-reliance, a discovery of one's singularity, a commitment to mobility, choice, and change."

After being fired from Harvard University, Leary was allowed to use a 2500-acre estate and 64 room mansion owned by Peggy, Billy and Tommy Hitchcock, heirs to the Mellon Gulf Oil fortune. The property was located in Dutchess County in the north of New York City. This property became the place of services and New Age fervour. Residents would give themselves to the experiences offered, delving deeper into the mind through transcendental meditation, sex games, and psychedelic drug experimentation.

Timothy Leary and others became the new faces of what can only be described as 'Psychedelic Religion', yet another offshoot of the eugenics (human genetics) tree. Through the door of psychology, mysticism was introduced to and invaded the minds of nations. Through this pseudo-science, there were no definitive results or further advances into the issues of the soul or mind, simply the further advancement of self-focused hedonistic experiences sold under the banner of love, freedom and enlightenment. To describe this movement as counterculture is a good effort at describing this global phenomenon, but as lighted upon while browsing through the pages of historical content, a more fitting term for this generational shift is '[140]occulture' (a combination of the occult and culture).

A familiar pattern continues with Leary, who was also an admirer of the domineering personality Aleister Crowley and is recorded in an interview on PBS Late Night America stating that he continues the work of Aleister Crowley and is indeed an admirer of his. This should come as no surprise, Yeshua states,

---

[140] Blend of "occult" and "culture," coined by Professor Christopher Partridge.

"Even so, every good tree bears good fruit, but a bad tree bears bad fruit. A good tree cannot bear bad fruit, nor can a bad tree bear good fruit. Every tree that does not bear good fruit is cut down and thrown into the fire. <u>Therefore by their fruits you will know them</u>."
Matt 7:17-20 (NKJV)

> *Answer B* [141]*"The brain is the key, the brain is the source, the brain is God. Everything that humans do is neuroecology."* – **Timothy Leary**

Lafayette Ronald Hubbard - Scientology
(L. Ron Hubbard)

Fiction writer and founder of Scientology.

"Why should anyone want to know anything about the human mind? And, for that matter, why should anyone believe that knowledge of the human mind is either unobtainable or undesirable? Why should men ostensibly seeking answers to the mind stray so far from it as to examine rats and entirely avoid looking at human beings? And why should anyone pretending to treat the mind stray so far afield as electric shock?"

So, what does the founder of Scientology have to do with anything? Well, it's amazing how the thread just keeps on connecting the most unlikely people.

From the accounts of his childhood and adulthood there are questions that surround the authenticity of most of his claims. However, what we have to do is to look at what was written and any events that could be corroborated by other

---

[141] Change Your Brain by Timothy Leary ISBN: 1-57951-017-5 (Ronin Publishing) pg. 4.

individuals. Not an easy task as this man has a long list of illustrious anecdotes and a prolific list of writings which entered him into the Guinness Book of Records. Despite his fiction writing ability Hubbard had a fascination with the world of religion. Hubbard's interests would lead him to the young star of the occult movement called Jack Parsons. A relationship which would last for a short period of time, ending with Hubbard having an affair with Parsons' girlfriend Sara Elizabeth "Betty" Bruce Northrup Hollister (Parson's wife's younger sister) who later became Hubbard's second wife.

Sara, like Hubbard and Parsons, was a member of the Ordo Templi Orientis (O.T.O.), an organisation that was headed by Aleister Crowley. Hubbard and Parsons would eventually part company but not before Parsons was swindled out of money by Hubbard and was to play a major role in the development of the Hubbard book, [142]*"Dianetics: The Modern Science of Mental Health."* A book that provides a system that claims to cure illnesses, yet another individual that delved into the 'science of the mind'. Of course, he was criticised for not having real medical data to support the claims made and indeed continued to suffer with many of the ailments that Dianetics was said to heal. Here is an extract from his book,

---

[142] In the 1930s and '40s he published short stories and novels in a variety of genres, including horror and science fiction. After serving in the navy in World War II, he published Dianetics (1950), which detailed his theories of the human mind. He eventually moved away from Dianetics' focus on the mind to a more religious approach to the human condition, which he called Scientology. After founding the Church of Scientology in 1954, Hubbard struggled to gain recognition of it as a legitimate religion and was often at odds with tax authorities and former members who accused the church of fraud and harassment. He lived many years on a yacht and remained in seclusion for his last six years.

[143]*"Dianetics (Greek dia, through, and nous, mind or soul) is the science of mind. Far simpler than physics or chemistry, it compares with them in the exactness of its axioms and is on a considerably higher echelon of usefulness. The hidden source of all psychosomatic ills and human aberration has been discovered and skills have been developed for their invariable cure."*

Once again Crowley is seen as a mentor to Hubbard and clearly held high esteem in Hubbard's mind which is confirmed in a lecture Hubbard gave on the 1st of December 1952 called *"The Philadelphia Doctorate Course."* Here is a quote taken from the lecture,

[144]*"Now he could simply say I have action. A magician, uh... the magic cults of the 8th, 9th, 10th, 11th, 12th centuries in the Middle East were fascinating. The only modern work that has anything to do with them is a trifle wild in spots, but it's fascinating work in itself, and that's work written by [Aleister] Crowley, the late [Aleister] Crowley, my very good friend. And uh... he... he did himself a splendid uh... piece of aesthetics built around those magic cults. Uh... it's very interesting reading to get ahold of a copy of a book, quite rare, but it can be obtained, THE MASTER THERION, T-h-e-r-i-o-n, THE MASTER THERION by Aleister Crowley. He signs himself The Beast, the mark of the beast six sixty-six. Very, very something or other, but anyway the... Crowley exhumed a lot of the data from these old magic cults."*

It is strange that there should be ongoing debates on a scholarly level regarding Hubbard's occult connections and influences when there doesn't appear to be any secret of his admiration of the practice or indeed the use of occult rituals. The question is not if Scientology's founder used Crowley's occult

---

[143] Dianetics: The Modern Science of Mental Health, by Hubbard, L. Ron, 1911-1986.
[144] L. Ron Hubbard, Philadelphia Doctorate Course (1952)

principles in Dianetics and the founding of Scientology, but can they be considered different in origin as though they sprung from distinct root systems. The answer is categorically, no.

Hugh Urban in his article, [145] *'The Occult Roots of Scientology'*, sums it up in the following way,

> *Hubbard appropriated "countless odds and ends" from a wide range of religious, occult, psychological and science fiction ideas available in the 1950s' spiritual marketplace, weaving them together into his own surprisingly successful synthesis. Thus, in his early Dianetic practice we can see clearly the influence of Freud, Jung and other thinkers available in the mid-twentieth centuries, as well as the influence of popular self-help works such as Norman Vincent Peale's best-selling* **The Power of Positive Thinking** *(1952).*

However, The God of Abraham, Isaac and Jacob puts it like this when speaking to Israel.

"There shall not be found among you anyone who makes his son or his daughter pass through the fire, or one who practices witchcraft, or a soothsayer, or one who interprets omens, or a sorcerer, or one who conjures spells, or a medium, or a spiritist, or one who calls up the dead."

Deuteronomy 18:10-11 (NKJV)

Jack Parsons – Rocketeer and Thelema

"She will come girt with the sword of freedom, and before her kings and priests will tremble and cities and empires will fall, and she will be called BABALON, the scarlet woman....And women will respond to

---

[145] Urban, Hugh B. "The Occult Roots of Scientology?" Nova Religio: The Journal of Alternative and Emergent Religions, vol. 15, no. 3, 2012, pp. 91–116. JSTOR.

her war cry, and throw off their shackles and chains, and men will respond to her challenge, forsaking the foolish ways and the little ways, and she will shine as the ruddy evening star in the bloody sunset of [Götterdämmerung], will shine as a morning star when the night has passed, and a new dawn breaks over the garden of Pan"

In November 2022, scientists discovered new details on a distant planet known as WASP 39b which is said to revolutionise the search for alien life on other planets. The discovery was achieved by using NASA's James Webb Telescope, designed to use infrared astronomy and being the largest telescope in space. Listed amongst other astounding feats of science and technological breakthroughs, NASA has fired rockets into space and put a man on the moon, a goal once considered the work of science fiction. However, have you ever stopped to ask how NASA came to be synonymous with space?

Well, NASA is an acronym for the National Aeronautics and Space Administration, which is a federal government agency responsible for the civil space programme, aeronautics and space research. Since the cold war between Russia and America, NASA became the agency which rose to the challenge of placing a man on the moon to surpass Russia's achievement of successfully launching a cosmonaut, Yuri Alekseyevich Gagarin into space on 12 April 1961. It has since stood at the forefront of space travel and exploration, and has the only national laboratory in space. Its discoveries are used to create products for the public and it continues to explore the boundaries of space with its Moon to Mars exploration. This is to the credit of committed, hardworking individuals with a sense of national pride and determination. However, something is missing in this narrative, like everything else we have uncovered. Erased from the pages of history is one of the most significant figures in the space programme story who was the catalyst for space travel in the west. His name may not appear when scanning search engines regarding US space programmes but he was pivotal to its future success. Yet this is where things get a little weird, so hold onto your seats.

John (Jack) Parsons originally called Marvel Whiteside Parsons was raised by a wealthy family in Los Angeles, Pasadena after his father left the family due to adultery. Los Angeles being the place where Thelemists had already set down roots complete with their new age spiritualism, earth culture/religion and occult practices.

At a young age, Jack developed an interest in science fiction and rockets but did not do well in his early education. He did, however, make friends with a schoolmate called Edward Foreman and both of them had the common issue of not doing well at school. Together they would experiment with fireworks in their backyard, developing a relationship that would be relevant to their later passion for rockets. Jack and Edward Foreman shared a common interest in the works of Jules Verne, who can also be remembered for his stories, *'Journey to the Centre of the Earth'* and *'Twenty Thousand Leagues Under the Sea'*, and pulp *Amazing Stories* magazines. Together they would eventually progress to build their own solid fuel rockets even though they both continued to fail in their education. However, it is this fusion of science and rockets with the occult lifestyle of Jack Parsons that has received little airtime until recently and for obvious reasons. Yet this interweaving thread of rockets, science and the occult eventually led to the creation of the original 'suicide squad' made up of Jack Parsons, Edward Forman and Frank Malina, a graduate student they would meet at a company called Caltech. Here is where they would become known as the 'suicide squad' due to their reputation of blowing things up and causing unpredictable and sometimes dangerous damage on campus.

Parsons would later be introduced to Thelema through the invitation of a couple called John and Frances Baxter. It is said that he attended a Gnostic mass where he met some individuals that may not immediately resonate with you but it is worth noting some of the additional early proponents of this cult, such as Regina Kahl, Jane Wolfe (an actress), John Carradine (horror movie actor), and Harry Hay (founder of the first gay rights group in the USA).

This interwoven thread of rockets, science and occult curiosity that developed into a lifestyle introduced Jack Parsons to the likes of Aleister Crowley and L Ron Hubbard. His subsequent thirst for more and this combination of rocket exploration and occultism created a character and outcome that those who know about this strange character and his exploits attempt to distance themselves from.

Jack Parsons is known to have achieved numerous breakthroughs in the world of rockets as one of the founders of NASA's Jet Propulsion Laboratory, originally known as CALCIT Rocket Group. His rise to prominence straddled parallel tracks; on the one hand, he had an obsession with rockets and explosions, an experience that was engulfed in his vision of breaking through the atmospheric boundaries of planet Earth in the exploration of other domains. On the other track was his pervading appetite for the occult where explosions and leaving planet earth or transcendence were spiritual experiences. This man was the embodiment of what it means to be an occultist with aspirations that manifest themselves in the physical realm. Both worlds were one to him and reflected in his lifestyle, but even today people try to grapple with his profession and spirituality as very separate things. It is clear to see that his 'all in' attitude spilt over into everything he occupied himself with including unthinkable hedonistic practices in his home (which was the parsonage for Thelema) and during his journey of discovery in the laboratory. To add to this unusually hidden character, a little-known fact is that Jack Parsons also believed in population control in his own way, but this placed him on the outside of certain circles. Of course, he would not rest until his thoughts were publicly aired so he published a book in 1971 called Population Versus Liberty, in which he outlines,

[146]*If it is true that harm could come to a society through the exhaustion of natural resources, pollution of the environment, stress, poverty, hunger, and violence, because of over-population, could the law have anything to say about it? Although the law is not at present, and, as it stands, probably could not be used for the purpose of population control, there seems little reason to doubt that the potential is there.*

During his decline from the stage of notoriety he worked on stage effects and eventually died from an explosion while working on one of his creations. Some speculate about it not being an accident, others to the contrary.

Here is the influencer, the hedonist, progenitor and believer in modern space travel in the form of metaphysics and more. Who would have guessed it? The NASA space program owes its origins to this man. Yet, we continue to see the repeated pattern of distancing the programme from its occult roots. Too strong a description? I doubt it, after all is it too strong to have suggested the implementation of a counterculture was the result of a group of Earth worshippers, Thelemists and others? Yet here we are witnessing the outworking of a dark presence established through the active occultists that embedded themselves in the community. It is no accident or conspiracy theory that the whole region became a stronghold for the 'do what thou wilt' movement in this locality and beyond. This is a literal example of the strand of science that appears to speak the language of human discovery but is then revealed as an extremely confusing form of indoctrination. Accepting the 'science' without discernment leaves you in danger of accepting

[146] Population Versus Liberty, by Parsons, Jack 1971, p. 141.

the giver of this new knowledge all in the name of technological advancement.

The real point here is that we assume that science is science and it all emanates from a good place. Hopefully, this example goes some way to identifying a wolf in sheep's clothing and convinces us to accept that the elephant in the room is real.

> [147]*Answer A: An end to the pretence, and lying hypocrisy of Christianity. An end to the servile virtues, and superstitious restrictions. An end to the slave morality. An end to prudery and shame, to guilt and sin, for these are of the only evil under the sun, that is fear. An end to all authority that is not based on courage and manhood, to the authority of lying priests, conniving judges, blackmailing police, and an end to the servile flattery and cajolery of minds, the coronations of mediocrities, the ascension of dolts.*
> **Jack Parsons**

New Psychiatry

[148] *"Positive psychology is a relatively new field that focuses on enhancing well-being and optimal functioning rather than ameliorating symptoms, and complements rather than replaces traditional psychology. Common themes in positive psychology*

---

[147] Manifesto of the Anti-Christ by Parsons, Jack
[148] Chakhssi, F., Kraiss, J.T., Sommers-Spijkerman, M. *et al.* The effect of positive psychology interventions on well-being and distress in clinical samples with psychiatric or somatic disorders: a systematic review and meta-analysis. *BMC Psychiatry* **18**, 211 (2018).
https://bmcpsychiatry.biomedcentral.com/articles/10.1186/s12888-018-1739-2

include savoring, gratitude, kindness, promoting positive relationships, and pursuing hope and meaning."

Farid Chakhssi, Jannis T. Kraiss, Marion Sommers-Spijkerman & Ernst T. Bohlmeijer

[149]*"Humanistic psychology is a perspective that emphasizes looking at the whole person, and the uniqueness of each individual. Humanistic psychology begins with the existential assumptions that people have free will and are motivated to achieve their potential and self-actualize."*

Humanistic Approach In Psychology (Humanism): Definition & Examples By Saul Mcleod

Psychiatry and psychology are branded as 'new' under this wholesale remarketing campaign by taking the old philosophies and mixing them some more with current trends and spiritual explorations of the mind. These two areas have gained such popularity that corporations, educators, recruiters and of course 'church leaders' are employing the techniques and theories as a plausible solution to selecting the right character types, resolving personal issues and directing the next generation to a safe place.

Yet, after a closer examination of the people behind the theories and methodologies, there is a clear sign of how quickly and deeply their influence has buried itself in the ground of self-determination. It is also interesting to note that the language used to promote the chosen path continues to morph into an appealing, caring representation of possibilities, providing the individual with a kind of inner exploration for salvation. To fully appreciate the web of glamourised intelligent contributions it is simply a fact that we must first find some

---

[149] Humanistic Approach In Psychology (Humanism): Definition & Examples By Saul Mcleod, PhD Updated on February 16, 2023

place of objectivity. Without this, it is impossible to see what is in front of us and equally impossible to discern between the obvious realities and culturally accepted practices endemic in the industries of the mind.

In this section, we will examine the world of 'new psychiatry and psychology', from the perspective of the modern idealists who unashamedly propagated a particular brand of secular humanistic religion, kept alive by the plasma pumping arteries of occultism and the desperation of human need.

Sigmund Freud, 1856-1939: The Father of Psychoanalysis

[150] *"First and foremost, Freud was the discoverer of the first instrument for the scientific examination of the human mind. Creative writers of genius had had fragmentary insight into mental processes, but no systematic method of investigation existed before Freud. It was only gradually that he perfected the instrument, since it was only gradually that the difficulties in the way of such an investigation became apparent. The forgotten trauma in Breuer's explanation of hysteria provided the earliest problem and perhaps the most fundamental of all, for it showed conclusively that there were active parts of the mind not immediately open to inspection either by an on-looker or by the subject himself. These parts of the mind were described by Freud, without regard for metaphysical or terminological disputes, as the unconscious."*

Although we can talk at length about Sigmund Freud, it is his perspective on the unconscious that is important. As the creator of psychoanalysis, as it is called, there is a world of thought around this that is relevant to the following pages.

[150] The Interpretation of Dreams by Freud, Sigmund, 1856-1939

During his lifetime he was exposed to so many aspects of discovery which were esoteric and unchartered in the realm of science or medicine. It seems almost strange to think that leading figures in their field of training could somehow merge two worlds to form what most people accept as a solid, tangible fact.

In this instance, Sigmund Freud's theories on the mind have managed to garner the cloak of truth at the expense of truth. The whole idea of psychoanalysis is centred on the conscious and unconscious mind of an individual, the emphasis being on the unconscious. Psychoanalysis is used in the treatment of 'mental disorders' and is broken down into various theories and techniques. It carelessly reinforces the belief that anyone can circumnavigate the mind of another provided they are armed with Freud's tool kit:

- **Theory** on - The Psyche
- **Theory** on - Psychosexual development
- **Theory** on - Religion
- **Theory** on - Female Psychology
- **Theory** on - Defence Mechanisms
- **Theory** of - Personality
- **Theory** on - Talk Therapy
- **Theory** on - The twisted 'Oedipus complex'

And last, but not least,

- **Theory** on - Dream interpretation.

Note that each area mentioned is prefixed with the word **'theory'** which makes it abundantly clear that there are no foundations that can be relied upon when considering these notions. Yet, strangely, possibly through some form of indoctrination, we regurgitate statements like, *'Whoops, that was* *a Freudian slip',* (which he calls [151]**parapraxis**) and we measure each other's character with a quick reference to the 'ego' if someone is considered to be too selfish or obstinate.

The point here is that humanistic psychology with all its bizarre strands owes its underlying problem to its roots and Sigmund Freud's theories were not created in a vacuum; they have their origin in a long history of spiritualism. Consider this: dream interpretation has been around for centuries finding its voice in divination, no, not prophecy, divination. A form of witchcraft that seeks to gain answers to questions that are otherwise hidden from our reality; using rituals, incantations, psychedelic drugs, and other means in an attempt to open up another reality. This includes but is not exclusive to, the prediction of future events. Of course, Satan is only too pleased to oblige. However, the question we should ask ourselves when engaging in these activities is, where do the answers come from? Are we to assume that they come from our inner selves, our subconscious, or do they come from the gods? No, if there is any activity not contrived by human involvement then the response can only come from spirits. The Bible refers to these entities as spirits or demons regardless of the identity they hide behind and, yes, they do mimic real people. So, you know that deceased Grandmother that you said keeps speaking to you...?

So Saul disguised himself and put on other clothes, and he went, and two men with him; and they came to the woman by night. And he said, "Please conduct a séance for me, and bring up for me the one I shall name to you."

Then the woman said to him, "Look, you know what Saul has done, how he has cut off the mediums and the spiritists from the land. Why then do you lay a snare for my life, to cause me to die?"

---

[151] In psychoanalysis, a minor error in speech or action, such as a slip of the tongue, a slip of the pen, an action slip, or a slip of memory.

And Saul swore to her by the Lord, saying, "As the Lord lives, no punishment shall come upon you for this thing."

Then the woman said, "Whom shall I bring up for you?"

And he said, "Bring up Samuel for me."

When the woman saw Samuel, she cried out with a loud voice. And the woman spoke to Saul, saying, "Why have you deceived me? For you are Saul!"

And the king said to her, "Do not be afraid. What did you see?"

And the woman said to Saul, "I saw a spirit ascending out of the earth."

1 Samuel 28:8-13 (NKJV)

Sigmund Freud, with his cocaine addiction and troubled mind, was a mirror image of the people he claimed to be helping. Yet, he is another person who is revered as an expert.

Carl Jung: New Psychiatry / Psychoanalysis

"Then a most disagreeable thing happened. Salome became very interested in me, and she assumed I could cure her blindness. She began to worship me. I said, "Why do you worship me?" She replied, "You are Christ." In spite of my objections she maintained this. I said, "This is madness," and became filled with skeptical resistance. Then I saw the snake approach me. She came close and began to circle me and press me in her coils. The coils reached up to my heart. I realized as I struggled that I had assumed the attitude of the Crucifixion. In the agony and the struggle, I sweated so profusely that the water flowed down on all sides of me. Then Salome rose, and she could see. While the snake was pressing me, I felt that my face had taken on the face of an animal of prey, a lion or a tiger.!!"

Carl Jung

The name Carl Gustav Jung is synonymous with Sigmund Freud, and they were close friends until the later breakup over differences in ideas. These two men were pivotal in elevating the mind to a place of popularity that would transform the landscape of mind sciences. When I stumbled into the character of Carl Jung there was nothing about psychology or psychoanalysis that bore any interest to me whatsoever. However, the discovery of Carl Jung answered many questions that I had relating to what seems to be a resurgence in Jungian philosophy. He seems to pop up everywhere alongside some of the other old but new psychiatrists and psychologists.

From the opening quote by Carl Jung, we can see an immediate picture of his mindset and his perspective on dream interpretation (to mention one area) and the supernatural. It also reveals his thoughts on a subject which is popular inside and outside of Christian circles, the idea that man can transcend and become god. Should this be a surprise? Not really. As Carl Jung was among the Ascona contingent and he was open to exploring the occult and other forms of the same. Yet, say anything defamatory against him and you run the risk of being on the receiving end of an attack as Richard Noll discovered when he wrote a book called *'The Jung Cult, Origins of a Charismatic Movement'*. I hasten to add that Richard Noll is not a Christian but has successfully mined the real character and motivations of this complex personality. So, let's take a brief walk through the philosophy that has created the Jung Cult, a movement that has disciples in counselling centres near you.

We have read a brief exert of Carl Jung's perceived 'deification' — an experience that many other world seekers are yearning for, be it in the form of leaving the planet to join a passing UFO or transcending into a fleshless form through a final rite before death. This is blasphemous to say the least and reveals an attitude that was not uncommon during this period. However, the spiritual, supernatural element is never mentioned when dialoguing about his theories. His passion for Hellenistic mysteries and embedded forms of occultism in his theories are brushed under the carpet to avoid tarnishing his public image and credibility. The truth is his philosophy is everywhere and there is no getting away from it. Yet the body of evidence paints a picture of a man who was on a mission to change the world using a form of spirituality that is not at once obvious. His obsession with all things mystical is expressed through the delivery system of psychology in the form of psychoanalysis which was loaded with mythological material relating to Mithraic mysteries *(a Roman mystery religion centred on the god Mithras)*. Was it a scientific treatment for people who were experiencing issues of the mind? By any stretch of the imagination this is not true. As explored by Richard Noll, Jung's correspondence with Freud reveals so much about his thoughts on psychoanalysis. It is far removed from our assumption that this was somehow a scientific application of research-led discoveries begun by Sigmund Freud and continued by Carl Jung.

For example, if one were to search for a definition of psychoanalysis online one would soon discover definitions such as,

[152]*"psychoanalysis, method of treating mental disorders, shaped by psychoanalytic theory, which emphasizes unconscious mental processes and is sometimes described as "depth psychology." The psychoanalytic movement originated in the clinical observations and formulations of Austrian psychiatrist Sigmund Freud, who coined the*

---

[152] Britannica, The Editors of Encyclopaedia. "psychoanalysis". Encyclopedia Britannica, 2 Mar. 2023, https://www.britannica.com/science/psychoanalysis. Accessed 7 March 2023.

term psychoanalysis. *During the 1890s, Freud worked with Austrian physician and physiologist Josef Breuer in studies of neurotic patients under hypnosis. Freud and Breuer observed that, when the sources of patients' ideas and impulses were brought into consciousness during the hypnotic state, the patients showed improvement."*

(See the earlier section on mesmerism). Though Sigmund Freud is recognised as the creator of psychoanalysis, Carl Jung's perspective on psychoanalysis elevated it to another insidious level. In his letter to Freud on 11 February 1910, Jung makes the following comments,

[153]*"I imagine a far finer and more comprehensive task for [psychoanalysis] than alliance with an ethical fraternity. I think we must give it time to infiltrate into people from many centres, to revivify among intellectuals a feeling for symbol and myth, ever so gently to transform Christ back into the soothsaying god of the vine, which he was, and in this way absorb those ecstatic instinctual forces of Christianity for the one purpose of making the cult and the sacred myth what they once were – a drunken feast of joy where man regained the ethos and holiness of an animal. That was the beauty and purpose of classical religion, which from God knows what temporary biological needs has turned into a Misery Institute. Yet what infinite rapture and wantonness lie dormant in our religion, waiting to be led back to their true destination! A genuine and proper ethical development cannot abandon Christianity but must grow up within it, must bring to fruition its hymn of love, the agony and ecstasy over the dying and resurgent god, the mystic power of the wine, the awesome anthropophagy of the Last Supper – only this ethical development can serve the vital forces of religion. But a syndicate of interests dies out after 10 years."*

To unravel what he was saying it is necessary to provide some context leading up to these comments.

---

[153] The Freud/Jung letters: The Correspondence between Sigmund Freud and C.G. Jung, edited by William McGuire, p. 294

In short, an invitation had been given to Carl Jung to join the 'International Order for Ethics and Culture' but he questions its purpose and philosophy, believing that psychoanalysis is the new religion for modern society. In this letter he posits a position that looks for another approach to answer the question surrounding the usefulness of these organisations, including the one to which he was invited. From this standpoint he introduces his esoteric experiences into the body of work that we describe as 'treatment', exposing all and sundry to the musings of yet another individual who believes he has discovered a new religion that will save the world. His exploration of occult practices led him to the experience described in the opening paragraph and many other instances that he records in his diaries. He delves into his dreams, searching for understanding and explanations and experiences all manner of encounters that he feels unable to share with others. When he shares his thoughts with Sigmund Freud, even Freud rebukes him, refusing to be associated with Jung's ambitions of starting a new religion.

So, psychoanalysis isn't a therapy, it is a religion borne out of occult philosophy, Carl Jung being its self-proclaimed leader. Once again, he like others had spirit guides, one of whom was called Philemon. In *'The Red Book of C. G. Jung; A Journey Into Unknown Depths'* there is reference to this which explains it in more detail.

[154] *"CHAPTER NINE*

Philemon

---

[154] The Red Book of C. G. Jung: A Journey Into Unknown Depths by Walter Boechat.
Walter Boechat is a medical doctor from Brazil who also trained at the C. G. Jung Institute in Zurich. He is a former member of the Executive Committee of the International Association for Analytical Psychology, and a founding member of the Jungian Association of Brazil.

In his book of memoirs Jung wrote: "Philemon and other figures of my fantasies brought home to me the crucial insight that there are things in the psyche which I do not produce, but produce themselves and have their own life" (1963, p. 176).

The appearance of Philemon represents the culmination of Jung's pilgrimage in search of the self. Philemon is referred to in Memories, Dreams, Reflections *as equivalent to the guru figure in Indian religion. Jung relates how he had a real-life experience with a guru when he was visited by an Indian intellectual who was one of Gandhi's disciples. The visitor revealed that he had had a guru, and Jung asked him who this was. He answered that his guru was called Sankaracharya. Jung was surprised: "You don't mean the commentator on the Vedas who died centuries ago?" His visitor then explained "matter-of-factly" that this was not at all relevant and that the guru experience is an inner experience. At that moment, said Jung, "I thought of Philemon".*

Now, this may come as no surprise considering what you have just read, but the Carl Jung that we hear about and claim to know is a caricature of the real man. So let us pause a moment to list some of his experiences or characteristics that we do not get to see too often.

- As a child, he grew up in a house which had regular paranormal activity.

[155]*"Then I myself went, and found a door which led to my mother's room. There was no one in it. The atmosphere was uncanny. The room was very large, and suspended from the ceiling were two rows of five chests each, hanging about two feet above the floor. They looked like small garden pavilions, each about six feet in area, and each containing two beds. I knew that this was the room where my mother,*

---

[155] Memories, Dreams, Reflections by Jung, C. G. (Carl Gustav), 1875-1961, pp. 213, 214.

who in reality had long been dead, was visited, and that she had set up these beds for visiting spirits to sleep. They were spirits who came in pairs, ghostly married couples, so to speak, who spent the night or even the day there.

- He believed that he had two personalities which he named number 1 and number 2.
- His grandfather was the rector of the University of Basel and a Grand Master of the Swiss Lodge of Freemasons.
- In addition to the above, his doctorate was on *'The Psychology and Pathology of So-Called Occult Phenomena'*. This became the basis of his theories regarding the need to work at an unconscious level as this was where most of the issues were. It is the idea that the unconscious has part personalities, which he called 'complexes'. Personalities can reveal themselves through occult phenomena. It was through a séance that Carl Jung engaged in, that he developed his initial thoughts on this matter but that was not at the exclusion of ongoing contact with spirit guides and occult teachings which are related in his book *Memories, Dreams and Reflections*.

Is this the leading figure of psychology that you know and reference in your marketing material? Does he take the uppermost place on your website or in your boardrooms? Even with the knowledge that he was raised in occult surroundings, you could argue that this did not have a bearing on his theories, you could choose to remain in complete denial over the whole issue because all of the references made could be copied and pasted together to make any point that is contrary to common opinion. So, before we move into some of those theories, here is a portion of a letter Jung wrote to Freud, dated 8 May 1911 followed by another on 12 June 1911, which allows him the opportunity to tell us what's on his mind.

[156]*"Jung writes, "The meeting in Munich is still very much on my mind. Occultism is another field we shall have to conquer — with the aid of the libido theory, it seems to me. At the moment I am looking into astrology, which seems indispensable for a proper understanding of mythology. There are strange and wondrous things in these lands of darkness. Please don't worry about my wanderings in these infinitudes. I shall return laden with rich booty for our knowledge of the human psyche. For a while longer I must intoxicate myself on magic perfumes in order to fathom the secrets that lie hidden in the abysses of the unconscious."*

[157]*And, a month later, astrology again (12 June 1911): "My evenings are taken up very largely with astrology. I make horoscopic calculations in order to find a clue to the core of psycho-logical truth. Some remarkable things have turned up which will certainly appear incredible to you. . . . I dare say that we shall one day discover in astrology a good deal of knowledge that has been intuitively projected into the heavens. For instance, it appears that the* **signs of the zodiac are character pictures, in other words libido symbols** *which depict the typical qualities of the* **libido** *at a given moment." Freud's reply (15 June 1911) sounds rather fatigued: "In matters of occultism I have grown humble since the great lesson Ferenczi's experiences gave me.' I promise to believe anything that can be made to look reasonable. I shall not do so gladly, that you know. But my hubris has been shattered."*

The [158]libido is defined by Carl Jung in a manner that makes it palatable to the open-minded researcher, counsellor,

---

[156] Psychology and the Occult by Jung, C. G. (Carl Gustav), 1875-1961 p. ix
[157] Psychology and the Occult by Jung, C. G. (Carl Gustav), 1875-1961 page ix
[158] In 1912, at the age of 37, Jung published the original version of this work, which marked his divergence from the psychoanalytical school of Freud. The volume was titled 'Wandlungen und Symbole der Libido' (Transformations and Symbols of the Libido); in 1916, it was first published in English with a rather different title: Psychology of the Unconscious. It has become Jung's most widely known and influential work. On one hand, in its author's words,

and general practitioner but there is a major problem here. As he puts it, it is in *'the abyss of the unconscious'*, the realm of *'astrology'*, *'mythology'*, the *'land of the darkness'* and the *'signs of the zodiac'* that we can somehow understand the human mind. Using the occult to figure out how the human mind works is an insurmountable leap to make and yet his supposed discoveries and application of these theories are worshipped as breakthroughs in 'research' instead of failed spirituality that is offered to the unsuspecting. This could be stood on the same platform as the many cults that ended with the death of their followers as this is nothing short of religious dogma.

To move on, let's also include an equally important extract which tells us about the origin of his inspiration for his theories.

[159]*'I was compelled from within, as it were, to formulate and express what might have been said by* <u>Philemon.</u> *This was how the* Septem Sermones ad Mortuos with its peculiar language came into being.'*

(*translated as [160]*'Seven Sermons to the Dead'*)

His account expands on the information provided by his spirit guide Philemon, and he describes what happened to him and his family when this entity (demon) imparted it to him,

---

it is "an extended commentary on a practical analysis of the prodromal stages of schizophrenia" Symbols of Transformation by C.G. Jung, (inner paragraph of book cover).
[159] Memories, Dreams, Reflections by Jung, C. G. (Carl Gustav), 1875-1961, p. 190.
[160] *"The Sermons contain hints or anticipations of ideas that were to figure later in his scientific writings, more particularly concerning the polaristic nature of the psyche, of life in general, and of all psychological statements. It was their thinking in paradoxes that drew Jung to the Gnostics. That is why he identifies himself here with the Gnostic writer Basilides (early second century AD) and even takes over some of his terminology – for example, God as* **Abraxas**. *It was a deliberate game of mystification."* Page 378

[161] *"It began with a restlessness, but I did not know what it meant or what "they" wanted of me. There was an ominous atmosphere all around me. I had the strange feeling that the air was filled with ghostly entities. Then it was as if my house began to be haunted. My eldest daughter saw a white figure passing through the room. My second daughter, independently of her elder sister, related that twice in the night her blanket had been snatched away; and that same night my nine-year-old son had an anxiety dream. In the morning he asked his mother for crayons, and he, who ordinarily never drew, now made a picture of his dream. He called it "The Picture of the Fisherman." Through the middle of the picture ran a river, and a fisherman with a rod was standing on the shore. He had caught a fish. On the fisherman's head was a chimney from which flames were leaping and smoke rising. From the other side of the river the devil came flying through the air. He was cursing because his fish had been stolen. But above the fisherman hovered an angel who said, "You cannot do anything to him; he only catches the bad fish!" My son drew this picture on a Saturday.*

In this atmosphere of demonic inspiration and transference of dark intel, Carl Jung received the information that shaped his therapies and that of future practitioners. He does not hide where his ideas came from, but it is probably in more recent times that we have been allowed to gather and review some of his records.

To help you recognise the theories when you next attend an event, training course or therapy session, a brief definition has been added below the following subheadings followed by extracts from his book Memories, Dreams, and Reflections, which we have taken the last quotation from. While reading, remember who he said gave them to him.

---

[161] Memories, Dreams, Reflections by Jung, CG (Carl Gustav), 1875-1961, p. 190.

- **Psychological functions (Pairs of opposites)**
Definition: Carl Jung posited that personality types are split into four functions all of which are arranged in opposites. They are **Intuition (Ni), Sensation (Se) Thinking (Te),** and **Feeling (Fi).** In addition to this are the additional functions divided under Extrovert and Introvert.

> [162] *"The pairs of opposites are qualities of the pleroma which are not, because each balanceth each. As we are the pleroma itself, we also have all these qualities in us. Because the very ground of our nature is distinctiveness,"*

- **Individuation**
[163]Definition: The process in the analytical psychology of CG Jung by which the self is formed by integrating elements of the conscious and unconscious mind.

> [164] *"Individuation means becoming a single, homogeneous being, and, in so far as 'individuality' embraces our innermost, last, and incomparable uniqueness, it also implies becoming one's own self. We could therefore translate individuation as 'coming to selfhood' or 'self-realization.'"*

---

[162] Page 381
[163] "Individuation." Merriam-Webster.com Dictionary, Merriam-Webster, https://www.merriam-webster.com/dictionary/individuation. Accessed 11 Mar. 2023.
[164] Memories, dreams, reflections by Jung, CG (Carl Gustav), 1875-1961, p. 395

> [165]*"Though the four hexagrams were put into the mandala on purpose, they are authentic results of preoccupation with the I Ching. 'The phases and aspects of my patient's inner process of development can therefore express themselves easily in the language of the I Ching, because it too is based on the psychology of the individuation process that forms one of the main interests of 'Taoism and of Zen Buddhism."*

- [166] **Abraxas**

Not a theory, but central to Jung's beliefs was that of Abraxas who, in Gnosticism, is considered to be above all other deities. This image of Abraxas compliments the Gnostics' belief that the material world is evil and the spiritual realm is sacred. So, in this context, the opposing view of Christianity is challenged by the belief that salvation comes through the elevated mind i.e., *gnosis or esoteric knowledge*. It is, therefore, no coincidence that Carl Jung, through the black awakening of his generation, placed Abraxas as a central character in his numerous encounters with 'the spirits' identified as Philemon,

---

[165] The archetypes and the collective unconscious by Jung, CG (Carl Gustav), 1875-1961, page 340
[166] **abraxas,** also spelled **Abrasax,** sequence of Greek letters considered as a word and formerly inscribed on charms, amulets, and gems in the belief that it possessed magical qualities. In the 2nd century AD, some Gnostic and other dualistic sects, which viewed matter as evil and the spirit as good and held that salvation came through esoteric knowledge, or gnosis, personified Abraxas and initiated a cult sometimes related to worship of the sun god. Basilides of Egypt, an early 2nd-century Gnostic teacher, viewed Abraxas as the supreme deity and the source of divine emanations, the ruler of all the 365 heavens, or circles of creation — one for each day of the year. The number 365 corresponds to the numerical value of the seven Greek letters that form the word abraxas. Britannica, The Editors of Encyclopaedia. "abraxas". Encyclopedia Britannica, 27 Feb. 2023, https://www.britannica.com/topic/abraxas-sequence-of-Greek-letters. Accessed 11 March 2023.

Ka or other names. In his writing, there is also a play on the title 'God', almost as though this would deceive some into believing in his expression of spirituality, people who may otherwise distance themselves from his specific notions of salvation.

- **Myers-Briggs personality or spirituality test**

This section would be incomplete without mentioning the Myers-Briggs testing used by professionals and ministries. Katharine Cook Briggs (1875-1968) and her daughter Isabel Briggs Myers (1897-1979) were followers of the Jungian psychological types which resulted in the 'introspective' psychometric test. This test is widely used and is trusted as a scientific approach to determining character types. Of course, those that understand Jung's alchemistic, astrological and spirit guidance approach to his work will understand that the MBTI has subsequently founded its methods on a foundation which is the equivalent of reading astrological star signs. This makes the MBTI test a tool of mystical sorts rather than scientific. This is an important distinction to make.

- **Four Colour Energies – Cool Blue / Fiery Red / Earth Green / Sunshine Yellow**

Using the intel provided by the spirit guide Philemon combined with the infamous colour energies borrowed from Hippocrates, the personality type test is formed. This is a popular mechanism for people who are desperate to have a generic method of labelling themselves and others. Interestingly, once a group of individuals has been selected and comfortably placed in any one of these categories, the competition soon heats up to highlight a colleague's inability to manage or a colleague's inferiority due to their shy demeanour confirmed by the colour energies.

The roots of this method are as divisive as the method itself. By design, it invites the uninitiated to open the door to occult mysticism while whetting the appetite to pursue further knowledge on self-actualisation.

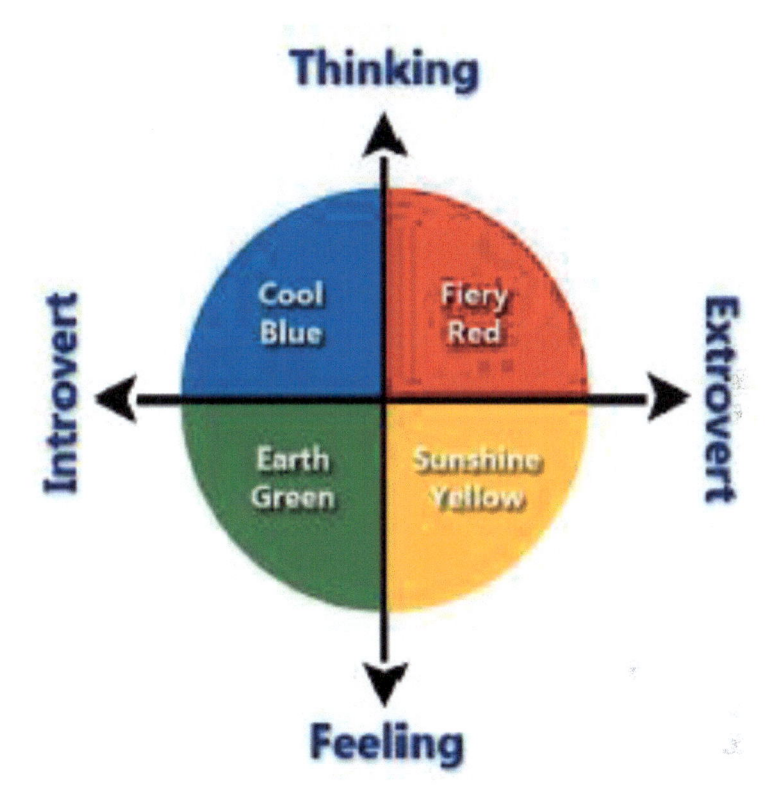

Thinking / **Introvert** / **Extrovert** / **Feeling**

- Cool Blue
- Fiery Red
- Earth Green
- Sunshine Yellow

In light of the very strange and often overtly occult tones of this secular religion of psychoanalysis, its presence in the root system of the eugenics tree coalesces with its deceptive tones of self-determination. At first, it appears to be a distant, objective world of thought, dedicated to fulfilling its mantra of wellbeing, but in the end, duping its recipients into accepting the occult as salvation. These are not my words. Here is a conversation which Carl Jung has with his soul, but we understand the nature of his conversations, right? The extract is taken from Carl Jung's *The Red Book: Liber Novus* page 211,

"On January 5, 1922, he had a conversation with his soul concerning both his vocation and Liber Novus......

[Soul:] No, listen! You should not break up a marriage, namely the marriage with me, no person should supplant me ... I want to rule alone.

[I:] SO you want to rule? From whence do you take the right for such a presumption?

[Soul:] This right comes to me because I serve you and your calling. I could just as well say, you came first, but above all your calling comes first.

[I:] But what is my calling?

[Soul:] The new religion and its proclamation.

[I:] Oh God, how should I do this?

[Soul:] Do not be of such little faith. No one knows it as you do. There is no one who could say it as well as you could.

From colour coded characteristics borrowed from Hippocrates to psychological types and archetypes, extroversion, introversion, collective unconscious and persona, the question remains, who will bow at this altar for a renewing of their soul and mind at the behest of Carl Jung, the god-man and embodiment of Homo-Deus? Whatever your answer, his influence is unprecedented and has found legitimacy amongst the literati of the 21st century and beyond, embedded in Gnostic services and asserted from new-age pulpits this cult is yet to be refuted and the boardrooms are yet to expunge its sermons. What is to be said of the medical surgeries and universities that align this form of occultism as a legitimate tool to be used on vulnerable, broken and damaged individuals? However, this question finds little strength in debate as many still defend the Jungian roots as though they are the embodiment of truth. It is a religion of sorts that has been born wearing the mask of truth but hiding the real face of its character, which is Deception.

Is Carl Jung the only one pursuing such an inner journey of man becoming a god? Sadly not, as there were and are others who are as damaged but open to a new form of spirituality.

> [167]*Answer C: "One does not become enlightened by imagining figures of light, but by making the darkness conscious. The latter procedure, however, is disagreeable and therefore not popular."*
> **Carl Jung**

Abraham Maslow - Humanism in Psychology and Empirical Spirituality

Positive Psychology - Saving the World by a New Spirituality

But know this, that in the last days perilous times will come: ***For men will be lovers of themselves,*** *lovers of money, boasters, proud, blasphemers, disobedient to parents, unthankful, unholy, unloving, unforgiving, slanderers, without self-control, brutal, despisers of good, traitors, headstrong, haughty, lovers of pleasure rather than lovers of God, having a form of godliness but denying its power. And from such people turn away! For of this sort are those who creep into households and make captives of gullible women loaded down with sins, led away by various lusts, always learning and never able to come to the knowledge of the truth.*

---

[167] The Collected Works of C.G. Jung, Volume 13: Alchemical Studies by C. G. Jung, edited and translated by Gerhard Adler and R. F.C. Hull.

I Timothy 3:1-7 (NKJV)

In addition to the Carl Jung narrative, we might recognise the hierarchy of needs pyramid used in various instances of training and 'self-actualisation' programs as an aid to understanding 'self' and the needs of others, be they children, adults, office staff and the list goes on. Once again, this repetitive message of searching for a new spirituality undergirds the philosophy of Abraham Maslow and Carl Rogers. The reality is, you could choose any individual in the arena of psychology during this era and alight upon the same self-destructive root. The journey is always inwards, and the solutions supposedly lie within the unconscious in one form or another. The contradiction becomes evident when the individual that has made these truth claims is put under the spotlight. Repeatedly, these individuals carry the insecurities and issues that they claim to help others overcome while practising their occult theology and exploring its influence at the expense of those most in need. Sadly, the symbolism of the same root theology permeates our lives from home, to places of education and even our places of work. The ultimate in each example seems to direct the individual to an ultimate state of mind that can only be described as transcendence, full self-actualisation.

It is not necessary to go into detail regarding Abraham Maslow and Carl Rogers as both share the award for introducing Humanistic Psychology as though it was somehow different and separate from other forms of psychology. However, it is safe to say that their search was for a new form of spirituality that would save the world. Yet the recurring theme of delving into the occult box of tricks for the answer is hard to believe if it were not for their own words that declare it.

[168]We can no longer rely on tradition, on consensus, on cultural habit, on unanimity of belief to give us our values. Of course, we never should have rested on tradition - as its failures must have proven to everyone by now – it never was a firm foundation. It was destroyed too easily by truth, by honesty, by facts, by science, by simple, pragmatic, historical failure.

Only truth itself can be our foundation, our base for building. Only empirical, naturalistic knowledge, in its broadest sense, can serve us now.

[169]It used to be that all these questions were answered by organized religions in their various ways. Slowly these answers have come more and more to be based on natural, empirical fact and less and less on custom, tradition, "'revelations," sacred texts, interpretations by a priestly class. What I have been pointing out in this lecture is that this process of a steadily increasing reliance on natural facts as guides in making life decisions is now advancing into the realm of "spiritual values." Partly this is so because of new discoveries, but partly it is so because more and more of us realize that nineteenth-century science has to be redefined, reconstructed, enlarged, in order to be adequate to this new task. This job of reconstructing is now proceeding.

In Abraham Maslow's case, the hierarchy of needs became enshrined in the shape of a pyramid *(which does not appear in his notes)* and three years before his death the American Humanist Association (AHA) named Maslow humanist of the year. The AHA's motto is 'Good without God.' A contradiction in terms really, as the ultimate of self-actualisation in the hierarchy of needs is the same as Carl Jung's spirit guide approach which culminates in man becoming 'god.'

---

[168] Religions, Values, and Peak-Experiences by Maslow, Abraham H. (Abraham Harold), p. 9
[169] Page 52

SELF-ACTUALIZATION
morality, creativity, spontaneity, acceptance, experience purpose, meaning and inner potential

SELF-ESTEEM
confidence, achievement, respect of others, the need to be a unique individual

LOVE AND BELONGING
friendship, family, intimacy, sense of connection

SAFETY AND SECURITY
health, employment, property, family and social abilty

PHYSIOLOGICAL NEEDS
breathing, food, water, shelter, clothing, sleep

While these and others venture off into the wilderness searching for an alternative form of religion clad in pseudo-scientific clothing, people everywhere are going deeper into themselves. In direct contrast to the words of The Messiah and the Apostles in the Bible we are encouraged to love ourselves more before we can love others, when the reality is we already love ourselves too much, making it impossible to see anyone else or to see past the inner darkness that constantly overwhelms and engulfs us. Not true? Well ask yourself this; when was the last time that you were on the receiving end of someone else's sarcastic remarks, or you were prevented from doing something that you were passionate about? In that instance, did you respond by accepting their slight of you because you loved yourself so much? Or did you respond in a manner that was more in line with your thoughts of *'this is unacceptable'* and refuse to stand for it. If your response was the latter, then you have just proven that you love yourself. This is demonstrated by the decision you made to protect yourself as a human being and to defend your right to choose, think or act. In a way, a form of *'self-*

defence.' However, if this is left unchecked, and it often is, it can mature into something that lacks any form of boundary whatsoever.

It isn't an accident that Rabbi Paul wrote about this to Timothy when he was inspired to state, 'men shall be lovers of themselves' as it is clearly displayed in this age. What's the answer? Well, keep reading and let's finish the journey to find out.

Answer D: *A positive self image and healthy self esteem is based on approval, acceptance and recognition from others; but also upon actual accomplishments, achievements and success upon the realistic self confidence which ensues.*
Abraham Maslow

Mental Illness

Thomas Szasz, a leading Psychiatrist, professor at the State University of New York Upstate Medical University, and fellow of the American Psychiatric Association states in his book 'The Myth of Mental Illness,'

[170]*"Until the middle of the nineteenth century, and beyond, illness meant a bodily disorder whose typical manifestation was an alteration of bodily structure: that is, a visible deformity, disease, or lesion, such as a misshapen extremity, ulcerated skin, or a fracture or wound. Since in this original meaning of it, illness was identified by altered bodily structure, physicians distinguished diseases from non diseases according to whether or not they could detect an abnormal change in the structure of a person's body. This is why, after dissection*

---

[170] 'The Myth of Mental Illness' pp. 11, 12

of the body was permitted, anatomy became the basis of medical science: by this means, physicians were able to identify numerous alterations in the structure of the body which were not otherwise apparent. As more specialised methods of examining bodily tissues and fluids were developed, the pathologist's skills in detecting hitherto unknown bodily diseases grew explosively. Anatomical and pathological methods and criteria continue to play a constantly increasing role in enabling physicians to identify alterations in the physicochemical integrity of the body and to distinguish between persons who display such identifiable signs of illness and those who do not.

It is important to understand clearly that modern psychiatry and the identification of new psychiatric diseases began not by identifying such diseases by means of the established methods of pathology, but by creating a new criterion of what constitutes disease: to the established criterion of detectable alteration of bodily structure was now added the fresh criterion of alteration, of bodily function; and, as the former was detected by observing the patient's body, so the latter was detected by observing his behavior. This is how and why conversion hysteria became the prototype of this new class of diseases - appropriately named "mental' to distinguish them from those that are "organic," and appropriately called also "functional" in contrast to those that are "structural." Thus, whereas in modern medicine new diseases were discovered, in modern psychiatry they were invented. Paresis was proved to be a disease; hysteria was declared to be one.

It would be difficult to overemphasize the importance of this shift in the criteria of what constitutes illness. Under its impact, persons who complained of pains and paralyses but were apparently physically intact in their bodies-that is, were healthy, by the old standards-were now declared to be suffering from a "functional illness." Thus was hysteria invented. And thus were all the other mental illnesses invented each identified by the various complaints or functional-behavioral alterations of the persons affected by them".

In addition to Thomas Szasz's articulation on the subject, the [171]CEP or Council for Evidence-based Psychiatry makes the following observations in a paper called *'Unrecognised Facts about Modern Psychiatric Practice'*.

"There are no known biological causes for any of the psychiatric disorders apart from dementia and some rare chromosomal disorders. Consequently, there are no biological tests such as blood tests or brain scans that can be used to provide independent objective data in support of any psychiatric diagnosis."

After the CEPs opening statement, it is undergirded by the following quote,

[172]*"A simplistic biological reductionism has increasingly ruled the psychiatric roost... [we have] learned to attribute mental illness to faulty brain chemistry, defects of dopamine, or a shortage of serotonin. It is biobabble as deeply misleading and unscientific as the psychobabble it replaced."*

Andrew Scull, Professor of History of Psychiatry, Princeton University, in The Lancet

In Andrew Scull's article he explores the complex web of psychiatric institutions and psychiatric development which includes the lead up to his above quotation in which he makes a revealing point about the subject of mental illness. He directs the reader to the statement of the US National Institute of Mental Health which declared the 1990s as "the decade of the brain" and as he puts it,

"A simplistic biological reductionism increasingly ruled the psychiatric roost. Patients and their families learned to attribute

---

[171] © Council for Evidence-based Psychiatry 2014
[172] A psychiatric revolution Scull, Andrew, The Lancet, Volume 375, Issue 9722, 1246 - 1247

mental illness to faulty brain biochemistry, defects of dopamine, or a shortage of seratonin..."

The information drawn out by these and other researchers, who are not Christians I may add, should ring alarm bells that wake us up to a reality that we have purchased with our world influencing 'self' initiatives. However, if what they are saying is considered it could make a difference to someone on a journey of understanding and possibly help them avoid the mistake of creating or accepting a diagnosis that may not be applicable in the first place.

The CEPs paper is split into thirteen key points for exploration. The thirteen points are,

1. No known biological causes
2. Myth of the chemical imbalance
3. Diagnostic system lacks validity
4. Psychiatric drugs cause altered mental states
5. Antidepressants have no benefit over placebo
6. Worse long-term outcomes
7. Long-lasting negative effects
8. Negative effects are often misdiagnosed
9. Psychiatric drug withdrawal can be disabling
10. More medicating of children
11. Regulator funded by industry
12. Conflicts of interest
13. Manipulation and burying of drug trial data

In case there should be any element of doubt there are 192 citations at the end of this document, providing the reader with a huge database of reference material for personal investigation. Of course, the big question is, *'If mental illness is a myth, misnomer, biobabble then the cause of our issues must reside elsewhere, right?'* This is a mountainous thought that will split contemporary opinion, especially as society is being ushered down a road manufactured by modern 'experts' of the mind. But as we now know, the evidence will retain its position as the elephant in the room until the fatal day when someone, somewhere, talks about it.

In a world of painless ease and escapism, 'mental illness' has become a mixing pot for new programmes which conveniently embed themselves in our homes, communities, offices, boardrooms and even congregations. Entering wherever someone will accept their solutions, as though these solutions were a collective Noah's Ark designed to provide a haven from the ensuing flood tide of human emotion and breakage. Sadly, for many recipients, this vehicle is nothing more than an eternal prison with no means of parole or escape, while for others, they stand on the cliff edge of an unthinkable reality while gazing listlessly into an abyss of despair and hopelessness.

Ironically, the symbol used to represent the Third Reich is the swastika, which comes from the Sanskrit 'svastika', which means "good fortune" or "**well-being**." A mantra that has become synonymous with our overall healthy state of mind and body.

Medicine

In today's world of medicine (one of the roots), illness is not always viewed as something to diagnose solely through asking questions, examining records, getting to know the patient and any specific physical problems, but many within the profession are making a diagnosis beginning with your place of cultural origin. This approach is based on [173]'Medical Eugenics'.

---

[173] Tabery, J. (2014, April 29). Genetics. Retrieved October 1, 2022, from https://eugenicsarchive.ca/discover/encyclopedia/535eec197095aa00000002 2c

So, in this context, if you walk into a doctor's surgery as a dark skinned individual, your appearance has already been factored into the process of diagnosis and logged in the mind of the practitioner. The familiar opening question would be something like, "Is there anyone in your family who has this condition?"

In addition, to support this diagnostic model, statistics are provided that indicate you are more prone than other cultural groups to have acquired a particular illness, 'genetically'. All of this without knowing who you are? Now apply this same approach to prenatal screening which is to determine the health of the foetus by considering your heritage and cultural origin. Surely, if this is the process of diagnosis you are already predisposed to a potential misdiagnosis due to a racially biased model rooted in eugenics and not science?

Antipsychotics. The Problem or the Cure?

NB: Do not stop taking your medication without consulting your Doctor or Health Professional first.

"These drugs, when they do have effects, work more like substances that temporarily alter our state of mind, such as caffeine or cannabis. These pills, in other words, don't cure us they simply change us. They can throw us temporarily into a foreign state of mind, into an altered version of who we are."[174]

[175]*"Ritalin and other stimulants are prescribed to millions of adults and children diagnosed with ADHD. Stimulants affect dopamine along with other neurotransmitters, and as a consequence of this it has been suggested that ADHD is related to dysfunction in the dopamine system. However, there is no convincing evidence that ADHD is caused by dopamine abnormalities. Moreover, the characteristic effects of stimulants, which include improved attention at low doses, occur in everyone regardless of whether or not they have an ADHD diagnosis."*

Have you noticed how we are obsessed with speaking to the next generation about how they can *"be anything, do anything and say anything?"* A message that is reinforced in the endless movies that have helped to deconstruct the family unit and

---

[174] Quoted in Davies J., Cracked: why psychiatry is doing more harm than good (London: Icon (2012))

[175] Council for Evidence-based Psychiatry 2014

position the child (with super intelligence and/or superpowers) as the force that saved the home (and the world) from descending into chaos at the onslaught of alien entities. Screaming at the top of their voice, "*Mum, Dad come on, move now or it will eat ya...!*" Ok, so I've stretched it a bit there, (or is that an example of [176]hyperbole?) but you know what I mean, right? Whatever happened to the super... **'man'**, wonder... **'woman'**, bionic...**man** or bionic...**woman**? Not that I'm advocating you watch any of these for all sorts of reasons, but isn't there something wrong with our current cultural picture or am I the only one that thinks this is strange?

Yet with everything we are telling our children, it is evidently clear that they are being set up for failure, not just in job opportunities, and education, as is often the focus, but life in general. In their tender teenage years, they are thrust into roles of global proportions under the banner of *'you can be and do anything if you put your mind to it'* with a lifetime experience of approximately seven teenage years (if you exclude the time it took to learn to crawl, walk, speak, and think independently). This is not a slight on their importance or ability by any means as there are young adults, teenagers who have been born into the most atrocious situations that many of the adults around them have never experienced but let us not think this is a qualification for using them as mascots for the world's ills. A world which is responsible for creating their circumstances through wars, corruption, global greed etc.

At the same time, the one thing that every human being (including our children) needs to function, is being targeted by relentless programmes of the mind. It has seeped into every area of a child's existence and adults make it impossible to breathe.

---

[176] Exaggerated statements or claims not meant to be taken literally: he vowed revenge with oaths and hyperboles | [mass noun] : you can't accuse us of hyperbole.

Playing the role of the 'mental health police' trained to observe the smallest change in behaviour, as was the case of an eight-year-old child called Gillian Lynne, later known as Dame Gillian Lynne.

In her autobiography, [177] she mentions that by the time she was eight that it was clear that she suffered from,

[178]*"some kind of excess of energy. So much so that I was a real pain to everybody. Nowadays I dare say I would have been labelled hyperactive and my diet would be scrutinised, and a pill given, but back then the approach was quite different... I was nick-named 'wriggly-bottom' at home."*

In her autobiography, she continues to explain that her parents didn't know what else to do about her behaviour, so they took her to a local doctor, a doctor who knew her and any ailments she suffered as a child. Contrary to the modern model of an almost self-diagnosis approach and the often distant doctor-patient relationship today, this doctor observed her closely as her mother gave a long speech about the annoying symptoms of her daughter. What happens next should challenge every modern practitioner to think about their role in the health of their patients regardless of timescales, job titles, threats of being struck off and the like.

"The doctor fixed me with his highly intelligent beady eye, unobtrusively put on some music and said to my mother, 'Mrs Pyrke, I would like to have a word with you outside please. Young lady, you stay in here.'

Out they went and the minute they had gone I started to dance to the music, even going up on his desk because it seemed like a wonderful vantage point for jumping off from. What I hadn't noticed

---

[177] A Dancer in Wartime: One Girl's Journey from the Blitz to Sadler's Wells by Lynne, Gillian Publication date 2011
[178] Page 12, 13

was that his door was one of those beautiful old glass ones with etched designs, through which the doctor and my mother were watching. Mummy told me afterwards that the doctor had said, 'There is no trouble with this child, Mrs Pyrke. She is a natural dancer – you must take her immediately to dance class."

Dame Gillian Lynne's mother listened to the doctor's wise advice and took her daughter, the 'next day', to Miss Sharp's class for young ladies in the ballroom of the Bell Hotel in Bromley. After the observations of Miss Sharp, an experienced teacher, Mrs Pyrke was invited to bring her daughter to attend a regular Friday class. Gillian Lynne states,

"When Daddy arrived home a little after us, we both spoke to him at once and soon he joined us in our euphoria. Our bungalow was a happy place to be that night, though I am sure that later, as one overexcited child was sent early to bed, serious discussion was had as to how my parents could afford these lessons."

From here she went on to become a world-renowned dancer with performances and accolades that filled at least eleven sides of A4 sheets of paper. Incredible.

If you have understood anything to date, the big question we must all ask ourselves is, 'how many gifted children have we already destroyed under the guise of this label of ADHD?' Not to mention all the other 'mental illness' labels that we have conveniently stuck on the foreheads of our children without the proper, wise counsel of someone who sees beyond the annoyances you may be experiencing? The answer to this question demands a responsible and immediate call to action before it's too late.

In addition to my cursory observations, a recent survey by ADHD UK found that *a total estimate of 2.6 million people in the*

UK has ADHD (708,000 children, 1.9m adults). [179] The organisation Mind tells us that 1 in 4 people will experience a mental health problem of some kind in England and 1 in 6 people report experiencing a common mental health problem. Ok, so let's put this together in a way that makes obvious sense. [180] The UK population in mid-year 2020 was estimated to be close to 67 million people (67, 026 300 million). So, that equates to, 16.7 million of the general population who will experience a 'mental health' problem of some kind and, 11.2 million people of the population who report having experienced a 'common mental health' problem. By subtracting those diagnosed with ADHD from those who reported experiencing a common mental health problem, this equates to 11.2 million minus 2.6 million leaving a figure of 8.6 million who had problems that were not categorised as having ADHD. However, they will fall under some other categorisation of mental illness.

Whichever way you do the maths, the statistics are constantly reinforcing the message that the UK's population is experiencing an epidemic of the mind. An epidemic as defined in the Merriam-Webster dictionary as *'affecting or tending to affect a disproportionately large number of individuals within a population, community, or region at the same time'.* This is impossible to believe given the previous history of the development of mental illness, however, there is something else going on here.

Dr Peter Breggin is known as the conscience of psychiatry, a psychiatrist and opponent of the ADHD diagnosis and prescribing medication to children. His involvement in this field includes his wife Ginger Breggin and together they were responsible for stopping US federally funded programmes which targeted black inner city children using psychosurgery,

---
[179] https://www.mind.org.uk/information-support/types-of-mental-health-problems/statistics-and-facts-about-mental-health/how-common-are-mental-health-problems/#References
[180] https://www.ons.gov.uk/

eugenics and other means of behavioural control. In a paper, he writes the following,

[181]"*I began to see a pattern that I call medication spellbinding. Technically, the new scientific concept is called intoxication anosognosia: not knowing that you are intoxicated. Medication spellbinding has four basic effects.*

***First,** people taking psychiatric drugs rarely realize how much the drugs are impairing them mentally or emotionally. They often do not recognize that they've become irrational, depressed, angry, or even euphoric since beginning the medication.*

***Second,** if they do realize that they are having painful emotional feelings, medication spellbinding causes them to blame their feelings on something other than the drug. They may get angry at their husbands, wives or children, and become abusive. Or they might blame themselves and become suicidal. Often they confuse the harmful drug effect with their emotional problems and attribute their emotional distress to "mental illness."*

***Third,** medication spellbinding makes some people feel that they are doing better than ever when in reality they are doing much worse than ever. In one case, a man who was high on a combination of an antidepressant and a tranquilizer happily went on a daylight robbery spree in his hometown wearing no disguise. Another otherwise ethical citizen happily embezzled money while documenting the details in easily accessible company computer files. Both men thought they were on top of the world.*

---

[181]The Conscience of Psychiatry: The Reform Work of Peter R. Breggin, M.D. *is the first biography of Dr Breggin's work. Edited and sponsored by the International Center for the Study of Psychiatry and Psychology*

Fourth, some people become so medication spellbound that they lose control of themselves and perpetrate horrendously destructive actions. My book opens with the story of an otherwise kind and gentle man who became agitated on an antidepressant and drove his car into a policeman to knock him down to get his gun to try to kill himself. In another case, a ten-year-old boy with no history of depression hung himself after taking a prescription stimulant for ADHD. He documented the dreadful unfolding events while speaking in a robotic monotone into his computer.

Particularly striking to me, of those who have survived, none of the people I have evaluated has ever perpetrated again after stopping the offending medication. There has been zero recidivism in the cases I have evaluated and who have stopped taking the medication."

If we understand what has been happening, we will see that our attention is being directed to an 'illness' which requires medication, instead of recognising the often disastrous side effects of mind-bending drugs in themselves. Combine this with the messages of self-determination and a child that fails to meet the high ideals without any foundations on which to stand, if they do not achieve their promised expectations, it is inevitable that they will eventually be in crisis.

Unlike the preachers of such ideals, these children are yet to become men and women, they are yet to discover that life is not the same for all and hard work or intelligence is not the guaranteed solution to progress in life. Ultimately, without opportunity and without the ability to think, one is already trapped in a prison forged in the mind potentially leading to disastrous outcomes.

So, what will the next 10 years look like when the children of this age become the evidence of our superior ideas and theories, including the indoctrination of medicating the unseen mind/emotions? Will our denial of knowing the truth be enough to recover the loss that millions will suffer, or will we carry out our due diligence now confessing our sins before the one who knows our game? Will we continue to vehemently defend our position, failing to realise that we have missed the vitally important point? Which is, that we have successfully lobbied for the prevention of lab tests on animals under the banner of animal cruelty, but we have failed to prevent the experimentation of drug use on our children. Who is fighting for them?

To keep this in context, please remember not to confuse this discourse on medication with the treatment of physical ailments. There is a difference.

Population Control

(See earlier Chapter- The Evangelists)

*"It is generally agreed that lower forms of life must give place to higher types, and when the pioneer of civilization makes his way into the forest, he must of necessity destroy the man-killing animals living therein. Exterminating warfare is also waged against the savage members of the human race wherever they oppose the establishment of conditions necessary for the development of the more highly organized types. Of course, where improvement by instruction and subsequent cooperation is possible, this extreme of annihilation need not be practiced, **but unless it can be shown that there is room enough on earth for both savage and civilized, the savage must go.**"*

'The fear of growth' is now central to modern society and continues to grip the news headlines and politics. This is not new and continues as a central theme taking its lead from Thomas Malthus as did Margaret Sanger and her cohorts. The emphasis, however, has placed 'saving the planet' centre stage, turning a subject that was once an obvious tool for controlling the numbers of those deemed 'unfit' into an excuse for prioritising the planet over the sanctity of preserving human life. However, on the other hand, we are crying out for more housing, better health for a healthy workforce, and a reduction in immigration to protect the local economy. It appears that fear rules and the intellect is king in this ever-growing root system.

This fear, as promoted by the early evangelists, lives on and is leading most people to openly accept their teaching without considering what is on the table. Inevitably, one fear leads to another.

Save the Planet Lose the Child / Age Reduction

For You formed my inward parts;
You covered me in my mother's womb.
I will praise You, for I am fearfully and wonderfully made;
Marvelous are Your works,
And that my soul knows very well.
My frame was not hidden from You,
When I was made in secret,
And skillfully wrought in the lowest parts of the earth.

Psalm 139:13-15 (NKJV)

The ensuing gladiatorial battle of opposing world views openly collides on the global stage, fighting for the right to determine who should live and who will die. Anxious onlookers frantically wave their branded banners for their preferred champion in the hope that a win would secure a gamester's swag of huge reward.

Ill-informed of the trouble their interfering forbears had caused in honour of this public onslaught, the sword of accusation recklessly swings back and forth to the cheers of an overconfident crowd, determined to win at any cost. As the heated battle intensifies, the balance of opportunity swings back and forth. In one brief moment, the momentum of the short sword of feminism alights upon the defence of the opposition, disarming the deliberating woman with chants of *'take charge of your own body'* in disregard for the tiny life within. In the next instant, the wieldy sword of human rights crashes in with obvious threats of annihilating any opposition to assisted death programmes borrowing from the mentality that reintroduced this devilish idea through the doctrine of evolution. Not to mention the brutal axe of conspiratorial mind play which set the tone for the battle itself, destroying every opposing thought in its way. It's all over.

However, the double-edged sword of the Spirit decimates the action of all its opponents by cutting through the very thoughts of man and exposing the inner workings of self-preservation dressed as care for all. Amid a baying crowd, this exposed body of falsehood is now left defenceless and unarmed, causing the bloodthirsty to call for death while the remaining voices demand that life be spared.

Over the confused and insistent mob, a cloud of uncertainty descends like storm clouds lighting upon a once sunny place. To the observant bystander, the sinking noise diminishes under the realisation that someone has to decide who lives and who dies. Who could that someone be that has all knowledge of the past, the present and the future of each life that is destined to enter this world's reality? Who will define what is life and which child is deserving of it? What model of selection will determine which soul should die due to its dilapidated state after 60+, 70+, even 80+ years on the planet? In this humanistic endeavour to usurp the throne of authority in these delicate matters of life and death the Apostle John during his time of incarceration on the island of Patmos observed a legally sealed scroll which came with a similar problem of 'who is worthy?'

"And I saw in the right hand of Him who sat on the throne a scroll written inside and on the back, sealed with seven seals. Then I saw a strong angel proclaiming with a loud voice, "Who is worthy to open the scroll and to loose its seals?" And no one in heaven or on the earth or under the earth was able to open the scroll, or to look at it. So

I wept much, because no one was found worthy to open and read the scroll, or to look at it."

Revelation 5:1-4 (NKJV)

This cataclysmic, world changing release of a prophetic reality could only find its legitimacy in the hands of a righteous, selfless individual. One who had nothing to gain from the action of opening what was hidden but someone who had already given their life to save a life. Above all, this individual could not be governed by personal inconveniences, wealth opportunities and agendas.

But one of the elders said to me, "Do not weep. Behold, the Lion of the tribe of Judah, the Root of David, has prevailed to open the scroll and to loose its seven seals."

The reality is, that regardless of the arguments surrounding abortion and euthanasia, the unworthy face of humanistic kindness exploits the narrative to introduce new laws and new forms of morality. Sadly, at the expense of the individuals who are wrestling with an immediate and often overwhelming problem that demands a just, wise and unbiased response. So, I ask again, who is worthy?

This brings into question the likes of Margaret Sanger's and Marie Stopes' advocacy of an abortion pill which, had it been administered by all mothers in the last 100 years, would have resulted in the abortion of some of the world's renowned children. People like [182]Andrea Bocelli whose mother was told that her child would be born with a disability, or Steve Jobs [183]whose mother was 23 years old when she could have had him aborted due to the relationship her family disagreed with, but

---

[182] https://www.andreabocelli.com/
[183] Levy, Steven. "Steve Jobs". Encyclopedia Britannica, 20 Feb. 2023, https://www.britannica.com/biography/Steve-Jobs. Accessed 25 February 2023.

instead gave him up for adoption. Of those that survive such an ordeal, how many genuine future influencers have we resigned to a lacklustre existence at best with a feeling of hopelessness reinforced by the adage that 'you are not fit to live' and how many have we lost under society's general position that they are 'worthy to die'?

The sanitisation of this subject has caused all of us to view life as a fad, sometimes an inconvenience resigning the human being to the same destiny as the obsolete technological gadgets of yesterday. A true representation of evolution's tenets of *'why care for the weak when you can dispose of them?'* Hallelujah for the characteristic of 'The Root of David', who casts our sins (and not us) into the sea of forgetfulness in the hope that we will see the light.

As far as the east is from the west, So far has He removed our transgressions from us.

Psalms 103:12 (NKJV)

Modern Art

"...painted directly through me [by these spirits], without any preliminary drawings, and with great force. I had no idea what the paintings were supposed to depict; nevertheless I worked swiftly and surely, without changing a single brush stroke."

Hilma af Klint

Hilma af Klint was an artist and mystic with a deep interest in the things of the occult as a teenager and later became involved with Theosophy which appealed to her desire to go beyond the bounds of conservative art and into the realm of the unconscious. A theme that would influence her work and development as an abstract artist. Through seances and communicating with entities they called 'The High Masters', Hilma af Klint (and her group) would use Hilma af Klint as a conduit to produce automatic works of art. This was a technique used in spiritualism but through automatic writing, which also requires a spirit to communicate through words written by the conduit's hand but with the will completely disengaged. In other words, this type of engagement is the act of psychics as one would expect in séances.

As we have been discussing Ascona and the period of global change, it is recognised that this approach to automatic art was not uncommon but was used by surrealists during the 1920s. The term used in the art world to describe this is automatism, a technique Sigmund Freud would use to explore the unconscious mind of patients, used in dream interpretation and other aspects of a patient's observation. This is a tool which comes under the banner of the occult and this era of striving for a superior expression of the mind making automatism an easy tool for exploring the invisible world of possibilities.

So how did this become a tool in Christian conferences and church services as a legitimate tool for becoming a channel for God's anointing? At what point does The God of Israel authenticate an abstract piece of art as glorifying and life-transforming using automatism?

Just to ensure that you understand these are not my words or a theological stance on the matter, here is a quotation from [184] André Breton *(born February 18, 1896, Tinchebray, France – died September 28, 1966, Paris)*, who was a French poet and co-founder and principal theorist of the surrealist movement. His manifesto called the *'Manifeste du surréalisme'* is noted in the Encyclopedia Britannica as one of several manifestos that played an important role in the history of social movements. Of course, he shared an interest in Sigmund Freud's work on the unconscious and met Freud in 1921. In his manifesto he describes surrealism as follows:

"Pure psychic automatism by means of which one intends to express, either verbally, or in writing, or in any other manner, the actual functioning of thought. Dictated by thought, in the absence of any control exercised by reason, free of any aesthetic or moral concern."

Hans Arp (see *The First Hippie Colony*) is one of those surrealists that used automatism, and so did André Masson and of course André Breton through automatic writing.

This subject is worthy of further exploration as there are issues surrounding the introduction of similar practices within the congregations of God. There are, of course, deep and

---

[184] Britannica, The Editors of Encyclopaedia. "André Breton". Encyclopedia Britannica, 14 Feb. 2023, https://www.britannica.com/biography/Andre-Breton. Accessed 5 March 2023.

meaningful explanations offered by advocates of this practice, but it is a practice that is lacking any biblical foundation, nonetheless. Maybe it's because we romanticise art and all expression of it that we find it easy to rationalise its use as a 'gift of the Spirit' expressed through Christian surrealism, ignoring the 'psychic' aspect of this practice. Is this any different from other areas of expression that we have discussed so far? Not really, as there is a clear distinction between the method and origin of the work of surrealists, in contrast to the gift to draw or paint the world around us by engaging the mind, vision and natural attributes God gave us. To believe otherwise is like asking an Architect to design and detail a building without engaging the mind, resulting in a structure that is both abstract and impossible for anyone to live in as its only purpose is to satisfy and harbour the messages of spirits outside of the designer's world of consciousness. Wait a minute! Some designers did that right; [185]Salvador Dali? Oh, the irony.

"*Surrealism is destructive, but it destroys only what it considers to be shackles limiting our vision.*"

Salvador Dali

---

[185] As an art student in Madrid and Barcelona, Dalí assimilated a vast number of artistic styles and displayed unusual technical facility as a painter. It was not until the late 1920s, however, that two events brought about the development of his mature artistic style: his discovery of Sigmund Freud's writings on the erotic significance of subconscious imagery and his affiliation with the Paris Surrealists, a group of artists and writers who sought to establish the "greater reality" of the human subconscious over reason. To bring up images from his subconscious mind, Dalí began to induce hallucinatory states in himself by a process he described as "paranoiac critical."

Syncretism - So What's New?

Religion

"So He brought me to the door of the court; and when I looked, there was a hole in the wall. Then He said to me, "Son of man, dig into the wall"; and when I dug into the wall, there was a door. And He said to me, "Go in, and see the wicked abominations which they are doing there." So I went in and saw, and there — every sort of creeping thing, abominable beasts, and all the idols of the house of Israel, portrayed all around on the walls."

Ezekiel 8:7-10 (NKJV)

The scripture that you have just read paints a clear picture of what may be described as syncretism. This is not a biblical word, but it does accurately describe what was revealed to Ezekiel by God. So, what is Syncretism? The Oxford Dictionary offers a definition which may help us understand it a little better. Syncretism is,

[186]*The combining of different religions, cultures, or ideas; an instance of this:*

'We are seeing a new syncretism that is uniting parts of different religions.'

This definition emphasises that it is the coming together or fusion of different worlds, be they religious, cultural, or otherwise. A simplistic way of applying syncretism to a biblical context such as the one just described, may be broken down into three areas, the outcome being the result of the first two. Please note this is an aid to understanding and not a dogmatic formula.

The Instruction

1. **Exclusivity:** This place of worship was for the worship of the God of Israel alone.
2. **Purity of Worship:** The Torah (teachings) given to Israel forbid the worship of other deities or spirits in any form.

The Choice

3. **Axiomatic - You Choose:** This is an act of choice. No one is excluded. The choice is reflected in our actions as much as our words. The choice determines the outcome, for example, to worship another is equivalent to saying, *"we do not need God, there is a better deal on the table."* Self-worship, idol worship etc all fall into this area.

[186] (Definition of syncretism from the Cambridge Advanced Learner's Dictionary & Thesaurus © Cambridge University Press)

The Outcome

4. **National Crisis:** This type of religious fusion leads to confusion and ultimate national collapse.
5. **Opportunistic Takeover:** If we choose another we move outside of the boundaries of God's protection. ([187]Deuteronomy 28:36). As in the Garden of Eden, there is always someone ready to take the place of God, but don't forget, unlike God, they will take you for everything you hold dear, physically and/or emotionally.

So in light of this, the hidden occult practices of the nation that Ezekiel witnessed stood out as a stark reminder of human depravity, an image that must have been indelibly imprinted in his mind. Standing in glaring contrast to the view of pure worship that marked Ezekiel's call to service described as follows,

[188]*"Now it came to pass in the thirtieth year, in the fourth month, on the fifth day of the month, as I was among the captives by the River Chebar, that the heavens were opened and I saw visions of God. On the fifth day of the month, which was in the fifth year of King Jehoiachin's captivity, the word of the Lord came expressly to Ezekiel the priest, the son of Buzi, in the land of the Chaldeans by the River Chebar; and the hand of the Lord was upon him there.*

Then I looked, and behold, a whirlwind was coming out of the north, a great cloud with raging fire engulfing itself; and brightness was all around it and radiating out of its midst like the color of amber, out of the midst of the fire. Also from within it came the likeness of four

---

[187] The Lord will drive you and the king you set over you to a nation unknown to you or your ancestors. There you will worship other gods, gods of wood and stone. 37 You will become a thing of horror, a byword and an object of ridicule among all the peoples where the Lord will drive you. (Deuteronomy 28:36 NIV)

[188] Ezekiel 1:1-6 (NKJV) Scripture taken from the New King James Version.

living creatures. And this was their appearance: they had the likeness of a man. Each one had four faces, and each one had four wings..."

Ezekiel was someone who became accustomed to walking with God yet, irrespective of this close walk with God he was unaware of the evil that was being summoned by the nation from the one place that was central to God's presence amongst them. A Holy place of national worship and importance, The Temple. At the time that Ezekiel was taken on this tour in a vision, the nation had been decimated and no one understood why. They now found themselves in exile and here is Ezekiel being shown the reason for their demise. In the mix is the worship of Tammuz forms of ritualistic rites, men and women functioning as prophets and prophetesses speaking out of their own hearts. This included the act of being led by the Elders to turn their backs on the temple and turn their faces towards the east as they worship the sun (Ezekiel 8:16), a practice that the community at Monte Verità embraced.

Let's make no mistake about it, this nation was called to be stewards of 'The Way' as the Bible describes it, a responsibility that came with global attention and equal accountability. As students of [189]**'The Way,'** we are advised to make a careful note of these defining events so that we do not become puffed up in our pride in the belief that we are above such primitive behaviour. There is much we can learn as we are reminded once again by Rabbi Paul.

Moreover, brethren, I do not want you to be unaware that all our fathers were under the cloud, all passed through the sea, all were baptized into Moses in the cloud and in the sea, all ate the same

---

[189] *However, I admit that I worship the God of our ancestors as a follower of* **the Way***, which they call a sect. I believe everything that is in accordance with the Law and that is written in the Prophets,*
Holy Bible, New International Version.

spiritual food, and all drank the same spiritual drink. For they drank of that spiritual Rock that followed them, and that Rock was Christ.

Now all these things happened to them as examples, and they were written for our admonition, upon whom the ends of the ages have come.

1 Corinthians 10:1-4 & 11 (NKJV)

So, to the disciples of 'The Way', what does God see today? In our self-proclaimed, advanced society that relies on occult values, do we still believe that we can self-actualise by searching within? Have we traded the precious things of God like [190]Esau who sold his birthright, (the key to his family's destiny) in exchange for the immediate satisfaction of his hunger in the form of homemade stew? Unfortunately, this trade-off happens too often leaving the onlooker in a place of uncertainty and confusion. There is something about this façade of spirituality that is alluring and appealing to some innate desire to go deeper into the things of the spirit, but which spirit and who is the author?

Unclear answers mean that the line between safe and unsafe, cult tragedies and biblical freedom remains dangerously obscure leading one to believe there is very little difference. However, it is because of the mixture of the clean with the profane that we are left vulnerable to life destroying power bases. For example, the Manson Family (known as the Family) of the 1960s occulture of love led by Charles Manson, a person

---

[190] *Now Jacob cooked a stew; and Esau came in from the field, and he was weary. And Esau said to Jacob, "Please feed me with that same red stew, for I am weary." Therefore his name was called Edom. But Jacob said, "Sell me your birthright as of this day." And Esau said, "Look, I am about to die; so what is this birthright to me?" Then Jacob said, "Swear to me as of this day." So he swore to him, and sold his birthright to Jacob. 34 And Jacob gave Esau bread and stew of lentils; then he ate and drank, arose, and went his way. Thus Esau despised his birthright. Genesis 25:29-35 (NKJV)*

whose followers believed him to be a manifestation of Jesus. Unsurprisingly, they were based in California and engaged in the mind-bending drug taking activity explored by Leary, Huxley and others, eventually leading to murders. There is also the 1970s Peoples Temple Jonestown massacre led by Jim Jones, which took the lives of over 900 people (men women and children) in a mass suicide pact by drinking poison mixed with 'Kool Aid'. What about the Movement for the Restoration of the Ten Commandments of God, the Kanungu cult, founded by Credonia Mwerinde and Joseph Kibweteere? An apocalyptic movement that massacred 700 people by locking them in a church and setting fire to the building. Shocking right? Yet this does not include the Branch Davidians at Waco in 1993, the Heaven's Gate cult of 1997, the Mymensingh family of nine who wanted to experience the pure life of Adam and Eve, so threw themselves under a train, and of course the most devastating and equally disturbing Shoah (Holocaust), a massacre which took place in plain sight taking the lives of millions of people.

So, for those of us who are thinking we are immune to anything that has been mentioned so far, let's look through the hole in the wall as Ezekiel did and let's see if the activities in our places of worship bear the same symbolism and, therefore, the same guaranteed outcome.

Music

Worship Matters

Crossover music has been a phenomenon in the Christian world for decades and has also been a point of debate and disagreement for just as long. However, it is in more recent years that this subject has gained renewed momentum and with it equally confusing points of view.

So, before we move on, let's briefly look at a few characters in the Bible to set our thinking off in the right direction. The first is an obvious character in this area of discussion, the son of Jesse, David. Now is there anywhere in the Bible that describes David as a crossover artist who was so popular that he travelled the world performing for his fans, singing their favourite songs and signing their parchments, *"To X, your superstar, David, future King of Israel"*? How about the Hebrew boys Shadrach, Meshach, and Abed-Nego who were exiles in Babylon and had been promoted to manage the affairs of Babylon? When faced with the threat of execution for not bowing to a demonic image on the queue of the music played by a handpicked symphony, did they bow down to the image at the sound of the music? Did they say? *"We think the music is so inspiring so we will bow but, you've gotta work on your theology O king. Hey, but God understands."* If your answer is no, then you've answered correctly. If you answered yes, well...?

Let's be clear, there were no record companies in sight, no contract deals to be made, no televised live productions in the Tabernacle in the wilderness as the sacrifices were offered, or production teams in Jerusalem during the feast of Shavuot to record Peter and his brethren under the genuine power of the Holy Spirit. There was one focus and one focus only (when in line with God) and that is the worship of God.

Now before you wonder if there is anything wrong with record labels that bring true worshippers into your homes, please use some wisdom here. The issue is how these areas have been completely exploited without anyone noticing the subtle change. For the genuine seeker, it has been used to share the good news that The Messiah of Israel saves. For the genuinely called out preacher, teacher, or worshipper, the message has reached into areas that personal travel cannot. But some caught a glimpse of something that would generate a huge amount of wealth and could also be used to promote another gospel. Ask yourself another question, why would a godless society want to record a modern, sanctified artist to sell records to an uninterested audience? Why would they invite the equivalent of Miriam who played the tambourine when Israel crossed the Red Sea to provide backing percussion to the latest and greatest artist? There is no correlation and at a base level, it makes little sense until we look at the motives.

The music industry is only one aspect of this picture, but it is an area that carries a large amount of influence and is merging religious beliefs, artists and opportunities. Ok, so let's break things down into manageable chunks but in no particular order, examining the areas with 'ministry' as the focal point.

The HipHop Occult Culture

True indeed, I'd like to welcome the rebirth of the Goddess

Word up it's all about knowledge of self

The Truth - Lyrics of KRS-One,

It was through a DVD that was handed to me during the early days of exploring 'The Hidden Tree' that HipHop and other connected areas came into focus. At the time, any new ideas in the form of Christian material were met with healthy scepticism. Not because I didn't trust the giver, but simply because there were so many strange ideas that were floating around under the banner of 'revival' and 'spirituality'. So, disconnecting from reports of anything 'new' became my default unless proven otherwise. However, one day I decided to do the courteous thing and watch the DVD. As I watched, a slow, overwhelming, and troubling realisation came over me. HipHop was one of the new roots of the Hidden Tree. What was relayed I can only describe as a type of magnifying glass which was focused in on the attributes of a single root, zooming in on its origin and place within the pre-existing, complex root system.

The DVD was called, 'The Truth Behind HipHop V' by EX Ministries, G Craige Lewis. Now I hasten to add that 'The Truth Behind HipHop V' caught my attention then and is the one recording that still stands out amongst other recorded expositions on the subject. Before this, anything that I could find on the subject of music was focused on the dangers of 'Rock Music'. Of course, these materials went some way to exposing the influences behind them, but it was missing a whole group of music listeners who did not relate to 'Rock Music'.

How had I not heard about this DVD before? Also, how is it that following its discovery I was now meeting people at other functions who were talking about and having meetings with the DVD as the centre of attention? One thing I knew, I could not have planned all these elements better if I had tried.

As I continued to watch the DVD, it went into great detail on the introduction and impact of HipHop amongst young adults, exposing the experience of black young adults who would once have avoided the occult altogether. This was due to their Christian heritage and aversion to some of the strange behaviour of known rock bands at the time. However, fast forward to our era and the same people groups are voluntarily engaging in previously unacceptable forms of expression and lifestyles, partly due to HipHop. An expression of music that is generally brash, disrespectful, demeaning, loaded with overt occultism, interwoven with profane language, sordid performances and unapologetic, anti-biblical visuals and speech.

Following this discovery, it's as though the light had been switched on and would not be switched off. I began to notice the release of one new video after another that was creating a media buzz. Without any hard work, it was obvious to see that the artist was reinforcing an occult message. There was no filter, no embarrassment, just a clear confirmation that Satanism had gone mainstream in the black community. Was this at the exclusion of other ethnicities? Of course not. This was syncretism at its worst. The noticeable shift in musical expression traversed all communities, as the record industry recruited young adults black or white, including those from Christian backgrounds. On more than a single occasion, the transition of originally 'Christian' artists would be so vast that it was too obvious to miss, shifting from a shy withdrawn individual with little hope of a musical career to the full-on embodiment of vulgarity and profanity as though they had swallowed an identity changing pill.

Yet, they are the idols on the walls of most places of worship, they are the ones that are invited to stand in support of the elders who metaphorically turn their back on the Temple while leading the congregations in the worship of the sun and Gnostic mass. Topping off the experience with a baptism in ritualistic ice-cold water while throwing up a Baphomet one moment and preaching Jesus the next. Finally, to dominate the pulpits that were once reserved for the dedicated man or woman of God. It seems so incredible that it is impossible to move on without asking, how did this happen? Possibly a slightly naive question given the land that we have travelled but it is still an appropriate question, nonetheless.

Now, here is a detail that you may or may not know but it is worth repeating. We have identified the tree and its root system as a religious edifice complete with its roots, branches, and everything else that makes it an organic form. So how does HipHop fit into this if it is simply a genre of music? What relevance is this to the subject at hand? Let me answer these questions beginning with an excerpt from 'The Gospel of HipHop' bible,

[191]*"The concluding point here is that as Hiphoppas we can establish a new nation, a new tribe, even a new race; it's been done before and we are positioned at this time to do it again. However, before the creation of our Hip Hop nation, we as Hip Hop scholars studying and building Hip Hop as a sustainable community are going to have to reexamine our very existence as a People and above these arbitrary race distinctions, finally create and then define ourselves for ourselves. This would be the true history of Hip Hop – the story of our triumphant SELF-CREATION!"*

When the HipHop bible was launched, HipHop was officially recognised as a religion. There could be no dispute about it and KRS-One would certainly not refute it now. Those that attempt to maintain that it is simply a genre are in denial about what they are involved with. With a careful review of HipHop's tenets, we will notice that its characteristics share the same DNA as the musings of Aleister Crowley, Carl Jung, Carl Rogers and all the other advocates of esoteric knowledge. Firstly, it views Christianity as an obsolete faith ready to be replaced by the religion of HipHop. Secondly, it harbours the notion of Hiphoppas being 'gods' which feeds into the same language as other aspects of the root system we have already explored. Finally, call it self-determination, self-actualisation, or collective consciousness, at a fundamental level it is the same religion as all the other mystic, Gnostic religions that are found in the Hidden Tree (the overarching religious system or framework). Once again in the words of the Gospel of HipHop,

[192]*However, WE ARE GODS! And the absence of such self-knowledge is actually the trigger that sets the universe in motion*

---

[191] Track 4: 441, The Gospel of Hip Hop: The First Instrument by KRS-One
[192] The First Overstanding – Real HipHop, 14

toward self-knowledge. Mystery (not ignorance) is indeed the greatest motivator toward knowledge. As it turns out, not totally knowing our ancestral past has created the possibility of starting a new and even brighter future. We can create and re-create ourselves right now!

Finally, it claims to be establishing a new culture spelt 'Kulture', a similar assertion that earlier mystical, cult leaders have made due to their search for another form of spirituality.

[193]*I AM HIP HOP! And upon this faith (our belief in ourselves as Hiphoppas) we can achieve Truth. Through Hip Hop we have a paradigm by which to create ourselves and document our own body of Hip Hop knowledge and history. Our faith in ourselves as a community of conscious Hiphoppas is what we call Hip Hop's culture or Hiphop* **Kulture***.*

This is the essence of HipHop and the primary reason that its overtly dark symbolism and expression has been carefully designed to appeal to an audience outside of rock music. It is bizarre to think that a new religion founded on ancient mysticism is still being tailored to suit our specific tastes in spirituality. Which is like a school student demanding that the teacher avoid giving them a headache over maths because they don't like the subject, or alternatively, a student rejecting the notion of school education altogether because it doesn't fit in with their feelings about life. These are derisory notions that do not exist in any semblance of reality and are mostly promoted by broken people who have nowhere to go but to look inward into the dark places of the soul for apparent answers. This can only ever lead to more trouble as it is yet to be seen how the inventors of such inward searching have overcome their own issues of suicidal tendencies, emotional instabilities, physical ailments and last but not least, freedom from their very real demons. However, a similar position has permeated Christian worship with a belief that we are creators of our own destiny

[193] The First Overstanding – Real HipHop, 23

through fashioning a personal flavour of the Bible that edits out what we do not like. Emboldened by the platforms, public profiles and superstar connections, artists stand before an all seeing God and proclaim their newly fashioned form of worship in the confidence that it will set people free from all forms of oppression. But I dare say that the sons of Sceva (and others) had more hope of success than the current contingent, having the firm belief that their family heritage as descendants of priests, rubber stamped with the name of Jesus (as a technique), would somehow yield the 'peaceable fruit of righteousness' in the world's spiritual battlefield. Let the record speak for itself,

> *Then some of the itinerant Jewish exorcists took it upon themselves to call the name of the Lord Jesus over those who had evil spirits, saying,* **"We exorcise you by the Jesus whom Paul preaches."** *Also there were seven sons of Sceva, a Jewish chief priest, who did so.*
>
> *And the evil spirit answered and said,* **"Jesus I know, and Paul I know; but who are you?"**
>
> *Then the man in whom the evil spirit was leaped on them, overpowered them, and prevailed against them, so that they fled out of that house naked and wounded. This became known both to all Jews and Greeks dwelling in Ephesus; and fear fell on them all, and the name of the Lord Jesus was magnified.*

Acts 19:13 -17

When considering *'the Paul that demons knew'*, the preacher, Leonard Ravenhill aptly states,

> [194]*"He had no side issues, no books to sell. He had no ambitions — and so had nothing to be jealous about. He had no*

[194] Why Revival Tarries by Ravenhill, Leonard. p. 164.

reputation — and so had nothing to fight about. He had no possessions — and therefore nothing to worry about. He had no "rights" — so therefore he could not suffer wrong. He was already broken — so no one could break him. He was "dead" — so none could kill him. He was less than the least — so who could humble him? He had suffered the loss of all things — so none could defraud him. Does this throw any light on why the demon said, "Paul I know'? Over this God-intoxicated man, hell suffered headaches."

Christian artists seem to believe they can successfully achieve what no other generation has ever been able to do, by merging the worship of a Holy God with that of another. There is no correlation as Ezekiel and many others witnessed and the end is always the same; destruction. The person that was once a wonderful voice with a beautiful personality forgets that old age is coming; good looks and a sweet voice will not be enough to answer the challenges this lifestyle choice is guaranteed to bring. Ultimately, the accuser of the brethren who set everything up as he did for Adam and Eve will one day return to let you know that you have served your purpose and he has no further use for your services.

There is only one solution to this, and it involves the whole body of the Messiah and requires an unreserved dedication to Him. We may also have to take the lead from Nehemiah when he was heading up the transformation of Jerusalem. It required a plan from The God of Israel and the courage only He can offer. Listen to what Nehemiah the reformer had to say,

"Now before this, Eliashib the priest, having authority over the storerooms of the house of our God, was allied with Tobiah. And he had prepared for him a large room, where previously they had stored the grain offerings, the frankincense, the articles, the tithes of grain, the new wine and oil, which were commanded to be given to the Levites and singers and gatekeepers, and the offerings for the priests. But during all this I was not in Jerusalem, for in the thirty-second year of Artaxerxes king of Babylon I had returned to the king. Then after

certain days I obtained leave from the king, and I came to Jerusalem and discovered the evil that Eliashib had done for Tobiah, in preparing a room for him in the courts of the house of God. And it grieved me bitterly; therefore I threw all the household goods of Tobiah out of the room. Then I commanded them to cleanse the rooms; and I brought back into them the articles of the house of God, with the grain offering and the frankincense.

Nehemiah 13:4-9 (NKJV)

Nehemiah's actions seem radical and unfeeling but what would you do if you found out that while you were away the dangerous enemy of your family, friends, children, wife, husband, oh and the God you serve decided to take up residence in the one place that is reserved for you and your God? Would you allow them to continue to have a nice sleep every night and make them a lovely breakfast in the mornings or would you instinctively see it for what it was and exit them via the nearest door making sure to have the place cleaned up and rededicated for the service of God?

These false worshippers stand in the presence of a Holy God, the same God who said to Ezekiel,

"...For they say, 'The Lord does not see us, the Lord has forsaken the land."

Ezekiel 8: 12 - last part (NKJV)

The prevalence of collaboration between artists is one of the most destructive avenues that the enemy of souls has used to infiltrate and undermine the body of Messiah and its message. While the offer of godhood looms in the background waiting for the right moment to capture the heart and mind of a gifted and sometimes publicly recognised soul. The temptation to join forces with the Tobiahs and Sanballats who openly taunted the work of God when it seemed like a meaningless programme of rebuilding, must be guarded against if we are to extract ourselves from the deeper problems that we have already created. There is only one way to be sure that we are singing from the same song sheet and that is, [195] *"You must be born again."*

New Age Ministry

Worship Teams

The natural progression of this dialogue leads us to consider the style and type of worship that congregations are exposed to every week. It doesn't take much for the material that has been consumed in private to reach the ears of a captive audience during worship time. So, when service attendees experience something tantamount to new age philosophy in Christian services, this should not be surprising.

Since the explosion of the occult culture, there have been masses of material and conferences that have promoted a new age/humanistic philosophy. We read newspaper articles, listen to radio broadcasts and watch video interviews on the subject, and it all confirms that there are serious attempts to completely remove Yeshua from every aspect of the biblical narrative inside and outside of congregations. Through the strategic deconstructing of everything that was once the bedrock of society, 'self-determination' in all its forms is demanding its place on the throne of hearts everywhere. Of course, there are many quarters where this has not been successful, and long may

---

[195] *Jesus answered and said to him, "Most assuredly, I say to you, unless one is born again, he cannot see the kingdom of God." Nicodemus said to Him, "How can a man be born when he is old? John 3:3-4 (NKJV)*
Scripture taken from the New King James Version.

it continue, but there is a predicament that is compounded by us 'not knowing' the difference between the truth and the lie.

Our lifestyles have been corrupted with the philosophy of humanism, we have undeniably traded in what we were once stewards of by taking the lead from a society that embraces *'new thought'*, *'do what thou wilt'*, *'if it feels right, it's ok'* as its mantras. 'Positive thinking' and forms of meditation and self-actualisation are seen everywhere, including from the platforms occupied by 'worship leaders' and the like. Not possible? Well, don't take my word for it. The next time you are offered a training course on leadership and spiritual gifts, take a look at the programme and find out about the origin of the methods. Or, carry out an online search for programmes that are being offered to congregations that are aimed at improving or preparing candidates for worship teams — you may be surprised at what you will find.

Now these are not your superstar worship teams that you see every day on your television or computer screens. No, these are everyday congregations that are trying to make a difference in their local community. The mega worship teams already have their place, and it is obvious they are not backing down from anyone or anything outside of their record deals and public fan base. Borrowing from the same mystic roots of the past to offer alternatives to the authentic worship born out of walking the path of the saints. Moving the listener to embark on a journey of inner healing through popular music absent of any Yeshua focused sentiment.

Instead, in conjunction with the musical experience, on offer are courses to improve your worship team using all the theories we touched upon in the section under psychology. The courses and/or tests are applauded as tools that have produced incredible results, helping ministers tailor their services to each personality profile, and providing a personalised spiritual experience. In other circles, the ability to improve ministry teams by using Maslow's hierarchy of needs is promoted as the solution to worship teams' overall performance. Performance is the operative word which is the direct result of excluding God from the central process of individual and community growth. Of course, there's money to be made in these programmes and in an age where our most admired Bible teachers seem to know less about God and more about psychology and 'inner consciousness' and making money from the Bible, it is no wonder that there are few authentic life-changing God encounters to behold in the media, and yet God has not stopped working and He isn't finished yet. However, the real keynote is that we are so busy chasing the cloud of 'revival' out of sheer desperation to 'experience' power trips that we have forgotten that He is so personal that there is no need for an introduction through paid marketing, airtime or algorithms. He does not need to be legitimised by a popular individual if He so chooses. It is purely because of His love for His creation that He has always wanted to walk with us and work through us in bringing about the transformation of the world He so lavishly bestowed upon us.

This is another form of syncretism that is shaping what individuals think while apparently leading you in the worship of The Messiah, rocking you back and forth with the melodic tones of,

My hope is built on nothing less

than Jesus' blood and righteousness.

I dare not trust the sweetest frame,

but wholly lean on Jesus' name.

while clutching the humanistic manual of personality colours and archetypes in the hope that we will not forget our designated 'better self'. Information that is seemingly critical to us understanding our capabilities in the context of a team. How ludicrous is this when each follower of Yeshua has been designated their attributes by Him for the benefit of the community of believers? A community that makes up the body of The Messiah and therefore makes the application of otherworldly philosophies to this body a contradiction in terms.

So how can a measure that has nothing to do with righteousness become the measure for individuals who are to lead in spiritual songs? This holds no water in the lifestyle of the disciples of Yeshua and it is a dangerously misleading practice.

Thankfully, we have numerous accounts of people who surpassed the limiting measures of sinful humanity and we do well to be reminded of them. Take, for example, Moses in the book of Exodus who did not consider himself leadership material. He was not defined by the Myers-Briggs Type Indicator or exposed to the dark intel provided by entities conjured up from another realm. What would he have done if God agreed with our self-centred, soulish methods of profiling? It makes one shudder to think.

The only thing that matters here is what God says to him. So, what place do our theories and self-made religious beliefs have in God's business and who would be brazen enough to suggest such a thing?

Then Moses said to the Lord, "O my Lord, I am not eloquent, neither before nor since You have spoken to Your servant; but I am slow of speech and slow of tongue."

So the Lord said to him, "Who has made man's mouth? Or who makes the mute, the deaf, the seeing, or the blind? Have not I, the Lord? Now therefore, go, and I will be with your mouth and teach you what you shall say."

But he said, "O my Lord, please send by the hand of whomever else You may send."

Exodus 4:10-13 (NKJV)

What would Israel have said if Moses had turned up with nothing more than a personality test result and a bucket load of theories full of superior intellectualism, while declaring it a miracle, a sign, and a wonder that he had finally discovered his better self? All of which in today's world, would confirm him as prepared and ready to oversee the national needs of millions of people. Let's be honest, would he have been confident enough to turn up uninvited to meetings with the son of a Pharaoh that he once grew up with, having reneged on his position as an adopted prince of Egypt following his murder of an Egyptian? The Moses, who as a baby, was superstitiously believed by Pharoah's daughter (his adopted mother) to be a gift from the gods because she found him in the river Nile. Would he have been confident to meet his [196]brother by adoption, now reigning as Pharaoh in place of his deceased father, revered as god over Egypt with the clear understanding that Moses was an enemy of the state. Can you imagine? Instead, the account reads like this,

Then Moses answered and said, "But suppose they will not believe me or listen to my voice; suppose they say, 'The Lord has not appeared to you.' "

So the Lord said to him, "What is that in your hand?" He said, "A rod."

And He said, "Cast it on the ground." So he cast it on the ground, and it became a serpent; and Moses fled from it. Then the Lord

---

[196] Then the daughter of Pharaoh came down to bathe at the river. And her maidens walked along the riverside; and when she saw the ark among the reeds, she sent her maid to get it. 6 And when she opened it, she saw the child, and behold, the baby wept. So she had compassion on him, and said, "This is one of the Hebrews' children."

7 Then his sister said to Pharaoh's daughter, "Shall I go and call a nurse for you from the Hebrew women, that she may nurse the child for you?" Exodus 2:1-7 (NKJV)

said to Moses, "Reach out your hand and take it by the tail" (and he reached out his hand and caught it, and it became a rod in his hand), "that they may believe that the Lord God of their fathers, the God of Abraham, the God of Isaac, and the God of Jacob, has appeared to you."

Exodus 4:1-5 (NKJV)

Moses' confidence and calling were shaped by the intervening hand of the original potter, the God of Abraham, Isaac, and Jacob. Moses was not permitted to take anything that was in any way connected to the religious or supernatural ideals of Egypt. The success of his mission could not be reliant on anything that he believed to be superior thought or forms of enlightenment taught by this culture. After years on the run, Moses' training was different on all fronts and surpassed anything that Egypt had ever seen. Its sole purpose was to strip Moses of self-reliance and all forms of mystic notions. A form of training that is still ongoing for those that do not fit into the mould of the world around them. People who are indeed in the centre of God's will but outside of the norms that society has pervaded as advanced. Well, the Exodus is worthy of careful study and consideration as it is another instance of mysticism at its peak, during a period when the family that Moses descended from was no longer credited as the reason for Egypt's survival. But due to the rise of a Pharaoh that did not know [197]Joseph and

---

[197] So the advice was good in the eyes of Pharaoh and in the eyes of all his servants. 38 And Pharaoh said to his servants, "Can we find such a one as this, a man in whom is the Spirit of God?"
Then Pharaoh said to Joseph, "Inasmuch as God has shown you all this, there is no one as discerning and wise as you. You shall be over my house, and all my people shall be ruled according to your word; only in regard to the throne will I be greater than you." And Pharaoh said to Joseph, "See, I have set you over all the land of Egypt." Genesis 41:37 - 41 (NKJV)

Joseph eventually brought his family to live in the land which he was given rule over. A family which eventually grew into the size of a nation and were

his contribution through righteous judgement, this Pharaoh took it upon himself to turn the growth of these people into an asset that could be used to build his empire. The end is predictable. Egypt, a superpower, was brought to its knees through nationalistic pride.

I dare not venture too far down the road to discuss the issue of Saul who became Paul. A man with credentials as long as his arm slaughtered or imprisoned anyone that did not agree with his theology, met on the road by his Jewish Messiah who spoke to him in Hebrew, surrounding him in his glorious light and then sending him home blind to experience the trip of a lifetime (without hallucinogens). An authentic three-day journey into his character (without the aid of Jungian psychology). When he was ready, Ananias was sent to pray for him, at which point Paul received his sight and was baptised, being transformed by the work of the Holy Spirit. Also, Peter (Mark 14:66-72) could not stand his ground at the crucifixion of Yeshua and lied under the cross-examination of ordinary folk. No longer a vehement defender of his Rabbi Yeshua, but now an embarrassed and broken denier of the same. This process brought him into contact with the [198]resurrected Messiah who was not condemning him but restoring him to a better place of service, a service without self at its heart. Transformed by the act

---

given the nations statutes at a meeting with God (YHWH) in the wilderness. Their official birthplace as a nation. The congregation born in the wilderness, the first gathering of its kind in the world under the visible, powerful guiding hand of God.

[198] For I delivered to you first of all that which I also received: that Christ died for our sins according to the Scriptures, and that He was buried, and that He rose again the third day according to the Scriptures, and that He was seen by Cephas, then by the twelve. 6 After that He was seen by over five hundred brethren at once, of whom the greater part remain to the present, but some have fallen asleep. 1 Corinthians 15:3-6 (NKJV)

of forgiveness [199]Peter later stood up as the spokesperson in the centre of another unprecedented move of God that had not been witnessed in this manner since the earlier reformations in the Torah. The evidence would not be complete if we did not mention the righteous women of the Bible who did not gain status through the intervention of humanism through feminism but stood in their Messiah-given right under the banner of holiness, courage, and forgiveness as sisters and proclaimers of 'The Way'. Women such as [200]Mary Magdalene who was bound by seven demons and set free by Yeshua. A woman who was present at every major event in the lead up to the crucifixion, during the crucifixion and after. A transformed woman whose character remains intact regardless of recent attempts to sully it and the complete work of salvation evident in her life.

Every one of those mentioned became a role model in dispute resolution, leadership, and teamwork. Once changed through the salvation of The Messiah their courage and boldness stood up even in the face of death. Can we honestly say the same about what we are offering to our trainees in the congregations? Can we honestly say that we are helping to establish characters of fortitude? Then maybe it's time to stop trying to peddle the darkness in the light.

---

[199] Peter stood up with the eleven apostles. He shouted, `You men of Judea and all who stay in Jerusalem, listen to me! I will tell you the truth. You think that these men are drunk. That is not so. It is only nine o'clock in the morning. The thing that has happened is what the prophet Joel told about. Acts 2:14-16 (NKJV)

[200] and certain women who had been healed of evil spirits and infirmities — Mary called Magdalene, out of whom had come seven demons, Luke 8:2 (NKJV)

Now when He rose early on the first day of the week, He appeared first to Mary Magdalene, out of whom He had cast seven demons. Mark 16:9 (NKJV)

Through prophetic training schools, worship seminars, ministerial conferences, meditation classes and the absence of biblically sound theology, worship has been sanitised, or would it be better to call it *'Satanised'*. Spray painting over words like holiness, sin, repentance, humility, and the name of Yeshua (Jesus) in songs leaving us devoid of the things of God. This is not a trade off or a discussion about old and new songs or an objection to the tradition of inspired songs because we are encouraged to enjoy all things that are right if they are biblically sound.

"speaking to one another in psalms and hymns and spiritual songs, singing and making melody in your heart to the Lord,.."

Ephesians 5:19 (NKJV)

No, this is about the influences of eastern mysticism and pagan worship that have crept into the worship experience. However, the term 'worship' has also been lost in the white noise of visually and emotionally impactful entertainment, absent of the necessary credentials to be called true worship. Thankfully, the Bible (our manual on life) tells us this,

But the hour is coming, and now is, when the true worshipers will worship the Father in spirit and truth; for the Father is seeking such to worship Him. God is Spirit, and those who worship Him must worship in spirit and truth."

John 4:23-24 (NKJV)

Now you can breathe another sigh of relief. It is here in black and white that provision has been made for the individual that worships God in 'spirit and in truth'. This is one of the foundational definitions of worship. Hallelujah! I bet you were worried that there was a precondition that you must have music playing ability, own smoke machines and expensive stage lighting and a natural ability to move a crowd (*a form of manipulation when reliant on 'self' as the crowd pleaser*). Thankfully, it is impossible to worship God without it being in spirit <u>and</u> truth.

What Should We Say About Music Awards?

In case you still haven't realised it, the subject of music is quite an emotive one. Like everything else, there is a strange recurring image of Christian artists at the biggest award events in music, such as The Grammys. I began seeing images of popular Christian singers/bands popping up to receive awards at the same event alongside secular bands. So, what's so strange about that? Well, I hadn't appreciated that a trend had been developing at the awards ceremony, which was being reported year after year, drawing attention to live stage performances with overt satanic symbolism. Of course, this could probably have been media stunts to improve declining ratings but even so, there was openly defiant and deviant imagery being portrayed during these performances.

On the other hand, the imagery of Christian bands receiving awards at the same ceremonies became somewhat of a knotty issue. At this point, you can probably hear the floodgates of reason slowly creaking open under the swelling force of what initially seemed like a gentle wave of questions. Without warning, the sweeping tide crescendos into a tsunami, bursting open the weirs of understanding. Each movement was accented with a rapid call and response, I was astounded to find that I soon slipped into a soliloquy (*a monologue addressed to oneself where thoughts are spoken out loud, basically to an audience of one*).

- *How does any band or group sit through that?*
- *Why would they subject themselves to openly satanic performances?*
- *Is their award a celebration of Jesus in Christian music?*

- *Who nominates them?*
- *Who votes for them?*
- *Who is sponsoring these events?*
- *How or when are these Christian artists receiving their awards?*
- *Why are Christians arguing over these performances? Were they forced to watch? Hmmm?*
- *Who came up with the idea anyway...?*
- *Light shining in darkness...? Isn't that taking biblical Hermeneutics a little bit far? Don't you think...?*

Without any applause or satisfactory resolutions, the pendulum of incredulity swung ferociously the other way, landing upon the final force of unwavering disbelief, which broke the floodgates.

- Will someone go and find a real preacher? Something's gone wrong and it's not the Bible.
- Have I got any mp3s from these guys???
- They vote on what, the best soundtrack?
- In comparison to what?

You would be forgiven for thinking all music awards are a celebration of the artists' contribution to 'worship' and the spreading of the gospel. But there are obvious indicators that we have descended into the realm that does little to elevate God and does everything to fit into a world of notoriety and acceptability.

In the realm of the biggest awards event for music, there are serious questions about the artists that are recognised on this stage. It also brings into question our need for this type of artist in our music collection. When all is said and done, and when we have concluded our biblical semantics, there are only more questions that can settle the matter.

Would Yeshua have sat through events like these to receive an award for sharing the good news? Of course not. Furthermore, would He subject himself to listening to their lyrics which reimagine the lifestyle of His followers and His teachings? Would He be accepting of the exploitation of the vulnerable or innocent who are not able to discern between the truth and a lie?

I dare say that He, like Nehemiah, share the same passion for what is right and Holy. There is no place for self-gratification at the expense of His words. His words are as He is, the same yesterday, today and forever.

"Now the Passover of the Jews was at hand, and Jesus went up to Jerusalem. And He found in the temple those who sold oxen and sheep and doves, and the money changers doing business. When He had made a whip of cords, He drove them all out of the temple, with the sheep and the oxen, and poured out the changers' money and overturned the tables. And He said to those who sold doves, "Take these things away! Do not make My Father's house a house of merchandise!" Then His disciples remembered that it was written, "Zeal for Your house has eaten Me up."

John 2:13-17 (NKJV)

Preachers / Teachers and the Gifted

*But to **each one of us** grace was given according to the measure of Christ's gift. Therefore He says:*

"When He ascended on high, He led captivity captive, And gave gifts to men."

Ephesians 4:7, 8 (NKJV)

The congregation of Yeshua is made up of many parts, all related to the advancement of one global body, built upon one foundation and pursuing a single goal. If you were to hear this from a pulpit today you might be tempted to think that the preacher was talking about a *'one world religion'*, but this is far removed from the message the Apostles and Prophets taught and preached. Their commitment was to the covenants and walk of faith entrusted to them by God and His Son Yeshua. Their call to action encourages all believers who have received such grace to move from passivity to activity in The Holy Spirit under the guidance of The Holy Scriptures. This is enveloped in such statements as, *'to each one of us grace was given according to the measure of Christ's gift.'* The statement made by Paul reinstates the position of *'us'* without compromising the *'you'* and yet it does not elevate the 'us' at the expense of 'you', which is in complete contradiction to the *'self'* philosophy that we have come to love so much.

When we are back in right standing with Yeshua under this simple yet powerful truth the man-made boundaries are neutralised and 'self' is dethroned, paving the way for the legitimate expressions of 'The Holy Spirit', later described as *'gifts' of the Holy Spirit,* through ordinary people.

Let's be honest though, and far be it from us to join the club of *'conspiracy theorists'* at the exclusion of biblical truth, but we have collectively accepted the [201]*'shaman'* in the pulpit, the

---

[201] Shamanism, religious phenomenon centred on the shaman, a person believed to achieve various powers through trance or ecstatic religious experience. Although shamans' repertoires vary from one culture to the next, they are typically thought to have the ability to heal the sick, to communicate with the otherworld, and often to escort the souls of the dead to that otherworld. The term shamanism comes from the Manchu-Tungus word šaman. Diószegi, Vilmos and Eliade, Mircea. "shamanism". Encyclopedia Britannica, 20 Dec. 2022, https://www.britannica.com/topic/shamanism. Accessed 25 March 2023.

'psychic' in the prayer room, the *'guru'* in the Bible class and the *'positive thinker'* in the prayer line. In a way, voting for the teachings of people like Phinehas Quimby, (considered to be) the founder of the *'New Thought'* movement, who believed that everything is in the mind, such as our health, prosperity, good and evil. He is yet another foundational character who was a catalyst for different cults that we have with us today, but we prefer to embrace his model of *'wellbeing'* over the biblical approach to transformation for all. Here is an example of some of the ideas he was happy to share with anyone that would listen,

[202]*HOW DOES THE MIND PRODUCE DISEASE?*

"I will give the symptoms of a person who called on me to be examined. The upper part of his body above his hips felt so large that his legs were not strong enough to carry the weight, therefore he complained of weakness in his knees. **This idea of weakness was in his mind***, for there never was any strength or knowledge in his knees of themselves, any more than there is power in a lever of itself.*

If the lever, or legs, had to create its own power his body would never move. Therefore, if his body ever moved, it must be by some power independent of his knees or legs. There is such a thing as pressure, but pressure is not power, for it contains motion and motion is another element. These two elements together we call mechanical power, so mind agitated is called spiritual power."

It's kind of strange to read thoughts like this but many Christians have come to believe it, without questioning it. Glued to our television screens, we are filled with ideas from these heretical preachers, genuinely believing that we are going to

[202] The Quimby Manuscripts, 1921, p. 182

transform our lives for the better by applying their newly discovered knowledge, which for all intents and purposes, turns the problem inwards pointing towards an inner problem of the mind. Making everyday experiences such as, a lack of finance, the absence of healing after prayer, the failed opportunity, simply a matter of how and what we think. Now let's think about it *(excuse the pun)* and excuse me for repeating it. But, if wealth or health was decided by positive thinking, I doubt that anyone would miss the opportunity to spend hours correcting their *'thought life'*. If it were a simple matter of focusing on what we want through mental ascent then all of us would be billionaires, physically superior, living comfortably in the most idyllic places in the world, without harassment, without global poverty, in fact without any issues whatsoever. Reality check...how could this ever be true, yet we encourage it in our congregations and many people believe it. The disappointment that someone wasn't healed is levelled at a *'lack of faith'*. Which is code for, *'you were not positive enough, you wavered in your mind.'* The lack of finance in the prosperity, word of mouth, sorry,... word of faith circles is because *'you did not give in faith but doubted'*, which is code for *'you were not positive enough, you wavered in your mind.'* The problem is placed squarely into the lap of the offender, *'name it and claim it'* or *'speak it into existence'*, they are told. Which is code for, *'you are gods, you have the power.'*

Another issue to consider here is the hot topic of *'spiritual gifts'* and effective *'ministerial teams'*. An obvious area of conflict between the legitimate activities of the Holy Spirit and that of false spirits. The problem is, how do we know which is authentic?

Firstly, a Holy Spirit filled congregation will obviously know the voice of the Holy Spirit. This sounds almost too simple to miss, but this is a basic principle of the biblical faith and one that has been compromised by manipulative teachings. In Acts Chapter 2 an authentic move of The Holy Spirit was described in detail to help the reader understand some of the characteristics of The Holy Spirit. The same could be said of the onlookers, and visitors to Jerusalem during the Feast of Shavuot who also required an understanding of what was taking place. How was that need met in the absence of a printed copy of the latter portion of the Bible, 'The Renewed Covenant'? Clarity was given through someone who had encountered The Messiah, someone who had been baptised in His Holy Spirit and who also understood the Hebrew Scriptures. A person who had been transformed by the work of The Holy Spirit and humbled by their own obvious weakness. In this instance, it was the disciple and Apostle called Peter.

But Peter, standing up with the eleven, raised his voice and said to them, "Men of Judea and all who dwell in Jerusalem, let this be known to you, and heed my words. For these are not drunk, as you suppose, since it is only the third hour of the day. But this is what was spoken by the prophet Joel:

'And it shall come to pass in the last days, says God, That I will pour out of My Spirit on all flesh;

Acts 2:14-17 (NKJV)

Pay careful attention to the first line of the opening sentence, *But Peter, standing up with the eleven*. His role in the context of this visitation was not to become the recipient of the day's offering/collection or to gain an advantage by establishing a new ministry rubber stamped by a very real expression of The Holy Spirit. No, his role was to stand <u>with</u> the congregation of male and female believers, to expound the wonderful works of Yeshua's kingdom and provide understanding to a convicted, yet perplexed audience.

Another very important aspect of this event which may be easily overlooked is that of the message which was rooted in the Hebrew Scriptures. After all, it was the Messiah who instructed his disciples to wait in Jerusalem knowing that there was going to be a meeting between The God of Israel and His chosen people once again, just as He had done at their first meeting at Sinai. Therefore, it made sense that it was a Jewish preacher on this day, a decision that we should be grateful to Yeshua for. Had this been entrusted to the kind of *'shaman'* preacher that we are familiar with today, the outcome would have been devastating for everyone. There was no way that this would be allowed to happen at such an important kingdom event, in Jerusalem, the spiritual capital of the world.

Can you imagine any of our prosperity gospel preachers standing up <u>with</u> the eleven in a manner which made them equal to their brothers and sisters in the Way? What do you think they would do if they saw thousands of people turning up for this annual event, do you think they would see needy souls, or do you think they would salivate over the potential for a day's profit at the expense of the true worshipper? This is the reason that the work of the Holy Spirit is dependent on the contribution of all persons and not the exclusivity of one person. The congregation's legitimacy and success rely on the foundational teachings given by The Messiah to all, expressed through each individual and lorded by none. Leaving us with a huge distinction between the hierarchical system that provides obvious benefit to a single individual in contrast to the organic body that has Yeshua as its head.

This is why we are instructed to 'test the spirits', advice that can be misconstrued due to our appetite for things of the supernatural and apparent aversion to that which is biblical.

Beloved, do not believe every spirit, but test the spirits, whether they are of God; because many false prophets have gone out into the world. By this you know the Spirit of God: Every spirit that confesses that Jesus Christ has come in the flesh is of God, and every spirit that does not confess that Jesus Christ has come in the flesh is not of God.

And this is the spirit of the Antichrist, which you have heard was coming, and is now already in the world.

1 John 4:1-3 (NKJV)

For a follower of Yeshua there is no escaping it, there will always be a counterfeit to the authentic as we saw with Simon the sorcerer. Therefore, it is inevitable that open confrontations between both sides will ensue. Although, there is a way that we can save ourselves and others a lot of pain. Simply follow the advice and do your homework. The Bible gives us some basic pointers if we are new to the way,

- Do not believe everything you see that is labelled a manifestation of The Holy Spirit
- Do not be afraid to prove that the manifestation is of God. Many are claiming *"God told them to..."* If this is true, then God will not be offended by your being cautious. Please do not confuse this with resisting the work of the Holy Spirit as Rabbi Paul did prior to his conversion.

Also, get to know the Spirit of God. How?

- Firstly, the Spirit of God has no problem with the fluidity of God i.e., that He came in the flesh as Yeshua (Jesus).
- Secondly, a rejection of The Jewish Messiah, Yeshua (Jesus) is tantamount to rejecting everything God is. He is Echad (One, single).

"Hear, O Israel: The Lord our God, the Lord is one! You shall love the Lord your God with all your heart, with all your soul, and with all your strength.

Deuteronomy 6:3-5 (NKJV)

Jesus answered him, "The first of all the commandments is: 'Hear, O Israel, the Lord our God, the Lord is one."

Mark 12:29 (NKJV)

- Finally, the Spirit of God cannot be against Himself. There is a spirit which is in direct opposition to everything God is. This is referred to as the spirit of the Antichrist or Anti-Messiah.

Based on these fundamental points, you can safely say that the following truth statements are false. Foundational statements that undergird the preaching and teaching of popular individuals who themselves have usurped the titles Apostle, Pastor, Preacher, Prophet, Teacher, and Healer for financial benefit:

- **The Law of Attraction:** Whatever you ask the universe for you will receive it back. First mentioned by Helena Blavatsky (the occultist) in the 1800s but has other historical roots.

- **You are God:** Popularised by modern prosperity, word of faith preachers but originating in the book of Genesis when Satan manipulated the truth with a lie.

    [203]"*...For God knows that in the day you eat of it your eyes will be opened, and you will be like God, knowing good and evil.*"

- **Oneness** (this is different from biblical unity): The belief that everything is at one with the universe and everything is spirit, therefore, we can restore world peace through a form of unification absent of disagreement. The statement regularly misquoted by Christians '*...do not judge me*', finds a comfortable home in this philosophy.

---

[203] Then the serpent said to the woman, "You will not surely die. For God knows that in the day you eat of it your eyes will be opened, and you will be like God, knowing good and evil." Genesis 3:4-5 (NKJV)

- **Your Truth:** *"You believe what you like and I believe what I like. Hey, we all have our own truth."*

    This is completely contrary to the teaching of Yeshua who said,

    "I am the way, **the truth,** *and the life. No one comes to the Father except through Me.*

    John 14:16 (NKJV)

- **Dream Interpretation:** A belief that we can understand and elevate ourselves through the unconscious. Dreams are a way of achieving this. This is not the same as the scenario with Joseph, Daniel, and other accounts where God spoke to national leaders in a dream and gave the interpretation to his servants. In these instances, God is the originator and the revealer.

    The type of dream interpretation promoted by Carl Jung has demonic origins and is at the root of this literature. Therefore, to be engaging with your dreams in search of secret knowledge is not even close to biblical spirituality. Yet there is a plethora of books like this under the title 'Christian' which are marketed to Christian audiences everywhere.

- **The Devil is a Lie:** The devil is who you make him to be. He is an invention of the mind.

    This idea seemed to go viral a few years ago and was featured in a HipHop artists label in 2013. The problem with this notion is that it does not get the last word in the title correct. It should read, *"the Devil is a liar"*.

    You are of your father the devil, and the desires of your father you want to do. He was a murderer from the beginning, and does not stand in the truth, because there is no truth in him. When he speaks a lie, he speaks from his own resources, for he is a liar and the father of it.

John 8:44 (NKJV)

Of course, there are many more areas of theological error, but I think you get the point from the examples given. To enter a lengthy dialogue about this kind of deliberate twisting of the Bible should be avoided unless there is a genuine desire to know where the error has occurred. We do best to follow wise counsel and reconsider the type of teaching (and teachers) that we have dedicated ourselves to. The writer in the Book of Psalms puts it like this,

"Blessed is the man who walks not in the counsel of the ungodly, Nor stands in the path of sinners, Nor sits in the seat of the scornful; But his delight is in the law of the Lord, And in His law he meditates day and night."

Psalm 1:1,2 (NKJV)

Of course, when the word 'meditate' is used here the writer is not referring to Yoga or mysticism as spiritual gurus may choose to deduce, it is the position or posture of placing God's teachings, The Torah, at the centre of one's lifestyle, reflecting on its words day and night. This is more than a ritualistic reflection as the writer refers to this process as being a delight, making it a relational position. Reminiscent of God's reassurance to Joshua who was to carry on the leadership of Israel following the death of Moses,

This Book of the Law shall not depart from your mouth, but you shall meditate in it day and night, that you may observe to do according to all that is written in it. For then you will make your way prosperous, and then you will have good success.

Joshua 1:8 (NKJV)

So, if we have been shipwrecked by the preaching that we have believed and applied without any thought, prayer or consideration for the source, before we blame society, the Pastor, The Creator and anyone else *(who may be unfortunate enough to be present at the moment of accusation)*, let's remember that we are guilty of ignoring our spiritual drinking habits. With a kind of religious stupor, we have drunk heartily at the fountain of 'humanistic philosophy', believing that in it we will experience the thirst-quenching properties that only pure water provides. On and on we have plunged our heads into the depths of this mirky, toxic water, filling our minds and bodies with the theories of dead men and demons. This may help you understand why there are so many Christians in crisis? So, to conclude, let's borrow the words of the Psalmist and Rabbi Paul,

"Blessed is the man who walks not in the counsel of the ungodly,

Psalm 1:1- First Part (NKJV)

O wretched man that I am! Who will deliver me from this body of death?

Romans 7:24 (NKJV)

Politics

The backdrop of the 21st century is marked by the continued merging of the ordinary person with a system of religious thought. In addition to this is the notion of being free from indoctrination and therefore, the freedom to provide objective thought or analysis on any given subject. Also, these ever-present influencers that ebb and flow in our daily lives cause us to follow one trend today and another tomorrow, or a passion for one political party today over another tomorrow. The truth is, we are not as free from indoctrination as we like to think. Take the pandemic for example, where friends, families and colleagues descended into the saturated airwaves of opinion. People that had grown up together, shared birthday parties, started businesses together, and lived in a neighbourhood for years suddenly found themselves on opposite sides of the fence based on the most curious ideas. The masses were ushered along in the river of debate only to conclude at the end of it all that we can go back to normal as though nothing had ever happened. During this time everyone that had engaged with each other in a confrontational manner was left to pick up the pieces of the relationships they once had.

The real factor in this globally impacting event is the same short word we have been using repeatedly throughout this section, 'self'. You know what I mean, and you probably said it yourself, "*I will do what I want? I'll do what is good for me? Who cares if you don't like it? If I want to go out I will. Anyway, why haven't you taken the jab yet? If you don't take the jab, you are responsible for everyone else getting the virus...*

All of this in the centre of never before experienced crisis which threatened the lives of millions of people; men, women and children. However, there is a flip side to this which is the ease with which we all turned on each other. Let's be honest, this was a massive display of a single, global belief that everyone had bought into. It was as though someone had pressed a button that activated a new personality in everyone. Then as quickly as it started it was all over with the simple announcement that restrictions are removed, and life continued as normal. Now if that isn't a form of indoctrination, I don't know what is.

So here we are, the best and the brightest, independent thinkers of our time incapable of objectivity of any lasting degree. Proven by ideals that were tested under the application of an invisible fire and found woefully lacking, disintegrating in the heat of a crisis. So here we are, looking into the future, worn out by fear and political agendas, struggling to buy food, fuel and other necessities of life but still bowing at the altar of self-sufficiency. While we have been busy and distracted by these unforeseen occurrences the tree of apostasy has blossomed once again, stretching its reach into the heavens to make itself the only thing that gives humanity a sense of purpose.

To make matters worse, politics and religion have revived in a historic alliance creating a unified school of thought that points towards a future without God. Of course, there isn't anything new about that, but there is something ominously new about the 'how'. In the past, some individuals promoted their flavour of how we should live by using their influence in politics and using legislation as a tool. However, through these thoughts, whether political or otherwise, there is an emergence of collective thought with a singular goal, this time driving forward its political and religious agenda with renewed determination and force. The subjects of birth control, population control, technology revolution, psychology, mental testing, earth culture, history, race, immigration, anthropometrics, mind sciences, sexuality, human experimentation, genetics and all the other old and new roots of the tree are now central to policy making and legislation.

Francis Galton, John Davenport, Margaret Sanger, and Julian Huxley (along with others) set the agenda many years ago but if it had been possible, they would have implemented their draconian measures sooner rather than later. It was impossible for them to fully realise their goal during their lifetime, nevertheless, their utopia is being realised and actioned by new personalities now.

While scanning through the material produced by the personalities documented in the earlier chapters, a consistent connection between words and phrases they created could be traced to its application today. Logically, this led to the conclusion that the word 'Transhumanism' (coined by Julian Huxley) should also be traceable from its point of origin to present day usage.

In other words, has transhumanism sprung up as a new root or was this purely a work of fantasy on my part? There had to be evidence. Now you must understand, at the beginning of this exploration it was difficult to comprehend a world where transhumanism held any credibility whatsoever. It was an oddity to think that Julian Huxley could have coined a phrase that would become the source of future, global developments yet this was his dream. It held extremely strange notions about humans and our ability to improve ourselves, to become 'superhumans' if you like, through further intervention in social eugenic, human genetic like fashion. This was, in my mind, a work of fiction, but something about it would not release me to dismiss it completely. The logic is, if all the other areas that formed the root system of what was known as eugenics are present in the new form of human genetics, then as strange as it sounds, *'transhumanism'* had to be there too. It didn't take long or much searching to discover in the same year of applying this logic, in black and white, the announcement that for the first time in history the US had a presidential candidate running for the White House under the banner of the 'Transhumanist Party'. The goal of the party being to raise the profile of the transhumanist agenda, knowing fully well that they would not win the campaign, but the beliefs that were central to transhumanism would be brought into focus in the public domain.

Julian Huxley had envisioned a world that would be built on his UNESCO manifesto, and now here we are witnessing its implementation alongside the other root beliefs he and others had written about. The spirit that was at work through the early false evangelists and apostles was raising up new voices, new ideas, new strands of the ancient philosophies and we are the recipients of it. Here we are seeing the outworking of a political and religious application of past influencers, born from the seed of Darwinism, and fashioning itself under science and technology. Here is an example of what we are alluding to embedded in two quotations,

1st Example

*"I believe in **transhumanism**": once there are enough people who can truly say that, the human species will be on the threshold of a new kind of existence, as different from ours as ours is from that of Pekin man. It will at last be consciously fulfilling its real destiny."*

2nd Example

*"As a **secular transhumanist** — someone who advocates for improving humanity by merging people with machines — I don't believe in death anymore. At least, I don't believe in biological death's permanency the way most people do."*

In contrast, it is impossible to tell the difference between the authors of these quotes but be it safe to say that the first was by Julian Huxley of yesterday and the second by a new transhumanist advocate of today. By simply removing the text written in bold letters, you would struggle to say that they were not written by people with religious beliefs. That is simply because transhumanism is a religion.

Too Good to Be True

Here is another reminder of a quote from Julian Huxley,

[204]*The human species can, if it wishes,* **transcend** *itself — not just sporadically, an individual here in one way, an individual there in another way, but in its entirety, as humanity. We need a name for this new belief. Perhaps transhumanism will serve: man remaining man, but transcending himself, by realizing new possibilities of and for his human nature. (Page 21)*

I find the language of Julian Huxley of interest in the context of the current Transhumanist party. He believes that humanity can transcend itself, which seems to imply that we can simply better ourselves, which if taken at face value doesn't seem like a bad idea. But what does this mean? What are the core beliefs of the Transhumanist Party?

- They believe that 'Life Extension' is achieved through the progress of science and technology.
- They support a cultural, societal, and political atmosphere informed and animated by reason, science, and secular values.

---

[204] Huxley, Julian. (1968). Transhumanism. Journal of Humanistic Psychology - J HUM PSYCHOL. 8. 73-76. 10.1177/002216786800800107.

- They support efforts to use science, technology, and rational discourse to reduce and eliminate various existential risks to the human species.

Ok, so far, so good?

Now, remember the email that I received with the transcript of the final age of evolution?

(See the chapter Homo Deus – Man Is God, Man merges with machine, Transition from 20th to 21st Century (Third and Fourth Industrial Revolution)

Also, do you remember some of the advances that were said to be possible through the merging of man with machines? Let me remind you,

"Bringing things we once prayed for or only imagined into the real world"

(Extract from the email).

Well, transhumanism (h+) is the embodiment of an alternative salvation model which masquerades as separate and different from all other expressions of the root system. However, it is impossible to separate it, it shares the same DNA as the tree itself. Through its futuristic image, it can draw together all the different facets of a science-based salvation or philosophy that appeal to the modern, self-directed mind. With the intervention of 'god-tech' enhancements and the discarding of the biblical faith, a transhumanist will strive to elevate the decaying human body with its mental attributes into a place of immortality, making Francis Galton's wildest dreams seem like child's play. It is through the door of transhumanism that we are being drawn to embark on a journey into 'dark intel', it is also through this door that the mind sciences are joining forces to reproduce the darkness that captivated Jack Parsons from a young age; and what shall we say about the drug-induced psychic revelations in search of empirical spirituality that will become commonplace through the eventual legalisation of mind-bending drugs including the over the counter drugs? Not forgetting the devastating effect that such a religion will have on children who will be born into a world where humanity is a self-proclaimed god, where death is an obsolete word in the secular dictionary, replaced by the twisted application of the word 'immortality' and where you are free to do what you want as long as it feels right. Have I covered it all?

In this new era of false evangelism, it seems that there are no limits to the places this new religious offshoot will go. The Silicon Valleys of this world are the perfect places to groom and develop and execute the transhumanist philosophy.

At every corner in every home, on every street, business or place of recreation, the altars of worship are perfectly positioned, waiting for the final call. Be it worn on the wrist, sat on a desk, or placed in the pocket, what we innocently consider to be the future is gradually distancing us from reality and gently guiding us into a place of 'virtual' reality with the promise of no more unhappiness. You can almost imagine the words of Timothy Leary ringing on every device, *"Turn On, Tune In, Drop Out"*, as young and old are transfixed by the screens of a seemingly innocent device. With every passing moment, the need to be connected becomes more and more pronounced, faster and faster we touch type and voice call, feverishly reacting to the multiple 'pings' that ring out of our devices. Oblivious to the freedoms that are slipping away under the additional promises of safety, security, and opportunity.

Do you think this is an exaggeration or another fanciful commentary? If so, the next time you visit your city centre, stand in the shopping mall when it is busy and watch what people are doing when they pass by. Then take a few paces to the local technology store which is selling the latest devices. Now observe what people are doing there. Are they busy talking to each other or is their attention fixed on an electronic device..., do you see them? If so, what you are witnessing my friend is the technological revolution and it hasn't taken long to turn us into tech junkies.

Trans-religions

Tech Religions Put Down Their Roots

For such are false apostles, deceitful workers, transforming themselves into apostles of Christ. And no wonder! For Satan himself transforms himself into an angel of light. Therefore it is no great thing if his ministers also transform themselves into ministers of righteousness, whose end will be according to their works.

2 Corinthians 11:13-15 (NKJV)

The word *'trans-religions'* is a word that simply means you can have faith but also embrace any number of other faiths at the same time. A word that may not be familiar yet but will most certainly gain traction soon. Combine this word with *'syncretism'* and you pretty much have what 'you' want. In other words, 'self' will be the singular yet collective core that determines and defines what some will believe. In this context, to say, *'we shouldn't be doing that, should we?'* is the kind of question that will hold very little water in the presence of the *'me'*, *'myself'* and *'I'* clan. There will be no room for absolutes, no room for anything outside of the vehicle called the brain, and only enough space for personalised spiritual preferences with human desire at their centre.

If you still have any doubts about the transhumanism agenda, we probably need to delve deeper into the stream of religious development, all of which is 'transhumanist' in nature. We will look at some of the churches or organisations that have been established in recent years.

Terasem

'We explore and promote geo-ethical technology for human life improvement and extension.'

Terasem is from the Greek 'Earthseed'. It is a movement that was founded by Bina and Martine Rothblatt, who was known as Martin before his gender realignment in 1984. According to a Times article published online in 2014, their son, Gabriel Rothblatt encouraged them to start their own religion which he became a Pastor of.

If you are interested in knowing their core beliefs, they are as follows,

1. Life is purposeful.
2. Death is optional.
3. God is technological.
4. Love is essential.

Terasem could be considered a denomination of transhumanism as it alludes to the same tenets but simply chooses to emphasise its own prescriptive approach to being a member. As with all of these personalised religions meditation, yoga and other ritualistic practices are the accepted norm, but there is an underlying belief that regular connections with the 'collective' will somehow usher in good energy or peace on the planet. In the list of core beliefs, mankind is evidently in charge of creating their own god through technology with the philanthropic values included to make the wider beliefs acceptable to a wider audience.

The Terasem movement speaks about the technologies that are being created to deliver an ultimate merging of man with machine, which is referred to as the singularity. A point at which humanity transcends its biological limitations.

The Church of Perpetual Life

The Church of Perpetual Life is the first transhumanist church in the world, founded in 2013 by Bill Faloon, just a year before the first transhumanist candidate Zoltan Istvan entered the political race for the White House. The irony of this establishment is (as with all religious movements) that they also have prophets, services, pews, a pulpit and a setting that mirrors that of a traditional Christian church. The church recognises two people as prophets: Nikolai Fedorov and Sir Arthur C Clarke.

Nikolai Fedorov was a Russian Orthodox Christian, philosopher, and cosmist who was born in 1829 and died in 1903. He is an obvious choice for such a position amongst transhumanist disciples due to his anti-death philosophy which included life extension, physical immortality, and resurrection of the dead through science. One of Fedorov's contemporaries is Konstantin Eduardovich Tsiolkovsky, who was mentored and taught by Fedorov during his 25-year period at the first public Russian museum and library, called the Rumyantsev Museum.

Tsiolkovsky is believed to be responsible for developing the theory of rocketry and is considered by others to be the man behind the idea of space stations, space planes, multi-stage rockets, interplanetary communications and the colonising of the Milky Way Galaxy, to name just a few.

Konstantin Eduardovich Tsiolkovsky was another in the line of mystics that were looking for answers to the future, which led him to search for alternative salvation for humans, a familiar pattern for worshippers of science. He believed the answer lay somewhere in the cosmos and his vehicle to get there was rocketry. Now, if this sounds familiar it is because he and Jack Parsons shared the same goal and both were involved in influencing their nations (and the world's) space programmes.

In an article by the historian Michael Hagemeister called, *'Konstantin Tsiolkovskii and the Occult Roots of Soviet Space Travel'*, he makes the following statement relating to the definition of occult and its application to the Russian Space Programme,

The word "occult" has two meanings: firstly, it means "hidden" or "concealed", but it can also mean "esoteric" and "supernatural", relating to the transcendental, magic preternatural world. Both meanings apply to "the occult roots of Soviet space

travel": *the previously hidden, repressed, and therefore unconscious roots of the Soviet space program and its connection with the world of the supernatural.*

Tsiolkovsky, (as was Fedorov) was an early futurist whose language and philosophy are present amongst the futurists of today. People who are obsessed with interplanetary travel and elevating humanity from a sad place to a happier, peaceful existence. According to these individuals and Tsiolkovsky, human existence on Earth is in danger due to overpopulation *(a eugenics idea)*, [205]asteroid impact, the Earth's inner core exploding and the extinction of the sun. However, the bigger question lay in waiting for someone to alight upon it and that was, *how were humans going to survive the conditions of space and other planets with the bodies that we currently have?* This is a question which tracks us back to the original Darwinian consideration of, *why care for the weak,* and the active improvement of the human race advocated by the early evangelists of *'social eugenics'.* Without the acceptance of the earlier tenets of eugenics, the Tsiolkovsky utopia could not ever be realised. So, being from the same root, his outcomes would naturally include the pursuit of a superhuman race that we saw in the Third Reich and other individual or political persuasions that cared to follow the same beliefs. A brief list of beliefs which have retained their influence and expansion under transhumanism includes,

- Controlled selection of the fittest.
- Artificial reproduction.
- The disposal of the unfit before birth. i.e., *defective genes / genetically modified babies.*
- The disposal of the unfit after birth. i.e., *the degenerate gene/euthanasia programmes.*

[205] *Konstantin Tsiolkovskii and the Occult Roots of Soviet Space Travel.* Michael Hagemeister. p. 138

To develop this further under transhumanism we may also include,

- Body enhancement.
- A desire to have old age officially classified as a disease.
- Brain Implants to enhance intelligence.
- The preservation and resurrection of the dead through cryonics and science.
- The transfer of consciousness to a man-made host body.
- The merging of man with machine/technology.

Before we return to the mentor of Tsiolkovsky, we have since discovered that the town where Tsiolkovsky lived, called Kaluga, was to Russia what California was to America. It was a prominent centre for the Russian Theosophical movement where Helena Blavatsky's influence made significant inroads. As Hagemeister points out there was little research into the influence of Theosophy on Tsiolkovsky's work at the time, but it is now considered certain that his work incorporated several of Theosophy's ideas,

> [206]*The influence of Gnostic, Theosophical and spiritualist teachings on the philosophical work of Tsiolkovskii has been hardly researched up to now because it was to a large extent taboo in the Soviet Union. The provincial town of Kaluga, in which Tsiolkovski lived, was – as Maria Carlson has demonstrated – the most important center after St. Petersburg of the Russian Theosophical movement at the beginning of the 20th century. It can now be regarded as certain that Tsiolkovskii knew the writings of the Theosophists, of which many were published since 1905 in the Kaluga 'Lotos Publishing House', and incorporated several of their ideas and formulas – such as "cosmic thought" "cosmic consciousness", "citizen of the universe" or the description of the "heavenly worlds and their inhabitants" – into his "cosmic philosophy", an essential*

---

[206] Konstantin Tsiolkovskii and the Occult Roots of Soviet Space Travel. Michael Hagemeister. Page 143.

component of which was the aspiration to achieve a "holistic worldview" (tsel'noe mirovozzrenie), a "synthesis of science, religion and philosophy". Indeed, Tsiolkovskii's claim that he received messages from super evolved beings is remarkably similar to the alleged communication with the "Mahatmas" or "Ascended Masters", whom Madame Blavatsky claimed to consult.

This isn't surprising as Tsiolkovsky, like Jack Parsons, was a practitioner of magic sciences and the leader of the US branch of the OTO, Ordo Templi Orientis. Remember Aleister Crowley?

It is Nikolai Fedorov that proposed a new phase of evolution using science and technology to create the 'Kingdom of Heaven' by eliminating the 'death' problem, which he considered to be embedded in a false Christian teaching. In addition, his views included the replacement of body parts with artificial organs in the quest to eliminate decay and death. Of course, if according to Fedorov, death were eliminated then there would remain a global overpopulation problem. His solution is that we move from the Earth and occupy the galaxy in an interplanetary system created by humans for superhumans. This 'cosmic evolution' which is central to the occult doctrine of the universe is better described as 'cosmic philosophy'. A theme that is accepted as inspiration by the transhumanist church.

So, what about Sir Arthur C Clarke, the selected prophet of the transhumanist church? Here is a British writer who has gained notoriety in the transhumanist movement possibly because of his predictions on the future of technology using what is known as Clarke's three laws of forecasting,

1. *When a distinguished but elderly scientist states that something is possible, they are almost certainly right. When they state that something is impossible, they are very probably wrong.*

2. *The only way of discovering the limits of the possible is to venture a little way past them into the impossible.*
3. *Any sufficiently advanced technology is indistinguishable from magic.*

The laws of predictions make a guess at what the future holds in the world of technology, but the future of humanity does not reside in the superstitious world of cosmic philosophy.

Way of the Future Church of AI

[207]*"We believe in science (the universe came into existence 13.7 billion years ago and if you can't recreate/test something it doesn't exist). There is no such thing as "supernatural" powers. Extraordinary claims require extraordinary evidence."*

While we are seeing an upsurge in people and groups creating their own religion, the cofounder of an autonomous trucking company Otto (bought out by Uber) called Anthony Levandowski founded a church to worship artificial intelligence. Levandowski is also the man behind the Google self-driving car programme.

It is hard to believe at first but the Way of the Future Church was registered as a religion with AI as its god. An action that is really old news in the technology world. However, reading through the website's thoughts on AI you would think that he was referring to a newfound friend that requires your compassion and understanding. It is fair to say that anything outside of the world of science (which we now know is steeped in the supernatural) is considered unprovable, therefore, unreal. Yet we are willing to bow the knee at our

[207] Taken from their website prior to removal. 16th November 2017

inventions which we then name as a god. Of course, this is nothing new, it has been done many times before. We are slow learners.

And there you will serve gods, the work of men's hands, wood and stone, which neither see nor hear nor eat nor smell.

Deuteronomy 4:28 (NKJV)

Now when the people saw that Moses delayed coming down from the mountain, the people gathered together to Aaron, and said to him, "Come, make us gods that shall go before us; for as for this Moses, the man who brought us up out of the land of Egypt, we do not know what has become of him."

And Aaron said to them, "Break off the golden earrings which are in the ears of your wives, your sons, and your daughters, and bring them to me." So all the people broke off the golden earrings which were in their ears, and brought them to Aaron. And he received the gold from their hand, and he fashioned it with an engraving tool, and made a molded calf.

Then they said, "This is your god, O Israel, that brought you out of the land of Egypt!"

Exodus 32:1-4 (NKJV)

The Christian Transhumanist Association

[208]*"We believe that the intentional use of technology, coupled with following Christ, can empower us to grow into our identity as humans made in the image of God... In this way we are Christian Transhumanists."*

---

[208] https://www.christiantranshumanism.org/ number 5 of the Christian Transhumanist Associations affirmations.

This brief list of new religious denominations would not be complete without seeing what some Christians are doing. Are they also joining the wave of new religions in the hope that death may be avoided or are they reading their Bibles in the hope that scripture may support the straddling of the obvious divide between transhumanism and biblical Christianity?

Unsurprisingly, there is a contingent that believes they are participating in the work of God to 'cultivate life and renew creation' through the transhumanist agenda. Like every other attempt to confuse the lines between two opposite kingdoms the title 'Christian' is used to legitimise what is a religion tailored to suit the 'self'.

This association has the same credentials as the other trans-religions and is by design misleading. In their *'Statement of Principle and Action,'* they begin with a reference to Jesus' statement and then apply poor hermeneutics to legitimise their personal beliefs.

- *We focus on that which is transcendent.*
- *We pursue greater coherence of mentality, physicality, spirituality.*
- *We seek the betterment of the world.*

If you are not aware of the goal of transhumanism you may think that everything the association is saying is about the God of the Bible and His will for His creation. Yet, the first of the three statements uses a word that has been alluded to by occultists, transhumanists and cosmists. That word is *transcendence;* it is probably more familiar in the word pairing of *'transcendental meditation'* made famous by the cult leader Maharishi Mahesh Yogi. It is strange to see this word in purportedly Christian material as a goal for humanity as this word is usually applied to God, not necessarily in biblical literature but in the fact that He alone stands outside of the biological and spiritual constraints of His fallen creation. When applied to a world without God at its centre, its proposition only relates to the self-determination of humanity, a point that has been made on numerous occasions throughout this book. Therefore, particularly for those that are called Christians, it would be more honest to relinquish their title and accept transhumanism as an alternative to the path they originally accepted. To attempt a fusion of Christianity with Transhumanism is equivalent to merging the light with the dark, an impossible and foolhardy proposition even for people of faith. The distinctions we are given in the Bible are there for specific reasons and require no assistance from our finite, reckless minds. Within its pages, it defines the body as that of the Messiah, a body that is not artificially constructed or scientifically developed but spiritually and mysteriously joined together under the banner of His death and resurrection alone. As Paul puts it,

"...*There is **one body** and one Spirit, just as you were called in one hope of your calling; one Lord, one faith, one baptism;"*

Ephesians 4:4-5 (NKJV)

Evolutionary Leaders

This movement is worth mentioning under this heading of trans-religions as it plays the role of preparing individuals for all the other aspects of transhumanism that we have talked about. The Source of Synergy Foundation was started by Diane Williams in 2006 and continues to invite individuals to become part of collective consciousness. This movement is described by them as a service to conscious evolution.

Through the evolutionary project, they are focused on preparing individuals and organisations to become part of the collective to transform themselves and the world. Deepak Chopra and the late Barbara Marx Hubbard are founding members of the Source of Synergy Foundation, but it is Barbara Marx Hubbard who is seen as an authority on various subjects surrounding consciousness and the awakening of the Earth's nervous system. With little effort, we see a belief emerging that a new kind of human being is being born.

Within this group of educated people, there is a preparation going on that is calling and preparing people for this perceived transformation. Once again, your particular religious persuasion is not a barrier to being an evolutionary leader.

Religion and The Theory of God

The fool has said in his heart, "There is no God." They are corrupt, They have done abominable works, There is none who does good. Psalm 14:1

The big question surrounding this belief system is, how is it possible for an anti-God movement to be engaged in Christian activities? You see, the areas of influence in the root system are simply a means to an end, they are not the tree but simply a source of nutrients for the tree's growth. This, by definition, means that God is not present in their thoughts at all. In their world, there is no supernatural authority outside of the human mind or experience unless you believe in the universe as your source. Psalm 14:1 puts it succinctly, the fool has said in his heart, "There is no God."

Transcendence

Singularity
The transition unknown (Fifth Industrial Revolution)

For all of the talk about evolution as the result of free thinking, enlightenment and reason, we are now permitted to witness the removal of its shabbily branded scientific seed coat, a carefully crafted outer layer designed to hide its malevolent character, and with it the revelation of its true mystical nature and identity. This single seed has been the epicentre of a multiplicity of sinful agendas, laws, wars, and crimes against humanity and at its core the essence of the serpent's nature. The trail of devastation leads us from the fall of humanity in the Garden of Eden to the debased slave trades and on to the experimentation, execution, and close annihilation of the covenanted Jewish people, landing finally in the lap of modern occult culture. Unrelenting, the result is a world that has become the playground of culpable spirits, cults, and advocates of the elevation of man to godhood.

There have been consistent recurring themes which have pointed us to a specific demonically enthused goal, which is described as a final transition or transcendence. From the very beginning of this complicated map of discovery Satan has peddled his philosophy as the deal of a lifetime in direct opposition to the relational mandate of God (YHWH), *Then the serpent said to the woman, "You will not surely die. For God knows that in the day you eat of it your eyes will be opened, and you will be like God, knowing good and evil."*

Genesis 3:4, 5 (NKJV)

The falsification of this subtly crafted sales pitch is the reason people of all age groups are signing up for his insurance-backed guarantee, all living in the hope of finding a shortcut to eternal security. Included in the package are the false promises of supernatural interventions, enlightenment, power encounters, success techniques, a personal spirit guide and the ultimate pathway to godhood. Although, there is one thing that remains securely hidden until the contract is fully ratified. You know, the part of the contract that is written in the smallest print possible so that you cannot read it with the naked eye. If you were able to, you would immediately recognise the nature of its special lifetime cover '… *your life for life.*' There are no exceptions to this rule, so when one chooses to go into business with the serpent, be prepared for the inevitable outcome, death. His only concern is to use your carnality, your soulish desire, and your obsession for greatness to establish his end goal. Nothing else matters to this prince of darkness, not even your committed service.

Due to this, we are speeding towards the ultimate goal of this strange but real network of cosmic philosophy. Its disciples have said it repeatedly, their actions have supported it and their victims are a testament to the source of its inspiration. This philosophy is not ashamed to be seen, experienced or talked about but brashly parades itself manipulating its way into every facet of human life. This is particularly difficult to comprehend in light of our repeated mention of objective thought, intelligence, and evidence-based theories while on the other hand embracing concepts that are nothing less than occult spirituality.

To our detriment and ignorance, this new form of global religion is already present in the form and stature of the hidden tree. Its unification is evident in 'god-tech,' a tool of cosmic philosophy, and its doctrine is revealing characteristics that we do well to familiarise ourselves with.

Deliver Us from Transhumanism

[209]*As the cosmic evolution developed, the perfected human race, which would inhabit the entire universe, would lose its corporeality and turn into a kind of energy or radiation (luchistoe chelovechestvo), and thus become "immortal in time and infinite in space."*

Konstantin Eduardovich Tsiolkovsky (who we spoke about earlier) shared the same belief as Gnostics, which is that some of humanity will become so highly developed that they will transform into bright rays of light...

Wait a minute, transform into what...? Rays of light?

It is hard to believe that in a rational, intelligent society we will mock the idea of God who created the heavens and the Earth, but we will fully embrace the proposition that through some strange, and self-appointed means, we will one day transform ourselves into rays of light. Of course, whatever anyone thinks about the plausibility of the latter makes no difference to the drive to achieve this goal. So they are, standing on the edge of the abyss staring into a cosmic reality alongside a long line of cosmic disciples, some alive and many long since gone. What is it that these people all have in common?

---

[209] 'Konstantin Tsiolkovskii and the Occult Roots of Soviet Space Travel' p. 139

Francis Galton, Julian Huxley, Charles Davenport, Clarence Gamble, Margaret Sanger, Marie Stopes, DH Lawrence, George Bernard Shaw, John Harvey Kellogg, Aleister Crowley, Jack Parsons, L Ron Hubbard, Aldous Huxley, Timothy Leary, Hitler, Helena Blavatsky, Sigmund Freud, Carl Jung, Abraham Maslow, Carl Rogers, Nikolai Fedorov, Konstantin Eduardovich Tsiolkovsky and many others that are not mentioned?

The answer is simple and has been present from the very beginning, **'transcendence'**. At each stage of this evolutionary theory the pursuit of a superior human race was always central, nodded to in statements like *'the survival of the fittest.'* Later to progress from stage to stage.

So why was this not obvious? The reason is, the separation of these individuals by time and location dissipates the overall picture but, once they are brought together it is the morphing of the religious form and the draw of 'professional' titles that make the obvious difficult to see. So, some may refer to this goal as the fifth stage of the Maslow Pyramid while others lean towards [210]nirvana. Whichever word you choose to use, the word that draws all variations of alternative spiritually together is *'transcendence'*. This is the heart of the matter and

---

[210] nirvana, (Sanskrit: "becoming extinguished" or "blowing out") Pali nibbana, in Indian religious thought, the supreme goal of certain meditation disciplines. Although it occurs in the literatures of a number of ancient Indian traditions, the Sanskrit term nirvana is most commonly associated with Buddhism, in which it is the oldest and most common designation for the goal of the Buddhist path. It is used to refer to the extinction of desire, hatred, and ignorance and, ultimately, of suffering and rebirth. Literally, it means "blowing out" or "becoming extinguished," as when a flame is blown out or a fire burns out. Lopez, Donald S.. "nirvana". Encyclopedia Britannica, 26 Dec. 2022, https://www.britannica.com/topic/nirvana-religion. Accessed 11 April 2023.

transcendence is the final goal of evolution, a man-made stage. Or is it?

Tsiolkovsky believes that once humanity has committed to the technological advancement of the human body, the human form will eventually transform into rays of light. This is intriguing because in this idea alone there is a perceived supernatural element to the experience, as it assumes that the mind or consciousness will transform, the human body will be elevated outside of its biological limits and somehow the dream of these false prophets is realised. Conversely, there is an element of spiritual fantasy attached to it. As we see in Rabbi Paul's letter to the congregation in Corinth, false teachers of eternal matters will always present themselves as authoritative spiritual guides and if necessary, disciples of Yeshua (Jesus). To the listener, this may not be easily detected, but there is a further statement that Paul makes that relates specifically to Satan, who can mimic the form of God's ministering angels of light. This is something to take note of because mimicking light is Satan's domain.

For such are false apostles, deceitful workers, transforming themselves into apostles of Christ. And no wonder! For Satan himself transforms himself into an angel of light. Therefore it is no great thing if his ministers also transform themselves into ministers of righteousness, whose end will be according to their works.

2 Corinthians 11:12-14 (NKJV)

Please note that this kind of light is not life giving, it does not have within it the ability to save any human being from themselves or anything else for that matter. It is a false manifestation of the work of The Holy Spirit. It is for this reason that people (Christians or others) are left bereft after years of practising the philosophy or techniques passed on to them by these biblically classified false prophets, teachers and Apostles who give their allegiance to this false light. In particular, where congregations are steeped in new-age occultism there are always conflicts over fundamental biblical beliefs.

Cosmic philosophers understand the requirements to achieve this state and the cloak of 'science' flanked by philanthropy is used to dupe us into believing that the future is safe in the hands of the preachers of mankind's ascension through technology.

It would seem that the slogan of eugenics is not an abstract thought after all but a goal in itself, a public declaration of a hidden desire to recover something that was lost or never obtained in the first place.

The Masters of the Universe?

In case you haven't worked it out yet, if humanity succeeded to bypass the physical body, made from the earth, where do you think that leaves everyone else that by definition is classed as unfit? Where do the defective fit into this noble exploit of transcendence? If a new master race of deities is achieved who will serve who? What will happen to nations and their differences? Who will decide the fate of another human being? Will it be based on nationality? Will it be based on gender? Maybe not as this is being redefined to leave us without a definitive identity. What about financial status? Yes, this has always worked, hasn't it?

We do not have to travel too far back in time to see in full colour the result of this blasphemous concept. Many believed they were the saviours of a master race then and there are many alive who believe the same now. Between them a form of sensual wisdom is exchanged followed by an overconfident pat on each other's back.

This wisdom does not descend from above, but is earthly, sensual, demonic. For where envy and self-seeking exist, confusion and every evil thing are there. But the wisdom that is from above is first pure, then peaceable, gentle, willing to yield, full of mercy and good fruits, without partiality and without hypocrisy.

James 3:15-17 (NKJV)

Although, there is still a problem. You see, judgement on humanity did not exclude the Earth at the time of the flood in Genesis 6:5 and 9:17 but what led to it? Well, this is the biblical account,

Then the Lord saw that the wickedness of man was great in the earth, and that every intent of the thoughts of his heart was only evil continually. And the Lord was sorry that He had made man on the earth, and He was grieved in His heart. So the Lord said, "I will destroy man whom I have created from the face of the earth, both man and beast, creeping thing and birds of the air, for I am sorry that I have made them." But Noah found grace in the eyes of the Lord.

Genesis 6:5-8 (NKJV)

The context of the flood is a universal, global event. It was actioned because of the level of human wickedness and the evil inventions of humanity's heart. But, if God is described as straightforward in His approach to those that love Him and those that hate Him then we can accept that His response in the Genesis account is weighted according to the actions He witnessed.

"Therefore know that the Lord your God, He is God, the faithful God who keeps covenant and mercy for a thousand generations with those who love Him and keep His commandments; and He repays

those who hate Him to their face, to destroy them. He will not be slack with him who hates Him; He will repay him to his face.

Deuteronomy 7:8-10 (NKJV)

So, we have judgement on the whole land, a global event that no one except those appointed to be with Noah would escape. Following the flood, we are drawn to the single language that the population spoke. Within this framework and after a global disaster one would think that it would make sense to walk a little more carefully than before, but we are moved to the plain of Shinar where the unification of language, technology, and the desire for more became the inspiration behind a city and a tower that would reflect humanity's greatness and also serve as a place of security from separation. Yet this monumental act of self-determination (in the light of past events) was enough for God to take necessary action. If left to their own devices, everything that entered the imagination would be pursued without boundaries. Here is where language was introduced to limit the free flow of ideas and cooperation.

This still may not make complete sense until we bring the same dynamics into our time. Modern history is littered with things created through the imagination of humanity's heart. This is from the same sinful place where our ancestors devised their plans. That hunger to demonstrate our greatness, to remove the need for an eternal God is driving the world out of its mind, literally. Now, we are busy building modern structures into the heavens using the occult as a vehicle. We are changing the structure of the human body to fashion it after our imagination and lusts, we are exposing the innocent young of the world to this era's agreed position on gender, from the age of three upward. Is this something you would encourage if you were the creator of the people who promote these things in the name of the collective? As with the flood, judgement is certainly on the land and there will be a renewing of all things but this time by fire.

In the Bible, there is a familiar account of a battle between the King of Kings and the global powers of the earth that are against this King. This will be a final battle, an end time battle between the Kingdom of Yeshua and the Kingdom of Darkness. The real question is not whether it will happen but whose side you will be on when it all comes down.

Whatever the state of the human race, when Yeshua lights up the cosmos with His presence the god-tech of this age will meet the ruler of the universe in an exchange that will silence the question of self-determination. With Satan as the captain of this earthly army of genderless combatants armed with the latest technological inventions, everything the world has created will be pointed at the heavens to stop the one who truly is the ruler of the universe. His description is clear, His presence real and His intention unquestionable.

I saw heaven opened, and look! a white horse. And the one seated on it is called Faithful and True, and he judges and carries on war in righteousness. His eyes are a fiery flame, and on his head are many diadems. He has a name written that no one knows but he himself, and he is clothed with an outer garment stained with blood, and he is called by the name The Word of God. Also, the armies in heaven were following him on white horses, and they were clothed in white, clean, fine linen. And out of his mouth protrudes a sharp, long sword with which to strike the nations, and he will shepherd them with a rod of iron. Moreover, he treads the winepress of the fury of the wrath of God the Almighty. On his outer garment, yes, on his thigh, he has a name written, King of kings and Lord of lords.

Revelation 19:11-16

Lekh-L'kha

Get Yourself Out of Here

Now the Lord had said to Abram, "Get yourself out of here! From your country and from your father's house to a land that I shall show you. And I shall make a great nation of you, and I shall bless you and make your name great and you will be a blessing. And I shall bless those who bless you and curse the one who curses you: And in you will all the families of the earth be blessed.

Genesis 12:1-3 (ONM)

If you have made it this far on the twisting roadmap of the world and its history, you may be asking, *'So, what was that all about?'* You may even be wrestling with the subject matter under the conviction that something has to change. But let's be honest, your response may also be, *'it's ok, I'll think about it tomorrow'* or, *'I've heard it all before, c'est la vie, such is life'.* The truth is, you are allowed to think about what you have read, at length if necessary; you are allowed to reflect on the detail in each line and between the lines. I would encourage it, to be sure you understand the message. But what you are not permitted to do is procrastinate, you are not allowed to find reasons to delay what you know to be right. Now that is a problem.

If the testimonies of all the people that claimed to be met by a spirit guide are easy for you to believe, then what does that say about you, when you immediately rejected the things expressed in the Bible dismissing them on the grounds of fantasy, *'just a story'* or even worse, *'scientists don't believe it.'* Friend, what does it say about you? Of course, you have seen for yourself how things are not always as they first appear especially when intellectualism is involved. Therefore, we must take seriously the fact that God who created all things can and does speak. However, He does not require us to employ some kind of technique to get his attention. He is not an energy or a force that requires you to take a particular position to receive a download from the cosmic universe. No, there is no place for pagan rituals or practices in the presence of a Holy God. Think about this the next time you witness a gathering of Christians and pagans on Stonehenge at the time of the summer solstice or when you attend a service where the preacher impresses the congregation with a supernatural ability to tell you your bank account details through the aid of a spirit (not the Holy Spirit I may add). Consider the real issue at hand here.

As a liberal Christian, it is possible to believe anything that comes to mind and to act upon it based on a divine authority you think you have been given. This is all very interesting at best, but in the realm of eternal questions, what God thinks is what carries the weight of eternal finality. So, who would you pay attention to? The preacher that stands on the hill with his hands raised to the sun, saying, *'It's ok, join in, have a great time'* or, would you do the smart thing and run the other way, just in case this religious magnet of knowledge has never read the Bible and is clueless about the things of God (YHWH).

For the most part, we may deliberate at length on the grounds of what <u>we think</u> is acceptable Christianity, but we must be careful not to walk under the illusion that we are aspiring transcended beings working towards the day when we will become rays of light. A notion that gives a whole new meaning to the song *'This little light of mine, I'm gonna let it shine'*.

Equally, if we have convinced ourselves that God is in attendance at such diabolic services, tailored to suit our pernicious ways, it may be worth pausing the sound system for a moment..., and guess what...? He's not there.

The safest thing that we can do in this deliberately confusing world of spirituality is to follow the instruction of the only one who understands what's going on. His instruction to Abram was, *"Get yourself out of here!"*

To the Congregation at [211]Corinth, it was *"Come out from among them and be separate"*, and to anyone else that reads and understands the unveiling of Yeshua to John it is, [212]*"Come out of her, my people, lest you share in her sins, and lest you receive of her plagues"*.

The Hidden Tree is a metaphor for the secretive, connected plan which is deviously woven into the history, struggle and suffering of humanity. A history which has been darkened by the evil hand of the serpent, enthused by an insatiable appetite, and triggered by the first bite of the forbidden fruit in the unspoilt environment of Eden. It was not by choice but by inspiration that this image became the selected symbol to reveal the image of the human heart and to lay it bare for all to see. Examining this organic form in a three-dimensional manner seemed to expose more and more world affairs that at first had no correlation to each other and then after a myriad of threads would reappear in what seemed to be an obscure, unexpected place. After all, what would HipHop have in common with the intelligentsia of Europe? How could slavery relate to the modern era of freedom and human rights when the evidence on the ground keeps on telling us that nothing has changed?

It's Time to Move On

Your Body, Your Mind, Your Choice

---

[211] 2 Corinthians 6:17
[212] Revelation 18:4 (PART) NKJV

I beseech you therefore, brethren, by the mercies of God, that you present your bodies a living sacrifice, holy, acceptable to God, which is your reasonable service.

And do not be conformed to this world, but be transformed by the renewing of your mind, that you may prove what is that good and acceptable and perfect will of God.

Romans 12:1-2

There is no escaping it, we have chosen a path that is resistant to anything that resembles truth in the hope that our resistance to it will allow us to fill the world with our truth. The evidence tells us every generation is weakened and broken by the exploits of the previous, helpless and hapless under the weight of this ignominious baton of perceived truth. At every step, its weight crushed the love of life that each innocent child was once born with, confiscating their minds, bodies, and wills in the process. No, God sees this parasitic aberration of nature complete with its toxic fruit and subversive roots and in His infinite wisdom, He has made provision for it. He affords us the freedom to choose once again while planting His vineyard amid a corrupted creation. A vineyard that would have a single vine, a true vine ready and waiting to give life where it had been stolen, to restore hope where it had been devastated and to remain constant when everything else changes.

It is my prayer that you understand the magnitude of what we are facing today. Where we once considered events and challenges revealed in the Word of God as 'future' we are now living in that future, sometimes oblivious to the fact that many things have and are coming to pass daily. Even during the compilation of this book, it has been astounding how quickly each area has advanced making it impossible to include all that one sees in front of them.

What more can be said about the revival of other wild exploits which are shaping our world under the banner of 'saving it for future generations.' Including geo-engineering, plant-based food substitutes, insect based food substitutes, the turning of the human body into an interface, brain implants, nanorobots in healthcare, the Higgs Boson machine, and the list goes on.

In reality, the big questions are being thrust on us all and there is nowhere to hide but in the search for answers. Answers that were and still are uncomfortable but necessary if anything is to be resolved.

We need to extricate ourselves and our families from the obvious philosophies that are creating many of the problems they are claiming to resolve. But this action may leave us feeling vulnerable, isolated, and possibly even afraid of what will happen next. If this is your experience, do not worry. God has made provision for you already.

The True Vine

Standing In the Place of the Nations

"I am the true vine, and My Father is the vinedresser. Every branch in Me that does not bear fruit He takes away; and every branch that bears fruit He prunes, that it may bear more fruit. You are already clean because of the word which I have spoken to you.

John 15:1-3

Our Place of Safety

This vine has been there from the beginning, dressed, ready, maturing and growing in plain sight. He waits for your undivided attention gently cultivating the nutrients you will most certainly need when you come to the end of your – *'self'*. It is by definition and character opposite to the Hidden Tree. Also, The True Vine is in the past, present and the eternal future. He stands amid the world as the delivered nation of Israel.

You have brought a vine out of Egypt; You have cast out the nations, and planted it. You prepared room for it, And caused it to take deep root, And it filled the land.

Psalm 80:8, 9

He stands as the Son of God, yet a descendant of Israel. Bearing fruit for the benefit of all.

and was there until the death of Herod, that it might be fulfilled which was spoken by the Lord through the prophet, saying, "Out of Egypt I called My Son."

Matthew 2:15

There shall come forth a Rod from the stem of Jesse, And a Branch shall grow out of his roots.

Isaiah 11:1 (NKJV)

Everyone that is joined to this anointed vine also becomes the bearer of much fruit. In this is a divine exchange of giving and receiving.

"I am the vine, you are the branches. He who abides in Me, and I in him, bears much fruit; for without Me you can do nothing."

John 15:5 (NKJV)

My friend, as a disciple of Yeshua all retracted human rights are restored, reclaimed and protected. In Him no parasites are waiting to take advantage of our weaknesses or naivety and no works of darkness demanding your life for life. No, this vine is true in all aspects of the word, and all of this was prepared before the foundation of the world. Shall we say more? The beautifully tended branches on this liberated Vine, are by nature life giving to anyone who chooses to connect with it.

The Prophets point us to this vine, the Apostles became part of this vine, and the Gentiles were grafted into The Vine. Is it any wonder that the Serpent would attempt to destroy such a wonderful work of grace? Is it any wonder that a decaying power-hungry world would want to replace its beauty with that which can be controlled? Yet here we are, centuries later, still beholding the beauty of The True Vine.

And he came and dwelt in a city called Nazareth, that it might be fulfilled which was spoken by the prophets, "He shall be called a Nazarene."

Matthew 2:23

But one of the elders said to me, "Do not weep. Behold, the Lion of the tribe of Judah, the Root of David, has prevailed to open the scroll and to loose its seven seals."

Revelation 5:5

"I, Jesus, have sent My angel to testify to you these things in the churches. I am the Root and the Offspring of David, the Bright and Morning Star."

Revelation 22:16

The Feast of Passover

Leading up to the Feast of Passover, Yeshua and His disciples were together fellowshipping and dialoguing about various things of importance. Of course, Yeshua was fully aware that His time of crucifixion was approaching. In the account of John, we are invited to sit in the [213]Seder as observers to a monumental series of events.

1. We are given a snapshot of The Messiah's thoughts towards 'His own', a term that is full of so much that is right and righteous. He loved His own who were in the world, He loved them to the end.
2. The devil is recorded as being present at this important time in the Jewish calendar. Now he wasn't there to enjoy the Seder, he was there to ensure Judas Simon Iscariot, one of the disciples completed the deal to hand over The Messiah.
3. Yeshua washed the disciple's feet and when met by Peter's feeling of unworthiness, they had a discourse on cleanliness, humility, and service. Elaborating on the need to serve each other.
4. Yeshua speaks about His betrayal at the hand of one of His disciples, causing some concern amongst them. At this stage Satan came into Judas.

---

[213] (Hebrew: "order") religious meal served in Jewish homes on the 15th and 16th of the month of Nisan to commence the festival of Passover (Pesaḥ). Though Passover commemorates the Exodus, the historical deliverance of the Jewish people from Egyptian bondage in the days of Moses (13th century BCE), Jews are ever mindful that this event was a prelude to God's revelation on Mount Sinai. For each participant, therefore, the seder is an occasion to relive the Exodus as a personal spiritual event. Britannica, The Editors of Encyclopaedia. "seder". Encyclopedia Britannica, 3 Apr. 2023, https://www.britannica.com/topic/seder-Passover-meal. Accessed 13 April 2023.

5. They are instructed to love one another as He, Yeshua had loved them.
6. Simon Peter denies the Messiah.
7. Yeshua speaks to them about being the Way to the Father.
8. He promises them the gift of The Holy Spirit.

All of this in preparation for the penultimate lesson on His identity as The True Vine. In a clear and steady fashion, He breaks down the nature of The Vine, He paints these wonderful word pictures about the process that is applied to any branch that is in the Vine, and He draws in the disciples to understand their place of safety and security. As if this were not enough, He lays it on thick about the aggression they would experience because of their relationship with Him, The Vine, but reassures them that they will be equipped. The Holy Spirit will come, their sorrow will be turned into joy, they will overcome the onslaught of the world because He has overcome the world.

Are these the words that a true leader would impart to his companions? Absolutely. Did they understand everything that was being said to them? Absolutely not. But the manner in which Yeshua concluded their fellowship before He was arrested is the act that we must all remember. When He had finished speaking to them, He lifted up His eyes to heaven and He prayed the most remarkable and encouraging prayer for those He loved, while simultaneously including those that would come to follow Him because of the message His disciples would speak.

[214]*"I do not pray for these alone, but also for those who will believe in Me through their word; that they all may be one, as You,*

---

[214] Jesus spoke these words, lifted up His eyes to heaven, and said: "Father, the hour has come. Glorify Your Son, that Your Son also may glorify You, as

You have given Him authority over all flesh, that He should give eternal life to as many as You have given Him. And this is eternal life, that they may know You, the only true God, and Jesus Christ whom You have sent. I have glorified You on the earth. I have finished the work which You have given Me to do. And now, O Father, glorify Me together with Yourself, with the glory which I had with You before the world was.

Jesus Prays for His Disciples
"I have manifested Your name to the men whom You have given Me out of the world. They were Yours, You gave them to Me, and they have kept Your word. Now they have known that all things which You have given Me are from You. For I have given to them the words which You have given Me; and they have received them, and have known surely that I came forth from You; and they have believed that You sent Me.

"I pray for them. I do not pray for the world but for those whom You have given Me, for they are Yours. And all Mine are Yours, and Yours are Mine, and I am glorified in them. Now I am no longer in the world, but these are in the world, and I come to You. Holy Father, keep through Your name those whom You have given Me, that they may be one as We are. While I was with them in the world, I kept them in Your name. Those whom You gave Me I have kept; and none of them is lost except the son of perdition, that the Scripture might be fulfilled. But now I come to You, and these things I speak in the world, that they may have My joy fulfilled in themselves. I have given them Your word; and the world has hated them because they are not of the world, just as I am not of the world. I do not pray that You should take them out of the world, but that You should keep them from the evil one. They are not of the world, just as I am not of the world. Sanctify them by Your truth. Your word is truth. As You sent Me into the world, I also have sent them into the world. And for their sakes I sanctify Myself, that they also may be sanctified by the truth.

Jesus Prays for All Believers
"I do not pray for these alone, but also for those who will believe in Me through their word; that they all may be one, as You, Father, are in Me, and I in You; that they also may be one in Us, that the world may believe that You sent Me. And the glory which You gave Me I have given them, that they may be one just as We are one: I in them, and You in Me; that they may be made perfect in one, and that the world may know that You have sent Me, and have loved them as You have loved Me.

Father, are in Me, and I in You; that they also may be one in Us, that the world may believe that You sent Me.

John 17:20 (NKJV)

A Salutation

Finally, brethren, farewell. Become complete. Be of good comfort, be of one mind, live in peace; and the God of love and peace will be with you. Greet one another with a holy kiss. All the saints greet you.

The grace of the Lord Jesus Christ, and the love of God, and the communion of the Holy Spirit be with you all. Amen.

11 Corinthians 13:11-13

It is common in the literature of the Bible to see a concluding statement or paragraph after messages of correction, rebuke, warning etc, messages that were well received and others that were vehemently resisted. This was a key signature of Rabbi Paul's letters to the congregations and individuals as expressed following strong words of warning, direction, oversight, and attestation.

Similarly, it is important to leave you with some final cautionary words and a salutation which I trust is appropriate to the matter at hand.

So, if you have accepted Yeshua as your Messiah, you will already be on your way to discovering more about His

---

Scripture taken from the New King James Version.

"Father, I desire that they also whom You gave Me may be with Me where I am, that they may behold My glory which You have given Me; for You loved Me before the foundation of the world. O righteous Father! The world has not known You, but I have known You; and these have known that You sent Me. And I have declared to them Your name, and will declare it, that the love with which You loved Me may be in them, and I in them."

wondrous purpose and calling for your life. If, however, you have not considered this whole matter of salvation to be a puzzle too simple to be worthy of your attention then I would encourage you to think again. It is imperative that you at least consider what is in front of you.

Also, this book can never outshine the evidence, practicality and spirituality of the words found in The Holy Bible. Therefore, it cannot and should not be perceived as a replacement for the truth that is revealed in the pages of God's teaching, as revealed to the nation of Israel. We understand this to be the Tanakh (the Hebrew Scriptures), the foundation of the Messianic faith. It is out of love and respect that we as Gentiles should maintain a place of humility in the knowledge that one of the greatest transitions that the world was blessed to witness was activated through the birth, death, and resurrection of the Jewish Messiah. It happened during years of oppression, humiliation, sickness, and dictatorial leadership. At the appointed time Yeshua was sent to restore the broken covenant with Israel and then to open the door for the Gentiles globally. This single unifying act became the declaration of independence for a new movement rooted in the Tanakh. Its application is expressed in the life of Yeshua and His disciples, recorded and documented for unborn generations, all the while living amid a world in crisis.

In comparison, it seems as though the world has not moved on much since these righteous followers left it. Yet, in every generation on every continent, in freedom and persecution, the movement of Messiah moves on. Sharing from the words that the pioneers of 'The Way' left us to help us understand the ways of The Creator.

So, whatever our thoughts on the biblical faith, many things are marked out in this whole matter which we must face head on. To shy away from it or to resist it is tantamount to missing the one opportunity you may have been given to follow The Messiah. Reminiscent of the [215]rich young ruler who was offered an opportunity of a lifetime but could not see The Messiah beyond the things he held dear.

Allow me to leave you with the words from Ecclesiastes 12:13 (KJV)

*Let us hear the conclusion of the whole matter: Fear God, and keep his commandments: **for this is the whole duty of man.***

---

[215] Now behold, one came and said to Him, "Good Teacher, what good thing shall I do that I may have eternal life?" So He said to him, "Why do you call Me good? No one is good but One, that is, God. But if you want to enter into life, keep the commandments."
He said to Him, "Which ones?"
Jesus said, "'You shall not murder,' 'You shall not commit adultery,' 'You shall not steal,' 'You shall not bear false witness,' 'Honor your father and your mother,' and, 'You shall love your neighbor as yourself.' " The young man said to Him, "All these things I have kept from my youth. What do I still lack?"
Jesus said to him, "If you want to be perfect, go, sell what you have and give to the poor, and you will have treasure in heaven; and come, follow Me." But when the young man heard that saying, he went away sorrowful, for he had great possessions.
Matthew 19:16-22 (NKJV)

Glossary of Terms

To expand on this is so important because the term 'religion' is placed in the root system.

1) **Idiots**: those so deeply defective as to be unable to guard themselves against common physical dangers.

2) **Imbeciles**: those whose defectiveness does not amount to idiocy, but is nonetheless so pronounced that they are incapable of managing themselves or their affairs, or, in the case of children, of being taught to do so.

3) **Feeble-minded persons**: those whose weakness does not amount to imbecility, but who yet require care, supervision, or control for their protection or for the protection of others, or, in the case of children, are incapable of receiving benefit from the instruction in ordinary schools.

4) **Moral imbeciles**: those who display mental weakness coupled with strong vicious or criminal propensities, and on whom punishment has little or no deterrent effect.

Appendix

Eugenics Record Office, Bulletin 10A

This is the front and rear cover of the bulletin. The names of Directors and the tenets of the committee are included. You will notice a couple of familiar names: Alexander Graham Bell (the inventor of the telephone) and **Charles Davenport, mentioned in earlier chapters (The Root System).**

Eugenics Record Office
Cold Spring Harbor, Long Island, N.Y.

BOARD OF SCIENTIFIC DIRECTORS
ALEXANDER GRAHAM BELL, Chairman   WILLIAM H. WELCH, Vice-Chairman
LEWELLYS F. BARKER   IRVING FISHER   E. E. SOUTHARD
CHARLES B. DAVENPORT, Secretary and Resident Director

The functions of this office are:
1. To serve eugenic interests in the capacity of repository and clearing house.
2. To build up an analytical index of the traits of American families.
3. To train field workers to gather data of eugenic import.
4. To maintain a field force actually engaged in gathering such data.
5. To co-operate with other institutions and with persons concerned with eugenic study.
6. To investigate the manner of the inheritance of specific human traits.
7. To advise concerning the eugenic fitness of proposed marriages.
8. To publish the results of researches.

A. Publications of the Eugenics Record Office, Cold Spring Harbor, Long Island, N.Y.

I. MEMOIRS.
1. The Hill Folk. Report on a rural community of hereditary defectives, Florence H. Danielson and Charles B. Davenport. August, 1912. With 3 folded charts and 4 text figures, 56 pp. quarto. 75 cents.
2. The Nam Family. A study in Cacogenics, Arthur H. Estabrook and Charles B. Davenport. August, 1912. With 4 charts and 4 text figures, 85 pp. quarto. $1.00.

II. BULLETINS.
1. Heredity of Feeble-mindedness, Henry H. Goddard. April, 1911. (Out of print.)
2. The Study of Human Heredity, Charles B. Davenport and others. May, 1911. (Out of print. Reprinted in Bulletin No. 7.)
3. Preliminary Report of a Study of Heredity in Insanity in the Light of the Mendelian Laws, Gertrude L. Cannon and A. J. Rosanoff. May, 1911. (Out of print.)
4. A First Study of Inheritance in Epilepsy, C. B. Davenport and David F. Weeks. November, 1911, 30 pp., 33 charts, 11 tables. 20 cents.
5. A Study of Heredity of Insanity in the Light of the Mendelian Theory, A. J. Rosanoff and Florence I. Orr. October, 1911, 42 pp., 73 charts, 2 tables. 15 cents.
6. The Trait Book, C. B. Davenport. February, 1912, 52 pp., 1 colored plate, 1 figure. 10 cents.
7. The Family History Book, C. B. Davenport, in collaboration with Geo. S. Amsden, William F. Blades, Florence H. Danielson, Mary O. Dranga, W. E. Davenport, A. H. Estabrook, H. H. Goddard, Winifred Hathaway, W. M. Healy, August Hoch, E. R. Johnstone, H. H. Laughlin, Ruth S. Moxcey, Elizabeth B. Muncey, Helen T. Reeves and David F. Weeks. September, 1912, 16 figures and 5 plates, 101 pp. 50 cents.
8. Some Problems in the Study of Heredity in Mental Diseases, Henry A. Cotton. August, 1912, 59 pp., 9 figures, 5 folded charts. 15 cents.
9. State Laws limiting Marriage Selection examined in the Light of Eugenics. C. B. Davenport. June, 1913, 66 pp., 2 folded charts. 40 cents.
10. Studies of the Committee on Sterilization.
   (a) Study Number One—The Scope of the Committee's Work, by Harry H. Laughlin. February, 1914, 64 pp., charts, tables. 20 cents.
   (b) Study Number Two—The Legal, Legislative and Administrative Aspects of Sterilization, by Harry H. Laughlin. February, 1914, 150 pp., 4 charts, 7 tables, 6 folded tables and map. 60 cents.
11. Reply to the Criticism of Recent American Work by Dr. Heron of the Galton Laboratory, by C. B. Davenport and A. J. Rosanoff. February, 1914, 1 text figure, 43 pp. 20 cents.

III. REPORTS.
1. The Eugenics Record Office at the End of the Twenty-seven Months' Work. Harry H. Laughlin, July, 1913, 32 pp., 1 map, 1 chart, 10 figures. 10 cents.

B. PROBLEMS IN EUGENICS.
Complete Text of the papers read before the First International Eugenics Congress, London, 1912. Octavo, 490 pp., cloth. $2.75.
The foregoing publications are for sale (postpaid) by the Eugenics Record Office, at the prices named.

C. HEREDITY IN RELATION TO EUGENICS.
By Dr. Charles B. Davenport. Octavo, 298 pp., 175 illustrations and diagrams and 2 plates, cloth. $2.00. By Mail, $2.15. Henry Holt and Company, 34 West 33rd St., New York, N.Y.

D. SCHEDULES FOR FAMILY RECORDS.
1. Family Traits.
2. Musical Talent.
3. Mathematical Talent.
4. Tuberculosis.
5. Index to Germ Plasm.
6. Genealogical Cards.
7. Special Trait Chart.
8. Harelip and Cleft-palate.

These schedules are sent free in duplicate to such persons as will undertake to fill them out and after retaining one copy for their own use will file the other with the Eugenics Record Office.
Address all Orders for Publications and all Requests for Free Blank Records to
EUGENICS RECORD OFFICE,
Cold Spring Harbor, Long Island, N.Y.

Race Crossing in Jamaica

This is an extract from the book which outlines the measures used throughout the tests. Inadvertently, it provides a snapshot of the areas that the eugenics religion used as a doctrinal guide when examining the human makeup. Some of these measures are discussed in the 'Materials' chapter.

CONTENTS

Part I. Introduction

1. History of this investigation

2. The island of Jamaica and the historical development of its population

3. The adult population studied; localities and institutions where measurements were taken:

    a. Mico College
    b. Shortwood Training College
    c. Gordon Town
    d. Glengoffe
    e. Brownsville and Emboma
    f. Seaford Town
    g. Grand Cayman Island
    h. Fire Department, Kingston
    i. Police Depot, Kingston
    j. General Penitentiary, Kingston
    k. Kingston Whites
    l. City Creche, Kingston

4. Community procedure

5. Individual procedure

6. Method of classifying individuals of adult series

7. **Anthropometry:**

(1) Weight; (body lengths); (2) stature; (3) suprasternale height; (4) right tragion height; (5) omphalion height; (6) right acromion height; (7) right radiale height; (8) right stylion height; (9) right dactylion height; (10) right iliocristale height; (11) right anterior iliospinale height; (12) right tibiale height; (13) right internal malleolus, sphyrion; (14) span; (15) sitting vertex height; (16) sitting suprasternale; (17) kneeling height; (18) kneeling suprasternale height, (arm length, direct measurement) ; (19) acromion-stylion length, (trunk breadths) ; (20) biacromial breadth; (21) transverse diameter of chest; (22) anteroposterior diameter of chest; (23) bicristal breadth; (24) interspinal breadth; (25) trochanter breadth; (horizontal depths) ; (26) of tragion; (27) of glabella; (28) of subnasale; (29) of gnathion; (girths); (30) chest, at rest; (31) umbilical; (32) right upper arm; (33) lower arm, max.; (34) lower arm, min.; (35) thigh, max.; (36) calf; (37) ankle; (38) neck; (head girths) ; (39) horizontal; (40) head arch, sagittal; (41) head arch, transverse; (head diameters) ; (42) head height; (43) head length, A. P. max.; (44) head breadth, max.; (45) bizygomatic breadth; (46) minimum frontal breadth; (47) bigonial breadth; (facial features) ; (48) nose depth; (49) nose salient; (50) nose bridge; (51) ear salient; (52) outer angles of the eye; (53) inner angles of the eye; (54) nose breadth; (55) mouth width; (56) maximum length of right pinna; (57) breadth of pinna; (58) trichion to gnathion; (59) nasion to gnathion; (60) nasion to stomion; (61) nasion to subnasale

8. Physical observations

    a. Drawing of hand
    b. Drawing of foot
    c. Dynamometer
    d. Teeth
    e. Hair form — diameter of curl
    f. Eye color

g. Fingerprints
h. Palm prints
i. Other observations

9. **Social data**

10. **Psychological testing**

   a. General procedure
   b Musical capacity: Pitch, intensity, time, consonance tonal memory, rhythm; procedure in giving test and tabulation of results
   c. Form discrimination test
   d. Form substitution test
   e. Copying geometric figures and drawing a man
   f. Criticism of absurd sentences
   g. Repetition of seven numbers
   h. Cutting figure out of folded paper
   i. Ball and field
   j. Manikin test
   k. Knox moron test
   l. Knox cube imitation test
   m. Army alpha test

Part II. Anthropometric findings on adults

1. Age

2. Stature

3. Weight

4. Sitting height

5. Relative sitting height

6. Biacromial breadth

7. Chest girth

8. Transverse diameter of chest – sitting suprasternale height (torso height)

9. Intercristal breadth

10. Intercristal breadth – biacromial breadth; trunk breadth index

11. Chest girth – stature; body build

12. Summary on trunk, or torso, of Blacks, Browns and Whites

13. Height of head-and-neck

14. Neck girth

15. Absolute span

16. Relative span

17. Acromion-stylion (net arm length)

18. (Acromion-stylion) – stature

19. Length of upper arm

20. Upper arm length – gross arm length

21. Lower arm length

22. Lower arm length – gross arm length

23. Brachial index; lower arm length – upper arm length

24. Hand length

25. Hand breadth

26. Hand index

27. Summary on upper extremity

28. Leg length

29. Stature minus sitting height

30. Leg length, from anterior iliac spine minus 40 mm

31. Relative kneeling height

32. Stature minus kneeling height

33. Tibiale height

34. Calf girth

35. Ankle girth

36. Ankle girth – tibiale height

37. Ankle girth – calf girth

38. Foot length

39. Foot index

40. Summary on lower extremity

41. Head height

42. Head breadth

43. Head length

44. Head height – head breadth

45. Head height – head length

46. Cephalic index. Head breadth – head length

47. Minimum frontal breadth – head breadth; transverse fronto-parietal index

48. Cranial capacity

49. Discussion of cranial dimensions

50. Interpupillary distance

51. Interpupillary distance – face breadth

52. Face length – face breadth

53. Nasal breadth

54. Nasal height (nasion to subnasale)

55. Nasal index

56. General discussion of nose form

57. Pinna length

58. Pinna breadth

59. Pinna index

60. General discussion of pinna form

Part III. Physical Observations, physiology, correlations

61. Tooth defects

62. Papillary patterns

63. Palmar dermatoglyphics (by Inez Dunkelberger Steggerda)

    a. Introduction
    b. Methods of formulation
    c. Results and discussion
    d. Summary

64. Eye colour

65. Skin colour

66. Hair colour

67. Hair form — diameter of curl

68. Hair on hands

69. Hair on arms

70. Tongue furrows

71. Bite

72. Strabismus

73. Laxness of wrist joint

74. Strength of hand grip with dynamometer

75. Blood groups of the Jamaicans (by Dr Laurence H Snyder)

76. Blood oxidation

77. Basal metabolism (by Dr FG Benedict)

78. Correlations between physical traits:

    a. Sitting vertex height and stature
    b. Sitting vertex height and span
    c. Cephalic index and span
    d. Weight and relative sitting height
    e. Relative kneeling height and weight
    f. Arm length and leg length (height of anterior iliac spine minus 40 mm.)
    g. Body weight and foot index
    h. Chest girth and foot index
    i. Foot index and hand index
    j. Nose index and skin color
    k. Summary of correlations

Part IV. Psychological tests

1. **Musical capacity**

    a. Pitch
    b. Intensity
    c. Time
    d. Harmony or sense of consonance
    e. Tonal memory
    f. Rhythm
    g. Summary on musical capacity
    h. The West India Band

2. **Form discrimination**

    a. Discrimination of circles
    b. Discrimination of triangles
    c. Discrimination of octagons
    d. Summary on form discrimination

3. Copying geometric figures

4. Drawing of a man

5. The reconstruction-of-manikin test

6. Folded and notched paper test

7. Knox moron test

8. Form substitution test (Woodworth and Wells)

    a. Number complete
    b. Number of mistakes

9. Knox cube imitation test

10. Repetition of seven numbers

11. Criticism of absurd sentences

12. Army Alpha test

a. Test I
b. Test II
c. Test III
d. Test IV
e. Test V
f. Test VI
g. Test VII
h. Test VIII
i. Summary on Army Alpha test

13. Correlation between grades in rhythm and drawing geometric figures

14. Relative social traits

15. Teachers' estimates of athletic ability, leadership and scholarship

16. Summary of observations on mental tests

Part V. Developmental Studies

A. Methods and materials

1. Jamaica schools

2. Seaford Town and other schools

3. Age

4. Field procedure

5. Laboratory procedure

    a. Ratios calculated
    b. Racial classification

6. Description of instruments and measurements

a. Weight
b. Standing vertex height or stature
c. Span
d. Sitting vertex height
e. Chest girth
f. Head length
g. Head breadth

7. Jubilee hospital and the city crèche

B. Results

1. Measurements of growth

    a. Stature
    b. Weight
    c. Absolute chest girth
    d. Body build
    e. Absolute sitting height
    f. Relative sitting height
    g. Absolute span
    h. Relative span
    i. Summary and discussion of section 1

2. Indices of growth

    a. Body build
    b. Head length
    c. Head breadth
    d. Cephalic index
    e. Summary and discussion of section 2

3. Growth of children under five years of age

    a. Growth of infants under one year of age
    b. Summary and discussion of section 3

4. Size and shape of heads of new-born negroes

5. Summary of developmental level of 23 coloured infants (by Arnold Gesell)

Part VI. Family Studies

1. Kameka family

2. The J. family

3. The P. family

4. A study of sibs in an inbred community

5. A study in identical twins

    a. The Webster twins
    b. The Salmon twins
    c. The Ebanks twins
    d. Summary on identical twins

6. Two mulattoes

Part VII. General Discussion

1. Variability

    a. Fisher's Rehoboth bastards
    b. Sullivan's half-blood Sioux
    c. Wissler's Negro-Whites in U. S.
    d. Rodenwaldt's Mestizos of Kisar
    e. Dunn's Hawaiian hybrids

2. Evidence of dominance

3. Evidence of hybrid vigour

4. Sexual Dimorphism and its racial differences

5. Mutations in man

6. Do races differ in mental capacity?

7. Comparison of mental traits of Blacks, Browns and Whites

8. Summary of conclusions

Hitler's Testimony Before the Court for High Treason

TRANSLATION OF EXTRACT OF DOCUMENT 2512-PS
(cont.)

for the purpose of protecting the Party propaganda, but
not to fight against the State. I have been a soldier so
long that I know it is impossible to allow a Party Organization to fight against the disciplined organization of
the Armed Forces, or against the Freikorps and Police.
When meetings are disturbed and disrupted, only then does
the State step in and dissolve the gathering. But in this
way those attempting the disturbance achieve their aim.
In the beginning therefore it was only possible to carry
on at all, if one took one's own steps against such a pan-
tomime. That was the sole purpose of our Sturmabteilungen
(S. A.). It is obvious that a movement of many thousands
of people cannot be judged on the statements of individuals.

The President then drew the attention of the Court to:

the Happenings in München in 1923

Hitler: I don't know whether I may speak about them.

President: I believe the Public is fully informed today of these
occurrences. You, witness were sentenced on 1 April 1924
to five years confinement in a fortress for high treason.
Furthermore it was also said at the Party Rally (Parteitag)
in Nürnberg in September 1923 that the Party was a fighting organization and that force would certainly be used.

Hitler: At that time, the S.A. were going to be changed into
a military organization. I myself did not make them into
soldiers, they were forced into being soldiers (Nicht ich
habe damals die Abteilungen in die Kasernen hineingefuehrt
sondern sie sind hineingefuehrt worden). The situation
was such that the latent state of war between the Reich
and Bavaria had to break out. But I asserted in 1925 that
the happenings in 1923 must be completely forgotten and
that the movement must be led back to its basic aims. I
published a decree completely prohibiting arms for the S.A.
On no account were they to assume a military character.
Rather should all the S.A. serve exclusively to protect
the movement from other Parties. All military exercises
were forbidden and if a platoon was in possession of arms
and one single one of them had a weapon in his possession
without a license then these platoons were dissolved and
their members expelled. I did everything to prevent the
organization from assuming any kind of military character.
This was particularly difficult at a time when one tried
to equal the Fascists as best one could, and because of
the inward pleasure it gives the German people, to carry
a gun. I have always expressed the opinion that any attempt to replace the Reichswehr would be senseless. (In
an excited voice) We are none of us interested in replacing
the Reichswehr, I have only one wish, that the German Reich
and the German people imbibe a new spirit.

As the witness became more and more excited, the
President warned him to discontinue this public propaganda
and to confine himself to actual evidence.

Hitler: Naturally a movement which aspires to take over the
State will bring to the forefront the idea of being able
to defend oneself.

We want to make sure once and for all that out
of the present German Reichswehr a great German
People's Army is formed.

- 2 -

TRANSLATION OF EXTRACT OF DOCUMENT 2512-PS
(cont.)

There are thousands of young men in the Reichswehr of the same opinion. But that does not mean the replacement (of the Reichswehr). Nevertheless we regard the realization of this conception as the first essential for the future of Germany.

President: You could hardly attempt to carry out these ideals, purely by legal means. There is something else inferred in your program even if it is only between the lines.

Hitler: It would not be possible to lead such a great organization as ours, if we wanted to issue secret directives in addition to our public announcements. It would also be impossible after it had been publicly announced that no military exercises were to be carried out, never theless to carry out these. On questions of this kind only my orders are valid. All my political opponents and the State can control my speeches and directives. But above all this my basic principle holds good: if a (party) regulation conflicts with the Law, it is not to be carried out. I am even now punishing the failure to comply with my orders. Countless Party Members have been expelled for this reason; among them Otto Strasser.

Otto Strasser actually toyed with the idea of revolution. I never declared myself in agreement with this.

The President then put statements to the debate, which had been made by the NSDAP author Reinhold Muchow. In these it was said that those countries with older constitutions had already had their revolution. But that Germany was on the threshold of a revolution and that this imminent revolution could only be National Socialist.

Hitler: I think Mr. Muchow only wanted to illustrate a general spiritual movement. But I may assure you that if the Nazi movement's struggle is successful, then there will be a Nazi Court of Law too, the November 1918 revolution will be atoned, and there'll be some heads chopped off. (Cheers from the gallery, the President asked that the applause be discontinued and said: We are in Court and are here to seriously dispense Justice).

President: (to the witness Hitler) What do you mean by the expression "German National Revolution".

Hitler: The expression "National Revolution" should always be considered in a purely political sense. For the Nazis it is simply an uprising by the oppressed German people of today.

President: Do you mean independent movement, or one instigated by a Party?

Hitler: Naturally a movement will always represent an uprising, but it does not need to prepare it by illegal means. If we were to have two or three elections today, the Nazi movement would have the majority in the Reichstag and would prepare the Nazi revolution then.

President: You mean the spiritual (revolution)? And if we understand something different by this, you will say "We can't do anything about that."

- 3 -

TRANSLATION OF EXTRACT OF DOCUMENT 2512-PS
(cont.)

Hitler: Germany is being strangled by Peace Treaties. All German legislation today is nothing more than an attempt to foist the Peace Treaty onto the German people. The Nazis do not consider the Treaty as a law, but as something forced upon us. We do not want future generations, who are completely innocent, to be encumbered by this. When we fight this with all the means at our disposal, then we are on the way to a revolution.

President: Even by illegal means?

Hitler: I will declare here and now, that when we have become powerful (gesiegt haben) then we will fight against the Treaty with all the means at our disposal, even those which are illegal from the world's point of view.

The President then referred to another phamphlet by Helmuth Brückner, in which it says "Reform is only a half measure, revolution goes all the way."

Hitler: The German National Peoples Party is an opposition party just as we are. But the German National Peoples Party is a reform party. The Nazi movement sees as the core of the State, that which is summed up in the term "people" (Volk). Therefore we cannot be compared with other Parties. But it cannot therefore be said, because we used other methods - therefore by force - Our propaganda is the spiritual revolutionizing of the German people. This change is at least as gigantic as that brought about by the Marxist ideology. It is a completely new world. Our movement has no need of force. The time will come when the German nation will get to know our ideas. Then 35 million Germans will stand behind me. Whether we take over the Government today or form an opposition is immaterial to us. The next election will increase the number of Nazis in the Reichstag from 107 - 200. There will come a time when people will be glad that there is such a movement, the members of which are now trembling before the Court. Our opponents are interested in representing our movement as anti-state, because they know our goal is to be attained by legal means. Nevertheless they realize that our movement must lead to a complete change of State.

President: What relation does this bear to the so-called

THIRD REICH?

Hitler: We honor the memory of the old German Empire, we have fought for it. But this State had an inner weakness from the very beginning. Out of it came the present Germany. It is the embodiment of Democracy and Internationalism. This second State wants to leave the German people no man behind, who will defend their rights before the world. We hope, therefore, for a new Reich in which all institutions - beginning with the organisation of the State itself down to those which serve to maintain the national life (Volkstums) - will lead the people towards a splendid future. It is only natural that this Third Reich will quarrel with the decadent forces of today. Consequently the attempts by our opponents to designate our methods as illegal and to attribute to us a trend which we do not have.. He who maintains that isolated quotations are proof of a point of view, which he cannot construe from regulations and Party orders, will find a thousand possibilities for this.

- 4 -

TRANSLATION OF EXTRACT OF DOCUMENT 2512-PS
(cont.)

I have in our movement countless millions of people, whose hearts bleed for Germany. These young men, themselves fighters, are pushed about, come before the Court, although they had only the best intentions. They are struck down and hounded by the "red" mobs. That these people make statements, which are not in accordance with the spirit of the movement, is understandable because of their youth.

President: How do you imagine the setting up of a Third Reich?

Hitler: This term only describes the basis of the struggle but not the objective. We will enter the legal organizations and will make our Party a decisive factor in this way. But when we do possess constitutional rights then we will form the State in the manner which we consider to be the right one.

Presiden: This too by constitutional means?

Hitler: Yes.

- - - - - - - - - -

CERTIFICATE OF TRANSLATION
OF EXTRACT OF DOCUMENT
NO. 2512-PS

17 November 1945

I, EVELYN GLAZIER, P/O, W.R.N.S., 37371, hereby certify that I am thoroughly conversant with the English and German languages; and that the above is a true and correct translation of Extract of Document 2512-PS.

EVELYN GLAZIER
P/O, W.R.N.S.
37371

The CBC Tenets as set out in Appendix C of
THE AUTHORIZED LIFE OF MARIE C. STOPES
BY AYLMER MAUDE

APPENDIX C.

THE TENETS OF THE C.B.C.

The objects for which the C.B.C. was founded are as follows:—

THE objects of the Society are (*a*) to bring home to all the fundamental nature of the reforms involved in conscious and constructive control of conception and the illumination of sex life as a basis of racial progress; (*b*) to consider the individual, national, international, racial, political, economic, scientific, spiritual and other aspects of the theme, for which purpose meetings will be held, publications issued, Research Committees, Commissions of Enquiry and other activities will be organized from time to time as circumstances require and facilities offer; (*c*) to supply all who still need it with the full knowledge of sound physiological methods of control.

As these objects indicate, **the scope of the Society is very wide, its interests far-reaching, and its possibilities of future development very elastic.** Even to-day the tenets which appear fundamental to different members of the Society will naturally vary, hence **no one of the following is binding on an individual member. General agreement with the objects of the Society suffices for membership.**

Nevertheless, it has been felt that it would be useful explicitly to state in concise form what may be described as the bedrock of general agreement in the Society. This is as follows:—

Appendix C.

1.—The hygiene of sex is as suitable and proper a subject for scientific and serious study as the hygiene of nutrition, locomotion, or any other human function.

2.—Owing to the shamefaced attitude which has until recently characterized our dealings with the subject, all the manifold data involved in the different aspects of sex life have not had the direct, scientific and physiological handling they deserve and require. We deplore this and shall endeavour to remedy it.

3.—We maintain that the highest spiritual development, the noblest intellectual illumination, and the sweetest romantic possibilities of individual sex experience, are not damaged by sound scientific knowledge, but contrariwise, are enhanced and elevated.

4.—We consider that in relation to the procreation of additional members of the community, the best possible knowledge of scientific and technical details should be available to those undertaking this important social duty.

5.—We believe that the haphazard production of children by ignorant, coerced, or diseased mothers is profoundly detrimental to the race. We believe, therefore, that parenthood should no longer be the result of ignorance or accident, but should be a power used voluntarily and with knowledge.

6.—We maintain that to achieve this result a knowledge of the simple hygiene of contraception is essential.

7.—We advocate no individual contraceptive measure as final or fundamental, but maintain that the **best** measures **available** at any time should be taught and known by the people.

8.—We desire to keep constantly in touch with all advances in science which may have a bearing on the practical details of contraceptive measures, and for this purpose we have organized a Medical Research Committee to keep our Society informed as to the current scientific position of the hygiene of contraception.

9.—AS REGARDS THE POPULATION AT PRESENT. We say that there are unfortunately many men and women who should be prevented from procreating children at all, because of their individual ill-health, or the diseased and degenerate nature of the offspring that they may be expected to produce. These considerations would not apply to a better and healthier world.

10.—There are many women unfortunately so constructed —suffering from weakness of certain organs—that they would risk death if they were to attempt to bear children, and who, therefore, should not bear them.

11.—There are unfortunately many couples so ill-provided with this world's goods, or with means to acquire them, that they cannot support further children, and therefore should not bear them. Women, owing to their own or their husband's incapacity to be self-supporting, may be permanently or temporarily in such a position owing to disaster or unemployment. The following Resolution was passed by our Society:

Resolution passed at General Meeting November 22nd, 1921.

"Both to spare your own personal distress and to avoid bringing a weakly child into the world, it is important that all should realize that no one should conceive in times of individual misery or ill-health. Of course wherever a child is already on the way, the best must be made of it. But sound and wholesome methods of Birth Control (Control of Conception) are known, and advice

Appendix C

will be given free by a qualified nurse to all unemployed married persons who present this slip at the Mother's Clinic, 61, Marlborough Road, Holloway, London, N. 19."

12.—The Society approves and welcomes the work done by the first British Birth Control Clinic (The Mother's Clinic, 61, Marlborough Road, Holloway, N.19), where the very poor and ignorant receive personal instruction ; but we consider that this public service should not be left to private enterprise to maintain, and hence that the Ministry of Health should supply suitable help and contraceptive instruction to working-class women at the many Ante-natal Clinics, Welfare Centres, etc., already in existence all over the country.

13.—We maintain that science has already made available contraceptive measures as safe and as simple to use as any other hygienic measures widely known and practised, such as brushing one's teeth, or the removal daily of a dental plate by one who has artificial teeth. We, therefore, maintain that knowledge and instruction in these matters for the normal and healthy is an **hygienic** and not a medical matter. The problem of controlling conception on the part of those who are diseased, abnormal and unhealthy is on the other hand a purely medical matter and may involve measures which this Society would not advocate for general use.

14.—We as a Society are at present working for the dissemination of the best possible hygienic knowledge to all who are intelligent enough to be capable of using it, but we recognize the grave National problem raised by the fertility of those too degenerate or too careless to be capable of using any form of contraceptive.

The Life of Marie C. Stopes

15.—We are convinced that children spaced by voluntary means have a less mortality, and that the mother of such children has time to recover her health and attend to the young child in a better way, than if the pregnancies follow rapidly one after the other, and we are therefore in favour of voluntarily spacing all the desired children of even the healthiest woman.

16.—In short, we are profoundly and fundamentally a pro-baby organisation, in favour of producing the largest possible number of healthy, happy children without detriment to the mother, and with the minimum wastage of infants by premature death. We, therefore, as a Society, regret the relatively small families of those best fitted to care for children. In this connection our motto has been "Babies in the right place," and it is just as much the aim of Constructive Birth Control to secure conception to those married people who are healthy, childless, and desire children, as it is to furnish security from conception to those who are racially diseased, already overburdened with children, or in any specific way unfitted for parenthood.

17.—We hold no fixed opinions concerning the total numbers either of individual families or of populations, desiring only that the **optimum** shall be attained.

Passed by the Executive Committee, C.B.C.

March, 1923.

Everyone who is interested in securing the best future for our Race should join the Society for Constructive Birth Control and Racial Progress. Apply for Membership forms to the Hon. Secretary, **C.B.C., 4-5, Adam St., Adelphi, London, W.C.2. Gerrard 4431.**

APPENDIX C.

THE TENETS OF THE C.B.C.

The objects for which the C.B.C. was founded are as follows : —

THE objects of the Society are (a) to bring home to all the fundamental nature of the reforms involved in conscious and constructive control of conception and the illumination of sex life as a basis of racial progress ; (b) to consider the individual, national, international, racial, political, economic, scientific, spiritual and other aspects of the theme, for which purpose meetings will be held, publications issued, Research Committees, Commissions of Enquiry and other activities will be organized from time to time as circumstances require and facilities offer ; (c) to supply all who still need it with the full knowledge of sound physiological methods of control.

As these objects indicate, the scope of the Society is very wide, its interests far-reaching, and its possibilities of future development very elastic. Even to-day the tenets which appear fundamental to different members of the Society will naturally vary, hence no one of the following is binding on an individual member. General agreement with the objects of the Society suffices for membership.

Nevertheless, it has been felt that it would be useful explicitly to state in concise form what may be described as the bedrock of general agreement in the Society. This is as follows : —

1. — The hygiene of sex is as suitable and proper a subject for scientific and serious study as the hygiene of nutrition, locomotion, or any other human function.

2. — Owing to the shamefaced attitude which has until recently characterized our dealings with the subject, all the manifold data involved in the different aspects of sex life have

not had the direct, scientific and physiological handling they deserve and require. We deplore this and shall endeavour to remedy it.

3. — We maintain that the highest spiritual development, the noblest intellectual illumination, and the sweetest romantic possibilities of individual sex experience, are not damaged by sound scientific knowledge, but contrariwise, are enhanced and elevated.

4. — We consider that in relation to the procreation of additional members of the community, the best possible knowledge of scientific and technical details should be available to those undertaking this important social duty.

5. — We believe that the haphazard production of children by ignorant, coerced, or diseased mothers is profoundly detrimental to the race. We believe, therefore, that parent¬ hood should no longer be the result of ignorance or accident, but should be a power used voluntarily and with knowledge.

6. — We maintain that to achieve this result a knowledge of the simple hygiene of contraception is essential.

7. — We advocate no individual contraceptive measure as final or fundamental, but maintain that the best measures available at any time should be taught and known by the people.

8. — We desire to keep constantly in touch with all advances in science which may have a bearing on the practical details of contraceptive measures, and for this purpose we have organized a Medical Research Committee to keep our Society informed as to the current scientific position of the hygiene of contraception.

9. — AS REGARDS THE POPULATION AT PRESENT. We say that there are unfortunately many men and women who should be prevented from procreating children at all, because of

their individual ill-health, or the diseased and degenerate nature of the offspring that they may be expected to produce. These considerations would not apply to a better and healthier world.

10. — There are many women unfortunately so constructed — suffering from weakness of certain organs — that they would risk death if they were to attempt to bear children, and who, therefore, should not bear them.

11. — There are unfortunately many couples so ill-provided with this world's goods, or with means to acquire them, that they cannot support further children, and therefore should not bear them. Women, owing to their own or their husband's incapacity to be self-supporting, may be permanently or temporarily in such a position owing to disaster or unemployment. The following Resolution was passed by our Society :

Resolution passed at General Meeting November 22nd, 1921.

"Both to spare your own personal distress and to avoid bringing a weakly child into the world, it is important that all should realise that no one should conceive in times of individual misery or ill-health. Of course wherever a child is already on the way, the best must be made of it. But sound and wholesome methods of Birth Control (Control of Conception) are known, and advice will be given free by a qualified nurse to all unemployed married persons who present this slip at the Mother's Clinic, 61, Marlborough Road, Holloway, London, N. 19."

12. — The Society approves and welcomes the work done by the first British Birth Control Clinic (The Mother's Clinic, 61, Marlborough Road, Holloway, N.19), where the very poor and ignorant receive personal instruction ; but we consider that this public service should not be left to private enterprise to

maintain, and hence that the Ministry of Health should supply suitable help and contraceptive instruction to working-class women at the many Ante-natal Clinics, Welfare Centres, etc., already in existence all over the country.

13. — We maintain that science has already made available contraceptive measures as safe and as simple to use as any other hygienic measures widely known and practised, such as brushing one's teeth, or the removal daily of a dental plate by one who has artificial teeth. We, therefore, maintain that knowledge and instruction in these matters for the normal and healthy is an **hygienic** and not a medical matter. The problem of controlling conception on the part of those who are diseased, abnormal and unhealthy is on the other hand a purely medical matter and may involve measures which this Society would not advocate for general use.

14. — We as a Society are at present working for the dissemination of the best possible hygienic knowledge to all who are intelligent enough to be capable of using it, but we recognize the grave National problem raised by the fertility of those too degenerate or too careless to be capable of using any form of contraceptive.

15. — We are convinced that children spaced by voluntary means have a less mortality, and that the mother of such children has time to recover her health and attend to the young child in a better way, than if the pregnancies follow rapidly one after the other, and we are therefore in favour of voluntarily spacing all the desired children of even the healthiest woman.

16. — In short, we are profoundly and fundamentally a pro-baby organisation, in favour of producing the largest possible number of healthy, happy children without detriment to the mother, and with the minimum wastage of infants by premature death. We, therefore, as a Society, regret the relatively small families of those best fitted to care for children.

In this connection our motto has been "Babies in the right place," and it is just as much the aim of Constructive Birth Control to secure conception to those married people who are healthy, childless, and desire children, as it is to furnish security from conception to those who are racially diseased, already overburdened with children, or in any specific way unfitted for parenthood.

17. — We hold no fixed opinions concerning the total numbers either of individual families or of populations, desiring only that the optimum shall be attained.

Passed by the Executive Committee, C.B.C. March, 1923.

Physicians' Juries for Defective Babies

SIR: Much of the discussion aroused by Dr Haiselden when he permitted the Bollinger baby to die centers around a belief in the sacredness of life. If many of those that object to the physician's course would take the trouble to analyze their idea of "life," I think they would find that it means just to breathe. Surely they must admit that such an existence is not worth while. It is the possibilities of happiness, intelligence and power that give life its sanctity, and they are absent in the case of a poor, misshapen, paralyzed, unthinking creature. I think there are many more clear cases of such hopeless death-in-life than the critics of Dr. Haiselden realize. The toleration of such anomalies tends to lessen the sacredness in which normal life is held.

There is one objection, however, to this weeding of the human garden that shows a sincere love of true life. It is the fear that we cannot trust any mortal with so responsible and delicate a task. Yet have not mortals for long ages been entrusted with the decision of questions just as momentous and far-reaching; with kingship, with the education of the race, with feeding, clothing, sheltering and employing their fellowmen? In the jury of the criminal court we have an institution that is called upon to make just such decisions as Dr. Haiselden made, to decide whether a man is fit to associate with his fellows, whether he is fit to live.

It seems to me that the simplest, wisest thing to do would be to submit cases like that of the malformed idiot baby to a jury of expert physicians. An ordinary jury decides matters of life and death on the evidence of untrained and often prejudiced observers. Their own verdict is not based on a knowledge of criminology, and they are often swayed by obscure prejudices or the eloquence of a prosecutor. Even if the accused before them is guilty, there is often no way of knowing that he would commit new crimes, that he would not become a useful and productive member of society. A mental defective, on the other hand, is almost sure to be a potential criminal. The evidence before a jury of physicians considering the case of an idiot would be exact and scientific. Their findings would be free from the prejudice and inaccuracy of untrained observation. They would act only in cases of true idiocy, where there could be no hope of mental development.

It is true, the physicians' court might be liable to abuse like other courts. The powerful of the earth might use it to decide cases to suit themselves. But if the evidence were presented openly and the decisions made public before the death of the child, there would be little danger of mistakes or abuses. Anyone interested in the case who did not believe the child ought to die might be permitted to provide for its care and maintenance. It would be humanly impossible to give absolute guarantees for every baby worth saving, but a similar condition prevails throughout our lives. Conservatives ask too much perfection of these new methods and institutions, although they know how far the old ones have fallen short of what they were expected to accomplish. We can only wait and hope for better results as the average of human intelligence, trustworthiness and justice arises. Meanwhile we must decide between a fine humanity like Dr. Haiselden's and a cowardly sentimentalism.

  HELEN   KELLER.
Wrentham, Mass.

New Age ~~Christian~~ Therapy Guide

Earlier we spoke about some of the tools that are used to elevate consciousness and measure intelligence. Still, there are lots of tools that we have accepted as okay and they are regularly integrated into the congregation's training programmes. The hope is that they will do what God's word apparently cannot do, and that is, tell us more about ourselves. *(See earlier chapters for a more in-depth explanation of each).* So, here are some classic areas which are intended to illustrate the point.

The problem	Suggested Modern Solutions
We all have different personalities, and this is the reason people clash with each other. This was also true of the disciples, right? If only they had our	• Myers-Briggs Personality Type Test (MBTI) to get a fuller understanding of your personality type. • **Psychometric testing**: To figure out if there is anything we should

understanding, Peter *(Galatians 2:11-13)* would not have clashed with Paul and Mark would have been welcomed to travel with Paul after a disagreement. *(Acts 15:38)*	know about an individual before placing them in a role of responsibility in the congregation. • **Colour Coded Character assessments** *(Carl Jung style)*: To identify the character and abilities of an individual.
Now in the second year of Nebuchadnezzar's reign, Nebuchadnezzar had dreams; and his spirit was so troubled that his sleep left him. *(Daniel 2:1 NKJV)*	• Maslow's Hierarchy of Needs will get to the core of everyone's issues. We can use this theory to create a solid base for growth and development. • **Psychoanalysis:** To resolve issues that deeply affect an individual, including trauma of the mind.
ⁱAnd Saul's servants said to him, "Surely, a distressing spirit from God is troubling you."	• **Meditation:** Not as described in the Psalm but rooted in eastern mysticism. • **Counselling:** An umbrella term popular in the church world of 'care in the community' but often shrouded in techniques learned from the 'humanistic' school of philosophy.

	• **Antipsychotics:** Mind-bending drugs used alongside these therapies? Just to help you (but not cure you).

Transhumanist Core Ideas and Values + Zoltan Istvan - 2015

1) Implement a Transhumanist Bill of Rights advocating for legal and government support of longer lifespans, better health, and higher standards of living via science and technology. Designate aging as a disease. Lay groundwork for rights for other future advanced sapient beings like conscious robots and cyborgs.

2) Spread a pro-science culture by emphasizing reason and secular values.

3) Create stronger government awareness and policies to protect against existential risk (including artificial intelligence, plagues, asteroids, climate change, and nuclear warfare and disaster).

4) Reduce the size and cost of the government by streamlining operations with new technology.

5) Implement policy for the phasing out of all individual taxes based on robots taking most jobs in the next 25 years. Advocate for a flat tax until we reach that point.

6) Advocate for morphological freedom (the right to do anything to your body so long as it doesn't harm others). Defend genetic editing and other radical science that can transform health care.

7) Advocate for partial direct digital democracy using available new technologies. Implement a Ranked Voting System.

8) End costly drug war and legalize all drugs. Spend saved money on rehabilitation.

9) Create government where all politician's original professions are represented equally (the government should not be run by 40% lawyers when lawyers represent less than 10% of the country's jobs). Create government where women run half of country too.

10) Significantly lessen massive incarcerated population in America by using innovative technologies to monitor criminals outside of prison. Spend saved money on education.

11) Strongly emphasize and create radical green tech solutions to make planet healthier.

12) Because most jobs will be lost to robots and software in the next 30 years, support and draft logistics for a Universal Basic Income for every American (taking care to devise a plan that does not enlarge the government). A properly set up UBI could eliminate welfare, social security, and dozens of other major government programs. Over the extreme long term, consider possibility of a Resource Based Economy.

13) Dramatically enlarge US space exploration agenda with increased government and private resources.

14) Develop international consortium to create a "Transhumanist Olympics".

15) Encourage private industry to develop and support usage of trauma alert implants or technology that notifies

emergency crews of extreme trauma (this will significantly reduce domestic violence, crime, and tragedy in America).

16) Develop science and technology to be able to eliminate all disabilities in humans who have them.

17) Insist on campaign finance reform, limit lobbyists' power, and include 3rd political parties in government. Implement term limits in all Government.

Mandate real time public surveillance and transparency of Government.

18) Provide free public education at every level; advocate for mandatory college education and preschool in the age of far longer lifespans.

19) Advocate for a more open and fair immigration policy, taking care to use technologies to help this.

20) Create a scientific and educational industrial complex in America instead of a military industrial complex. Spend money on wars against cancer, heart disease, and diabetes — not on wars in far-off countries.

Transhumanism Shaping the World and the Body

For example,

Genetically Modified Crops that are removing the ability to reuse seeds from their crops to plant the following years' crops. Meaning that control is placed in the hand of the inventor and taken away from the farmer, leading to a market which can profit wherever their GM seed is sold.

Svalbard Global Seed Vault. When this first came to light my initial thoughts were the same as anyone else's. Why? Of course, the reasons given then and now may allay any fears of 'conspiracy,' a word that is overused and often misapplied, but in the wider scheme of the goals of humanity a seed vault begins to look slightly out of place. Particularly in light of our past record of manipulations and confiscations. Couple this with the monopolising of grain through modifying its makeup and you can see what will potentially happen next. Like water and energy, food becomes the next thing to control and market for profit.

Genetically Modified Babies, a hot and sometimes heated topic of discussion, but once again taking advantage of a parent's concern for their unborn child and using the desire of a couple to have children. Once again, who really benefits? Where are the profits made? What are the long-term issues for the families and the children.

Gender Realignment: A personal choice, we are told, but with the reclassification of gender from male and female to a myriad of possible sexes we are potentially looking at generations who will have undergone the procedures through physical and technological means. This may render future adults incapable of having children hence, requiring an artificial womb of some kind to create the child of their choice. Now, this may seem extreme but we only have to consider what is in front of us to piece this together. Combine this with the previous point on GM babies and you can see where this is potentially going.

Atheism Goes to Africa

In 2015, the world's first atheist orphanage was set up in West Africa, Uganda called BiZoHa. The name is an acronym for the three founders, Biba Kavass, Zoltan Istvan, and Hank Pellissier.

So, transhumanism has come to Uganda to raise its orphaned children in the new salvation, science and technology.

Public Rituals

Around a similar time, the media was picking up on public ceremonies that were deemed strange. Such as the opening of the Gotthard base tunnel, the longest tunnel in the world, which put on a performance for dignitaries which had spirits, demons and other satanic symbolism.

Mental Health: The programmes for mental health exploded in the UK during my review of its history and impact on communities. Within a short time of sharing what was difficult to comprehend or believe, programmes were initiated at a rate that was concerning. Almost overnight it seemed as though everyone was talking about their mental health.

The theories of the psychologists were seemingly invited to educate Christians and counselling exploded with it. Once the documented thoughts of the psychologists' theories came to light, it was clear that their teachings on the mind were in direct conflict with biblical lifestyle. There were many things about this that just didn't sit right.

Of course, we then had a series of tragic incidents in schools and in Europe where people were suddenly being run over in a seemingly random event or a child was going into school to take revenge on other children. The connection of anti-psychotics or being under psychiatric treatment (which included the use of anti-psychotics) was evident on each occasion. This was not a coincidence.